Other books by GEOFFREY BIBBY

The Testimony of the Spade   *1956*
Four Thousand Years Ago   *1961*

THESE ARE BORZOI BOOKS
PUBLISHED IN NEW YORK BY ALFRED A. KNOPF

THE GAZELLE, MOST OFTEN LOOKING BACKWARD, IS SO COMMON ON THE SEALS
OF BAHRAIN AND KUWAIT (WHILE RARE ON THOSE OF MESOPOTAMIA OR THE
INDUS) THAT IT MUST HAVE BEEN REGARDED AS IN SOME WAY THE CREST OR
SYMBOL OF THE LAND OF DILMUN.

LOOKING for DILMUN

LOOKING for

DILMUN

by GEOFFREY BIBBY

ALFRED A. KNOPF   New York   1969

THIS IS A BORZOI BOOK
PUBLISHED BY ALFRED A. KNOPF, INC.

First Edition
Copyright © 1969 by Geoffrey Bibby

Library of Congress Catalog Card Number: 69–10704
Manufactured in the United States of America

TO THE MEMORY OF

His Highness Sheikh Sulman bin Hamad Al-Khalifah

Sir Charles Dalrymple Belgrave, adviser

Svend Unmack-Larsen, lord-mayor

Darwish Miqdadi, deputy director of education

Edward Skinner, vice president

Armand Eugène de Grouchy, director

Jette Bang, photographer

Frode Visti, conservator

Radi bin Ahmed, foreman

Ære være deres minde

FOREWORD

꘠꘠꘠꘠꘠

Four thousand years ago the "Lost Civilization" of Dilmun dominated the route to the Indies, the trade-ways between Mesopotamia and the civilization of the Indus Valley. And for fifteen
years it has dominated my life.

The search for Dilmun began as a fairly lighthearted archaeological adventure in 1953. I looked on it then, I think, more as an
opportunity for a nostalgic return to Bahrain, to which island
chance had brought me just after the Second World War, than as
a serious attempt to grapple with the Dilmun question—whose
existence, after all, was only known to a handful of Sumerologists.

But then the project grew with a momentum of its own, as
sheikhdom after sheikhdom on the oil-rich shores of the Arabian
Gulf took up the search for its own prehistory. Some six years after
it commenced the expedition was thirty strong and researching in
five separate lands. And I found that, like it or not, I was fated for
the rest of my life to be regarded as a specialist in the tiny field of
East Arabian archaeology.

In the process a lot of the gilt has been rubbed from the ginger-
bread.

Like Sindbad's Old Man of the Sea—in these selfsame waters—
the Dilmun Expeditions have firmly planted themselves upon my
neck. For fifteen years I have rarely spent an Easter or a Shrove-
tide with my family (and those who know Denmark will know
what I miss thereby). Christmas after Christmas is overshadowed
by last-minute preparations for an expedition which is to leave at

the beginning of January. In my garden the tilling and planting which should take place in March and April is hurriedly rushed through in May. And this for year after year.

It is difficult to sustain, in these circumstances, the romance of Archaeology, the glamor of the quest for the lost history of man. Especially as archaeology is hard work; many cubic yards of earth and stone must be moved for each even minor object found.

Thus, if the following account is prosaic, the fault is mine—I have lived too long with my eyes too close to the ground. For the glamor is indeed there. The thrill of discovery ever recurs, that sudden spreading glow of incredulous delight as you realize that the object you hold in your hand, or are uncovering beneath your trowel, is another piece of the jigsaw, extending the picture of what you already know and hinting of new vistas beyond.

The discovery of the city of the mound-builders of Bahrain, and its dating to 2000 B.C., the very period of Dilmun's zenith as a sea-trading power; the finding of the same people far to the north in Kuwait; the extension of civilization in the Arabian Gulf further and further back in time, to 3000 and then to 4000 B.C.; the emergence of a second, undreamed-of civilization on the Oman coast in Abu Dhabi; and the appearance of the same civilization a hundred miles inland at the foot of the Muscat mountains; these have been the highlights of the expedition's story, and they compensate for much.

Hardly a one of them has been my own personal discovery; and I need to emphasize that this book, though a personal record, is an account of the work of many hands. Over eighty archaeologists of half a dozen nationalities (though most of them Danes) have taken part in our excavations, as well as several hundred workmen from almost every Arab land. The story that follows makes clear, I hope, the debt the expedition owes to their devoted work. But our debt is far wider. There is hardly a government or an oil company in the Arabian Gulf which has not repeatedly come to our aid with grants of money, with loan of houses and tents, of transport and heavy equipment, of maps and instruments and air photographs, with analysis of samples or with radio-carbon dating. Many other firms and foundations, in Denmark and the Middle

East, have made us grants or placed their special facilities or abilities at our disposal, while behind us has always stood the Carlsberg Foundation. We have been singularly fortunate in our friends.

Special mention must be made of the amateur archaeologists, Arab, American and European, who ply their hobby along the Arabian Gulf. They are a modest and unassuming body of people, almost apologetic in their disclaimers of any ability to judge the significance of what they have found. And yet they are always the first in the field, explorers with an unrivalled local knowledge. We but follow in their footsteps, and our debt to them is beyond compute.

I owe too a personal acknowledgment of gratitude to Peter Glob, my companion throughout the course of the Dilmun expeditions. His sympathetic friendliness has won the hearts of sheikhs and villagers alike, his acumen has time and again pointed the way we should go. Together he and I have reconnoitred most of the territory in which we later worked. I could ask for no better comrade.

The expeditions continue, and no end is yet in sight. But we have, I feel, now reached a point where a coherent picture can be given of the civilizations which are now known to have existed in the apparent vacuum between the ancient Middle East and ancient India. While the book is, as I say, a personal record, and tells at least as fully what it has been like to dig in these new lands as what has been discovered, it is my hope that our colleagues in the quest will, pending the publication of the detailed and many-volume reports on the individual excavations, accept graciously this general survey of our work and results.

Qala'at al-Bahrain
4th April 1969

CONTENTS

DRAWINGS

(*Those marked* BHF *are by Bente Højholt Fischer.*
The others are by the author.)

MAPS

(by Bente Højholt Fischer)

PLATES

(following page 174)

*All photographs except Plates I, XVIIIa and XXa are the property
of the expedition and are reproduced with its kind permission.*

LOOKING for DILMUN

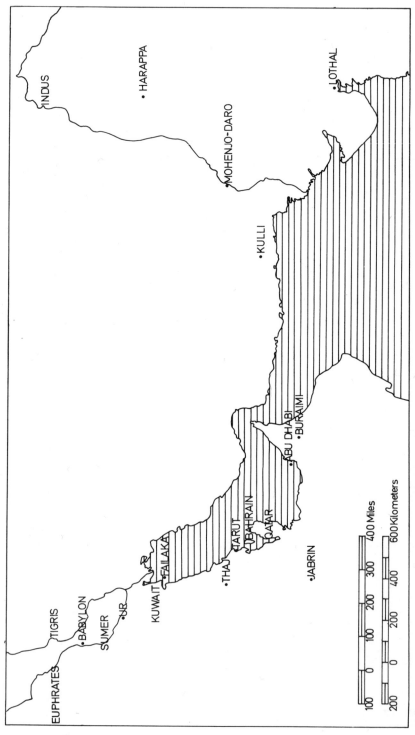

MESOPOTAMIA AND THE AREA OF THE INDUS VALLEY CIVILIZATION; AND THE REGION BETWEEN, WITH WHICH THIS BOOK DEALS.

CHAPTER ONE

ਟੇਟੇਟੇਟੇਟੇ

BACK TO BAHRAIN

We were digging a Viking causeway, as I recall it.

It was an idyllic spot, deep in the heart of Jutland, where a placid stream flowed through water-meadows below low green hills, and cattle scratched lazily against the posts that fenced off, precariously, our excavation from their pasture. It was the middle of a drowsy summer, the summer of 1953.

Across this valley, a thousand years ago, one of the major military roads of Viking Denmark had run, connecting the garrison camp of Fyrkat with the seaport of Aarhus. It had been part of the organized network of military preparedness that cast a new light—at least to an English archæologist but newly come to Denmark—on the seeming haphazardness of the Danish invasions of England during the century before the Norman Conquest. And where the road had dipped down to the marshy ground of the valley bottom the engineers of Sweyn Forkbeard's army had built a causeway, a road of stout oak planks laid crosswise over a fivefold row of lengthwise beams that in turn rested upon a brushwood bed and was tied down at fixed intervals by triangles of posts driven deep into the peat. It was a wonderful piece of engineering, preserved in its entirety by the waterlogged soil and lying a scant two feet below the greensward.

And it was not the only road to have crossed the valley at that

3

point. Below the Viking causeway three other roads, the upper also of wood and the two lower ones of cobbles, took the tale back another millennium and a half, to the end of the Bronze Age. Fifty yards to one side a mediæval post-road still made a discernible mound below the grass of the next meadow, and a hundred yards farther away a modern road ran on an embankment that raised it forever above the floods and freshets that had menaced seventy-five generations of wayfarers and overwhelmed, one by one, the five earlier roads.

Behind our backs as we worked—a local labourer, a girl volunteer, and I—to disentangle this sequence of highways stood the oldest traffic sign in Denmark. Where the road ended in a welter of flood-tossed timber, all that was left of a bridge or a planked ford across the Alling River, the Vikings had erected a warning sign, a standing stone carved with the head of a water-troll, with blank staring eyes and a beard apparently plaited of waving fronds of water weeds.

For as long as living memory went back the stone had lain face downward, half buried in the turf by the river, and, until a historian from the National Museum, in a routine search for runic inscriptions, had raised the stone two years before, no one had known of the troll's head carved upon it. Yet some memory of its existence must have been handed down, for among the people of the district the tale of the Aamand, the Man of the River, was well known. It was told that each year the Aamand craved a victim, that—before the causewayed road was built and the river straightened and deepened by the Fen Reclamation Authority— every year a man must die in crossing the river. Once indeed six years passed without the sacrifice being demanded, but then in the seventh year a coach foundered on a wild winter's night. And seven men were drowned . . .

On this warm July day it was difficult to credit the sinister reputation of the river crossing, and as the work of cutting and drawing the long central section through the four superimposed roadways progressed, our thoughts and eyes turned ever more often in the other direction, away from the river to where the inn stood—as surely a Viking hostelry must also once have stood—at the edge of the valley where the road began to curve down the hill to the bridge.

It was while we were eating our lunch at the inn that the telephone call came through, from the local correspondent of a Copenhagen daily. The Scientific Foundation had that morning published its list of grants for the next twelve months, and on the list there was a grant of four thousand dollars towards an archæological expedition from the Prehistoric Museum of Aarhus to the island of Bahrain. Could I tell them what it was all about?

I tried to marshal my thoughts. For there was a lot I could tell them about that little palm-clad island in which I had spent three years, and to which, it seemed, I was now to return. But it would not be easy to explain to newspaper readers who did not know the Arabian Gulf just what Bahrain was and why archæologists were interested in it. I took a deep breath and started in:

—Bahrain is a little island in the Persian Gulf. Or as the Bahrain islanders themselves prefer to call it, the Arabian Gulf. For the Bahrain islanders are Arabic-speakers, like all the inhabitants of the countries along the southern shore of the Gulf and on the islands off that shore.

Already I was getting off the subject. I swallowed, and went back to the beginning again:

—Bahrain is an island off the Arabian coast of the so-called Persian Gulf. It's a very small island, not more than thirty miles from north to south, and fifteen from east to west, but it is an independent nation, one of the smallest independent nations in the world. There are about 150,000 inhabitants, of Arab stock, Muslims, and they are ruled, autocratically but benevolently, by a paramount sheikh with a British adviser.

I was getting into my stride now, but was interrupted by questions.

—The ruler's name? He's called Sulman, His Highness Sheikh Sir Sulman bin Hamad bin Isa Al-Khalifah, K.C.M.G., K.C.I.E., and he is a little man in his late fifties with a carefully groomed black beard and a pair of very intelligent brown eyes. And the adviser? Sir Charles Belgrave, tall, cool, cheroot-smoking, very, very efficient.

5

—Did that mean that Bahrain was in fact a British protectorate?

I paused. This needed careful explanation, to a Danish audience. Not in the normal sense, I replied. A British protectorate, as I understand it, has a British governor, with armed forces at his disposal, governing in the name of, or in concert with, the native ruler. Bahrain isn't like that at all. Bahrain is in fact "protected" by the British. There is a treaty, nearly a hundred years old now, between the ruler of Bahrain and the British government which lays down that Britain guarantees the independence of Bahrain, and Bahrain in return undertakes to refrain from piracy and slave trading, not to make treaties with any other nation, and to allow herself to be represented abroad by Britain. But on the other hand the same treaty debars Britain from any interference in the internal affairs of the island, and so far as I have seen this proviso is very strictly observed.

—But what about the British adviser?

—Oh, that is a very different matter. Sir Charles is not an official of the British Foreign Office. He was simply appointed, as a young ex-officer, by Sheikh Sulman's father, to help him to plan a program of educational and technical progress, along Western lines, with the meagre revenue that Bahrain at that time possessed. His power and influence has increased, certainly, when the oil royalties began to come in, but he is in fact only a Bahraini civil servant. Even the fact that he is British is accidental.

But with the magic word "oil" the reporter had lost interest in Sir Charles Belgrave.

—Yes, oil was found in Bahrain in 1931. No one had guessed earlier that there was oil in the Gulf at all. Now, by Gulf standards, I suppose Bahrain hasn't got very much. Its production is surpassed very considerably by Kuwait and Saudi Arabia, and even by the next-door state of Qatar. But it's had a very nice income— somewhere between five and ten million dollars a year—for nearly twenty years now, and that has given it a chance to develop gradually into a very comfortable, fairly well educated, fairly prosperous little country.

—You sound as though you know Bahrain. Have you been there before?

—Yes, I spent three years there, the three years just before I came to Denmark in 1950. I was working with an oil company—not the one that extracts Bahrain's oil, but the one that was then developing the new field in Qatar, just across the water. They had an office in Bahrain, which I helped to run.

—And now you're going back—as an archæologist. Why? Is there anything of interest to an archæologist on Bahrain?

I smiled—gently. Yes, I said. There is the largest prehistoric cemetery in the world.

That afternoon I had difficulty in concentrating on Viking cause-ways. I was reliving the day on which I first saw the burial-mounds of Bahrain.

I had been in Bahrain about a fortnight. It was the middle of summer, and Bahrain was enveloped in the stifling blanket of sweat-dripping humidity which, so the old hands said, descended upon the island in June and never lifted again before October. They talked with sombre satisfaction of "the worst climate in the world," and in truth, arriving from England in July and landing by flying-boat in the steaming shallow waters that lay between Bahrain proper and the northern island of Muharraq, I had not felt in the mood to contradict them. I had been installed in a tiny whitewashed office in a large whitewashed building, and found myself in nominal charge of an organization engaged in supplying the necessities of life to three hundred men and more busy drilling for oil in the Qatar desert. Though I soon found out that my staff, of twenty or so Arab and Indian clerks and purchasing agents, were—fortunately—fully capable of running the whole organization without my interference, a perverted sense of the White Man's Burden had kept me to my desk, with every win-dow open and a ceiling fan singing above my head, signing requisition forms for everything from toilet-paper to three-ton trucks, and loading-notes for a fleet of dhows that sailed continu-ously with water from an undersea spring off Bahrain to waterless Qatar.

Then after ten days my chief, the only other Englishman in the building, was called to London for an emergency conference.

And three days later occurred one of the Arab feast-days on which it is the custom that the heads of the European firms in Bahrain call upon the ruler and offer him their congratulations.

Feeling very raw and thoroughly nervous, I summoned the general manager's large black limousine, and set off for the palace to pay my respects to an absolute monarch as temporary-deputy-acting-general-manager-in-Bahrain of one of the world's largest oil companies.

The summer palace lay ten miles away, to the south of the town. We had driven through the narrow streets of the bazaar quarter and past the tall new blocks of flats on the edge of town; and then for several miles through close-set palm groves, where the date-palms stood grey and dusty in the heat of the morning and where dark-brown men in loincloths washed their white donkeys, or occasionally a truck, in the deep irrigation channels that bordered the road. Then we rounded a bend, and came out into the desert.

For a moment my eyes had been dazzled by the white glare of sun on sand, after the gloom of the date plantations. And then, as they became accustomed to the light, I saw the mounds. On both sides of the road were groups of small round gravel hillocks, six to ten feet in height and very neatly circular. They grew more numerous. And larger. And closer together. Soon they began to blot out the horizon. In front and behind, to right and to left there was now nothing to be seen but mounds, some of them up to twenty feet high. They fell back as we dipped into a shallow valley, where only a single thirty-foot tumulus stood beside the road, and then, as we swung onto the slope that led up to the palace, I could see that the whole slope, three miles of gradually rising ground, was covered with mounds, crowded so thickly together that they were, so to say, treading on each other's skirts, the footings of one mound extending out over the footings of the next. As far as the eye could see to either side, a sweep of ten miles or more, there was no end to the mound-field; there must have been tens of thousands of mounds in view.

I had heard that there were burial-mounds on Bahrain, and I had intended—archæologist as I prided myself on being—to visit them someday. But this was something beyond my experience. These crowded, regular hillocks must be a phenomenon of nature, some sport of volcanic action or wind-drift. It was impossible that these scores of thousands of mounds could all be burials.

I looked at Ghuloom and pointed out of the window. Ghuloom was the general manager's driver, and not accustomed to acting as chauffeur for very junior general assistants. His dignity had been upset by my ordering out his cherished automobile, and he clearly believed that my usurping of his master's duties and privileges was blackest presumption. He had been silent throughout the journey, staring straight ahead. But now he unbent a trifle —after all, I was very new. "Grave-mounds, sahib," he said. "Grave-mounds of the Portuguese."

The audience with the sheikh was almost an anticlimax after that. I had passed the red-turbanned guards at the palace gate and crossed the courtyard to join the little procession of Europeans moving slowly forward to greet the sheikh. Sheikh Sulman had looked quizzically at me as I presented myself, and smiled conspiratorially as I apologized for my chief's absence in London, for Basil Lermitte was a favourite of his, even though he was working to ensure oil royalties for Sheikh Sulman's hereditary enemy, Sheikh Abdullah of Qatar. And I had been conducted to a seat in the huge audience hall, and the Negro servants poured the ritual bitter coffee from their brass coffee-pots, and, as short a time thereafter as etiquette would permit, presented the ritual burning sandalwood and the sprinkling of rose-water, which was the signal that we should leave.

On our way back to town, Ghuloom had stopped, without my asking, where the burial-mounds lay thickest. I got out, and climbed the highest of those nearby, my feet slipping on the hard-packed gravel, and sweat running down my face and reducing to a damp ruin the collar and tie and jacket that I had put on for my visit to the sheikh. From the top the view of the tumulus field was even more impressive. An unending vista of mounds was opened up. By far the majority of them were merely simple circular barrows, but occasionally one could be seen surrounded by a low ring-mound, as though in an attempt to keep the other mounds from pressing too close. And many of the mounds showed unmistakable signs of having been disturbed; shallow hollows, or sometimes deep cuttings, in the western slopes showed where robbers had dug down to the graves beneath.

As, at a distance of six years and from the position of a practising archæologist engaged in a routine Danish dig, I thought back to my first sight of the grave-mounds of Bahrain I found it hard to understand why I had not taken better advantage of three years spent on the island. During all that time I had only dug one of the grave-mounds, one of the smallest I could find. It had been a very amateur "dig," judged by the standards I had acquired in three years of digging Danish grave-mounds under expert supervision. Like the grave-robbers of an earlier age I had shovelled my way down from the top of the mound to expose the cap-stones of a burial chamber only just big enough to contain a body. I had prised up two of the cap-stones and rummaged through the few inches of dust and soil that had accumulated on the floor of the chamber below. And found nothing. Either other robbers had been there before me, or else the grave had been that of a person too poor to have anything buried with him—the exiguous mound above him could well suggest the latter.

Apart from that excavation I had left the mounds alone. Life in Bahrain was somehow not conducive to the pursuit of serious hobbies. During the summer no one save a very dedicated enthusiast could resist the after-work siesta, dozing the afternoon away under a ceiling fan or in the one air-conditioned bedroom with which some of the firms were beginning to equip their staff houses. During the winter the temptation was the opposite. Then the mild breezes from the north, and the sun, no longer the enemy, shining warm on the white sand and copper-green sea called to holiday rather than to endeavour. Evenings and weekends passed in sailing and swimming and tennis, in garden-parties and picnics and fishing cruises. It would have been a brave eccentric who refused all invitations and went off alone to dig. And a young executive in the oil business must not, I thought, be eccentric. I know better now.

Anyway, now I was going back to Bahrain. And this time as an archæologist, with no need to find excuses, or time off from business, to dig as much as I desired. And I was not going alone, but with a very experienced companion.

It is high time that my readers be introduced to Professor Peter Vilhelm Glob, commonly called simply P.V.

Since the birth of European archæology—which happened, by the way, in Denmark—a century and a half ago, Denmark has had a tendency to produce colorful archæologists. Christian Jürgensen Thomsen, who began his career as an import and export merchant and became an archæologist through rescuing a coin collection from the flames of the British bombardment of Copenhagen in 1807, went on to become the first curator of the Danish National Museum and to discover that prehistory could be divided into a Stone Age, a Bronze Age, and an Iron Age. Jens Asmussen Worsaae, who as a schoolboy had begun to assist Thomsen at the National Museum, quarrelled with his chief when poverty forced him to ask for payment for his work, and then went straight to the king of Denmark to ask for, and get, money for an archæological research program abroad. He became boon companion to the crown prince, the later archæologist-king Frederik VII, and came back in 1865 to succeed Thomsen as head of the National Museum. Sophus Müller, a fiery little Captain Kettle of a man with a goatee beard, had succeeded Worsaae at the National Museum, and, during his reign there, had acquired a legendary reputation as opponent of the senseless destruction of the grave-mounds of Denmark then taking place, and as the discoverer of the battle-ax-bearing invaders of Stone Age Europe from the East who were buried in them.

P.V. is in the tradition of men such as these, and indeed today sits in their seat, as head of the National Museum and the State Antiquary of Denmark. But at the time of which I write, in 1953, he was professor of archæology at the University of Aarhus and curator of the Prehistoric Museum of that city, the museum for which I work. A tall, burly figure, with a craggy face and a mane of fair hair which he never seems to find time to get cut, he is of a family of artists and himself a painter of unusual brilliance. And

11

he brings to his archæology, as to his painting, an astounding clarity of vision, an ability to see a pattern in an apparent mass of dissociate detail, and to see anomalies in an apparent pattern. This ability shows itself in the field, where P.V. will unfailingly pick up twice as many flint implements or painted potsherds as any other trained archæologist, and will invariably interpret correctly, apparently by sheer guesswork, the date and provenance and significance of what he finds. It can be vastly irritating to find P.V.'s guesses confirmed time after time by later discoveries of which he can have had no knowledge, and it is only after you have worked with him for years that you realize that behind the guesswork there is a phenomenal grasp of pattern, and of the place in the scheme of things where the objects found can and must fit in order to be as much artistically as scientifically *right*. In the sphere of planning, too, P.V.'s grasp of patterns and trends has irritatingly often resulted in him just happening to be around when new discoveries or opportunities for new and exciting projects crop up.

Bahrain was a case in point. No one could foresee that to attach an Englishman and a former oil executive to a Danish museum would result in an archæological expedition to the Middle East. But P.V., being P.V., could see that it would provide a break in the pattern of normal museum practice, and therefore could hardly fail to produce a result of some sort, which would certainly be interesting, probably amusing, and even perhaps important. Life is never dull when P.V. is around.

Of course I had talked about the grave-mounds of Bahrain.

P.V. and the four assistants that he had recruited—somewhat unorthodoxly every one—for his museum, and a sprinkling of wives, were sitting, as I recall it, over wine after dinner in the library of P.V.'s rambling old house. And Vibeke—who is my wife —had been talking about our life in Bahrain, and how *there* after dinner we used to drive out along the west road from Manama, the capital city, to areas of desert that we had found which were covered with millions of potsherds, and how we used to stroll around, as the sun went down behind the palm-trees, picking up pieces of glass bracelets, fragments of Ming porcelain, and occasional copper coins. And P.V. slammed his fist down on the table in front of him and said, "Let's run an expedition to Bahrain."

That had been a year and a half ago. For expeditions are not as easy as all that to arrange. I should explain, perhaps, that the Prehistoric Museum of Aarhus, Denmark, is not a wealthy foundation. Until two years before it had been a cosy little country museum, run by the local librarian in his spare time, and looked after by a white-haired old lady who opened the museum to visitors only when they rang the bell. It contained rather a good collection of nineteenth-century Danish paintings, and three rooms with glass cases full of flint axes and Iron Age pottery found in the neighbourhood. Then in 1950 the new University of Aarhus had established a chair of archæology and elected P.V. to fill it. And because P.V. was known not to be overly enthusiastic for purely academic and tutorial work they had given him the museum to develop into a research institute, and even scraped together sufficient money to allow him to bring with him from the National Museum a young and talented excavator and a very versatile conservator. But that was all. The other two members of the tiny staff, of whom I was one, were supernumerary, paid, when we were paid at all, from small grants laboriously acquired from literary and scientific foundations for individual excavations and for translation of books and articles.

The idea of the Prehistoric Museum, on its shoestring finances, entering the field of Oriental excavation, a field reserved up to now for institutions of the calibre of the Metropolitan Museum of Art of New York, the British Museum, the Louvre, and the Berlin State Museum, and the wealthier of the American universities, was completely preposterous—and completely irresistible. I wrote to Sir Charles Belgrave and asked whether the Bahrain government would approve of an expedition. And he wrote back that he had discussed the matter with the ruler, and Sheikh Sulman was full of enthusiasm for the idea.

But since then over a year had passed; and Sheikh Sulman was getting impatient. I had had to write to Sir Charles that our first application to the Scientific Foundation had been shelved "for reasons of government economy." Then we were informed, unof-

ficially, that a further application, the following year, of the size
that we contemplated would certainly be turned down too,
whereas there would be a good chance of a smaller contribution
being granted. There was a very considerable snag here; for our
original application had been for the amount which, after very
careful calculation, was the absolute minimum for which a two-
man expedition to Bahrain could be run.

In this impasse I wrote again to Sir Charles Belgrave and put
the position up to him as it was. And I asked him whether he
thought that His Highness might be willing to contribute to the
cost of the expedition.

Now, I should like to make it very clear just how completely
unheard-of such a proposal was. Governments in the Middle East
never contribute to foreign expeditions working in their country.
On the contrary. It has been for many years the general rule that
expeditions to the Middle East pay their own expenses, pay in
addition the salaries of the inspectors appointed by the countries
in which they work, and at the end of the "dig" hand over to the
government of the country everything they have found, with
copies of all their notes, drawings, and photographs. This system
is not as unreasonable as it sounds. The countries in which arose
the great civilizations of the ancient world are very conscious of
the fact that their best ancient monuments and most splendid
treasures grace the museums of France and Germany, Britain and
the United States. In the days, a century and a half ago, when the
great amateur archæologists of Europe, Botta and Layard and
the *savants* of Napoleon, were discovering apparently inexhaustible treasures of sculptured stone in Mesopotamia and Egypt, it
did not seem unethical that they should take back to their homes
the treasures which they found. And later, when the more scientific expeditions of Sir Leonard Woolley and Sir Flinders Petrie,
of Sir Wallis Budge and Robert Koldewey and Walter Andrae
were digging Ur and Abydos, Babylon and Nineveh, the new
governments of the countries of the Middle East knew very well
that if they wished their new national museums to be filled, they
must allow these Western experts to fill them. And the principle
of a fifty-fifty division of the objects discovered was generally

adopted. But of recent years the situation has changed. There are now Iraqi and Egyptian, Syrian and Lebanese, and Turkish and Palestinian archæologists of international standing, and these countries have skilled and well-equipped departments of antiquities quite capable of carrying out the most complicated and large-scale excavations within their own territories. If Western archæologists work in these countries, they do so for their own satisfaction and can no longer be considered as conferring a favour upon the country in which they work. It is therefore eminently reasonable that the national treasures which they find remain in the country to which they belong; and equally reasonable that they pay themselves for the work which they themselves choose to do. And in practice they are permitted to take back to their own museums and collections a large part of what they find, providing only that the specimens they are allowed to keep are not unique. But they have never, in all their history, received contributions towards the cost of their work from the countries in which they operate.

It was therefore with very great hesitation that P.V. and I had decided to ask the ruler of Bahrain for financial assistance—and with very deep gratitude that we received his reply, offering us three thousand dollars to assist our work, on condition that half the objects found should remain the property of the Bahrain government. When a little later the oil company that holds the Bahrain concession also offered us a contribution, and the Danish Scientific Foundation at last accepted our reduced application, the Danish archæological expedition to Bahrain was finally a reality.

This tripartite support for our expedition, with contributions from Danish foundations, from the government of the area, and from the oil companies operating there, has set the pattern for our subsequent work. We are very conscious of the quite phenomenal generosity with which our repeated applications for assistance have been met, and we have never made any secret of the fact that our tiny cramped museum would never have been able to enter the field at all, still less to mount expeditions of the size that we have sent out to the Gulf in recent years, without this constant and ever-increasing support. In the course of the years our archæological expeditions to the Arabian Gulf area grew until their yearly budget was vastly larger than that of the museum in which they started, and within six years after their beginning they formed one of the largest expeditions working anywhere at all in the field of archæology.

But in 1953 all that lay in the future. No plans could be made beyond the first expedition, for on its results would depend any future work. No plans could, in fact, be made at that moment at all. I have my Viking causeway, and P.V. was away, looking for the origins of the Eskimos in Greenland.

One thing could be done, though, while I waited for P.V. to return. I could get hold of the details of the work that had been done already on the problem of the Bahrain grave-mounds. I knew more or less what to look for; in the library of the British Political Agency in Bahrain there had been copies of some of the reports and references to others. And during my three years with my oil company I had looked into them and taken notes.

So when the autumn rains began flooding my Viking causeway I covered it up again with peat and took a belated summer holiday in England—and browsed through the bookshops opposite the British Museum. I was lucky. Although long out of print, second-hand copies were available of the reports of the three most important investigations made into Bahrain's antiquities. There was the report by Ernest Mackay, who later made a name for himself digging Mohenjo-Daro on the Indus, but who as a young man in 1925 had been sent from Egypt by Flinders Petrie, the greatest name in Near Eastern archæology, to solve the mystery of the Bahrain mounds. Mackay was an experienced archæologist who for four years, from 1923 to 1926, had been field director of the Oxford University and Chicago Natural History Museum excavations at Kish in Mesopotamia, and he had done a very competent job on the Bahrain mounds, opening nearly fifty of them, drawing plans and sections, and listing contents. Thanks to Mackay we had a very clear idea of what the mounds contained. He had shown that every one of them covered a stone-built chamber, lying roughly east-west with its entrance to the west. The majority of them were T-shaped, the crosspiece of the T formed by two alcoves, not so high as the main chamber, one at each side of the inner end of the chamber. There were variants, though, to this general rule, some chambers having no alcoves, or only one, some having two pairs of alcoves, one pair at each end of the chamber. And some chambers were "double-deckers," a second chamber being built above the first. The contents of the chambers were, frankly, disappointing. Such human bones as were found were in the wildest disorder; such pottery as was found was in most cases in fragments, and Mackay notes that often pieces of the same pot were found both inside and outside the chamber. And there was very little in the graves other than bones and potsherds, only some fragments of worked ivory and worked copper being recovered. Oddly enough, it never seems to have occurred to Mackay that these observations showed clearly that all the graves he opened had been plundered, and he went to great pains to try to explain in other ways the disorder in the chambers. The fragmentary skeletons, he claimed, must be re-burials of bones from an ossuary or charnel house; the presence of potsherds inside and outside the chambers showed that pots had been "ritually broken" before burial.

It is, of course, the duty of a professional archæologist to suggest theories to account for the facts which he digs up, always provided that he keeps what is theory clearly distinguished from what is observed excavated evidence (as Mackay did—and as I shall endeavour to do in this book), and we have no quarrel with Ernest Mackay for having theorized perhaps a little widely on what was perhaps a slender body of excavated evidence. But certainly some of his theories, in popular belief promoted by thirty years without contradiction to the status of established fact, have caused us some headaches in our work. For example, he notes the finding of ostrich-egg shells, cut and painted for use as drinking cups, and the fact that all the pottery found was round-bottomed; and on that bases the theory that the people buried in the grave chambers were natives of the Arabian main-land, where men still alive today can recall seeing living os-

triches, and wanderers in the desert sands, where round-bottomed vessels would stand more firmly than pots with flat bases.
And working from this, and from his theory of the reburial of
skeletons brought from elsewhere, added to the fact that he did
not personally observe any sites of ancient settlement in Bahrain,
he added the conclusion that Bahrain was not in fact inhabited at
all during the period when the grave-mounds were built (a
period that he sets with reservation as about 1500 B.C.), but was
solely used as a burial-ground for people living on the mainland
of Arabia.

This belief that Bahrain in pre-Islamic times had been solely a
necropolis, an island of the dead, has proved very difficult to
scotch, and for all our evidence that Bahrain in fact was a popu-
lous, civilized land at the time when it buried its dead in the
grave-mounds, visitors to our excavations still occasionally try to
demonstrate their knowledgeableness by quoting the burial-island
theory to us as revealed truth. That is one of the reasons why
the film which, some years later, was made by the Bahrain oil
company about our excavations was entitled firmly *The Land of
the Living*.

The other—and even more widespread—popular belief about
the burial-mounds is that they are Phoenician. But this cannot be
laid to Mackay's account, but rather to that of an earlier investi-
gator. Among the reports unearthed in London was that of a
Colonel Prideaux of the Imperial Government of India, who in
1906 had been instructed by that government to investigate the
Bahrain mounds. Prideaux was strictly an amateur, but an army
officer of considerable energy. And he tackled, with a large labour
force of local Arabs, the most formidable group of mounds on the
island, a collection of about a score near the village of Ali, a little
to the west of where I had first seen the mound-field forty-one
years later.

Whereas the majority of the grave-mounds are seldom more
than twice the height of a man, the mounds at Ali are stupendous,
the least of them as high as a three-story building. It cost us ten
years of hesitation before we ventured—unsuccessfully—to dig
even one of these tumuli; but Prideaux tackled eight of them at

once. His methods were, of course, by modern standards not beyond criticism—in many cases he contented himself with driving tunnels through the rock-hard gravel conglomerate until they met the central chamber. These chambers were very much larger than those later excavated by Mackay, but they followed the same plan and, like Mackay's, contained little, and that little in complete disorder. Prideaux, however, did realize that the scarcity and disorder of the contents were due to later robbery. Among the objects which he found were two gold rings and portions of two ivory statuettes. And it was these statuettes that gave rise to the belief that the tombs were Phoenician. For they were sent to the British Museum, where experts claimed that they showed a resemblance to certain ivories there which were believed to be of Phoenician workmanship. Less than ten years later it was shown that these ivories, which had been excavated at Nineveh in northern Iraq, had nothing to do with the Phoenicians, and in any case did not greatly resemble the Bahrain statuettes. But the damage was done; Prideaux had published, in good faith, the opinion of the British Museum experts, and the Bahrain grave-mounds were thereafter firmly believed to be Phoenician—though the Arabs of Bahrain, who could not read Prideaux's report, equally firmly believed them to be the graves of the Portuguese who had garrisoned the island in the sixteenth century A.D.

Prideaux's and Mackay's reports were bulky volumes that weighed down my suitcases as I packed to return to Denmark. The third report was a slim paper-back offprint from the journal of the Royal Asiatic Society, and it went without difficulty in my coat pocket, to be read on the voyage back across the North Sea. It was the earliest, and by far the most valuable, report of them all, a survey of the antiquities of Bahrain, carried out by a Captain Durand for the British Foreign Office in 1879.

Our respectful admiration for Captain Durand has increased steadily during our fifteen years of exploration on Bahrain. He was not an archæologist. The antiquities of Bahrain were not even his main reason for coming to the island—they were merely his cover. His antiquities survey was published the following year, but a bulkier report, on the contemporary economic and political situation on Bahrain, was—and still is—restricted, for internal Foreign Office consumption only. But his survey of the antiquities is a beautifully thorough job of work. Like those who were to come after him, he of course saw and described the immense mound-fields, and, before Prideaux and before Mackay, he opened one of the large mounds at Ali and described its construction, though he was inclined to doubt whether the structure it contained was intended for burials. But, unlike those who came later, he extended his survey to the rest of the island too, and pointed out many other features of probable historic significance. Time and again in our work we have discovered new sites for investigation and, on going back to Durand's survey, have

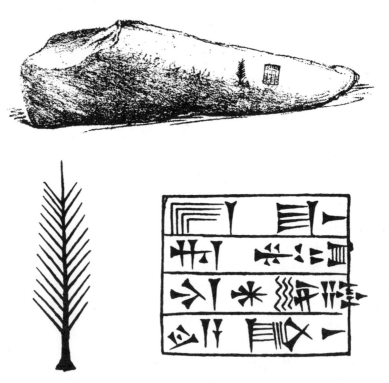

THE STONE CONE, FOUND BY CAPTAIN DURAND IN BAHRAIN IN 1879 AND NOW LOST AGAIN, WAS TWO FEET TWO INCHES HIGH. ORIGINALLY PART OF THE FOUNDATION OF A TEMPLE, THE STYLE OF ITS INSCRIPTION SUGGESTS A DATE OF ABOUT 1800 B.C.

found that he was there first, that he had stood upon our site and listed it as one which would repay closer investigation. To crown his work he discovered and brought back to England a cuneiform inscription, carved on a black basalt stone and built into the wall of a mosque. This inscription he published, and for many a year it was the only extant text from the prehistory of Bahrain. The stone had clearly been a foundation stone, and the inscription, in four lines, was disappointingly short. It read:

> *Palace*
> *of Rimum,*
> *servant of the god Inzak,*
> *man of (the tribe of) Agarum.*

Now, this inscription, for all its brevity, had certain points of significance, particularly centering on the mention of the god Inzak, and they have a bearing on the question of the possible identification of the island of Bahrain. The whole question is discussed at length in the next chapter. Here it need only be said that even at this point we were aware that our proposed expedition to Bahrain was going to involve us in one of the major controversies of Mesopotamian scholarship, the question of the location of the ancient land of Dilmun.

I arrived back in Denmark with the jigsaw pieces of a four-thousand-year-old puzzle in my luggage, to find a more contemporary problem awaiting me, a telegram from Greenland. P.V. wanted to know whether I thought the sheikh of Bahrain would be interested in a gift of a Greenland falcon.

On that point, at least, there could be no two opinions. I wrote to the sheikh's adviser, to be on the safe side, but replied immediately to P.V. that Sheikh Sulman would undoubtedly be delighted. Among the sheikhs and princes of Arabia falconry is a living sport, and there more than anywhere the odd resemblance between the courts of the sheikhdoms and the mediæval courts of Europe is striking. At the daily audiences of the sheikhs there are always retainers standing by with hawk on wrist, and outside the palace hawks and falcons are always to be seen on their perches, dozing motionlessly in the sun or, with wings flapping, tearing at a scrap of fur. The head falconer is one of the most important members of the sheikh's entourage, and in every palace the mews, where the falcons are kept, is one of the best-appointed buildings. Most weeks the sheikhs will be out for two or three days in the desert, hunting gazelle and bustard with their hawks and their swift selukis, and the rival merits of their hawks are eagerly discussed at all times.

Several species of hawk and falcon are employed in the chase, mainly peregrines and goshawks. But the pride of them all is the gerfalcon, the best of which are trapped in Persia, and the sheikhs give large sums for these birds. They are the largest and strongest of the falcons, and in mediæval Europe were reserved for those of royal blood. The rule, in fact, still obtains, and in consequence all Greenland falcons, which are gers, belong on capture to the Danish crown. To present a gerfalcon to the sheikh of Bahrain would thus be in every way to make him a royal present. But there was more to it than that. The ordinary gerfalcon is a magnificent bird, but brown in color with white mottling, like most birds of prey. But the Greenland falcon is pure white, save for the jet-black tips of its feathers. Such a bird had never been seen in the Arabian Gulf; it would be—simply—beyond price.

All this P.V. knew, or at least suspected, and when he had heard of three nestling falcons taken from an eyrie in the mountains near the ice-cap he had immediately acquired them for the Copenhagen Zoo—but reserved one of them for the ruler of Bahrain. As soon as he returned I went over to Copenhagen, and we selected the loveliest of the birds, a tiercel just beginning to assume its magnificent adult plumage, as our gift.

Time went fast from P.V.'s return until we were due to leave at the beginning of December. There was not much we could do in the way of material preparations. We were aiming to reconnoitre the island as thoroughly as we could, and then to dig at the places that seemed most promising. What these places would be and what their special problems would be and what special equipment they would call for we had no means of telling. Our equipment reduced itself to a stout builder's trowel and a two-metre rule each, a surveyor's level and a couple of cameras. What else we needed would have to be acquired on the spot or sent out to us. But I spent a lot of time writing letters to people I still knew out there, to my old company and to the manager of the BOAC hotel and to some of the local merchants. For we knew that we would need a place to live, and a vehicle of some sort, and sooner or later labourers. And our money was very strictly limited so that the sooner we could establish ourselves and get into the field the better.

We left on December 2 by air from Copenhagen, a grey day with low-lying clouds. We had had to pick our plane with care, as the Greenland falcon was to travel in the freight compartment and this had to be pressurized. Cold did not matter—it was built to take temperatures of forty below in Greenland—but it was as dependent on oxygen as we were. We were to fly direct to Beirut, and there change to another plane that would get us to Bahrain late the following day. There was quite a crowd to see us off, half of P.V.'s students and former colleagues from the National Museum; and Vibeke, looking rather wistful, because I had promised her when we left Bahrain three years before that we would return one day. And now I was returning. Without her.

After half an hour in the air we landed at Hamburg and were told that we could go no farther that day. All of southern Europe was blanketed in fog.

We were worried about the falcon. But the zoo people had told us, when we collected it, that it could easily take thirty-six hours without food; so we deposited it in a room comfortingly labelled "Live Freight" and hoped for the best. But the fog was slow to lift, and before we got away late next morning we knew that we had missed our connection from Beirut. We sent a telegram to Sir Charles Belgrave, asking him to tell the sheikh of Bahrain that the falcon and its two attendants would be late.

It was three o'clock the following morning before we touched down at Beirut—to find that our visas were improperly made out (one needed visas in those days for the Lebanon) and that we could not leave the airport. But now we found that we had entered the Arab world, and with a most potent ambassador. We had resigned ourselves to spending the rest of the night on the hard chairs of the transit lounge, but we explained that we had a white falcon with us and we were worried, because it had had neither food nor water for nearly two days. Immediately the atmosphere changed. Customs and immigration officials clustered round as the travelling cage was uncovered and the Greenland falcon blinked sleepily at the lights. A porter was sent to guide me to the airport restaurant, which was not open to feed human customers at that hour but whose duty cook, on hearing the story, immediately conjured up a pan of water and a juicy hunk of meat. Amid murmurs of approval in Arabic the falcon attacked the raw meat with vigor, and while it gorged itself the immigration officer apologized for the stupid mistake that the embassy in Copenhagen must have made in issuing invalid visas, stamped our passports with a flourish, and escorted us to a taxi, promising us that he personally would see to it that the white falcon was properly cared for until we returned. Within half an hour we had checked into one of the luxury hotels that airlines use to mollify benighted passengers and were sleeping away what was left of the night.

The next morning we discovered that the first plane to Bahrain left in the evening, and we sent off another telegram to Sir Charles. In the evening we collected our luggage, and the falcon, and boarded our machine. This time, though, we were travelling by an Arab airline, and there was no question of the most distinguished passenger being banished to the freight compartment. The travelling cage was placed on the forward two seats, by the door, and left uncovered, so that the white falcon could see, and be seen by, all who entered. The night trip was uneventful, and an early-morning stop at Kuwait only memorable for the lively interest which a party of sheikhs, who boarded the plane there, showed in the occupant of the front seat. And an hour later, with the sun well up, I could point out of the window and show P.V. the flat white outline of Bahrain spread out like a map below us as we went into the circuit to land at Muharraq airport.

It was three years and five months since I had last been there, and nothing had changed. As we walked over the Tarmac, the warmth of the December sun on our shoulders, the glare of the sand with the dusty grey-green of the palms beyond, and above all the faint smell in the rather damp air, the slightly acrid, tarry smell that is crude oil, sloughed off instantaneously the intervening years and brought a host of subconscious recollections up to somewhere just below the surface of my mind. Arabic phrases that I had not used or thought during the three years in Denmark came naturally to my tongue as customs and passport and health officials questioned us (and my Arabic has never been other than halting and laborious). It felt good to be back.

But before ever we reached the passport and customs officials, while we were still walking to the airport building with the travelling cage between us, a car drew up alongside and a tall Arab in long white *thaub* and white headcloth descended. "Mr. Glob and Mr. Bibby?" he asked in very good English. We assented. "I am His Highness's falconer," he said. "You have a falcon for His Highness?" We showed him the cage we were carrying. He motioned to two porters, and they took the cage and placed it carefully on the broad back seat of the car. "God be with you," he said, and got in beside the chauffeur. And the car turned and drove away.

P.V. and I looked after the departing car and then at each other. He could at least have offered us a lift into town, we thought. We had brought the finest gift that Denmark had to offer an Arab sheikh, and it had been taken off our hands without even a word of thanks or an offer of help. We were wrong, of course, but it was some years before we understood the Arab point of view. A gift for which a return is expected is no gift. To expect thanks, or especial courtesy, even to make a flourish or an official ceremony of giving is to detract from the gift. When, some years later, His Highness made *us* a gift of a gold watch and a complete Arab costume to each member of the expedition, one of his chauffeurs brought it, in an amorphous brown paper parcel, to the camp and left it, almost surreptitiously, with our servant. And when we suggested that we would like to write and thank Sheikh Sulman we were told that that would be a breach of etiquette.

Gifts should be bestowed by stealth, and never referred to by giver or recipient.

Anyway, there was a car waiting for us after all, sent by the adviser to take us to the BOAC hotel, where a double room was reserved.

A week later we were beginning to feel that we were getting nowhere, and at an uncommonly fast rate. We had called on a lot of people, the adviser, the director of public works, the bank manager, the manager of "my" oil company, the general manager and the production manager of the Bahrain Petroleum Company. We had walked miles along the dusty streets between the tall whitewashed windowless Arab houses of the capital, Manama, from one office to another in a town where no self-respecting European walks. And everyone we met was most interested, enquired when we were going to start digging, and was, I think, surprised that we did not have cut-and-dried plans and mountains of equipment. After all, we called ourselves an expedition, and somehow the term did not seem to fit two rather bewildered men with one suitcase each. When we had left the Bahrain Petroleum Company's office the production manager had said, cordially enough, "Well, we'll be seeing you again when you've something more definite to tell us." That seemed to express the general attitude. In the meantime we were living in a very expensive hotel because there was no other, and any travelling about the island had to be done by taxi. And our funds were being eaten away at an alarming rate.

Only in one respect had we been able to make a move in the right direction. We had discovered that the Bahrain Petroleum Company (Bapco to initiates) had complete air-photograph coverage of the island, and we had spent two days going over these with a stereoscopic magnifying glass. We had made a list of fifty-five sites where unnatural-looking mounds, unexplainable clearings in the palm plantations, or lines of ruined walls suggested that investigation on the ground might repay the trouble. And we had plotted the fields of burial-mounds on our map and made a rough estimate of their number, on a basis of the area covered by the mound-fields and the average density of mounds within the fields. The sum came out at a hundred thousand, a truly stupendous figure, more burial-mounds than in the whole of Denmark or all England. But we still could not visit the mounds or our fifty-five suspicious sites, until we had our own transport. It began to look as though we should have to buy a new jeep, which would make a very large bite into the reserve that we were keeping for excavation expenses.

Then all at once our luck changed. The manager of my old oil company, who was new since my day but who knew of my previous connection with his company, had written to his London office asking for their policy toward appeals for help from indigent archæologists, and he now got a reply allowing him to offer any help within reason. And the machinery began to move. This was the first time, but by no means the last, that we realized just what it meant to have an oil company behind you when opening up a new territory. It turned out that they were preparing to dispose of a large Humber station-car, specially built for desert transport, and it was written down on their books to a value of 170 dollars. We could buy it for its book value. And they would shortly have a furnished house vacant in their compound and saw no reason why we should not move into it, whereupon it would be reasonable for us to take our meals in their guest-house restaurant, at a nominal charge of a dollar a day (for which they "forgot" to bill us).

Three days later we took delivery of the powerful blue station-car, with its massive low-pressure desert tires, and celebrated the event by driving out to Ali, to look at the mounds which Captain Durand and Colonel Prideaux and Ernest Mackay had excavated between thirty and eighty years before. There they stood, just as the excavators had described them, with the sides of their cuttings still standing, and even the roofs of Prideaux's tunnels still unfallen. To archæologists used to digging in the peat bogs of Denmark, where all cuts have to be stepped and graded that the sides may not fall in on the digger, these perpendicular faces still standing after two generations were almost uncanny. We have since learned that the natural gypsum content of the Bahrain soil causes an exposed face to compact in the humid climate into an

27

almost cement hardness, and we have become accustomed to working immediately at the foot of perpendicular cuttings thirty and forty feet high. We have never had a face collapse, and hardly ever even a stone fall from such a face.

Our real work was now begun, and the reader may well be feeling—with the production manager of Bapco—that it is high time our plans and hopes and expectations at this time be more precisely described. That afternoon, on our first day of actual field-work, we had stood beside the results of the field-work of three predecessors. It was not unreasonable to ask what we thought we could do that they had not already done. We had been asked that question often enough, during the months of preparation, and we had got into the habit of replying that nothing at all was known of the history of Bahrain before the island was converted to Islam during the seventh century A.D., and precious little of its history thereafter until the Portuguese established their trading posts in the Gulf in the sixteenth century. Thus everything was grist to our mill, anything at all that could throw light on Bahrain in early Islamic and particularly in pre-Islamic times. The grave-mounds bore witness to the fact that Bahrain's pre-Islamic history had at some period been out of the ordinary and perhaps important, but to fit the grave-mounds into Bahrain's history was not our sole aim. Our aim, in fact, was to fit Bahrain into world history.

Now, the role of re-creator of history is one that no archæologist ever resists. In theory the archæologist is a technician, producing by his technique of controlled exploration and excavation the material on which the historian and the prehistorian can build up their picture of what happened. In practice the two processes are inseparable. Not only can the archæologist never resist the temptation to produce historical theories to fit the archæological facts, not only is he frequently the one best fitted to theorize about what he has found, but there is also a continuous feed-back, whereby the excavated evidence forms the basis of historical theories which are then tested by further excavation, confirmed or modified, and then tested again. We did not believe that we were better archæologists than our predecessors in Bahrain (though techniques had undoubtedly improved in the interval), but we believed that the theories that they had produced to fit Bahrain into world history had been inadequately tested. Mackay had claimed that Bahrain had, in the second millennium B.C., been a graveyard for the nomad tribes which he believed inhabited mainland Arabia at that time; and this theory was perfectly adequate "history"—if it were true. Prideaux had believed that Phoenicians had lived and died in Bahrain before they emigrated to the historical Phoenicia on the Levant coast of the Mediterranean, and this too would have been adequate history—had it been true; it would even have confirmed a statement

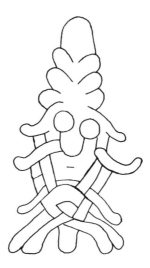

THE AAMAND.

by Herodotus that the Phoenicians in his day claimed that their ancestors came from the Arabian Gulf. Durand's theory—or rather the theory put forward in an appendix to his report by a very much more eminent authority—was much more circumstantial. "Let it be understood then," wrote Sir Henry Rawlinson in 1880, "that throughout the Assyrian tablets, from the earliest period to the latest, there is constant allusion to an island called Niduk-ki in Accadian, and Tilvun or Tilmun in Assyrian, and that this name, which unquestionably applies to Bahrein . . ." Sir Henry Rawlinson had an intuition that bordered on the uncanny, and even at that early date he had seen that Dilmun was a land of unusual importance in the minds of the ancient peoples of Meso-potamia. Later discoveries have shown that it occupied a unique position in their history and mythology, as the next chapters will try to show. And Rawlinson, for what it was worth, postulated that Bahrain could be Dilmun. The evidence at that time was slender. Whether it is stronger now is the question that this book seeks to pose.

It would be unfair to a distinguished scholar not to mention at this point Dr. Peter Bruce Cornwall, who during World War II excavated a number of the Bahrain burial-mounds and later wrote a very detailed thesis putting forward the evidence for an identification of Bahrain with Dilmun. The reason why he has not been mentioned hitherto is that when we began our work we knew little more than the bare fact that an American archæologist had worked for a time on the island. It was only some years later, and by rather devious channels, that we were able to obtain a photostatic copy of Dr. Cornwall's unpublished thesis and confir-mation of which grave-mounds he had excavated.

At the time, then, when our serious field-work was about to begin we were prepared to regard anything at all earlier than the Portuguese as worthy of investigation. Our terms of reference were simply to find out what had happened in Bahrain, from the time when man first set foot on the island until the beginning of recorded history a scant five hundred years ago. In theory we were just as interested in Stone Age implements or in early Islamic ruins as we were in the problem of the burial-mounds that had so monopolized our forerunners. But in practice we were well aware that there was one question that was bound to bulk larger than any other: that in seeking to bring Bahrain into the stream of world history we would be bound to find ourselves looking for Dilmun.

CHAPTER TWO

ༀༀༀༀༀ

"LIKE A FISH IN THE MIDST
OF THE SEA"

I have a feeling that people do not "discover lost civilizations"; but rather that, when the time is ripe, lost civilizations reveal themselves, using for the purpose whatever resources and people are to hand. This has, at least, been the case with Dilmun, which has gradually, over the last hundred years, swum back into the surface waters of world history, after being completely submerged for twenty-four hundred years.

For almost two and a half millennia Dilmun was in literal truth a lost civilization, lost as Assyria and Egypt and Babylonia never were, as even the Hittite Empire and Minoan Crete and the Sumerians were not lost.

That Babylon and Nineveh and hundred-gated Thebes had been capitals of mighty empires long before the time of the Greeks and Romans was information that had never been lost, that was known to the classical historians, to the monks of the Dark Ages, to the new scholars of the Renaissance. All that was lost was the location of these ancient capitals. That Crete had been a power in the Mediterranean before the rise of mainland Greece stood clearly written in the epics of Homer and the classical accounts of the legend of Theseus and the Minotaur. But the excavation by Sir Arthur Evans of the great palace at Knossos was needed, to show that the *Iliad* and the classical legends were not entirely works of fiction. That the Hittites and Sumerians had once been great powers was indeed completely lost to history—but the names at least survived. The Hittites and the land of Shinar stood recorded in the early books of the Bible.

But neither in classical history nor in biblical recollection nor in epic poetry nor in legend was any mention preserved of the land of Dilmun. For twenty-four hundred years no man ever heard the name of Dilmun, no extant book or paper or inscription bore mention of Dilmun.

And yet for more than two millennia before that, for just as long a period as Dilmun had been forgotten, its name had been a household word. It had been a country well known to traders and travellers, to historians and geographers, a country famous in romance and epic, in mythology and cosmogony. In these millennia the men of Dilmun roamed the known world. Their artifacts and inscriptions are found from Greece to the borders of Burma.

The way to Dilmun lay through the rediscovery of the civilizations of Assyria and Babylonia. Here the first systematic work began in 1842, when Paul Émile Botta was appointed French consul in Mosul, in northern Iraq. The tale has often been told of how Botta was fascinated by the huge mounds, called Nabi Yunus and Kuyunjik, which lay on the other bank of the Tigris from Mosul, and how he began to dig, first in Nabi Yunus and, when that was forbidden, on Kuyunjik. Three months' work at Kuyunjik brought little result, but aroused much interest among the local inhabitants. And one of them, a farmer from the village of Khorsabad some twelve miles to the northeast, noticed that all fragments of stone and brick bearing inscriptions were carefully collected, and told Botta that if he were interested in such things he should dig at Khorsabad, where there were thousands of them. Botta was sceptical, but sent a couple of workmen to dig at the village. And a little way beneath the surface they came on a wall lined with slabs of sculptured alabaster . . .

Forthwith Botta moved his workers to Khorsabad, and for eighteen months, with considerable obstruction from the Turkish governor of Mosul, excavated the palace that proved to lie beneath the village mound. A hundred rooms and corridors were unearthed, the majority with walls lined with bas-reliefs, carvings of battle scenes and religious processions, of gods and of kings, all in an art style never before seen. The ornaments and dresses of the human figures were of completely unknown type, the monsters depicted belonged to no known mythology, while the doorways were everywhere flanked by winged statues of bulls and lions with human heads. Between and upon the carved slabs were long inscriptions, engraved in a script composed of wedge-shaped signs.

Not long after the first ornamented slabs were exposed it became clear to Botta that the palace he was excavating had been destroyed by fire. And, alabaster being a form of limestone, the fired slabs began rapidly to disintegrate into powder when exposed to the air. While Botta attempted to draw the rapidly crumbling slabs, the French government sent out, post haste, an experienced artist who thereafter, as the excavation proceeded, drew with meticulous accuracy all the bas-reliefs and inscriptions. And by 1850, seven years after the excavation was completed, Botta was able to publish, in five volumes, a complete account and pictorial record of the Khorsabad palace.

During these seven years another excavator had made discoveries rivalling those of Botta. Austen Henry Layard had been on the scene first, in 1840, making an adventurous journey, with one companion, which aimed to reach India overland from the Mediterranean. They had travelled by horseback and without escort, and they had spent some time in Mosul and looked at the mounds of Kuyunjik and Nabi Yunus. They had made a detour to Baghdad and on the way had looked at other mounds farther down the Tigris, in particular one called Nimroud. Layard had been intrigued by the mystery of these mounds, with their surface debris of potsherds and inscribed bricks, and when the two companions reached Hamadan, in Persia, he decided to change his plans and return to Mosul. This journey had apparently been leisurely in the extreme, and when Layard reached Mosul again it was already 1842 and Botta had begun to excavate at Kuyunjik. Layard hurried on to Constantinople, at that time, of course, the capital of the Turkish Empire of which Mosul and the whole of Mesopotamia formed a part, and from there he tried to gain support for a British excavation of the buried sites of the Mosul area. For three years, as he says, "I spoke to others about excavations, but received little encouragement." These were the three years during which Botta was astounding the world with his revelation of a completely unknown civilization at Khorsabad, a civilization that the biblical and classical historians had, with one accord, identified as that of Assyria. "At last," says Layard, "in the autumn of 1845, Lord Stratford de Redcliffe, then Sir Stratford Canning, offered to incur, jointly with myself, for a limited period, the expense of excavations in Assyria, in the hope that, should success attend the attempt, means would be found to carry it out on an adequate scale." Layard left Constantinople immediately. "I crossed the mountains of Pontus and the great steppes of the Usum Yilak as fast as post-horses could carry me, descended the high lands into the valley of the Tigris, galloped over the vast plains of Assyria, and reached Mosul in twelve days."

It is not the purpose of this chapter to describe in detail the unveiling of Assyria and Babylonia. But briefly, Layard dug first, for two years, at the mound of Nimroud, now known to be the Calah of the Bible, and unearthed palaces rivalling those of Khorsabad. The same winged bulls and winged lions flanked in the same manner the doorways of halls lined with sculptured slabs. And everywhere among the reliefs of hunting and battle scenes were carved inscriptions in the wedge-shaped script of the Assyrians.

The British Museum now threw its weight into the scales. And Layard, with something like adequate funds at his disposal, decided, while continuing his excavations at Nimroud, to investigate the very much bigger mound of Kuyunjik. For although Botta had dug there with little success there appeared to be very little doubt that the mounds of Kuyunjik and Nabi Yunus covered the city of Nineveh itself, the capital of Assyria. In the summer of 1847, in the course of a single month's digging, Layard located at Kuyunjik a palace comparable to those of Nimroud and

Khorsabad. But his funds were exhausted, and he decided to return to London, after an absence of seven years. Two years later he returned, again with support from the British Museum, and in the course of eighteen months excavated at Kuyunjik "71 halls, chambers and passages . . . 27 portals, formed by colossal winged bulls and lion-sphinxes . . . and 9880 feet of bas-reliefs." And among the debris filling the sculptured chambers he found a large number of tablets of baked clay, covered with writing in the same wedge-shaped script as was found on the wall-slabs.

This was the first time that the long-familiar wedge-shaped, or cuneiform, script had been found inscribed on tablets, and the discovery opened wide perspectives. Although the script could not at that time be read, philologists had been working on its problems for a century and a half, and they were confident that they were nearing success. For the inscriptions dug up by Botta and by Layard were by no means the first cuneiform texts to be discovered and published.

On the northern shore of the Arabian Gulf, due north of Bahrain, lies Bushire, the largest port of Persia. And from it runs the main north-south land route through Persia, via Shiraz and Isfahan to the capital, Teheran, and to the Caspian Sea. A hundred and fifty miles along that route, forty miles northeast of Shiraz, lie the imposing ruins of a splendid city, known to the Persians as Takht-i-Jamshid, "the throne of Jamshid," or Chehil-Minar, "the forty pillars." They were first described for Europeans by the Venetian ambassador to the Persian court, Geosafat Barbaro, in 1472, and in 1602 the Portuguese ambassador Antonio de Gouuea first mentions the inscriptions which were to be seen upon the ruins. They were described in more detail by his successor, Don Garcia Silva Figveroa, in 1617, and it was Don Garcia who first correctly identified the ruins as the site of Persepolis, the capital of Darius the Great of Persia. Four years later, in 1621, the site was visited by a famous Italian traveller, Pietro della Valle (who also visited Babylon), and the first copy of a portion of the Persepolis inscriptions was made and brought to Europe. In the course of the seventeenth century two or three other short—and inaccurate—portions of the Persepolis inscriptions were published by European travellers, and in 1700 the term "cuneiform" (from the Latin *cuneus,* a wedge) was first used to describe the wedge-shaped script.

Serious study of the script only began, however, with the publication in 1778 of accurate drawings of three long trilingual inscriptions from Persepolis by Carsten Niebuhr.

Carsten Niebuhr has rather haunted our Danish expedition to the Arabian coast. The fact that he was a Dane, from the then Danish province of Schleswig, that he was a member—and the sole survivor—of a Danish scientific expedition to Arabia, and that that expedition was sent out by the king of Denmark just two hundred years before our expedition made us feel in many ways that we were merely carrying forward the work begun by this unassuming lieutenant of engineers.

The tale of this earlier Danish expedition has recently been told, in book form, by a member of *our* expedition (Thorkild Hansen: *Arabia Felix*), and—although this chapter is already piling digression upon digression—it is well worth telling briefly here. Six men, five scientists and one servant, left Copenhagen in 1761, with Egypt and the Yemen, in southwest Arabia, as their immediate goal. From there they were to proceed to Basra, and return overland through Mesopotamia and Syria. There was a professor of philology whose task was to study the languages and customs of the Middle East and to collect inscriptions and manuscripts; a Swedish professor of botany, a pupil of the great Linnæus, who was to collect plants and other natural-history specimens; an artist and copper-plate engraver who was to make illustrations of the countries and peoples met; a doctor, to study the diseases and medicines of the areas visited, and to look to the health of the expedition; a Swedish ex-soldier as servant; and Lieutenant Carsten Niebuhr, who was to act as surveyor and astronomer, to make maps and keep records of distances covered. As it turned out, apart from a portfolio of drawings by the artist, none of the objectives allotted to the first five members of the expedition were to be achieved by them. The philologist found no inscriptions; the collections of the botanist were largely lost and those not lost were dispersed; the doctor collected no medicines, failed to save the lives of four of the expedition's members, and finally died himself. The expedition would have been a disastrous and utter failure had it not been for the lieutenant of engineers, who, after the last of his companions had died of malaria and malnutrition in the Yemen and in India, carried through the planned overland trip from Persia to Denmark, taking on single-handed all the planned researches, collecting the specimens, copying the inscriptions, drawing the panoramas and portraits, and making the maps to cover everything of scientific interest met on the route. He arrived back in Copenhagen at the end of 1767, seven years after the expedition set out. For the last four of these seven years Niebuhr had worked and travelled alone. We had no reason to be ashamed of our predecessor in these latitudes.

It was the copies that Carsten Niebuhr made of the inscriptions of Persepolis that gave the impetus to the first real attempts to solve the riddle of the cuneiform script. Indeed, Niebuhr himself, though no philologist, made the first contribution, pointing out that the inscriptions were written in three different forms of cuneiform, the first of which only used forty-two different signs.

The conclusion was very quickly drawn that the three forms of cuneiform represented three different languages, all using a form of the cuneiform script, and that the first of them was alphabetic, each sign representing a letter, whereas the other two were probably syllabic, a different sign for each syllable giving naturally, as in Chinese, a larger number of signs. Logic suggested that in each three-language inscription the same message was in fact being given in each of the three languages, and that these three languages were probably the languages of the three major divisions of the Persian Empire, Persia proper, Susiana, and Babylonia. And effort was concentrated on the first script, obviously the easiest to "break," which was—rightly as it turned out—guessed to be Old Persian.

Now, it is outside the scope of this book to tell of the decipherment of Old Persian, or of cuneiform in general (and the story has been told many times already). Suffice it to say that progress was slow, though advances were made, and the names of Hystaspes, Darius, and Xerxes were identified, giving the phonetic values of fifteen signs. The trouble was that the Persepolis inscriptions were too short. Reading an unknown script is in many ways like breaking a cipher, and is largely a statistical process of collation of words and phrases, of finding out which signs occur most frequently and which combinations, or variations in combinations, of signs occur. The process is immeasurably easier if you have long messages with many signs at your disposal, and the eminent philologists who, in the early years of the nineteenth century, spent long hours and much ingenuity wringing the last drops of evidence out of the few three- and four-line inscriptions brought home by Niebuhr would have been better employed exploring Persia for longer inscriptions in the same scripts.

As it happened the Honourable East India Company saved them the trouble, when it seconded a twenty-three-year-old officer of its Indian army to the task of training and modernizing the Persian army. The officer was Henry Creswicke Rawlinson, and the year was 1833.

Just as the main south road in Persia runs from Teheran past Persepolis to the Arabian Gulf, the main west road runs from Teheran past Hamadan and Kermanshah to Baghdad. It is an ancient road, for Hamadan is the old Ecbatana, while at the western end of the road is not only Baghdad but also Ctesiphon and Babylon. Fifty miles west of Hamadan and twenty miles east of Kermanshah, the road skirts the end of a mountain range at Bisitun, running below a sheer rock face over 3,800 feet high. On this cliff, almost five hundred years before the beginning of the Christian Era and some 500 feet above ground level, Darius the Great of Persia had caused to be carved a large relief of himself as the conqueror of kings, and thirteen columns of inscriptions in the same three cuneiform scripts as occur at Persepolis. It was these inscriptions that attracted the attention of the young British major.

In 1835 and 1836 Rawlinson copied the greater part of the Old Persian inscription, which was the easiest of access, scrambling three and four times a day up the steep rock face to the foot of the inscription, balancing a short ladder upon the ledge, only eighteen inches wide, which ran along the foot of the inscription, and then standing upon the topmost rung of the ladder "with no other support," he tells us, "than steadying the body against the rock with the left arm, while the left hand holds the notebook and the right hand is employed with the pencil." By 1839, working on this hard-won material without any knowledge of the researches of the philologists in Europe, he had succeeded in deciphering nearly half of the inscription. In that year, however, the Afghan War recalled him to India and to Afghanistan, where he was mentioned in despatches and later appointed Political Officer in Kandahar in southern Afghanistan. It was not until the end of 1843 that he could return to his cuneiform studies. In December of that year he was appointed Political Agent in Baghdad.

This was the very year when Botta was startling the world with his discovery of inscribed alabaster slabs at Khorsabad farther north along the Tigris, and when Layard was trying desperately to raise funds for excavations at Nimroud and Kuyunjik. But Rawlinson had an appointment with Darius the Great, and the following summer he rode two hundred miles to Bisitun, to make a new and more accurate copy of the whole of the Old Persian and Susian inscriptions. The Susian text was more difficult to reach than the Old Persian, for here the foot-ledge was missing over a large stretch, and Rawlinson completed his copy balanced upon an upright ladder standing precariously upon a horizontal ladder bridging a sheer drop of several hundred feet. In the following year he revised his translation of 1839, and in 1846 it was published by the Royal Asiatic Society in London.

The following year, while Layard was excavating the first hoard of cuneiform tablets at Kuyunjik, Rawlinson was back at Bisitun, to try to get a copy of the Babylonian version of the inscription of Darius. This was a vastly more difficult task than that of copying the first two versions. For the Old Persian and Susian texts formed the lower register of the inscribed slabs, and the ledge below them could be reached via the irregularities of the precipice below. But the Babylonian text was inscribed upon slabs above the other two texts, and the smoothed surface of these lower slabs was quite impossible to climb. Above the inscriptions the rocks overhang the text, making access from above equally impossible. Rawlinson was at a loss, until a "wild Kurdish boy" volunteered to reach the inscriptions. Climbing up a cleft to the left of the inscriptions, he drove in a peg with a rope attached and, taking the other end of the rope, traversed across the almost smooth rock of the overhang above the inscription. At the other side he drove in another peg, and, with a loop of rope thus hanging free across the inscription, could fix up a "swinging seat, like a painter's cradle." From this, under Rawlinson's direction, he took casts in wet paper of the whole of the Babylonian text of the inscription.

With this material at his disposal Rawlinson returned to Baghdad, and for the next four years, first in Baghdad and then on a two-year leave in London (his first holiday in twenty-two years), he worked on the decipherment of the Babylonian language and script. It proved unexpectedly difficult, as many of the signs appeared to be capable of representing a large number of completely distinct syllabic sounds. And indeed, when he published his translation, first in lectures in London in 1850 and later in print in 1852, his interpretation was widely criticized on that score. If the signs had so many alternative values, it was said, the Babylonians could never themselves have known which ones were intended, and could not have read their own language . . .

In 1857, however, the critics were silenced, and Rawlinson's decipherment vindicated. In that year Rawlinson, and three other philologists who had been working, more or less independently of each other and of Rawlinson, on the problems of the Babylonian language, Hinckes of Ireland, Oppert of Paris, and Fox Talbot of London, were invited by the Royal Asiatic Society to submit separately, and in sealed envelopes, their translations of an inscription recently found during excavation by Layard's successor in northern Iraq. When the envelopes were opened a jury of five members of the society could report that the similarities between them were so remarkable, the rendering being often word for word the same, that there could be no doubt that the language of Babylonia and Assyria could now be read.

.   .   .

I make no apology for this long account of the first excavations at
Kuyunjik and Khorsabad, and of the reading of the cuneiform
script. Together they explain how, at the time when Layard and
Botta uncovered the palaces of an unsuspected civilization, with
their monumental inscriptions and their archives of clay tablets,
circumstances had conspired to bring about that the language in
which the inscriptions and archives were written was just on the
verge of being deciphered. Within a score of years of the excavation of the first slab at Khorsabad the history of Assyria, as
recorded by its own kings on the walls of their own palaces, was
known to the world.

And as an incidental by-product of the emergence of Assyria
and Babylonia into the full light of history, and certainly not
realized at the time, the stage was set for the reappearance of
Dilmun.

We have seen that the first monumental inscription to be found
in Mesopotamia was on the alabaster slabs excavated by Botta at
Khorsabad in 1842 and 1843. In 1850 these were published in
France, at the same time as Rawlinson in London was lecturing
on the translation of the Bisitun inscriptions. Four years after the
Royal Asiatic Society had proved that cuneiform could be read,
in 1861, a full publication, with translation, of Botta's Khorsabad
inscriptions appeared in France. They proved to be a full account, told nine times over in different words, of the events of the
reign of a certain Sharru-kin, king of Assyria; and they included a
description of the campaigns against Israel that established beyond a doubt that Sharru-kin was the Sargon, king of Assyria,
recorded by Isaiah.

This first correlation of the annals of a king of Assyria with the
Bible seized the imagination of the world, and it is hardly surprising that the rest of the inscription, full of the tale of campaigns
against other lands and other kings, most of them unknown,
received little attention. Certainly no one paid serious heed to the
closing phrases of an account of Sargon's campaign against a
rebel king of Babylonia, Marduk-apel-iddina, who is the Merodach-Baladan of the Bible. Sargon drove Merodach-Baladan out

41

of Babylon and pursued him into his southern realms of Chaldæa and Bit-Iakin. And, he says, "I brought under my sway Bit-Iakin on the shore of the Bitter Sea as far as the border of Dilmun," and he adds that "Uperi, king of Dilmun, whose abode is situated, like a fish, 30 double-hours away in the midst of the sea of the rising sun, heard of the might of my sovereignty, and sent his gifts." Dilmun had re-entered history—and nobody cared.

In the meantime Rawlinson had been busy. Now the acknowledged master of cuneiform, he had turned his attention to the clay tablets that Layard had brought home from Kuyunjik, and in the same year—1861—in which the Annals of Sargon were published in France Rawlinson published in London the first volume of tablets from the British Museum collection, in a series entitled "The Cuneiform Inscriptions of Western Asia." It was now known that the palace excavated by Layard in Kuyunjik was that of Assurbanipal, another king of Assyria well known from the Bible, and the cuneiform tablets proved to be part of the royal library of this king. But they were a very different proposition from the monumental inscriptions found engraved on the walls of the palaces. For one thing they were incomparably more difficult to read; they were in many cases fragmentary and written in a microscopic script. But they were also of a very different character. Whereas the inscriptions were clearly intended to give an easily readable account of the reigns of the kings who had caused them to be carved, the library was a jumble of records of widely different kinds. Among them were lists of cities, fragments of psalms and incantations, business records, copies of earlier inscriptions from other parts of the Assyrian Empire, portions of poems and myths, and even dictionaries, lists of signs with their variant meanings and pronunciations; some of them were even written in a new and unknown language, sometimes with Assyrian translation, sometimes without. And the sheer number of the tablets made the task of selection almost impossibly difficult, for by now about twenty-five thousand tablets had been recovered . . .

Just what principle Rawlinson followed in selecting the tablets for publication in the British Museum series is now unknown. It can hardly have been intentional that two of the tablets in the second volume, two in the third, and again two in the fourth mentioned this still insignificant land of Dilmun. They added little to the scanty information given in the inscription of Sargon of Assyria. Three appeared to be fragments of hymns or incantations, in very obscure terms, associating Dilmun with a variety of gods. One appeared to include Dilmun among a number of cities and regions subject to Assyria in the time of Assurbanipal. One was simply a list of gods, with the regions under their protection appended. In the list occurred the line:

"The god Enzak; the god Nabu of Dilmun."

This identification of Enzak (also listed elsewhere as Inzak) as the tutelary god of Dilmun was, as we know, to prove of significance later. The sixth mention of Dilmun was of greater immediate interest. It occurred on a tablet describing the career of King Sargon of Akkad, and states that he reached the "Lower Sea," which is the Arabian Gulf, and conquered Dilmun.

Now Sargon of Akkad is not to be confused with Sargon of Assyria. It was already clear from the text itself that Sargon of Akkad was immeasurably earlier than the Sargon of Assyria who reigned in the eighth century B.C. (Rawlinson even describes him in his publication of the tablet as "mythical"), and later research and discoveries have revealed Sargon of Akkad as the founder of the first empire in history, becoming king of Akkad, or Agade, in southern Mesopotamia, in 2303 B.C. (or thereabouts), some sixteen centuries earlier than his later namesake, and going on to conquer all the land between the Mediterranean and the Arabian Gulf.

The situation at that stage, twenty years after the first reading of cuneiform, was that some half dozen documents had been deciphered and published mentioning a land called Dilmun. They were all casual references, in documents containing casual references to dozens and scores of unidentifiable lands and cities. Even among the research workers who were now beginning to call themselves Assyriologists there was little profit or interest in chasing these unknown geographical names. The Assyriologists had other things to think about. As more and more of the larger cuneiform tablets from Assurbanipal's library were deciphered, they—and the world with them—began to realize that they were recovering a whole literature. Hymns and incantations began to fit together, and soon it became clear that some of them formed part of whole epic poems recounting the deeds of gods and heroes.

The epic poetry was, in later years, to have a bearing on the "Dilmun question." But when Captain Durand in 1880 published the results of his survey of the antiquities of Bahrain, there was no reason to believe that Dilmun was more than a little kingdom somewhere on the periphery of the Assyrian Empire. But Durand had found a cuneiform inscription on Bahrain, and therefore the Royal Asiatic Society, who published his report, asked the great Sir Henry Rawlinson to comment on the report.

Rawlinson's comment forms an article quite as long as the report itself, and it is fairly heavy going. He not only quoted all the cuneiform references to Dilmun then extant, but also all the later references to the Arabian Gulf in Greek and Roman writers, and he dealt in great detail, and with amazing prescience, with the possible role of Dilmun in the mythology and theology of the Babylonians. But his main argument was clear. The writer of the Bahrain inscription described himself as "slave of the god Inzak." The god Inzak was defined, in the British Museum tablet that Rawlinson had himself deciphered and published, as the "god Nabu"—in other words, the principal deity—"of Dilmun." And Dilmun, according to the annals of Sargon of Assyria, was the land whose ruler dwelt "30 double-hours away in the midst of the sea of the rising sun."

Rawlinson claimed that Bahrain was identical with Dilmun.

We must, I am afraid, look a little more closely at the evidence. Because some very eminent authorities have later disagreed with this identification. What Sargon of Assyria in fact said is that he conquered "Bit-Iakin on the shore of the Bitter Sea as far as the border of Dilmun." He later states that he conquered "Bit-Iakin, north and south, as far as" four cities "which are on the Elamite border," that he thereafter ordered one of his commanders to build a fortress at "Saglat, on the Elamite border," and only then goes on to say that "Uperi, king of Dilmun, whose abode is situated, like a fish, 30 double-hours away in the midst of the sea of the rising sun . . . sent his gifts."

Two things are clear from this. One is that, while the king of Dilmun lived on an island (for "like a fish" and "in the midst of the sea" are terms commonly used to describe islands), his realm also included part of the mainland, since it had a common frontier with Bit-Iakin. And the other is that the location of Bit-Iakin is vital to the question of where this mainland region lay. That Bit-Iakin lay to the south of Babylonia is attested by many phrases in the inscriptions, and Sargon also tells us that it lay "on the shore of the Bitter Sea" and that it had a common frontier, not only with Dilmun, but also with Elam. And Elam without a doubt was in present-day Persia, its capital, Susa, lying some 200 miles due east of Babylon. The question, then, is whether Bit-Iakin lay on the northern, Persian, coast or on the southern, Arabian, coast of the Bitter Sea. For on whichever side it lay, Dilmun must have been on the same side. A further complication lies in the possibility that the Bitter Sea itself, the Arabian Gulf, may not today have the same extent, in the delta area of the mouths of the Euphrates and Tigris, as it had at the time when Sargon of Assyria campaigned there.

We are in a better position now to answer these questions than Rawlinson was over eighty years ago. At his time it was believed that the Arabian Gulf in antiquity extended some seventy miles farther into Mesopotamia than it now does. But recent geological researches have shown beyond a doubt that this theory, still to be found in most textbooks, is unfounded, and that for all practical purposes we can regard the present-day coastline of the head of the Gulf as unchanged from that of Babylonian times. And in the 1920's the Annals of Sennacherib provided new information about the geographical location of Bit-Iakin.

Sennacherib was the son and successor of Sargon of Assyria, and shortly after his succession in 705 B.C. he had to take the field against the same Merodach-Baladan, king of Bit-Iakin, who had revolted against his father. He too, he tells us, conquered Bit-Iakin and reached the sea. And the inhabitants of the coastal towns of Bit-Iakin took to their ships and crossed the sea to seek refuge in Elam. This leaves no doubt that the coastal regions of Bit-Iakin lay on the Arabian side of the Gulf, and that the common frontier with Elam of which Sargon of Assyria talked lay in the region north of the head of the Gulf, somewhere in the lower Euphrates-Tigris area. Mainland Dilmun must then lie south of Bit-Iakin, farther along the Arabian coast.

We are, unfortunately, at this point still far from knowing precisely where Dilmun was. All we know is that it comprised part of mainland Arabia with access to the Arabian Gulf and also at least one island in that Gulf. We have, of course, one quoted distance, the "30 double-hours" of Sargon. It helps us little, though. For one thing numbers in the annals of the kings of Assyria are rarely trustworthy; for another, while we know that the island capital of Dilmun lay at one end of this distance we do not know where to measure *from;* and finally the actual unit of measurement is not very precise. But doing the best we can with what we have, we may guess that the 30 double-hours are to be measured from "Saglat, on the Elamite border," whither, it seems likely, Uperi, king of Dilmun, sent his gifts, and though we do not know where Saglat lay it cannot have been far north of the head of the Gulf. From there to Bahrain is 300 miles. Now, a "double-hour" is simply the distance that can be travelled in two hours, and it is normally used of a two-hour march. At that rate Bahrain would lie too far away, though not outside the range of normal inaccuracy of Assyrian measurements. But if a "double-hour" in the case of sea distances can mean a two-hour *sail* (and I am not sure whether the philologists will allow me this possibility) then the distance is almost embarrassingly accurate. With the north wind that blows four days out of five in the Gulf a speed of 5 miles an hour, or 4.3 knots, would be very reasonable indeed, and Arab dhows today, which are probably speedier than the ships of three thousand years ago, count the voyage from the Shatt al-Arab to Bahrain a good two-day sail.

We have then reached the conclusion that, unless we are to disregard completely the only geographical information we have, we must agree that Rawlinson's identification of Dilmun with

Bahrain is the guess that best fits the facts, though we must keep in mind that Dilmun was more than just Bahrain; it was also a still unidentified area of the Arabian coast.

A long while ago our impatient readers left P.V. and me preparing to explore Bahrain. But after the long discursion that has occupied this chapter we all, I hope, know more about what we had to look for. For if Bahrain was in fact Dilmun, or the seat of the kings of Dilmun, then we could expect towns—cities perhaps —of the people of Dilmun dating to the period during which we knew that Dilmun existed. And that was the period from Sargon king of Akkad to Sargon king of Assyria, from about 2300 B.C. to about 700 B.C. In fact we could do better than that. For since the time of Durand's and Rawlinson's report other historical inscriptions had come to light naming Dilmun. And we knew that the first-ever reference to Dilmun occurred in a tablet of Ur-nanshe, king of Lagash, in south Babylonia, who lived about 2520 B.C., and who claims that "the ships of Dilmun, from the foreign lands, brought me wood as a tribute." The latest-ever reference is in an administrative document of the eleventh year of Nabonidus, king of Babylonia, which is 544 B.C., mentioning a "governor of Dilmun."

Dilmun, then, was known to have existed for almost exactly two thousand years, and anything we found on Bahrain dating within those two thousand years would have a bearing on the history of Dilmun. So we set out to look for Dilmun.

It was a bright and windswept day. It was well on in December, not many days before Christmas, and there was a nip in the air very foreign to the usual balmy winter weather of Bahrain. The sky was a pale blue with high cloud. The usual haze that obscures the long view had been swept away, and across the narrow water to the west the ochre shore of Saudi Arabia could be plainly seen. A mile or so behind us the dark-blue bulk of our station-car stood out clearly against the yellow desert sand, where we had left it at the end of the oil-company track. Ahead of us hillocks of sand and parched scrub stretched up to the skyline where we knew the rim-rocks dropped to the central bowl of the island. We were on our way to a ruined building, far from any habitation, which the air photographs had shown out here in the southwestern desert area.

P.V., a little in advance, stooped down, and then turned and held out his clenched fist to me. "The expedition is off the ground," he said, and dropped a flake of flint into my out-stretched hand.

Now, I should explain that there are two main classifications of archæologists. There are those who are crazy about potsherds, and those who are crazy about flint. I belong to the first category, and P.V., though as good an all-rounder as I have met, belongs to the second. Your real flint enthusiast has a sort of second-sight. He can see worked flint, not merely at a distance where it is manifestly impossible to distinguish flint from stone, but, I am convinced, at anything up to an inch and a half below ground surface. And the fragment of flint that P.V. had picked up was unquestionably worked. It was only a "waster," a piece struck off in the course of fashioning some flint implement, but it showed the unmistakable bulb of percussion that can only be produced by the hand of man. We had found the Bahrain Stone Age.

Of course we had not found Dilmun. Worked flints found at ground surface are not in themselves datable. Flint does not age or decay. It only in certain circumstances even acquires a patina or a weathering that can make it certain that it was not struck the day before yesterday. And although patina, if present, does prove a considerable age, you cannot tell from it whether the flint is five hundred or fifty thousand years old. But as we ranged around for the rest of the morning gradually filling all our available pockets with fragments of worked flint, we began to make the acquaintance of the people who had worked the flint. Actual implements were few, perhaps a dozen in all—and all, as I recollect, spotted by P.V. And they were mainly scrapers and rather crude cutting tools. They were the tools used by hunters, to prepare skins and to work in bone, and despite their lack of any indication of age they clearly belonged to the general run of Middle Palæolithic cultures. They were probably not more than fifty thousand, but could hardly be less than, say, twelve thousand years old. And even that would make them nearly three times as old as the first mention of Dilmun.

But we had not come to Bahrain primarily to find Dilmun. We had come to find prehistory, and this was prehistory with a vengeance. P.V., who knew—and told me that evening—of the wide geographical gap separating the known Stone Age industries of Palestine and Africa from those of India, was already visualizing a link-up through an Arabian Stone Age; and I think it was on that day that we first began to think in wider terms than Bahrain Island. And the fact that the ruined building which we had come to look at turned out to be the remains of a mosque probably not more than a century or two old could in no way quench the glowing satisfaction of our first discovery.

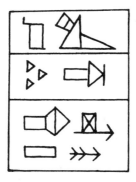

THIS INSCRIPTION OF UR-NANSHE, KING OF LAGASH ABOUT 2520 B.C., RECORDS THAT SHIPS OF DILMUN BROUGHT HIM WOOD FROM FOREIGN LANDS. IT IS THE EARLIEST DOCUMENT EXTANT WHICH MENTIONS DILMUN.

49

CHAPTER THREE

THE HIDDEN GARDENS

We were out every day from early morning until well after dark for the rest of the year, and some way into January. It was the cold season, and there would be a clammy chill in the air as we drove out of town. The mist would be hanging thick among the palm-trees, and the asphalt of the road would be black and slick with condensation. But before we were out of the date plantations the sun would already be groping through the mist, and over the desert the sky would be clear and the road rapidly drying. We would leave the asphalt road for a sandy track, P.V. driving and I trying hard to follow the route by our forty-year-old map and by the notes we had made from the aerial photographs. Often we would meet irrigation ditches, with a couple of date-palms felled across, as a bridge meant more for donkeys than for automobiles. And then most often we had to turn back and try a new route, though occasionally we essayed a crossing, the one who was driving following with painful accuracy—and with his tongue, as the Danes say, held level in his mouth—the signals of the other, as he guided the wheels onto the two narrow bridges. Sooner or later we would have to leave the car, and go on on foot. The objects of our journeys were various. Most often they were ruined buildings, three quarters covered with sand, with only a course or two of coral blocks still showing; or irregular mounds of sand that might well be the same thing at a later stage—now completely sand-covered. Once it was a hilltop fort, a ring of tumbled stones around the edges of an isolated mesa eroded away from the rim-rocks some way south of the oil town of Awali in the center of the island. Several times what we sought was the course of a *qanat*. The *qanats* are underground water-channels, dug out by hand and walled and roofed with slabs of stone, often running twenty feet and more below the surface. They extend for miles, running from the lower slopes of the central hills of Bahrain to the lowlands of the west coast, where a few poverty-stricken villages still exist and a little cultivation is still carried on. But the *qanats* no longer carry water for this cultivation, and following the water-channels uphill to their source we found out why.

There was no difficulty about following the underground channels. About every fifty yards circular stone "chimneys" led down to them from the surface, and the upper ends of these shafts, protruding one to four feet above the surface sand, formed long lines leading inexorably into the distance. Follow them for a mile or two and you see in the heat haze of the approaching noon a low brown wall and the grey-green of palm bushes beyond it. You come closer and finally climb the gentle slope of sand that almost laps the top of the wall. And then you see that the palm fronds are not the low bushes that they appeared to be. They are the topmost branches of tall trees. The wall surrounds a large oval area, anything up to two hundred yards in length, and the other side of the wall drops sheer a matter of twenty or thirty feet. In the whole area of the enclosure there is no sand. The limestone bedrock, pleasantly broken into low cliffs and smooth curving slabs, is patched here and there with grass and dotted with the score or so of palm-trees which we saw from afar. And in the hollows of the rock there are pools of crystal-clear water, in constant movement from the springs at their lowest depths, spilling over and forming chains of streams, with miniature waterfalls as they glide down over the faults of the rock.

Flights of steps led down the inner side of the walls, and P.V. and I frequently ate our lunch packets in one of these hidden gardens, lying in the shade of the trees and out of the wind that scoured the sand of the desert above. These gardens were the springs which once had fed the *qanats*. But they feed them no longer. The level of the waters has fallen, and the springs today only keep pace with the surface evaporation from the pools. At one end of the enclosure the entrance to the *qanat* could be seen, with its silted-up bottom no more than a foot above the water. But no water runs into the channel. Sometimes it was obvious that the water was too low ever to run again; sometimes it appeared that all that was needed was for the channel to be cleaned out along its length—by means of the "chimneys" undoubtedly built for that purpose—for the *qanat* again to be opened for irrigation. It will not be done. At the bottom of the mile-long slope, at the villages which the *qanats* once served, such agriculture as is still carried on is based on borings drilled down to the water-bearing strata, and on gasoline-driven pumps bringing up the water with a much smaller expenditure of energy and danger than went into the construction and maintenance of the underground water-channels.

But to the archæologist the *qanats* and the springs at their sources pose a problem. And the problem is not so much that of age as that of depth, the difference in level between the surface of the sand outside the protecting walls and the surface of the rock-gardens within. Has twenty feet of sand been dug away by hand over the enormous area needed to expose a matter of fifteen thousand square yards of bedrock and the springs that broke forth there? And was a twenty-foot wall then built and the sand piled back around it? And if so how had they known where to dig to find the springs? For if not there was only one other explanation. That we were standing there on the original ground surface. That once upon a time the whole hill slope had been naked rock at the level at which we stood, with springs in the hollows, and that the irrigation channels, probably indeed roofed from the start to prevent evaporation, had been dug at ground level or only a little below. In that case the sand had come later, and the wall around the springs, together with the "chimneys" giving access to the *qanats,* had been built up gradually, to keep pace with the encroaching sand. This would suggest that the sand was comparatively recent, how recent only an investigation into the age of the *qanats* could determine.

I must not arouse false expectations. We have never made that investigation. It is one of the many things on our list of "projects to be undertaken when we have the time and the money," and it stands high on that list. It would not be difficult, though it would be arduous. It would involve digging down *outside* the walls around the springs, in order to find the artifacts and potsherds of the original builders of the walls. It should be done. But it was only peripheral to our main problem, of finding the dwelling-places of the early inhabitants of the island. And we contented ourselves with collecting samples of the potsherds on the surface around the springs, and promised ourselves that one day we would come back and do more. We have never returned to these hidden oases.

Although we now told ourselves firmly that we were looking for settlement sites of the date of the builders of the grave-mounds or later, we found ourselves frequently making excuses to drive down to the southwestern areas of the island. We told each other that there might well be settlements there too, but somehow we always ended up looking for flint. There is a fascination about pacing slowly for miles over the empty desert, turning over stones with the camel-sticks with which we had equipped ourselves, in the hope of seeing the glossy surface of worked flint. We never came back without at least one new flint site to mark on the map and a bag of flint to add to our collection. The sites trended southward, and we followed them, into an area where there are notice-boards beside the desert tracks proclaiming that the southern portion of the island is the private hunting ground of the ruler of Bahrain, not to be entered without permission.

We had, a week or so before, called to pay our respects to His Highness, and had been received in the spacious throne room where I had first met the sheikh six years before. He had appeared very interested in our work, and had sent out for our Greenland falcon, which was brought in perched on the wrist of the falconer. He was already trained to the hood and the jesses, and raised his head attentively when the sheikh called his name

in a hoarse grunt. Sheikh Sulman had told us in detail of the
methods of catching the adult falcons—which he suggested we
should introduce into Greenland—and of how the hawks were
used in the hunting of gazelle and bustard. He had told us we
could go where we wished in his little kingdom, but even so we
were not sure whether his permission extended to his own private
hunting grounds.

Thus when one day we topped a ridge and saw, some hundred
yards away, a small building with several cars and trucks parked
nearby we felt it only polite to turn back and continue our search
for flint on the near side of the slope. But the Arab of the desert
has sharper eyes than we, and a few minutes later a tall Arab
strode down to us and told us that His Highness wished to see us.
Approaching, we found Sheikh Sulman sitting on a carpet spread
on the sand in front of the building, flanked by his body-guard,
who all appeared at first glance to be fierce-eyed, with jutting
aggressive beards and rifles held suspiciously loosely. But the
sheikh seemed to have no objection at all to being interrupted in
his hunting by a couple of European trespassers. He bade us be
seated, called for coffee, and asked us, in halting English, what
we had found. We showed him our flints, and tried to convince
him that they were in fact fashioned by man. He was uncon-
vinced, but responded by sending a servant to unearth from a
dusty corner of the hunting lodge several large fossil shells that
he said had been found in the neighbourhood. And then he
offered to take us to see the places in the south of the island
where, by tradition, there had been villages, before the water
supply gave out. He crooked a finger, and the long black limousine parked beside the lodge purred up behind us. We were
motioned into the broad rear seat and Sheikh Sulman climbed in
and wedged himself between us. The driver and an escort, bearing the sheikh's sporting rifle as well as his own Lee Enfield, took
their places in front, and we drove south. Looking back I saw two
large covered trucks pull away and follow us.

The south end of Bahrain narrows to a point, and distances in
the southern part of the island are therefore not long. After
twenty minutes' cruising on cushioned springs over trackless

country that would have chattered our teeth in our station-car and must have given the occupants of the trucks behind something to think about, we turned down a valley to a couple of palm-trees and a well. There were no ruins of houses to be seen, but for perhaps two hundred yards in every direction from the well the ground was littered with potsherds. I picked up a piece of typical blue-and-white glazed Ming china, such as I used to collect on my free afternoons in and around the Portuguese fort on the north coast of the island. "From the time of the Portuguese," I said impressively.

It had never occurred to Sheikh Sulman that a site could be dated otherwise than by written records, and he turned the sherd over and back, looking for the date inscribed on it. "Where is the writing?" he asked. I explained, haltingly, that there was no writing, but that pottery like this was made in China four hundred years ago and could only have been brought here by the Portuguese. Sheikh Sulman grasped the principle of dating sites by surface indications with the instantaneous comprehension that one hopes for and rarely finds in first-year archæology students. For the next half-hour he and P.V. and I quartered the site, picking up representative sherds of every type of pottery visible, meeting occasionally to compare notes and sherds and to speculate on the possibility of any of our collection being from before the Portuguese. I often saw Sheikh Sulman in later years, until his death in 1962, at official functions and receptions, or on visits to our excavations, but he has never impressed me as much as on that afternoon when, with his red-and-blue ankle-length *abba* flapping in the wind and with an almost boyish smile on his fiercely bearded face, he brought handfuls of potsherds for our inspection. Not a few kings have been archæologists of repute, and, given the training, I am sure Sheikh Sulman would have been a worthy addition to their number.

All that afternoon we drove from site to site collecting sherds, and each time we returned to the car we found the carpet rolled out beside it and the cook, who rode in one of the trucks, standing by with freshly brewed coffee in the brass coffee-pot. We would sit for ten minutes through the ritual three cups, eating sweet biscuits or sticky *halwa*, and then board the car again. The body-guard and the falconers would climb into their truck, the servants and the cook would whisk away the carpet and the coffee cups and get into the other truck, and the cavalcade would start off again. The sun was setting, and it was time for the evening prayer, when we got back to the hunting lodge. We said our farewells, took our bags of potsherds, entered our own, distinctly shabby-looking, station-car, and pressed the self-starter. Nothing happened. The sheikh, who had turned to Mecca to begin his *rakāt*, looked over his shoulder, and snapped his fingers. The escort, the falconers, even the cook, got behind us and pushed. After ten yards the motor fired and we drove away over the ridge. Sheikh Sulman was already back at his devotions.

Wherever we went we collected potsherds. Gradually our map became covered with numbered sites, and our rooms in our comfortable oil-company house became littered with piles of bags bearing corresponding numbers.

Potsherds have been called the alphabet of the archæologist. And that is because they so often tell the archæologist what it is that he is dealing with. It all looks most impressive to the uninitiated. In a barrow in England, or on the mound covering house ruins in Greece or a city in Mesopotamia, the archæologist picks up an insignificant scrap of pottery, and says, "Ah yes, a B Beaker burial" or "Late Mycenæan" or "Early Dynastic III B." And he will often add a very exact-sounding date to his identification, and a discourse on the origins and way of life of the people whose remains lie there. It is, of course, not clairvoyance. It revolves about the fact that pottery is a rather remarkable thing. Since about 6000 B.C., on latest reckoning, people have been baking clay to make receptacles. And from that time to this no community in the world has made pottery quite like that made by another community. The varieties in shape, texture, decoration, and mode of construction are apparently endless, and fashions and styling change continuously. In any one community at any one time there will be close similarity between all the pots made, but even in the most tradition-ridden community the type of pot made in a hundred years' time will be recognizably different. We must add to this that pottery is in very common use, is in most cases fairly cheap, and is constantly being broken. Even today it is very rare indeed for a piece of china to last a hundred years. And yet, oddly enough, pottery is practically indestructible. Where wood and cloth, leather and parchment, iron and even copper and silver will be dissolved in the soil in the course of periods varying from a few years to a few centuries, potsherds, together with stone and gold, will outlast the millennia.

All these facts combine to make potsherds far and away the most common objects found on any site where man has lived during the last five or six thousand years; and to make potsherds the easiest means of identifying the people who lived there as belonging to a definite community of a definite date. But there is one snag. The pottery does not in itself tell anything at all. In order to be able to call a potsherd Late Mycenæan someone must first dig Mycenæ, and discover there which types of pottery were used by the earliest dwellers on the site, by the later dwellers, and by the last dwellers. Only then can you label these types Early, Middle, and Late Mycenæan, and use these labels elsewhere where pottery of the same type is found. And if you wish to be able to date Late Mycenæan ware, there has to have been found together with that ware, somewhere, something that can be dated by other means, perhaps a *scarabæus* of a known Egyptian pharaoh or some charcoal that can be dated by residual radioactivity.

As our collections of bags of pottery from our various surface sites mounted up we found this snag obtruding more and more. For we found no Late Mycenæan or Early Dynastic Mesopotamian ware. Though we found many different styles of potsherds on the different sites, very little of it was known anywhere else in the world at all. And the few scraps that were of types known elsewhere were uncompromisingly modern. The oldest pottery that we could identify on any site was precisely that blue-and-white Chinese porcelain of the Ming Dynasty, dating to the sixteenth or seventeenth century A.D.

This result was not entirely unexpected. There had always

57

been a possibility that we might find potsherds of known Mesopotamian types in Bahrain, but we were, after all, over four
hundred miles from Ur and Eridu, the southernmost Mesopotamian cities excavated, and it was unlikely that the inhabitants
of Bahrain in Babylonian and Assyrian times had used the same
pottery as the Babylonians, or imported sufficient of it for it to be
found lying about the surface. What we had hoped to find was
the same type of pottery as had been found in the grave-mounds
by Prideaux and Mackay. We had the reports of these excavators
with us, and I had even seen a few sherds from Mackay's excavation at the British Museum. But we found now that these reports,
and even my recollection of the actual ware, were insufficient. All
excavation reports are full of drawings and photographs of pottery vessels and potsherds. And however well they are executed
they are always inadequate. Time and again, in the years that
followed, we were mislead by apparent resemblances between
the pottery we had found and pottery illustrated elsewhere,
and other people were misled by our descriptions and drawings.
We are constantly being shown potsherds found by explorers in
various parts of Arabia that appeared to the finders to resemble
those we have described. And in almost every case a single
glance is sufficient to show that the resemblance is illusory. For
the shape of a pot is only one of its characteristics. Colour and
texture, thickness of sherd, the precise admixture of gravel or
sand or straw as a binding medium, the hardness of firing, the
shade or consistency of the "slip" of liquid clay often used in the
final finish; all these things vary from one community or one
century to another, and even the best coloured illustrations
cannot supply all these details, nor reproduce the actual "feel" of
the potsherd type. While from the previous reports we could
reject the majority of our specimens as undoubtedly not of
grave-mound type, there were too many cases where we were in
doubt. We needed actual potsherds from the grave-mounds for
comparison. And these were, after all, easy enough to obtain.

Just after the New Year we decided to excavate two of the
grave-mounds in the hope of finding typical pottery.

We chose a mound-field in the northwest of the island, as far as possible from villages without being completely inaccessible by road. This was in the hope, vain as it proved, of finding unplundered graves. The mound-field was also far from the area on which Durand, Prideaux, and later Mackay had concentrated, so that we would at the same time be able to find out whether all the mound-fields contained tombs and artifacts of the same type. We picked two mounds, one large—about 12 feet high—and one only a little over half that height. And then we faced the problem of organizing the dig.

We asked the advice of an Iraqi contractor in Manama, and he took on the job for us. He supplied a gang of twenty workers with a foreman, arranged to drive them out to the site by truck each day, supplied a watchman, and a large black tarpaulin tent for the watchman, and a large circular galvanized tank for drinking water. We spent a day buying picks and shovels and measuring tapes and pegs and cord and builders' levels, and on January 9, 1954, we started work.

Although our main object was the contents of the graves we were too infected by the meticulous techniques of Danish tumulus excavation to trench straight in to the central chamber. Besides, this was our first dig on the island and we could expect visitors, including the people who had been giving us assistance and openly wondering when these Danish archæologists were going to begin digging. The usual technique for dealing with a tumulus is to remove the tumulus completely, a quarter at a time. When the first quarter is removed, leaving vertical walls of earth, these walls are drawn, to show all the phases of the build-up of the mound. The second quarter is then taken and the new face drawn. The third quarter provides a fourth face for drawing, and at this stage two complete sections through the mound have been drawn, at right angles to one another. Finally the fourth quarter is dug away and the ground plan of the original surface below the mound, which has been gradually drawn during the digging, can now be completed. Only at this point is the central chamber or central grave tackled. However, to save time and money, and in order to leave something to look at (for a completely excavated tumulus is after all no tumulus any more), we decided to make

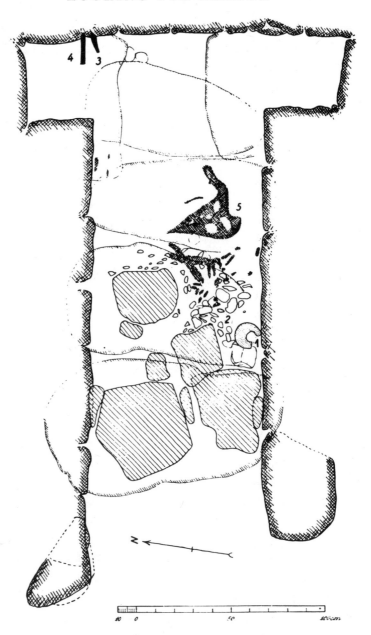

OUR FIRST BAHRAIN GRAVE-CHAMBER, ROBBED BUT WITH AN OSTRICH-EGG
BEAKER (1) AND THE SHERDS OF A RED POT (2) STILL LYING BY THE FEET OF
THE PARTIALLY PRESERVED SKELETON (5). THE HEAD-END OF THE CHAMBER
HAD BEEN CLEANED OUT BY THE ROBBERS, BUT THEY HAD OVERLOOKED TWO
COPPER SPEARHEADS STUCK IN THE WALL (3 & 4).

concessions to expediency. The smaller mound was cut completely in half, and only a single quadrant taken out of the larger.

The smaller mound in particular looked satisfactorily impressive when it was cut across. It could then be seen that a ring of stones had originally outlined the circumference of the mound, and in the vertical section through the structure of the mound almost every individual basketful of gravel could be seen lying where it had been tipped when the mound was built. In the centre of the section the stone slabs of the chamber projected out, with its entrance still blocked by two courses of cut stone. But the third course was missing, leaving a hole into the interior of the chamber. And in the section above, the outline of the tunnel dug down by grave-robbers to the entrance could be clearly seen. When we removed the entrance blocks the rest of the story was revealed. The stones of the missing third course lay just within the entrance, where they had been pushed in by the robbers, and beyond them the grave chamber was empty, except for a scattering of bone fragments. We began the thankless task of drawing a plan of what the robbers had left. The first to be drawn were the fallen blocking stones, and when they were plotted in we lifted them up to clear the way farther in. And as soon as we lifted them we saw the potsherds lying below them. Our mood changed at once, and we took out our trowels and brushes. As we brushed away the dust and drifted sand more fragments of red pottery came to view, and with them glossy ivory-coloured fragments that it took us some minutes to identify. Then we realized, both together, that they were pieces of the shell of a large egg, undoubtedly that of an ostrich. Among the shell and the potsherds lay bones, crushed by the falling stones but still obviously lying in position. After two days of painstaking work, crouched double below the low roof slabs of the chamber, we could see the outlines of the lower half of the skeleton take shape before us. It was the skeleton of an adult human, lying on the right side with the legs half bent. A little above the hips the skeleton ended, trodden to pieces by the robbers. But we had enough. We had the burial posture, and we had every sherd of a tall red pottery vessel. And we had the ostrich egg, showing clearly where the top had been cut away so that the egg could be used as a drinking cup, and even showing the traces of a band of red paint round the top of the cup. And the grave had a final prize for us. When we finally cleared our way to the head end of the chamber we found what the robbers had missed, two fine copper spearheads, driven into cracks between the stones just below the roof slabs.

The larger mound was of more intricate construction. To all appearances a gravel mound, it revealed just below the outer skin of gravel a series of concentric ring-walls, stepped inward so that the mound, when built, must have stood rather splendidly with white limestone walls forming three-feet-high steps below the final mound of gravel. This gravel mound hid the entrance to the actual tomb, a square stone-built shaft giving access to two chambers, one built above the other. But apparently the more splendid the tomb, the more thorough the plundering. Both chambers had been opened and ransacked. Apart from the usual scattering of bones—which was confined to the lower chamber—the mound contained only one small fragment of what had apparently been a copper mirror, and a sprinkling of potsherds, some of which could be assembled to form the greater part of a round-bodied vase with a short and narrow neck.

Anyway, we had our potsherds, which was all we had really hoped to find.

And they did not help us in the slightest. In all our collection of potsherds from the surface sites we did not find a single sherd that resembled the pottery from the grave chambers.

Now this could mean that Mackay's theory was right, that the people who built the grave-mounds had not lived on Bahrain. Or it could mean that we had not looked in the right places. But we had, after all, covered the ground pretty carefully—and the settlements lived in by the builders of a hundred thousand grave-mounds ought to be fairly thick on the ground. There was a third possibility: that the settlements were not on the ground but under it.

That settlements should lie below the surface is, of course, nothing new to archæologists. They spend most of their time digging below the surface. But the remains of ancient peoples do not get below the surface by some sort of natural law. They do not sink into the ground; they get covered . . . Now in the temperate climates in which we were accustomed to dig that can happen naturally. Grass and trees and bushes grow in the ruins of abandoned houses. A layer of turf and later of humus forms above the site and in the course of centuries only a low grass-clad mound marks the site of man's habitation. But in Bahrain no grass grows. On our flint sites we found the tools and weapons of Stone Age man lying on the surface just as they had been dropped thirty or forty millennia before. If the sites we now wanted were below ground something other than vegetational growth must have put them there.

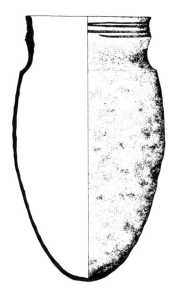

THIS ROUND-BASED, CYLINDRICAL-BODIED POT—IN THIN RED CLAY—IS THE DOM-INANT FORM IN THE BAHRAIN GRAVE-MOUNDS, WHILE ITS FRAGMENTS OCCUR ONLY VERY RARELY IN THE CITIES OF THE SAME PERIOD.

It could be sand. The evidence of the springs at the head of the *qanats* suggested strongly that in some areas of Bahrain thick deposits of sand had accumulated within historical times. On the other hand, the grave-mounds clearly still stood on the same ground surface as that on which they had been built—there were no mound-fields drowned or half-drowned in sand. The most likely explanation was the most obvious one, that our sites were overlaid by later settlements.

This is almost the rule in the Middle East. In lands where water is not universally available people at any period will tend to build their towns and villages where there is water. Towns will stand on the same site for thousands of years, and even if they are abandoned the same site will sooner or later be picked again for a new town. The houses and streets, the potsherds and discarded debris of one town will be covered by the houses and streets and debris of the next town, and these again by the third town. Theoretically none of the remains of the first town will lie on the surface at all. In practice people rarely live long on a site without digging holes, for cellars and grain-stores, wells and cess-pits and rubbish pits, or to quarry building stone from the house-ruins of their predecessors. And some of the buried material will thus find its way back to the surface. But it will be very little in comparison with the thousands of sherds and other remains left by the last occupants, and we could not be sure that they had not escaped our attention.

We must look, then, for sites that bore signs of having had several phases of occupation. And that, in Middle East terms, meant that we should look for "tells." *Tell* is an Arabic word and means a city mound. A town or city which has been occupied for a considerable period raises itself up on a sizable mound. The process of building on top of the ruins and rubbish of a previous town is a process of accretion, and each new building raises the level. In Mesopotamia, where the houses are built of mud brick, tells rise fast, and may well in the course of two or three thousand years reach a height of two hundred feet or more. In Bahrain, where stone was available for building, houses would last longer and the stone would be reused, so that the rate of growth would be much less. But even so a site with a long period of occupancy should have quite a conspicuous height.

We set out to look for tells.

CHAPTER FOUR

"THE LAND OF DILMUN
IS HOLY"

From the top of the low hillock we used to look longingly down
to the shade of the palm-trees to the north. Beyond the palms the
white houses and flat roofs of the village of Barbar could be seen,
and beyond the village the green waters of the Gulf looked cool
and inviting. It was well into April; three months had passed
since we had dug our grave-mounds, and every day the sun
seemed to climb higher and beat more fiercely down. On the top
of the hillock, where what breeze there was stirred the humid air,
the heat was to be borne, but twelve feet down, in the trench
through the centre of the mound, no air moved and the heat was
stifling. The trench ran north and south, so that at midday there
was no shade at all, and then even the wiry brown villagers
whom we had recruited from Barbar and Diraz gave up. Then we
would all lie under the palm-trees, while the sweat slowly dried
into white salt stains on our clothes, and eat green tomatoes from
the garden nearby. But when an hour had passed, and shadow
was beginning to creep across the bottom of the trench again,
Muhamed, the headman of Barbar village, would call the workers
back to their shovels and baskets, and for very shame we would
follow them back to work.

We told ourselves often that it was too late in the year for

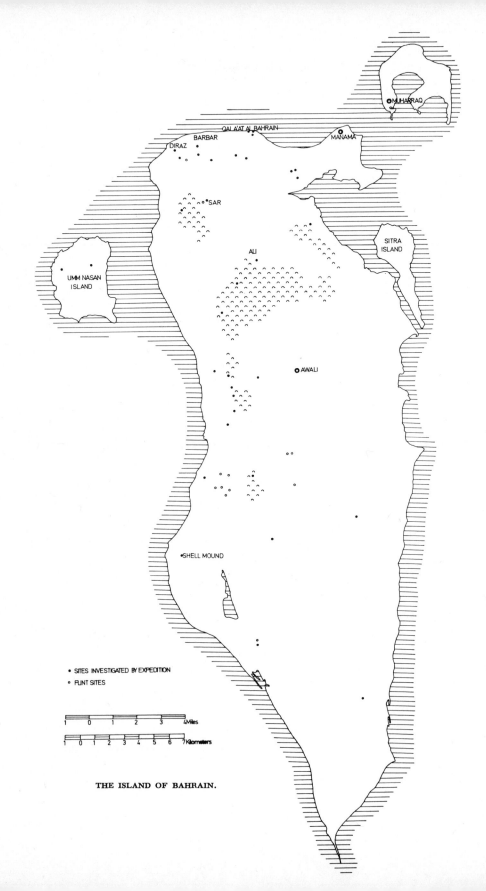

MUHARRAQ

QAL A'AT AL BAHRAIN

BARBAR

DIRAZ

MANAMA

SAR

SITRA
ISLAND

ALI

UMM NASAN
ISLAND

AWALI

SHELL MOUND

• SITES INVESTIGATED BY EXPEDITION

◦ FLINT SITES

1 0 1 2 3   4 Miles

1 0 1 2 3 4 5 6 7 Kilometers

THE ISLAND OF BAHRAIN.

digging. But we had a tell at last, and as long as our money held out we meant to dig it.

P.V., of course, had found it. We had dug at four other places first with no great success. The first one had looked promising. Sar, a village only a mile away from our grave-mounds, lay on top of a conspicuous and clearly artificial mound, and while I finished drawing my grave-mound P.V. had taken six workmen and dug a trial pit on the unoccupied western end of the mound. Immediately he hit drift sand, and for four days he dug heroically down through sand with a consistency like flour. All day long the sand drifted steadily down from the sides of the excavation, forcing continual widening of the hole if the workmen were not to be overwhelmed by the sliding masses. Finally at a depth of ten feet the bottom of the sand was reached and the remains of buildings were found. But the pottery among the buildings included glazed ware of undoubted Islamic date, and below it was the virgin desert. We moved our black tent north to Diraz.

Diraz is a village almost at the extreme northwest corner of Bahrain, and eastward from the village stretches a large area of sandy hillocks covered with millions of potsherds. Close in to the village is a remarkable circular hollow, ringed by sand-covered mounds on the top of which lie a hundred or so large squared blocks of stone. Local legend says that this hollow was once the largest well on Bahrain, filled in by one of the early Umayyad caliphs, Abdul-Malik bin Marwan, to punish the inhabitants of Bahrain for an attempted reversion to paganism. And indeed, when we dug in the centre of the hollow we came to a jumble of similar large blocks of stone and below them to water. To excavate there would have required continuous pumping, and we had no pump. While I started tracing a block of masonry jutting from one of the slopes of the hollow P.V. had taken his workers farther afield, to dig one of the hillocks half a mile away. There, too, he found drift sand just below the surface and moved to a new site even farther away. In the meantime I had found, behind my masonry, a flight of steps leading down into the hill of sand, and was following them down. I know no more exciting archæological discovery than a flight of descending steps. They obviously lead

67

somewhere, and one cannot avoid recalling Tut-ankh-amon's tomb. . . .

My steps led down to a well. It was quite a nice well as wells go. The actual well-head, flush with the floor of a tiny stone-built chamber at the foot of the steps, was one single block of stone, three feet square and a foot and a half thick, with a circular hole over two feet in diameter cut through it. The hole, like the chamber, was full of sand, but as soon as we began to dig it out fresh water seeped in. When the well was cleaned out the water found its level only an inch below the top of the stone. It was in fact a very fine piece of construction altogether, and rather puzzling if, as legend had it, the largest well on Bahrain lay just outside the head of the stairway.

In digging our way down the steps we had found two limestone figures of kneeling quadrupeds, about a foot and a half long. We began by calling them bulls but our workers said they were sheep. It was difficult to be certain, for in both cases the heads had been struck off, and were not to be found. But we did find where they belonged. At the head of the stairway, on either side, there was an empty pedestal just large enough to take one of the figures.

I am rather ashamed of this dig. Technically I suppose the excavation was done well enough; everything was drawn and photographed, and all the objects found, the two statues, a piece of an alabaster bowl, and thirty or so potsherds, were measured in and labelled. But I should have noticed that the potsherds did not include any of the glazed ware that should have been there if the well was actually of Islamic date. The pottery in fact was like nothing we had seen before. It was predominantly red in colour, with parallel horizontal ridges. It was not grave-mound pottery, but it was not Islamic either. And I packed it away and never looked at it again for two years. After all, the site seemed self-explanatory. Legend said that the site had been destroyed in the eighth century A.D. as a punishment for idolatry. And here was a destroyed site, complete with two idols with their heads knocked off. With the hindsight that fourteen more years of work have brought we can say now that the pottery from the Diraz well-chamber must be dated not to the eighth century A.D. but to the third millennium B.C.

Someday, when we have time and money—and pumps—I intend to return to Diraz and find out what it is that lies hidden beneath the tumbled limestone blocks in the hollow and beneath the sand hills that surround it. For it is by far the most promising site in Bahrain—partly because of its size and complexity, partly because much of the site is below the water-table, and water preserves much, woodwork and textiles and basketwork for example, which decays and disappears on a "dry" site.

While I was digging the Diraz well-chamber P.V. had been prospecting. Every afternoon he would leave his workmen to dig under the eye of their foreman and range over the surrounding countryside. And on one of these trips he had found the mound by Barbar village, just over a mile to the east of where I was digging.

Now, in that area there is a whole string of mounds, parallel to the coast and about a mile inland. They are huge heaps of sand, clearly artificial but larger than, and completely different from, even the biggest of the gravel grave-mounds at Ali. They have been noted before, by both Durand and Mackay, and one of them had even been dug into, by one of the British Political Agents. We had looked carefully at them, especially the one that had been excavated. But there seemed little doubt that they were grave-mounds, of a different type and therefore probably of a different date from the grave-mounds of the large mound-fields. They were very much too big for us to tackle, and were in any case unlikely to answer any of our questions, but much more likely to raise new questions to answer.

The Barbar mound was at the western end of this string of mounds, and differed somewhat from them. It was larger in area but smaller in height. But we would have assumed that it, too, was a burial-mound, were it not that P.V. noticed the corners of two very large blocks of shaped limestone protruding from the northern slope of the mound. One of these blocks showed the edges of two square depressions cut in the top. We were, I think, already beginning to realize that blocks of squared stone were indicative of a fairly respectable antiquity. In any case, this was the sort of thing we were looking for, a project where we could determine with a minimum of digging whether there was something worth a greater effort or not. P.V. took a couple of men off his excavation at Diraz and cleared the two blocks. They turned out to be very large indeed, two cubes of stone measuring four feet to a side and probably weighing over three tons each. And they stood on a paving of slabs of limestone.

P.V. moved his whole gang of workers to the site at once, and I followed with mine as soon as I could with a clear conscience leave my well-chamber. And we trenched in from the stone blocks towards the centre of the mound. It was an odd excavation —and it got odder. We were cutting a trench two metres wide, keeping the sides dead vertical, cut and scraped smooth with our trowels, so that any layering in the structure of the mound would be clearly visible. And these section cuts, as well as the material from the trench that our workers were removing in their coir baskets, showed completely sterile sand. And yet beneath our feet the stone paving went on. Now, as I have tried to make clear before, a tell, a mound covering a site where people have lived, is composed entirely of the debris of their living there, of the collapsed remains of their houses, of their rubbish, and of such furnishings of their dwellings as they did not take with them when they left; nothing more, except perhaps a little sand, blown in to fill the hollows and crannies in the ruins. A section through a mound of this sort shows stratified rubbish, stumps of walling, tumbled stones, all the way from bottom to top. But here there was sterile sand, already higher than our heads. And it was not wind-blown sand. We had already seen how yard-thick deposits of wind-blown sand could cover the sites of villages, but we had learnt to recognize the stuff the hard way; we could never have cut our vertical sections in its drift-fine consistency. This was much coarser sand, mixed with pebbles that no wind could have lifted so high. And it was even compacted, every two feet or so, with a thin horizontal skin of gypsum cement, and this was a technique that we had seen used in one of the larger grave-mounds at Ali, a device to prevent the lower layers of sand from sliding outward as more is piled on top. There was no doubt that this thick layer of sand on the Barbar mound had been deliberately placed there, heaped up by the hand of man.

For a long while we were more than half convinced that we were digging a grave-mound after all. A grave-mound sixty yards in diameter and only five or six yards high, and moreover floored in its entirety with stone flagging, was difficult to believe in, but it was equally difficult to believe in a building of that size deliberately covered to a depth of three or four yards with sand. It still is difficult to believe, but eight years of work have left no doubt at all that this is in fact what we have.

Our trench went on, and after nine yards we met a wall cutting straight across the line of the trench. It was of fine close-grained limestone, the blocks carefully cut to fit together without mortar, and it was only three courses high. Beyond it the stone flooring slabs continued. Eight yards farther on we met a further wall of the same type, and here it formed the rise of a step; the stone paving on the other side continued at a higher level. We were now approaching the middle of the mound, and the sand walls on either side of us were over ten feet high. After another six yards we met more stone blocks, equally carefully cut and laid to fit together, but this time they formed a circle, about six feet in diameter. We were in the centre of the mound.

It was now obvious that, whatever it was that we had found, it was worth going on with. We needed to complete our trench clean across the mound, and we wanted to enlarge our digging in the central area in order to find out what the circular structure was. But at the same time we did not want to get bogged down on one single site. In every free moment we had been continuing our reconnaissance trips over the rest of the island, and we had other projects now in view. Principally, we had found a very large tell, of completely orthodox character, with walls and floor levels right up to the surface of the mound. Of this very much more anon.

We telegraphed home for another man. It was by now the beginning of March and we had been three months in the field. Kristian was a classical archæologist, but he was also an architect, and as soon as he arrived he started on the job of making sense of the walls and pavings of the Barbar mound. P.V. and I still spent most of our time there too, but a few days a week we would take our favourite half-dozen men and dig elsewhere, P.V. on his "city" tell and I on some grave-mounds less than a mile from Barbar.

We had marked off an area ten yards square around the circular structure in the centre of the Barbar mound, and dug this down to the level of the stone paving. And now, in April, we could stand and look down into this excavation. And we knew what we had found.

We were looking down from a height of twelve feet upon the inner court of a temple.

It was not a temple of a type we had ever seen before, but there seemed no doubt about its nature. In the centre the circular structure was now revealed as an oblong platform framing two circles. Their purpose was still uncertain but they looked very much like plinths for twin statues. To one side of them stood an upright slab of stone and a foot or so away lay another, with the precise place where it had stood still marked in plaster on the stone paving. Both had hollows on the upper edge, and when the second stone was set up again it was obvious that they were the supports of a short bench or stool. In front of them stood an altar, a cubical stone with a square hollow on the upper surface, and in front of that again stood a stone with a round hollow leading into an open stone drain sloping down to a hole in the surrounding wall. In front of this whole complex there was a square pit in the courtyard, framed by slabs of stone standing on edge.

We recognized the picture. The most common scene depicted on the cylindrical seals of Mesopotamia is that of a god seated on just such a bench, with just such an altar before him, while in front of him stand the suppliants, bearing offerings to the altar, or pouring libations before the god, or else standing in an attitude of prayer, with their hands clasped in front of their breast. If we had needed further confirmation we found it when we excavated the pit in front of the altar. There, in a confusion which showed that the pit had been thoroughly rifled, we found the offerings. Among quantities of potsherds lay lapis-lazuli beads, alabaster vases, a

copper figure of a bird, and, the final proof, a little copper statu-
ette of a naked man, standing in just the attitude of supplication
represented on the seals. Such votive statuettes have been found
in large numbers in Mesopotamia, though there mainly of stone
or of terra-cotta, and they are always and only found in the
temples.

The whole picture made sense. And as we stood and looked
down on the slowly widening excavation we could almost see the
ceremonies that had taken place in the courtyard. The suppliants,
surely not looking very different from the cheerful swarthy villagers, bare to the waist and wielding their picks and shovels below
us, would be standing in line waiting to be presented by the
officiating priest to the deity on the throne. And in turn they
would lay their offerings on the altar and pour their libation, of
wine or beer or milk (or even blood?) into the hollowed stone.
The flies would cluster around them as they clustered around us,
and the same sun would beat down as they made their prayer—
for a son and heir, or for the recovery of a sick child, or for a good
harvest or fishing trip. And then they would pass on, perhaps, if
they could afford it, leaving a little suppliant figurine leaning
against the courtyard wall, to remind the god of their prayer even
after they were gone.

The deity on the throne was a little obscure to the eye of
imagination. It was hardly a statue, for the throne was life-size,
and yet could hardly bear the weight of a life-size figure in stone.
It was perhaps an image of wood, sheathed in copper, for we had
found quantities of twisted copper sheeting with rows of nail-
holes, and several hundred copper nails; or perhaps the chief
priest sat enthroned as the deputy of the god; or perhaps they
offered to the empty throne and the invisible presence of the god.

The circular plinths beside the throne equally defied the imagination. Was it here that the statues of the deities had stood, a god
and a goddess perhaps? I do not wish to raise expectations; we
have never solved that mystery. No images of the deities worshipped in the Barbar temple have been found during the eight
years in which we dug here. Only two enigmatic fragments of
stone have come to light, part of an arm and part of a shoulder of

a life-size limestone statue, with a hint of drapery and a criss-cross decoration of strings of beads. And they came from a rubbish heap, where the debris of an earlier, smaller temple had been thrown out when the temple we were looking at was built; and even that rubbish heap had been later disturbed.

We had a fairly good idea of when the temple at Barbar had been built. The little copper suppliant, with his large round eyes and shaven head, was very Sumerian in appearance. If he had been found in Mesopotamia he would certainly have been dated to somewhere between 2500 and 1800 B.C., and he could not be of very different date here. And one of the alabaster vases was of a shape known to have been used in Mesopotamia in the final centuries of the third millennium B.C.

The tentative dating made us very interested in the pottery that we were finding in increasing quantities, now that we were digging the centre of the temple. The sherds were remarkably uniform. Quantities of thin red ware, almost all decorated with low horizontal ridges about three quarters of an inch apart, all seemed to belong to almost globular, round-bottomed pots about a foot or a foot and a half high. We found very many fragments of the rims, and these showed that the pots had either been neck-less, ending in a broadened rim at the top of the egg-shaped body, or else had had a short neck with an outturned rim triangular in section. This "Barbar pottery," as we came to call it, was very distinctive, and would be easy to recognize if we met it elsewhere. I cannot explain why I did not at once recall that I had already met it, not many weeks before, in the well-chamber at Diraz. All we noted at the time was that, apart from the rounded bottoms, it had no resemblance to the pottery we had found in the grave-mounds.

But although we had thus not yet solved the principal object of our expedition, the third-millennium-B.C. temple at Barbar was a discovery of the very first rank, and as we began to pack our cases full of potsherds and specimens we knew that we would be back the following year to dig further at this and the other sites that we had located. It was highly significant that the first site of importance to be found on Bahrain should be a temple, and at that a temple with Sumerian affinities. And it is time to explain why.

At the time when Rawlinson, in 1880, wrote his commentary to Captain Durand's survey of the antiquities of Bahrain, Dilmun was, as we have seen, known as a kingdom beyond the borders of the Babylonian and Assyrian empires. Since that time Dilmun had achieved importance in quite a different way.

In actual fact Dilmun's unique position in Mesopotamian mythology was already presaged at the time when Rawlinson turned his attention to Bahrain. Just as the monumental inscriptions from the palaces of Sargon and Sennacherib and Assurbanipal had introduced the world to the lost history of the Assyrian Empire, so the library of Assurbanipal, with its tens of thousands of cuneiform tablets, had, as we have seen, brought again to the knowledge of man the literature of Mesopotamia, and in particular the great cosmological and epic poems of Babylonia and Assyria.

And just as with the royal inscriptions, so with this epic poetry it was the light that it threw on the Bible that most captured popular imagination. The years in which they were published were, after all, years when the Bible was under very heavy fire indeed. Darwin's *Origin of Species* had been published in 1859, and in the same year the authenticity of Stone Age tools had been recognized in the Somme gravels—together with and contemporary with the bones of animals long extinct. The biologists, with their theory of evolution, were attacking the story of the Creation, and the geologists, with their talk of Ice Ages, were questioning the concept of a Universal Deluge. Small wonder, then, that the Annals of the Kings of Assyria, recounting from, as it were, the other side of the fence many of the events of the later books of the Old Testament, were eagerly seized upon as counter-evidence for the truth of the Scriptures.

And then in 1872 an Assyrian account of a Universal Deluge had been found among the British Museum's stock of tablets from Assurbanipal's library.

The Deluge tablet was the eleventh "chapter" in the epic of Gilgamesh, the semi-mythical king of Erech, who spent many years of his life in a vain quest for immortality. And it told of his visit to the one mortal who had ever been granted immortality, Utu-nipishtim, the survivor of the Flood. And Utu-nipishtim, a rather garrulous old man, takes the opportunity to tell the whole story of the Flood. He tells how the gods decided to destroy mankind, but how Enki, the god of the waters under the earth, warned the narrator to build an ark and take on board his family and his livestock. For six days and nights the tempest raged, and on the seventh day the ark grounded, on a mountain-top in upper Kurdistan. A dove and a swallow were in turn sent out, but returned; and then a raven was sent out and did not return, showing that the waters had abated. Utu-nipishtim disembarked and offered sacrifice to the gods; and Enki interceded with the chief of the gods, that he never again should punish the whole of mankind for the sins of some. And Enlil, the great god, agrees and, going aboard the ark, touches Utu-nipishtim and his wife upon the forehead. "Hitherto has Utu-nipishtim been mortal," he said. "Now shall he and his wife be like the gods; and they shall dwell in the distance, at the mouth of the rivers."

This Assyrian story of the Deluge had such a number of points of resemblance to the biblical account that no one could doubt the common origin of the two. And it was clear even at this point that the Assyrian version must, like so much in Assurbanipal's library, be merely a copy of a much earlier version. But forty years were to pass before the earlier version was discovered, and only then did the relevance of the Deluge story to the Dilmun question become clear.

In 1899 and in 1900 the University of Pennsylvania was digging at Nippur, the site of a once-renowned city in lower Mesopotamia. In Sumerian times, and in the time of Sargon of Akkad, that first great Semitic conqueror, Nippur had been the leading religious centre of Mesopotamia, for the patron god of that city was Enlil, the first among the gods, and indeed the god who had decreed the Flood and granted immortality to Utu-nipishtim. In many ways the American excavations at Nippur marked a turning-point in Middle Eastern archæology. Here for the first time the principal emphasis was not on the discovery of statues and monumental inscriptions to grace museums, but on the uncovering of buildings in their entirety. This principle resulted in the discovery of the first ziggurat, the remarkable terraced mounds with a temple on the summit that were the chief features of the Mesopotamian cities. Each city had one ziggurat, and only one, dedicated to the patron deity of the city, and the ziggurat of Nippur, called *E-kur,* or "the house of the mountain," was dedicated to Enlil. At its foot lay the main temple of Enlil, and here Hilprecht, the leader of the expedition and himself an authority on cuneiform, unearthed the temple archive, a collection of 35,000 tablets, exceeding in number even the royal library of Assurbanipal.

Such a colossal number of tablets could not, of course, be translated and published in short order. Even now, two generations after the discovery, the greater part of the tablets are still unpublished, and discoveries of importance are still being made among them. Many of the tablets were in Sumerian, the language that preceded the Semitic Babylonian and Assyrian as at least the written language of Mesopotamia, and it was these tablets, in fact, that provided the basis for our knowledge of Sumerian. It is thus not surprising that it was only in 1914 that a tablet from Nippur was published giving part of the text of the Sumerian Flood story. The tablet was incomplete, only the lower third in fact being preserved, so that there were many gaps in the text. But the story is recognizably the same as that told by Utu-nipishtim to Gilgamesh, although the survivor of the Flood in the Sumerian version is not called Utu-nipishtim but Ziusudra. From our point of view the last part of the text is the most interesting. Where the Babylonian version tells us, as we have seen, that Utu-nipishtim was to be granted immortality and to dwell "in the distance, at the mouth of the rivers," the Sumerian version reads: "Anu and Enlil cherished Ziusudra, life like a god they give him, breath eternal like a god they bring down for him. Then Ziusudra the king, the preserver of the name of vegetation and of the seed of mankind, in the land of crossing, the land of Dilmun, the place where the sun rises, they caused to dwell." (The translation is that of Professor Kramer of Philadelphia.)

We must examine the last sentence rather carefully. The phrase "the land of crossing" is not readily explicable. And that is not the fault of the translator. The original Sumerian (*kur.bala*) is no clearer. *Kur* means "land" and *bala* is the verbal noun from a verb meaning "to cross," and used of crossing rivers and the like. "The place where the sun rises," on the other hand, is completely unambiguous, and has been used as an argument against the identification of Bahrain with Dilmun. Bahrain lies between southeast and south-southeast of Nippur, whereas a "place where the sun rises" must, it is claimed, lie approximately due east.

I wish to be fair to the opponents of the identification which—it must be obvious—we are inclined to uphold, for they are scholars whose learning and judgment none would challenge. Nothing is gained by pretending a certainty that does not exist, and we do not pretend to have found, as yet, any boundary stone inscribed "City Limits of Dilmun." And that is why this book is titled *Looking for Dilmun* rather than *The Discovery of Dilmun*. But I confess that I do not attach great importance to this argument about the direction of the place where the sun rises. For it is a well-known fact that the Sumerians and Babylonians used commonly three expressions to describe the Arabian Gulf. They called it the Lower Sea, the Bitter Sea, or the Sea of the Rising Sun. And it would be perfectly natural for them to call any place on or in that sea the "place where the sun rises."

With the discovery of this new Deluge text Dilmun became a much more important place than it had appeared to be from the references in the inscriptions of the Assyrian kings. It was the eternal home of the immortal ancestor of all mankind, and it must have been to Dilmun that Gilgamesh had come in his search for immortality. But why had the gods selected Dilmun as the home for the man they had saved from the Flood? There was no suggestion that Dilmun was the place where the ark had landed; on the contrary, the ark was stated to have landed in the mountains the whole length of Mesopotamia away.

Another text from Nippur suggested the reason, and at the same time showed the very special position which Dilmun occupied in the religion of Mesopotamia. This text, a large clay tablet containing 278 lines of cuneiform in six columns, was brought back by the excavators to the museum of the University of Pennsylvania, where it now lies. It was first published in 1915 but the translation then given was largely unintelligible, and it was only in 1945 that Professor Kramer, one of the world's great authorities on Sumerian and the curator of the Near Eastern section of the University Museum in Philadelphia, produced an adequate translation. The text is of a mythological poem and is normally known under the title of "Enki and Ninhursag," the names of the two protagonists in the poem. Enki we have met already, as the god who saved Utu-nipishtim from the Flood. He is one of the four chief deities of the Sumerian pantheon, the patron god of Eridu (which was the southernmost, and by tradition the oldest, of all the cities of south Mesopotamia), and the god of the Abyss. This needs further elaboration. The word "abyss" is perhaps the only Sumerian loan-word in the English language, and has changed its meaning somewhat during the thousands of years in which it has been current. Originally the Sumerian word *abzu* meant the waters under the earth. The Sumerians believed that the earth and the sea rested upon another sea, the *abzu*. Unlike the ordinary sea, which is salt, the *abzu* is of fresh water, and the two are kept quite distinct, both in belief and in actual fact, the bed of the salt sea preventing the two from mixing. The Sumerians believed that the *abzu* was the source of all fresh water, rivers finding their source in the underground sea, and wells and springs being holes, artificial or natural, reaching down to it. And Enki was the ruler and guardian of this fresh-water sea. Ninhursag was another of the four chief deities, and the only goddess among them. She was originally the great Earth Mother, the goddess of the land.

The events recounted in the myth of Enki and Ninhursag take place in Dilmun, and the poem opens with a eulogy of that land:

> *The holy cities—present them to him* [*Enki?*],
> *The land of Dilmun is holy.*
> *Holy Sumer—present it to him,*
> *The land of Dilmun is holy.*

The land of Dilmun is holy, the land of Dilmun is pure,
the land of Dilmun is clean, the land of Dilmun is holy.

After a few more lines in the same vein the text becomes more specific. Dilmun is holy because in it there is no preying of beast on beast, no sickness, and no old age:

In Dilmun the raven utters no cry,
the wild hen utters not the cry of the wild hen,
the lion kills not,
the wolf snatches not the lamb,
unknown is the kid-devouring wild dog,
unknown is the grain-devouring boar.
The malt which the widow spreads on the roof—
the birds of heaven do not eat up that malt.
The dove droops not the head.
The sick-eyed says not "I am sick-eyed,"
the sick-headed says not "I am sick-headed,"
its old woman says not "I am an old woman,"
its old man says not "I am an old man."

Thereafter apparently follows a request from the goddess Nin-sikilla to Enki to supply Dilmun with water. Nin-sikilla was a daughter of Enki, and we know from another poem that Enki had appointed Nin-sikilla to be the guardian goddess of Dilmun:

Father Enki answers Nin-sikilla his daughter:
"Let Utu (the sun god) stationed in heaven
bring you sweet water from the earth, from the water-sources
                    of the earth;
let him bring up the water into your large reservoirs (?);
let him make your city drink from them the water of abundance;
let him make Dilmun drink from them the water of abundance;
let your wells of bitter water become wells of sweet water;
let your furrowed fields and acres yield you their grain;
let your city become the 'dock-yard'-house of the (inhabited)
   land."

As Enki orders, so it comes to pass. And in this land of sweet water and growing crops the further events of the poem take place. Briefly, Ninhursag causes eight plants to grow in Dilmun. As Professor Kramer skilfully summarizes his long text, "she succeeds in bringing these plants into being by an intricate" (and, may I add, incestuous) "process involving three generations of goddesses all begotten by Enki and born without pain or travail." But Enki eats these plants, and falls sick with eight different ailments. Ninhursag, angered by Enki's action, withdraws from the company of the gods and threatens not to return until Enki is

A MESOPOTAMIAN CYLINDER SEAL OF ABOUT 2300 B.C., NOW IN BERLIN, SHOWS AN ENTHRONED GOD WITH HIS ALTAR AND A SUPPLIANT BEFORE HIM. BEAKERS OF THE TYPE HELD BY THE GOD HAVE BEEN FOUND IN THE BARBAR TEMPLE, AND THE DATE PALM MIGHT EVEN SUGGEST A CONNECTION WITH THE ARABIAN GULF.

dead. But the fox succeeds in persuading Ninhursag to return and she consents to cure Enki. This she does by giving birth to eight gods and goddesses, one to cure each of Enki's ailments. The last of these is the god Enshag. And Enshag is the Sumerian equivalent of Inzak, the god of Dilmun whose name was inscribed on the stone found by Captain Durand on Bahrain.

That is the story of Enki and Ninhursag—not a very uplifting or moral story, not even, by any standards except perhaps sheer age, of very high literary quality. But it is one of the oldest stories in the world. It was first written down nearly four thousand years ago, and it was probably quite an old legend even then. From our point of view, of course, its main interest lies in the fact that the events recorded in it take place in Dilmun. And it is really rather remarkable, considering the parochial nature of the Sumerian gods, that a land which throughout recorded history was regarded as a foreign country by the Sumerians and Babylonians plays such an important part in their mythology. The truth may be that Enki, the lord of the sweet water under the earth, was originally a god of Dilmun, and that the myth we have recounted came to Mesopotamia from there. Certainly it is now clear that the Sumerian and Babylonian inhabitants of south Mesopotamia believed that, at the dawn of time, the gods spent much of their days in Dilmun, and had blessed that land with sweet water and with vegetation, with health and with eternal youth. And when Enki had saved Ziusudra from the Flood and Enlil had granted him eternal life it was therefore natural that he should take up his abode in the blessed land where death was unknown. And there, it would seem, Gilgamesh at the dawn of history visited Ziusudra, coming in his quest for immortality to the land where that secret was already known. Here, admittedly, we are in the realm of speculation; nowhere in the Babylonian epic of Gilgamesh is Dilmun mentioned by name.

But that Dilmun was a holy land in the eyes of the Sumerians is not a matter of speculation. It is stated repeatedly, in as many words, in the myth of Enki and Ninhursag. And it was therefore very appropriate that the first major building contemporary with Sumer that we had found on Bahrain should be a temple.

CHAPTER FIVE

THE PORTUGUESE FORT

Two years had passed, and our camp was going up. Yunis and I had laid out its ground-plan four days before, and now Ja'far and his team of little old men were busy building. From where I sat, on the highest surviving portion of the ramparts of the fort, I could watch the men at work or, by turning my head, look out over the tell and over the miles of date-palm plantations. Or out to sea. The Portuguese had had a wonderful look-out point here.

The fort must have dominated northern Bahrain and the north-west approaches to Bahrain during the years when the Portuguese dominated the Arabian Gulf and the whole trade of the Indies. In 1498, six years after Columbus had discovered America, Vasco da Gama had sailed around Africa and discovered the route to India. During the following twenty years the Portuguese, under their great admiral, Affonso d'Albuquerque, established themselves along all the coasts from the Cape of Good Hope to Further India. In 1521 they conquered Bahrain and held it, with many vicissitudes, until 1602. It must have been shortly after 1521 that they constructed their immense fort on a prominent mound in the centre of the north coast of Bahrain.

In popular parlance, and on all the maps, the fort is always known as the Portuguese fort; but its official name, and the one we use in our reports, is Qala'at al-Bahrain, the Bahrain Fort. This is because the ruler of Bahrain, our very good friend Sheikh

Sulman, always used to claim that the fort was not in fact built by the Portuguese, but that they had merely adapted an Arab fort that already existed on the site before they came. Sheikh Sulman was, of course, no student of sixteenth-century fortifications, and we were long of the opinion that his belief in the priority of Arab fortification was dictated by a desire to minimize the influence of Europeans in the history of his country. We should have known better. Though the ruler's knowledge of the sixteenth century was no greater than our own, his instinct for strategic necessity was incomparably finer. He must have realized that such a commanding site could never have been left unfortified. And when, several years after our camp was built, we amused ourselves digging free one of the square corner towers of obvious European construction, we found that it abutted on an earlier round tower of equally obvious Arab construction.

But this discovery, like so many other discoveries, lay in the future as I sat that January afternoon of 1956 and watched our camp rising below. Around me lay the ruins of the fort. The whole of the interior was an immense area of tumbled stone and drifted sand, sloping steeply down from the edge of the ramparts to a fairly level sandy stretch in the centre. It was there, protected by the ramparts from the northerly winds that blow throughout the year, that we had laid out the camp. We had traced a long narrow rectangle in the sand, eighteen metres in one direction and four metres in the other. This was to be the living quarters, divided by eight cross-walls into nine small rooms, each two by four metres. Opposite these were to stand two smaller huts, the one a kitchen and the other the living quarters for the cook and mess boy that we were doing our best to recruit. And between the kitchen and the living wing, forming a third side to the rectangular layout, would rise a larger hut, our dining and work room. The size of all these rooms had been worked out carefully, in consultation with Ja'far. For the whole camp was to be in *barasti* construction, and Ja'far was the acknowledged expert in Bahrain on the construction of *barastis*.

A *barasti* is a palm-leaf hut, and its construction is a dying art. Even twenty years ago, when I first knew Bahrain, the villages among the palm plantations were built entirely of palm leaves, and even many of the houses in the larger towns were of the same construction. Now things have changed. A number of disastrous fires in the closely packed *barasti* suburbs of the towns have made this form of housing unpopular, and even caused the government to legislate against it. With the coming of electricity, and with it of fans and air-conditioning, to the villages the airiness of the *barasti* in the heat of summer is no longer a point in its favour. Most important, increased prosperity has made it possible for most villagers to afford stone-built houses. *Barastis* are now the dwellings of the poor—including archæologists.

One of the reasons why we were building our camp within the ruined ramparts of the Portuguese fort was that we could no longer afford to live in Manama. The expedition had grown. The Second Expedition, the year before, had been five men strong. All the oil companies had, most aggravatingly and understandably, wanted all their houses for oilmen, and we had rented a three-room house where, by putting beds in the kitchen and the attic, we had managed to squeeze ourselves uncomfortably in. This year the Third Expedition was to be nine, and the prospect of finding, and paying the inflated boom-town rentals of, accommodation for nine men, or rather eight men and a girl, in Manama had daunted our budget and our organizing abilities. We had decided to Go Native.

There were other reasons, very obvious from my look-out post on the rampart tower. For one thing the site was superb. A hundred yards to the north a white sandy beach edged the emerald-green waters of the coastal shallows, the colour deepening as the water deepened to a cobalt blue farther out. To east and west and south the pleasure gardens of the sheikhs approached to within a couple of hundred yards, the vivid green of the jasmine and hibiscus and pepper-trees underlying the grey-green of the palms. For another thing we would be living above the shop. The clearing around the fort, the white sandy mound some six hundred yards from east to west and three hundred yards southward from the beach, was our tell. Under it lay the remains of a city, or several cities. We had been digging in it for two years, but we had no idea, yet, how far back it extended in time. We meant to find out—this year if we could.

It was pleasant to sit up here and watch the activity below. We had ten men at work, work to which, once we had drawn out the plan of the camp, we could not contribute. They came from the village of Bani Jumra, whose inhabitants specialized in weaving and in building *barastis*. Apart from Ja'far, who was headman of the village, the local shopkeeper, and a *barasti* architect of some genius, they consisted of six youths who did nothing but fetch and carry, and three incredibly wizened and incredibly active old men who did the actual building. In addition there was a constant stream of donkey-carts, bringing loads of palm leaves, bundles of long stripped inner ribs of palm leaves, bales of jute cord, rolls of palm-leaf matting, and stacks of long thick poles, said to be mangrove and imported from India. All of these, the basic ingredients of the *barastis*, were piled up in the dry moat below the fort, and borne up, as they were required, by the six carriers.

The actual construction of the *barastis* was simple in theory and complex in execution. Not a single nail went into the building of the entire camp. But over a hundredweight of cord was used. First the framework of the long building was set up, with poles ten feet long standing vertically, one metre apart, with a third of their length rammed securely into holes in the ground. A row of longer poles, two metres apart, ran down the centre of the building. To the tops of these vertical supports poles were lashed horizontally to form the eaves and the ridge-pole of the peaked roof, with further poles sloping up from the eaves to the ridge-pole, all lashed together to form a rigid structure. Then came the turn of the inner ribs of the palm leaves. These were set vertically in the ground, about five inches apart, between the poles, except where the doors were left, and tied to the eave poles, and then more ribs were attached horizontally at the same interval, tied to the poles and to the vertical ribs at each point where they crossed. The side walls, the end walls, the eight partition walls, and the roof were all filled in with this neat trellis-work of naked ribs, the work going forward with incredible speed. And then the trellis was thatched. Bundles of palm leaves were painstakingly sewn onto the supporting ribs. One of the three old men prepared the bundles with a toothed iron sickle, and the other two placed them in position, one standing on either side of the wall and passing the cord back and forth on a large wooden needle made on the spot from a length of palm-rib. Thus the walls were filled in; the roof went even quicker. It was formed of two layers of plaited palm-leaf mats with a thick layer of banana leaves between. Ja'far assured me that this was adequate. When it rained, he explained, the banana leaves would absorb the moisture, and would swell to stop any holes there might be. (This was wishful thinking. We had very little rain that season—perhaps too little to cause the banana leaves to swell adequately. Certainly all the rain that fell on the roof found its way remorselessly inside, and the following season we improved on the local construction by covering the roofs with tarpaulins.)

Fascinating as it was to watch the camp going up, I could not spend all my time on the ramparts of the fort. Yunis and I had only a ten-day start on the main party, and there was much to do. Every day I took the land-rover that had replaced our first year's station-car, and went shopping in Manama. The camp had to be furnished. Mats for the floors and to hang in the doorways, bedsteads, chairs, kapok mattresses, sheets, and blankets had to be bought; and towels and crockery and cutlery, pots and pans and a kerosene stove, hurricane lamps and water-tanks and a water-filter, pillows and enamel washing bowls and a large red fire-extinguisher to stand in the middle of the yard. The list was endless.

While I shopped, Yunis stayed in camp to supervise the building, to dig a deep earth-closet, build a dry-stone rear wall for the kitchen, where the fire danger would be greatest, and construct two massive tables for the dining hall. Yunis was originally a carpenter by trade, and the tables he made were built to last out time. And they did, his time at least.

Yunis and Carsten Niebuhr would, I think, have had much in common. For Yunis was a practical man who could turn his hand to anything and who had fallen in love with the East. Many years ago, as a young man, he had worked his way, carpentering, to

Egypt, and since then he had spent more years in the Arab lands than in Denmark. And he had found his niche in life on archæological expeditions. He never learned to dig; but on Danish and Swedish, French and German and English expeditions he had done everything else, setting up camps, cooking, conservation, packing, repairing equipment. His Arabic was fluent, as was his English and French and German, and he was immensely popular with our Arab workmen. It was the Arabs who had given him the name of Yunis, finding his Danish name unpronounceable. He was already in his sixties when he built our camp, and for the next five years he was to run it for us. Then he left us for a more urgent job of archæology. He died in 1963, of a heart attack, while running the camp for the joint Scandinavian expedition working to save the sites in Nubia fated to be flooded by the High Dam at Aswan. And we still dine each year at the tables that he made in 1956.

And it was Yunis who made the first find of that season. Our ten days of grace were almost over. The walls of the dining hall were finished, only two partition walls of the living wing remained to thatch, and the kitchen was being built. Yunis needed more stone for the rear wall, and took it from a little stone hillock immediately behind his wall. Just under the surface he found a large stone cannonball, and then another, and then a third. When I came back from town I found a regular excavation in progress behind the kitchen. The walls of a small chamber had been cleared, and it could be seen that the entire chamber was full of cannonballs, stacked four deep. We estimated that there were over two hundred of them, all of stone, ten inches in diameter, and each of them weighing as much as a man could lift. We had built our kitchen practically on top of the arsenal of our Portuguese predecessors. They are still there. We left them exposed until our main party arrived two days later, and then covered them up again. We have often speculated since whether the cannon for which these round shot were intended also lie buried under the hill behind the camp.

Our ten days to build the camp only just sufficed. When Yunis and I drove out to meet P.V. and his five companions off the plane at Muharraq, the camp was just barely habitable. But the roofs were on the kitchen and the sleeping chambers, we were stocked up with food and drink, and we had a Persian cook and an Arab boy who were masters of improvisation, and who slept, without complaint, in the kitchen while their own hut was being built. During the next few days this hut was finished and the dining hall roofed, and finally a man-high fence was put up, running from each building to the next, and converting the seemingly haphazard group of huts into a neat rectangular structure surrounding a large sandy courtyard.

All that remained now, said Ja'far, was to celebrate the completion of the work. We asked how, and he said that if we would pay for a sheep they would take care of the rest. So we gave them their heads—and fifty rupees. And the same afternoon the three oldsters departed for Manama, and returned an hour later in a hired truck with a large black goat.

The ceremony that followed would not, I think, meet with the approval of orthodox Muslims, and almost certainly has its roots far back in the pre-Islamic religion of the island. Certainly when Habib bin Jasim, the oldest of the three old men, dug a shallow hole in the centre of the courtyard and, cutting the throat of the unfortunate goat, allowed its blood to drain into the hole, we recalled the stone we had found two years before standing in front of the altar-throne in the Barbar temple, with its deep hollow in the top leading out to the stone drain . . . The beast was then cleaned and skinned and partitioned, and handed over to the cook to be roasted, but the ritual was by no means over. A young palm-tree was planted in the hole that had been watered with the blood of the goat, the head of the animal was buried at the entrance to the camp, and one of the four legs at each of the corners of the camp. We were now, they explained, protected against the evil spirits, the djinns, who were known to infest ruins such as the Portuguese fort. And then we all sat down, the archæologists and the *barasti*-builders, the cook and the watchmen and the water-bearer, to a feast of goat's meat and chupatties—and tinned peaches and Coca-Cola from our provision store.

But all this occurred almost a week after our main party arrived. The intervening days had passed in showing the new members of the expedition where we had dug and where we were to dig. During the term of *barasti* building I had scarcely had a moment to look at our diggings, even though they lay literally but a stone's throw from our camp. But now the time had come to look more closely at our tell.

P.V. had discovered the city mound at the Portuguese fort during our first campaign two years before. In a way it was hardly a discovery. The Portuguese fort was one of the show places of the island, to which all visitors were taken. Vibeke and I had visited it many times during my oil-company days. We had collected the blue-and-white sherds of Chinese Ming porcelain, of the same sixteenth-century date as the Portuguese, which lie scattered over the area around the fort, in the vain hope of being able to put together a complete Ming bowl. And, like every other visitor, we had seen the clear evidence of buildings extending for several hundred yards around the fort, broken cement floors, fragments of squared stone, even the tops of walls showing level with the surface sand. And, like every other visitor, we had assumed that these remains of buildings were contemporary with the fort, the remains of a town or village that had clustered around the fort while it was occupied by the Persian garrison that the Portuguese had maintained here.

It was P.V. who pointed out the fallacies in this line of reasoning. One was that the embrasures and cannon-ports in the corner towers of the fort were clearly sited to command the ground on all sides of the fort, and they could only be effective if there was a clear field of fire all round the fort. Buildings in the area beyond the dry moat would have nullified this purpose and would certainly not have been allowed. Another and more important point was that the open country around the fort was raised ground, a broad plateau rising in places thirty feet or more above the general level of the surrounding country. And once that point was made it was obvious that the plateau was not natural, that it was a tell in the Mesopotamian sense, an accumulation of super-imposed buildings. And the hundred years or so of Portuguese occupation, or even the four hundred years from the time of the Portuguese to the present, could not have accumulated thirty feet of building and occupational debris.

It was in the month of April 1954 that P.V., on one of his exploration trips from the diggings at Barbar, had come to these conclusions about the Portuguese fort; and although our first season was well advanced and the heat already oppressive, he had taken five of his best workers from Barbar and started to dig at the new site.

Now a city tell is not a thing to be tackled lightly. Even a very small town covers quite a lot of ground, and this tell was no small town. With an area of almost forty acres it was a city that could bear comparison with the larger cities of Mesopotamia. It was, for example, about two thirds the size of Ur of the Chaldees, on which Sir Leonard Woolley had worked for twelve years without uncovering more than a fraction of the total area. And here there was no ziggurat, as at Ur, to tell us where we might find the most important buildings of the city. Haphazard digging could only give haphazard results, and years might go by before the portions of the town that might give the best results could be located. Yet a beginning had to be made somewhere, and the most important thing to determine was the history of the site, how far back it went in time. This could only be done by a deep digging, a *sondage* as the French call it, at some point in the centre of the city. P.V. picked a spot almost at the highest point of the mound, conveniently close to the deep moat surrounding the Portuguese fort, into which the earth he excavated could be tipped. He marked out an area four yards square and began to dig.

P.V.'s instinct rarely fails him, and at a depth of only three feet below the surface he came on the corner of a wall of large stone blocks. On cleaning up this masonry he found that two massive walls, three and a half feet thick, met at the centre of the northern edge of his *sondage*. He continued to dig down in the now restricted area inside the walls. And as he went down the walls, too, continued downward. They were composed of cut limestone blocks, up to three feet long, and in courses about a foot high.

Every day, when our work at Barbar and at my Iron Age grave-mounds was over, Kristian and I would drive to the fort to pick up P.V. and his workmen, and would stand on the edge of the excavation looking down into the ever-deepening pit. It was an excavation at which any ordinary archæologist would have baulked. The area left within the walls was scarcely six feet square, and to the south a perpendicular wall of earth three times as high as the excavation was wide seemed continuously to threaten to subside and bury the workers beneath. In the sweltering heat of a sub-tropical April the temperature at the bottom of the hole was scarcely to be borne. Only two men could in fact endure it, P.V. and Khalil bin Ibrahim. And Khalil was, in the opinion of the rest of our workmen, insane. He was an ex-pearl-diver and afraid of nothing. At Barbar he had distinguished himself by catching a live, and reputedly poisonous, snake by the tail and scattering the terrified workmen as he ran among them, waving the snake around his head, to show it to us. Now at the fort dig he, and he alone, insisted on digging out the deepening hole, piling the earth into the coir baskets to be handed up to the surface by the other workers perched on the wall-top or clinging to its stones. P.V. was beside him throughout, drawing each new level as it was met, collecting potsherds, and making notes. Eighteen feet they went down, and still the wall continued. It stood now fifteen feet above the bottom of the excavation, and its lower courses were even more massive than those above, some of the blocks being all of six feet long.

Then they came to a cement floor, broken through by two large oval holes. And digging down into these holes they found two bath-tubs. That at least was what they looked like when the rims first appeared above the earth. Three feet long, square at one end and rounded at the other, they were of thick earthenware, coated inside and out with bitumen. We had already guessed their function when, carefully removing the earth from inside, we found a human skeleton in each, huddled at the bottom, with its knees drawn tightly up beneath the chin. The bath-tubs were sarcophagi, earthenware coffins.

We had been speculating on the age of the immense walls ever since they had first appeared. But the sarcophagi told us that they were at least pre-Islamic in date. For the burials were certainly not Moslem, since they were in no way oriented toward Mecca, as all good believers are buried. And the burials were clearly later in date than the walls within which they lay and the floor through which their graves had been cut. And the floor was not even the original floor of the building. The holes for the coffins had been cut through two successive floors, and they rested upon a third.

That was all that could be said, at that time, about the *sondage*. At this point it had to be given up, as the work of extracting the two coffins used up all the time we had had left that first year.

The second year had given us a great deal more evidence—and no answers. Looking back over a dozen years of work one can see —as one cannot see at the time—that some years are interim years; not profitless, because in them essential work is done and essential progress made. But nevertheless at the end of them you are apparently no further forward, no nearer to knowing what that which you are finding means. Thus it was with the second year. It had of course been a shorter season. The first year we had been in Bahrain for a full five months, but we could not be away for five months every year. Even to an archæologist family life provides counter-claims and counter-attractions; and—more immediately unassailable—a professor cannot for years on end be absent from his university and from his students for five winter months. In 1955 we reduced our season to three months. But it was not that. Although we had only been out three months instead of five, we had been five men instead of three. And we had a deal more money. Sheikh Sulman and Sir Charles Belgrave, who advised him on finance, had doubled their grant. So had the Bahrain oil company. And the Carlsberg Foundation, that unique brewery which was willed as a going concern to Danish culture, which is run most efficiently by a board of professors and artists, and whose profits are devoted exclusively to pure art, pure science, and the purer of the humanities—the Carlsberg Foundation had decided to back our future work. The Pennsylvania University Museum, too, had sent Bob, their best young archæologist, with a cheque in his pocket. So we were in every way better equipped than the year before, and indeed in terms of cubic yards of earth moved we had achieved more. Yet all we had found were new questions, not new answers.

Kristian had gone on digging at Barbar. The whole of the

central court of the temple had been cleared, and three standing stones, one bearing a bull's head carved in the round and all with holes pierced through them, showed beyond a doubt where the sacrificial animals had been tethered. Excavations below the courtyard had proved, as we had suspected from our section trench the year before, that the temple had been built and rebuilt three times, but that it was the same people, and not many generations apart, who had built all three temples; the same round-bellied pots of red ware adorned with horizontal ridges were found from bottom to top of the excavation. In a corner of the courtyard of the second temple we had found one object that is still one of our best exhibits. In a heap of discarded copper bands and sheeting lay a magnificent bull's head of copper. It was a splendid work of art, with great splayed horns and flaring nostrils, but, more important, it was of a school of art clearly related to the bulls' heads of gold and copper that Leonard Woolley had found in the Royal Graves at Ur in Mesopotamia. There was some dispute among the experts about the date of the Royal Graves but—apart from Sir Leonard himself, who spoke for a fourth millennium B.C. date—the range of disagreement was between 2500 and 2200 B.C. So at Barbar at least we had something approaching a firm date.

At Qala'at al-Bahrain—the Portuguese fort—P.V., with Mogens to help him, had widened his appallingly narrow *sondage* and, with the greater elbow-room he had achieved, had driven two shafts down from the floor level of his great stone building a further ten feet to bedrock. But here the building itself was a hindrance. Its walls could neither be moved nor undermined, and the possible area for the deep *sondage* was therefore restricted to two holes little more than a yard square. Only sheer luck could have given anything conclusively datable from so small a sampling ground, and for once P.V.'s luck deserted him. Only a couple of sherds of painted pottery gave an impression of respectable age, and a flint flaking-core suggested that we might be getting back to the neighbourhood of the Neolithic, perhaps 3000 B.C. or earlier.

Bob, from Philadelphia, and I had started on the next stage in the exploration of the city mound. Now that the central *sondage* had shown that the site would repay further investigation, we had decided to cut in from the edge.

There are considerable advantages in digging into a tell from the side. There is not the same depth of earth to shift, and the earth can be disposed of more easily, without encumbering ground that you may wish to dig later. Moreover, the outer edge of a city may be a very interesting area, for it is there that fortifications may be found. On the other hand, if a city has grown outward from a smaller nucleus the remains at the edge may not be as old as the deepest layers in the centre, which is why the central *sondage* is a useful preliminary.

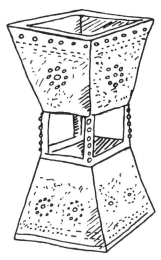

A MODERN INCENSE BURNER, OF BRASS-COVERED WOOD. WE FIND ITS PROTO-TYPE, OF CLAY OR STONE, BACK TO THE FOURTH CENTURY B.C.

For many reasons we chose the northern edge of the mound as our starting-point. There the mound ran right down to the beach, and it would have been by the sea that the earliest city would have lain. Besides, winter storms had here bitten deep into the mound and done a lot of our work for us. And indeed we were able to pick a spot where the waves had recently laid bare a short stretch of very fine masonry. It was possible that we had the city wall already discovered for us.

After two days' work I was quite sure that this was what we had. The wall that the sea had exposed curved back in a half-moon shape, and abutted on a very much more massive wall behind. Within a matter of hours of beginning the season's work we had been able to see what we were digging—a semi-circular turret jutting forward from a fortification wall. And the fortification wall was six feet thick, founded on bedrock, and preserved all the way up to the surface of the mound—which here of course, at the edge of the tell, was not nearly so high as at P.V.'s diggings in the centre. Even so, the wall rose ten feet high from the beach. Bob and I crossed the wall and, continuing the line of our trench due south, began to dig in the streets and houses of a vanished town.

The area that we had uncovered, during that second year, of the upper level behind the wall was quite impressively large. Beyond the wall we had found ourselves in a street, with footings of stone-built house walls on either side; and we had followed this street due south and soon had reached a little square. This was crazy-paved with stone slabs and sloped down to a drain in the centre. And as we cleared the square we began to notice a very odd feature about the town we were excavating. It appeared to be completely symmetrical. In the centre of each of the four sides of the square, streets identical to the one by which we had reached the square ran off in each of the other cardinal directions. And the plan of the rooms, and of the doorways into the rooms, on either side of each of the streets was identical. There seemed to have been a master-plan to this section of the town.

When we had ended our diggings the year before we had reached almost as far along the street running south from the square as the length of the street running north from the square to the northern turret. And I had speculated somewhat on what would happen when we did reach the same distance, whether the symmetry would be continued with another paved square, or whether the master-plan would show some radical change. I was not prepared for what we did in fact find.

And now the expedition was in Bahrain again. And, standing on the rampart above the magazine of Portuguese cannonballs, with the camp stirring to life behind me and the mounting sun in my face, I could watch the sea-mist clearing from the spoil-heaps and the trench of the year before. Another year's work was before us.

CHAPTER SIX

ৼৼৼৼৼ

THE ROMANCE OF ARCHAEOLOGY

Much happened in the third year. It was the year when we were besieged in the Portuguese fort; the year when the Seven-City Sequence was worked out; and the year when the grave-mounds were at last tied firmly into the growing framework of Bahrain prehistory. It was the year when we were given our Arab costumes by Sheikh Sulman, and the year when we first ventured out onto the mainland of Arabia. As we have seen, it was the year when we built the camp.

The camp made a great difference to our way of life. Formerly we had driven out to the sites each morning, and driven back in the evening to a house in a town, to electric light and refrigerators, to rooms with wooden floors and plastered walls and ceilings, with glass in the windows and with carpets and soft furnishings. And we had eaten European food in oil-company restaurants, food designed to remind expatriate Englishmen and Americans of their homelands. Now we were living square on top of our major site. Our floors were of earth covered with palm-leaf mats, our walls and our ceilings were of palm leaves. We became perpetually conscious of the weather. We slept—in our tiny two-by-four-metre cubicles—with the constant movement of air around our faces, for the flimsy walls allowed free passage for every breeze. We awakened to the pattern of sunlight filtered through the walls and roof. We washed in cool water carried in enamel bowls from the big round tank across the yard—and most of us abandoned shaving. In the kitchen the Persian cook, soon reinforced by a couple of boys from the local village, rapidly learned that the strange new sahibs had no desire for bacon and eggs for breakfast, but instead could consume buckets of coffee and loaf after loaf of bread with six different sorts of jam. And as we sat around the long table we could already hear the first of the "coolies" arriving outside, greeting each other and the watchmen as they selected their shovels and baskets from the pile against the camp fence. The Barbar team would be packing bags of fruit and bread and cheese, and selecting drawing boards and survey-or's levels and poles and cord and trowels, while Yunis or P.V. or I would be down by the moat, trying to coax one of the land-rovers to life in the damp morning air. For each day one of us had to drive the team out to Barbar and return with the vehicle. By the time we came back work would be in full swing on the fort site. Roll-call would be over, and the endless chain of baskets of earth already coming up from the diggings, to be emptied into the wheelbarrows and pushed out to the dumps. The workers would already be singing—they hardly stopped from morning to eve-ning—and, to one side of each dig, the oldest member of each gang would be building up the little fire to provide the embers for the water-pipe that would soon be going its periodic round.

In the camp all would be quiet. Yunis was away in town, in the other land-rover, buying provisions and six-inch nails and extra pencils and brushes. The cook was busy making the daily supply of bread in the kitchen, and a cake for afternoon tea. His young assistants would be cursorily sweeping out the dining hut. In one corner of the yard, under a privately rigged awning, Jasim was washing the potsherds that had been dug up the day before, laying them out on mats, to dry in the now-brilliant sunshine. And every quarter of an hour or so, Hasan would appear over the crumbled ramparts of the fort, bearing two buckets of water on a yoke from the spring by the edge of the tell, to replenish the big tank outside the kitchen.

About ten o'clock would come the "donkey-break." The market potentialities of sixty workmen had been quickly discovered by the pedlars of the surrounding villages, and the most regular visitor was the baker. Every morning his donkey-cart, loaded with chupatties and caraway bread and highly coloured cakes, came up over the brow of the tell, and all work stopped for half an hour while our workers bought bread and biscuits and sticky sweets. Our archæologists would come up to the camp for an extra cup of coffee, commonly loaded with hunks of thick sweet chupatties that had been pressed upon them by their workers.

At noon our Arabs, good Moslems all, break off for prayer, the most devout being led in their *rakāt,* the ceremonial prostrations in the direction of Mecca, by Sulman bin Yusuf, who is one of our less energetic workers, but a stately old man and, in his own village, a *mullah,* or lay priest. Following the short prayers they eat lunch, and we have soon learnt not to delay in leaving our diggings, but to hurry up to camp while prayers are in progress. For otherwise each group of Arabs, squatting around their billy-cans of rice and vegetables, will ceremoniously bid us join them as we pass. And while it would not be good form to accept the invitation, it taxes our meagre Arabic to the utmost to decline with due politeness and ceremony the courteous invitations—especially because the meal that the workmen have prepared over their fire looks vastly more appetizing than that which the cook has spread out upon our dining-hall table. There the fresh bread is flanked by a motley array of savagely opened cans, of bully beef and sardines and mussels and liver paste, which are almost all unanimously left untouched. The meal is saved by the bowls of hard-boiled eggs and the basket of locally grown salad and tomatoes and chives that have been brought in by our villagers from their gardens. And anyway lunch is a hurried meal, for after half an hour work begins again. We have tried many times to persuade our workers to take an hour for lunch, but they always prefer to shorten their lunch-break and stop work half an hour earlier in the evening. For many of them come from villages far afield, and some have well over an hour's walk or donkey ride back to their homes. So at half past four work ends; and a procession of workers carries tools and baskets of potsherds up to the camp.

As the last of the workmen depart the life of the camp begins.

Yunis arrives with the party from Barbar, and over tea and biscuits—and the cake—in the mess-hall the city-diggers and the temple-diggers compare notes and produce theories, to account for the lie of a wall or the presence of a sterile layer, which have to be defended against a barrage of counter-suggestions. Late-comers drift in, having stayed at their diggings after the workers left to bring a section-drawing up to date; others drift out, to wash and change and catch one of the land-rovers that, almost every evening, drives into town with those who want to visit the bazaar. There is much to be done before sunset, which falls early here on the edge of the tropics. Clothes have to be washed and notes written up. The pottery dug up the day before and washed today has to be examined, sorted, and bagged. If the tide is in there will be a bathing-party on the beach, while if the tide is out there are oysters to be gathered on the reefs at the far edge of the coral flats. Letters have to be read and written; from one of the rooms comes the rattle of a typewriter as some more enterprising author produces an article for his local newspaper back home on "The Romance of Archæology in the Middle East."

Around half past six the sun sets and half the camp will be on the ramparts to watch it. When we lived in Manama we were unaware of the splendour of the Bahrain sunsets, where the clouds change as you watch from white to pearl-pink and gold, and then to an ever-deepening red against which the palms stand out as though cut from black paper. As the glow fades and the dusk deepens, the lights of Manama and Muharraq wink on to the eastward across the bay, while overhead half the galaxy gradu-ally glows into light, with a crescent moon lying on its back and the Great Bear standing on its tail to the north and Orion striding the sky to the south. In the camp we have been given the freedom of the heavens, and we follow the courses of the stars and the phases of the moon with a very personal interest. The moon and the stars are, after all, the only street lighting we have, and in the dark of the moon it is dark indeed within the Portu-guese fort.

But now Saleh appears with the sizzling white light of the pressure lamps, to be hung in the mess-hall. And inside the sleeping rooms the softer light of the hurricane lamps begins to glow through the chinks in the palm-leaf walls. The party from town returns, to display their bazaar-purchases of brass coffee-pots and embroidered head-shawls. And in the middle of it all Abdullah sounds the call to dinner, striking the brass pestle against the brass of the coffee-mortar with a clear bell-tone.

Dinner is the main meal of the day and is fully Oriental, with fish or mutton and rice and fresh fruit. And it ends with dates and the unsweetened cardamom-flavoured Arab coffee, and long Indian cheroots. The meal goes on for an hour or maybe two, for this is the only time of day when the whole expedition is gathered, and there is more talking than eating. And, besides, the two largest breweries in Denmark have—independently and, it is rumoured, unbeknown to each other—given the expedition an unlimited supply of their beer, and Danes are great drinkers of beer. Even the mighty table which Yunis constructed rocks to the drinking songs of which Danish students have a vast repertoire, and the cook and his helpers—who are all good Moslems and never touch alcohol—sidle in to listen to the concert and to keep the coffee-cups filled. I should not, however, like to give an impression of nightly orgies in the camp. The day has been strenuous, and by nine o'clock the gathering around the table thins rapidly out. A few diehards may take a tour round the ramparts to look once more at the lights of Manama, but most retire to their rooms to read a while before they sleep. By ten o'clock the camp is still. Most lights are out, and only the faint rustle of the dry palm-leaf walls breaks the silence. For in the camp the wind is never still.

My long section trench, which I had begun the year before, began to move southward again. I was, you may remember, clearly digging my way through a fortified Islamic town. In the beginning, by the shore, I had met the city wall, with its turret; and then had followed a street southward to a paved square, and another street southward from that. And now, in almost the first day's digging of the new season, the trench met a wall, cutting clean across my southbound street. It turned out to be a thick wall, uncommonly thick for a wall in the middle of a town, almost thick enough to be a fortification wall. And then beyond it came a curving wall, and soon its shape became unmistakable. It was a semi-circular turret on the *southern* side of the thick wall, resembling exactly the semi-circular turret on the north side of the wall along the seashore.

It required little thought to see that my Islamic city was a myth. What I had been digging was an Islamic fort, and quite a small fort at that. Its north wall had lain along the shore, and now I had found its south wall scarcely sixty yards farther inland. And now everything fell into place. The odd symmetry of the streets and houses, on either side of the paved square, was perfectly understandable. The paved square was the central area of a square fort, with the symmetry extending not merely north and south but also east and west of the centre. Careful measurement on the ground allowed us to place where the corners of such a square fort would lie, and surely enough, when we dug at two of these points we found the round turrets that had defended these corners.

The question was now what to do next. We could expose the whole fort and thereby bring to light a quite imposing little monument. But that was not really what we were looking for. We knew from our diggings in the centre of the tell, which were now exposing more and more of the walls of the colossal building in which the "bath-tub" coffins had been found the first year, that the tell covered far older remains than my fort, which was incontrovertibly dated somewhere within the last thousand years by the Chinese copper coins and decorated glazed pottery found within its rooms. And our main aim was still to find out the history of the tell, to discover not who its last inhabitants had been, but who had first lived there, and how long ago, and what had happened since. We needed to go deeper into the tell, and deeper down too. I pulled my men in from the corner towers and set them to drive the original trench farther to the south.

It proved the correct decision. For for a space of at least twenty yards south of the wall of the Islamic fort there were no buildings of Islamic date of any sort. That was natural enough—

anyone building a fort would ensure that there were no buildings within bow-shot of its walls that could give cover to an attacker. In that cleared area we started to dig a line of square holes, five metres a side and with a baulk a metre wide between each, all the way down to bedrock. And in three successive holes we went all the twenty-four feet down to bedrock without finding a single trace of buildings, apart from one low wall slanting in from one of the baulks.

I have heard it said, by serious-minded archæologists, that the perfect excavation would be one in which nothing at all was found. I can see what they mean. Certainly structures are a nuisance. Build a wall, and you will make a foundation for it first; and you will dig a trench to put your foundation in. And when you dig a trench you will mix up the contents of a level older than you with the contents of the level you yourself lay down. And the stratigraphy is disturbed. And sure enough, sooner or later someone else will dig a hole through *your* level, to salvage the stones you used for your wall and use them for one of *his*. And the stratigraphy will be disturbed again. Anyway, it is hard work for an archæologist to remove a wall, and if it is an important building, like our Islamic fort or P.V.'s "palace" or the Barbar temple, you try not to remove the walls, and before you know where you are you have no room to dig down farther and examine the stratigraphy underneath.

So we were very glad of our holes with nothing in them. We dug them very carefully, watching out all the time for the slightest change in the colour or consistency of the soil, and switching our workers from hole to hole whenever we wanted a breathing space to scrape one of the levels clean with our trowels and make sure that we were not imagining things. And in copybook manner we kept the sides of our excavations vertical and scraped clean, and we drew diagrams of the vertical sides and numbered our levels with labels stuck into the earth face with six-inch nails. And we kept every scrap of pottery from each level, numbered according to our section diagrams. And we analyzed the pottery.

I was working with Toto that year. Toto was a Dutch girl, and the first woman to take part in our expedition. She had just finished a course at the London School of Archæology and had absorbed not a little of the technical perfectionism of that admirable and unique institution. Moreover she was a slave-driver. Promptly at three o'clock every afternoon she would hand over her excavation to me and go up to the camp. And when I came up at the end of the day's work all the potsherds from the previous day's digging would be laid out on the long table in the courtyard of the camp, each layer carefully separated from its neighbour, with all the rim sherds and base sherds and ornamented sherds in separate groups. Before sunset I was expected to have written a detailed analysis, anything up to two pages of close script, of the pottery of each level.

Now, as I wish to tell not merely how we reached our results, but what results we reached, I must go into some detail here. I have mentioned before that pottery is what tells you where you are in archæology. While its permutations and combinations are numberless, the potters of any particular time only actually manufacture a dozen or so different shapes of pots, and even this dozen will often have an underlying similarity, because they are made from the same clay and on the same wheel and baked in the same oven. The chance of the potter of one era producing a pot that can be mistaken for that produced by a potter of another era is so remote that it can be disregarded. Identical pots are of identical date, and not merely of identical date; they belong to the same "culture," by which we mean that people using the same pottery have the same cultural heritage and the same traditions and may be at least suspected of having an ethnic and political unity, of being a "nation" or a "country."

What we wanted to do with our pottery analysis was to distinguish "cultures" in our stratigraphic sequence; to find out the range of pots that the potters were making at each level. We wanted to find out whether these ranges of pots changed gradually from one to another, in a smooth progression of changes of fashions and techniques, or whether there were breaks in the sequence, when one range of pots abruptly gave place to a new and completely different range. For such breaks, if they occurred, would mirror fundamental breaks in the historical sequence.

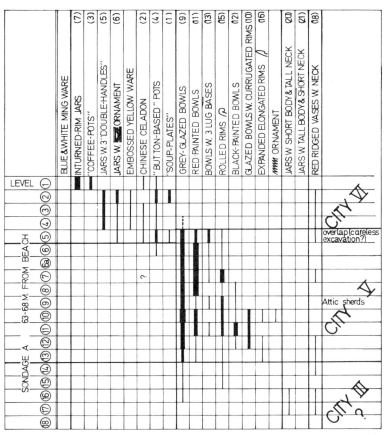

POTTERY ANALYSIS IN TWO ADJOINING *sondages* OUTSIDE THE NORTH WALL AT QALA'AT AL-BAHRAIN, SHOWING THE TWO CLEAR BREAKS IN SEQUENCE.

They would betoken either a gap in the chronology, a period when the site was uninhabited long enough for the pottery to change completely in character; or else a sudden replacement of one population, with one pottery tradition, by another population with a different tradition. And that could hardly mean anything other than foreign conquest.

So much for our aims. The method was equally clear-cut. We listed the salient characteristics of the pottery of each level in turn. On a large sheet of paper the characteristic features of the pottery of the uppermost level were noted at the head of vertical columns, and horizontal lines were drawn across the sheet in a number corresponding to the number of levels we had distinguished. On the line for level 1, crosses marked the presence in that level of the characteristics identified. Level 2 was similarly analyzed, and crosses marked where the same characteristics recurred. As new characteristics appeared new headings were added to further vertical columns. Two tabulations grew simultaneously, for Toto and I each had our square hole in the ground, and we made a separate analysis for each, though on the same sheet of paper and using the same pottery characteristics as key. As the work of digging and analysis went on, the list of pottery features along the top of the sheet and the number of levels down the side increased, and when we reached bedrock and finished the analysis of the final layer the pattern of the crosses slanting down the sheet was quite unmistakable. We had two complete breaks in the sequence; south of the little fort by the coast there was irrefutable evidence of three distinct phases of occupation.

Phase 1, the uppermost six levels of Toto's dig and the uppermost five of mine, had used a very variegated inventory of pottery which is easier to illustrate than to describe. There were (1) wide-rimmed "soup-plates," glazed and with a variety of arabesque patterns, generally balanced in some sort of radial symmetry, painted in black below the glaze. The glaze was in many cases badly preserved, sometimes completely vanished, and the colours of the original patterns had suffered severely. Particularly as the potsherds dried out in the sun the colours tended to fade, leaving only a grey-black pattern against a drab white. But sometimes original blues and greens and yellows would spring to life again as the sherd was dipped in water for a careful washing.

Apart from the "soup-plates" and an occasional deep bowl of similar ware there was only one other type of glazed ware, but this type was unmistakable and soon to be known to us very well indeed. It was a fine grey porcelain with an olive-green glaze that never showed any signs of deterioration under the action of the soil. It was so clearly modern in appearance that it was difficult to believe, when we had picked up the first specimens from the surface of the mound two years before, that it could be eight hundred or a thousand years old. But we knew that it must be that, for we knew what it was—Chinese porcelain, of the type known as celadon (2), first imported to the Arab world (according to contemporary Arab and Chinese writers) during the Sung Dynasty, A.D. 900–1150.

There was one type of vessel that we dubbed a "coffee-pot" just as soon as we recovered sufficient sherds to be able to reconstruct its shape (3). It resembled a wide-based vase with two handles, but one handle was hollow and functioned as a spout. This was the only type of vessel that was painted but unglazed, and the paint was always the same, dark-red lines and "ladders" on a pinkish white ground.

Four other vessels completed the stock-in-trade of the first phase: a little vase with four tiny handles and a very small base (4), a taller vase with three tall handles, the handles having the peculiarity that they were always formed of double or even treble bars (5), a round-bellied pot always decorated around the top of the body with an incised pattern of three wavy lines between two bands of three horizontal lines (6), and a three-foot-tall, though not very wide, storage jar with a rim which turned inward (7).

Seven types of vessels, then, characterized the uppermost six levels—and even of these the "coffee-pot" and the storage jar with the in-turned rim were late-comers, only occurring in the first two levels. There were, of course, sherds of other vessels than these, but not many where the form of the original vessel could even be guessed at—sherds of thin yellow ware with an embossed design clearly produced in a mould, and sherds with an

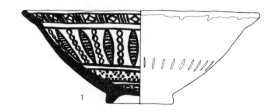

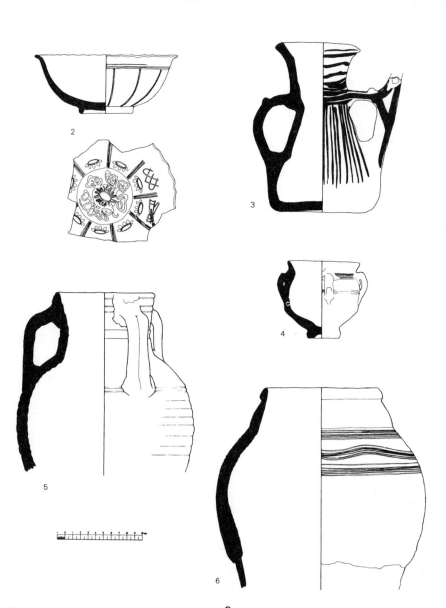

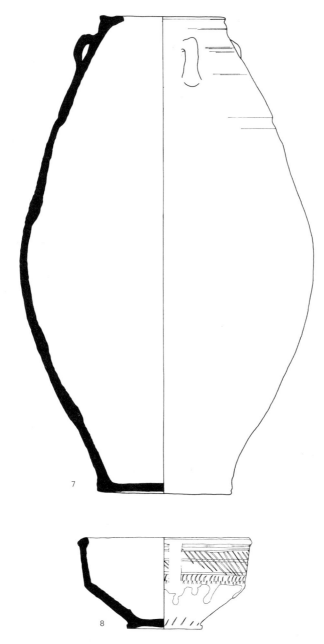

THE EIGHT MAJOR TYPES OF POTTERY COMPRISING THE "CULTURE" OF CITY VI AT QALA'AT AL-BAHRAIN, PROBABLY THE 12TH CENTURY A.D. THE NUMBERS REFER TO THE DESCRIPTIONS IN THE TEXT AND ARE ALSO SHOWN IN THE TYPE COLUMNS OF THE POTTERY ANALYSES.

incised design of triangles covered by a green glaze which we now know belong to deep "pudding-basins" (8).

I should be giving a wrong impression if I suggested that this inventory was any surprise to us. I had for a season and a half been digging up just this pottery. For this was the crockery found scattered everywhere in the rooms and streets of my Islamic fort, and it was already abundantly clear that the people who had built and inhabited that seashore fort had prepared and eaten their food from this kitchen and table ware. So if we could date the fort we could date the pottery. Or vice versa.

Below the levels we had now reached (level 5 in my dig, and level 6 in Toto's), the pottery changed completely; and for the next two metres, in which I distinguished nine layers and Toto ten, a completely different, but quite internally consistent, inventory of vessels came to light. We were tempted to call our new "culture" the "Corn-flakes People," for their tables were, it seems, dominated by shallow bowls. There was quite a variety of them. Some were glazed, with a bluish-grey crackled glaze apparently much more resistant to soil action than that of phase 1; others were painted, on the inside only and for about half an inch down the outside, either in a deep ox-blood red over an original straw-coloured ground, or in black over a base of grey. These painted bowls were as a rule partially burnished. Burnishing is a process achieved by rubbing with some smooth object, after the clay has dried but before it is fired, and it can often achieve quite a high polish. But these bowls were not polished over the whole surface, but in radial lines outward from the centre of the bowl. There were also plain bowls, neither glazed nor painted nor burnished. The bowls came in all sizes from two to five inches in height and five to nine inches in diameter. Common to them all was that their bases were either flat or furnished with three stub feet, whereas the vessels of phase 1 had all had ring-bases. The rims were fairly simple, often slightly incurved, and sometimes with one or two grooves just below the rim. I have drawn a selection of these bowls (9–13).

The people of phase 2 did not, however, live entirely on corn-flakes. We found sherds of round glazed bottles, with narrow

necks and two small round handles where the neck joins the body
(14). And there were coarser sherds of larger-necked vessels. We
could not then work out the shape of these vessels from the
scattering of sherds we had, but the rims were different from
anything in phase 1. They had two main forms, which we dubbed
the "rolled" rim (15) and the "expanded elongated" rim (16).
And that was phase 2. In general there was a lightness and
elegance about the pottery of this phase, in contrast to phase 1.
There was, though, little in the way of actual decoration; no
painted pottery designs, no moulded ornamentation, and very

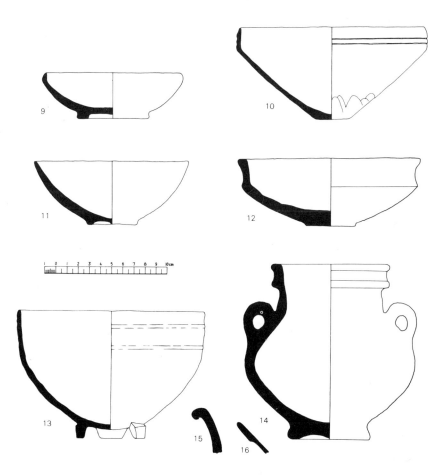

THE MAJOR TYPES OF POTTERY COMPRISING THE "CULTURE" OF CITY V, OF
THE CENTURIES AROUND 300 B.C.

little incised decoration. The only incised decoration, in fact, was a "saw-tooth" zigzag which we soon learned to regard as typical for this phase.

As the process of identifying and describing phase 2 objectively in terms of pottery types and rim shapes and ornamentation progressed, our scientific detachment began to wear thin. We very much wanted to know where we were, or rather when we were. And in the middle of the phase, in my layer 9 to be exact, two sherds turned up that gave the answer. They were as different from the normal run of sherds as the Chinese celadon had been from the ordinary sherds of phase 1. Of red clay, they were painted over with a jet-black varnish that had then been burnished to a degree that made them look polished. And one of them was decorated with a "roulette" pattern, as though a toothed cylinder had been run over the surface before firing. I was fairly sure that I knew what they were, but I took them to Kristian for confirmation—for Kristian is a classical archæologist, most happy when he is measuring Greek temples (we were to find the perfect excavation for him some years later). He took one glance at the sherds and handed them back. Attic ware, he said, black-on-red, third or fourth century B.C., probably late fourth.

To be presented with a date as accurate as that is not in accordance with the rules of pottery analysis. In fact, once you succeed in dividing your pottery into separate boxes called "cultures," you do tend, sooner or later, to find something in one of the boxes that can more or less date its contents; but pottery analysis is supposed to be workable even without this adventitious assistance. For at worst it gives its own *relative* chronology —at least you know that each culture is later in date than the one below and earlier than the one above, even if you have no idea of the *actual* date of any of them.

But it is always very exciting to get an actual date, especially one so exact as Kristian's. What made this occasion rather unusually exciting was the actual date he had given. There can hardly have gone two seconds after he said, "Late fourth century B.C.," before someone said, "Alexander the Great" . . .

We shall meet Alexander the Great later, and discuss his association with the Arabian Gulf at greater length. Let it be sufficient now to say that Alexander's biographer Arrian, who had access to the actual log-books of Alexander's admiral, tells that when Alexander reached India he built a fleet on the Indus River; and this fleet sailed back from India to Babylon along the Persian coast in the winter of 326-325 B.C. In the following three years, three voyages of exploration were made by Greek captains along the Arabian coast of the Gulf at least as far as Bahrain. These

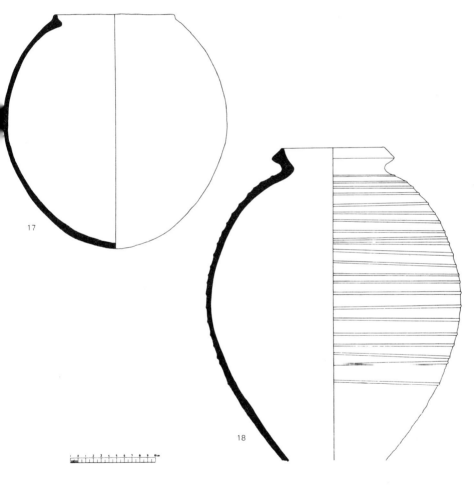

THE TWO MAJOR TYPES OF POTTERY OF CITY II, AS WELL AS OF THE BARBAR TEMPLES AND THE FAILAKA TOWNSHIP. TYPE 18 ALSO OCCURS FREQUENTLY IN THE GRAVE MOUNDS OF BAHRAIN. THEY DATE TO ABOUT 2000 B.C.

voyages were in preparation for a campaign against Arabia, which was abandoned on the death of Alexander in 323 B.C. Needless to say, our Attic sherds were immediately entitled "Alexander's tea-service," though we did not really believe that the sherds were necessarily brought to the island by one of the three Greek captains. In the years following Alexander's campaign, and perhaps even in the years before it, there can well have been extensive trade up and down the Gulf, and the presence of Attic ware does not necessarily imply the presence of Greeks.

Still, phase 2 was dated, and our thesis, that a complete change in pottery types probably betokened a chronological gap in the history of the site, stood proven. For the Chinese celadon found in phase 1 could not possibly be older than A.D. 900, and the Attic ware of phase 2 could not be later than 200 B.C. For over a thousand years between the two phases the site had lain deserted.

Below level 13 in my dig, and level 16 in Toto's, the pottery of phase 2 disappeared, and between this point and bedrock a new phase came to light, which I divided into five levels and Toto into four. It is perhaps inaccurate to call it a new phase—it proved tantalizingly difficult to pin down to the dozen or so sharply defined characteristics into which phase 1 and phase 2 had fallen almost of themselves. It *was* a new phase, but only for the rather negative reason that it was no longer phase 2. Every characteristic of phase 2, except the rolled rim and the expanded elongated rim, had disappeared, as had the general elegance and thinness of the ware. But in its place was an ill-definable collection. Perhaps sherds of a greenish clay predominated, but there were also bright red sherds with a cream-coloured wash, and ordinary straw-coloured sherds and sherds of a deeper warmer brown, fudge- or caramel-coloured. And there was a sprinkling of Barbar sherds.

Barbar sherds were what we had been hoping to get down to. At our temple site at Barbar, where Anders and Kristian and Peder were even now digging, we had an undoubted "culture," and a culture that could be dated, by the bull's head of the year before and the "Sumerian" mannikin of the first year, to somewhere about or before 2300 B.C. The pottery was eminently recognizable and very uniform—large vessels, as big as a pumpkin and shaped like an egg, of red clay and decorated with horizontal ridges perhaps half an inch apart. It will be recalled that there were two varieties of this pot; one in which the top of the pot was simply a round opening in the broad end of the egg, the rim being thickened around the opening (17), the other where there was a short neck at the broad end, ending in an out-turned triangular rim (18). We all knew these vessels of the "Barbar culture," and could recognize them blindfold. There was no doubt that the sherds occurring in Toto's and my lowest levels were of the "Barbar culture." But they were too few, perhaps fifteen or twenty sherds out of five or six hundred in a layer.

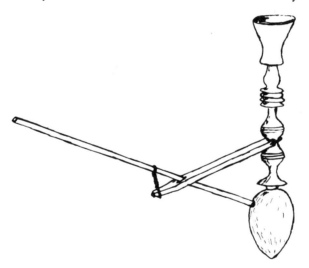

THE *narghila,* THE COCONUT WATER-PIPE, WHICH CIRCULATES AMONG OUR WORKMEN EVERY HALF-HOUR.

That was the sort of proportion of inconsistent sherds that we could normally expect to find "intrusive" in a culture level from the level beneath. There are always such intrusions; every time a hole is dug for a hut post or a storage pot, every time a stone or tree is uprooted, or a dog buries a bone, sherds from the level below will be mixed with the level then being formed. (This is why the archæologist has the rule of thumb that "a level is as old as the *latest* object in it.") But here there was no level below that could have intruded its Barbar sherds. We were digging in the fine white sand of the original foreshore, and below us was—uncompromisingly—bedrock.

There lay the answer, of course, though it took us a week to see it. The sand above bedrock was not an accumulated "occupation" level at all; it had been there before ever man had come to Bahrain. Phase 2 had been a typical series of occupation levels—although its houses must have been no more substantial than our own palm-leaf huts—but phase 3 was merely the foreshore debris *outside* the earlier cities, refuse of many periods trodden into the sand between the city and the shore. To find our "Barbar culture" we should have to dig, not farther down, but farther inland.

The season was by now far advanced. In a fortnight our party would be leaving. I decided to jump twenty-five metres and dig a new hole.

CHAPTER SEVEN

QATAR

Before I started my new sounding, P.V. and I took a holiday—
which we called an exploration. It happened this way.

Looking from the ramparts of our Portuguese fort we could see,
on clear nights, a red glow beyond the horizon to the eastward. It
came from the waste-gas flares of the Dukhan oil-field in Qatar.
And two years earlier Sheikh Sulman had taken us to a watch-
tower on a rock outcrop near the southeast shore of Bahrain, built
to keep watch on the Qatar shore and give warning of invasion
fleets. From the tower we had seen the Qatar coast, a yellow
streak beyond the turquoise blue of the straits between.

Qatar is the neighbouring principality to Bahrain, a peninsula
over a hundred miles long and fifty miles wide, jutting due north
from the Arabian coast and forming with that coast the deep
triangular bay at the entrance to which lie the islands of Bahrain.
I knew it well, for in my oil-company days my task had been to
keep the Qatar Petroleum Company's drilling staff supplied, from
Bahrain, with the necessities—and all too few of the luxuries—of
life, and I had been over many times. I had even been there on
the occasion when Sheikh Abdullah of Qatar had turned the
stop-cock that opened the flow of crude oil into the first tanker at
the loading jetty of Umm Said on the other side of the peninsula,
and afterwards when the sheikh feasted four hundred guests on
fifty sheep, roasted and laid out on mounds of rice in an immense

marquee. Now Abdullah had retired, and His Highness Sheikh Ali bin Abdullah Al-Thani, his son, reigned over the peninsula. And it was with his permission that P.V. and I now spent three days in Qatar.

The initiative had not been taken by us. But the noise of our doings was being bruited around the Gulf. The Arab is a great traveller, and a great raconteur. And the European in the East gets around too, and the cocktail party is as much a home of gossip as is the sheikh's daily court. So it was known throughout the Arab states of the Gulf that Bahrain was acquiring a Past. And in those countries such of the Europeans as had antiquarian leanings, and such Arabs as were interested in their forefathers (and what Arab is not?), had begun to speculate.

The initiative came from the commandant of the Qatar police. I had known Ron in the old days when he was an inspector in the Bahrain police, a tall, red-haired Scot; and I had seen him once, after he transferred to Qatar, in Arab dress with a jutting red beard, a hawk-like figure more Bedawi than the Bedouin. Now he sent us an invitation, offering to give us transport and guides to take us anywhere we wanted on the peninsula if we came over to reconnoitre. And the Qatar Petroleum Company offered to sail us across in their launch, and to house us during our stay.

It was a leisurely five-hour trip in the launch. For although Bahrain and Qatar are but thirty miles apart, the navigable channel through the shallow waters is tortuous, and we grounded more than once. In the early afternoon we turned into Zekrit Bay and at the jetty found a long black limousine and a two-ton truck waiting for us. We were to travel in state in the limousine, while the truck, with a corporal's guard of armed and khaki-clad police, was to follow after, loaded with gasoline, water, spare tires—and a winch to drag us out of any difficulty. For Qatar is true desert, with all the varieties of difficulties in which deserts abound.

We saw most of the variations in the following two days. After a night spent in the drilling camp at Dukhan we purred north the first day, among fantastically eroded chalk and limestone cliffs, and then up onto a rolling gravel plain. And almost immediately we saw, on the higher ridges of the plain, the unmistakable humps of burial-mounds. They were not numerous, nor so large as the mounds of Bahrain. These were mere flattish cairns of weathered stones. But they were undoubtedly pre-Islamic, for cairn burial is against the tenets of Islam.

For miles the cairns were the only things that broke the monotony of the landscape, an endless switchback of shallow gully and low rise, over grey pebbles and fractured rock. This was the real desert, very different from the sand areas of Bahrain, where the sea or the central hills were seldom out of sight. And yet gradually we realized that the desert was far from featureless. There were plants among the stones, sudden glimpses of tiny flowers; there were lizards, and it was inevitably P.V. who spotted a snake gliding away. Our driver suddenly pulled up with a jerk, and he and the corporal descended, to dig up a plant with a bulbous root which they had spotted from the truck, and to look around for more. P.V. and I stretched our legs, and looked for flint, but there was none. We went on. Over the next horizon there was a broad depression, and in the middle, where what rain falls each winter must collect, there were green bushes, and sandy soil and grass that for some reason carried me straight back to the furze-clad hills of Dartmoor. Perhaps it was the sight of the sheep grazing among the bushes, but the two low tents, striped horizontally in brown and white, on the slope beyond had never been seen on the Devon hills. At a word from the corporal the driver turned aside and pulled up by the tents.

Black-clad women had disappeared into the tents on our approach, leaving a cluster of small children, with black ringlets and brown ankle-length frocks, to gaze solemn-eyed as we alighted. As we came up two men came out of the tent, thin wiry brown men with short beards, clad in long grey-brown *thaubs* and red-chequered headcloths. They greeted the corporal with affectionate kisses on nose and forehead, and shook hands with us and the driver and the escort from the truck. The corporal explained that they were men of his own tribe, the Na'im, and motioned to us to sit down at the entrance to the larger tent. The younger man went into the tent, and returned to set before us a large wooden bowl of camel's-milk curds and a basket of dates.

We followed the example of our escort, and scooped up curds with the dates. It proved a surprisingly palatable combination.

In the meantime the older man blew up the camel-dung fire before the tent, set a blackened coffee-pot of water to boil, and poured out green coffee-beans upon a shallow long-handled metal ladle. He roasted the beans with practised hand over the fire, turning them from time to time with a short iron rake. Within minutes the roasting was complete and the beans poured into a brass mortar. The bell-tones of the pestle on the mortar as the roasted beans are pounded can be heard for miles across the desert and are said to be an invitation to any traveller within hearing to avail himself of desert hospitality. During the last strokes of the pestle a few berries of cardamom and two or three cloves were added and the contents of the mortar poured into the now-boiling pot.

P.V. and I had drunk this spiced coffee, black and unsweetened, many times before, on visits to sheikhs and merchants, but we had never witnessed its preparation. Now, as we sat sipping from the small handleless cups, with the fresh smell of the coffee-roasting mingling with the acrid smoke from the smouldering fire, and with the black goats grazing outside the tent mouth, we tried to explain to our hosts our purpose in driving over the Qatar desert. We were looking for flint, we said—we knew the Arabic word for flint—and for the houses and graves of the people of the Time of Ignorance, the time before the Prophet's revelation of Islam. They nodded; they had heard of archæologists, as has every Arab, and they told us of grave-mounds farther north, and of an old fort in the same region. How old, we asked? Oh, very old, they said, from the time of the Turks. We thanked them for the information; we knew that the "time of the Turks" was the period just before the First World War.

And indeed some half hour later we passed the fort, a crumbling ruin of weathered stone, clearly less than a century old. And a little later we pulled up at a more modern fort, a whitewashed stone building with the maroon flag of Qatar flying above it. It was a police post, and we were greeted by the police detachment as a welcome break in the monotony of their lonely watch.

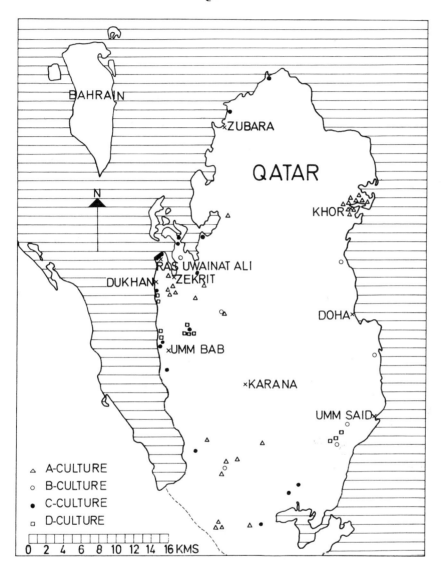

THIS MAP OF QATAR SHOWS MORE THAN THE BOOK TELLS OF OUR FINDS
THERE. THE FOUR SYMBOLS SHOW MAJOR SITES (THERE ARE ANOTHER 63 MINOR
ONES) OF THE FOUR STONE-AGE CULTURES IDENTIFIED. CULTURE A IS THE OLD-
EST, ALMOST LOWER PALAEOLITHIC; B IS CHARACTERIZED BY UNBARBED ARROW-
HEADS, C BY SCRAPERS, AND D, ONLY 6-7000 YEARS OLD, BY BARBED AND TANGED
ARROWHEADS. FLINT ENTHUSIASTS WHO WISH TO LEARN MORE MUST BEG OR
BORROW—OR EVEN BUY—VOLUME ONE OF THE EXPEDITION'S REPORTS, HOLGER
KAPEL'S *Atlas of the Stone-Age Cultures of Qatar* (AARHUS 1968).

Our escort had many friends among the little garrison, and we were immediately given mugs of hot sweet tea, to last us while coffee was brewed.

The post occupied a strategic position, on a ridge overlooking the coast. And below it, along the coast, stretched a deserted city, the city of Zubara.

We had been rather chary of visiting Zubara, for our motives might well be misunderstood, both by Sheikh Sulman of Bahrain and by Sheikh Ali of Qatar. For Zubara is the ancestral home of the sheikhs of Bahrain, a town in which the Al-Khalifah family had settled when, in the middle of the eighteenth century, they had moved south from the neighbourhood of Kuwait. For a score of years the Al-Khalifah had governed Zubara, before they had conquered Bahrain from its Persian overlords, and after their move to Bahrain they had retained their rights in this city on the coast of Qatar. In the 150 years and more since then, Zubara had been in dispute between the sheikhs of Qatar and Bahrain, the Al-Thanis claiming that the town was geographically part of Qatar, and the Al-Khalifah claiming that it was historically a dependency of Bahrain. The last armed clash between the two sheikhdoms had occurred within living memory, and it was on that occasion that the last of the inhabitants of Zubara, fearing reprisals and finding it impossible to carry on normal fishing and trading activities in a chronic state of war, had retired to Bahrain. The city, which had once rivalled Basra as a trading centre, lay now deserted on the northwest coast of the peninsula. And the police post was sited to give warning, in case the sheikh of Bahrain should decide to reassert his claim.

We had to see it. Although we ran the risk of being deemed Bahraini spies, there was a possibility that Zubara was an ancient town. Certainly it was older than Doha, the capital of Qatar and the only town of any size in the country.

It was eery to walk between the crumbled walls of this once-populous town. Feet sank in the yellow-grey sand that choked rooms and streets, sloping up almost to the top of the broken stonework. Not a roof remained standing in Zubara—except for the mosque. It was a multiple-domed building, resting solidly on a forest of pillars, and it illustrated to us as archæologists the lesson taught already by the Pantheon in Rome, St. Sophia in Constantinople, and indeed the arch of Ctesiphon outside Baghdad. The dome is everlasting; it depends upon no roof-beams, and it even protects the walls which support it. A domed building, like a pyramid, is a stable structure, and only the hand of man can pull it down. We ate our lunch packets in the shadow of the mosque, the only shade in Zubara. And after lunch we collected potsherds, though we could already see that Zubara was no ancient city. There was no tell, except one in the making. The buildings that were crumbling to ruins about us and being covered with sand would one day be an even flattish mound that future inhabitants of Qatar might well choose as a site for a new city. But these buildings were themselves built upon the naked rock and sand of the foreshore—there had been no city before the Zubara of the Al-Khalifah. The potsherds told the same story, though a sprinkling of blue-and-white Chinese sherds did suggest that the city might have existed in the seventeenth century, a hundred years before the Al-Khalifah came from Kuwait.

I think our escort was relieved when we resumed our journey. Our route lay now inland, across the whaleback of Qatar, a gravel and pebble plain of shallow ridges and hollows that the police vehicles took at speed, in a spray of stones.

After an hour the ridges began to trend downwards, and soon from their crests we could glimpse the sea ahead, the eastern sea, for the peninsula of Qatar in fact divides the Arabian Gulf into a western and an eastern basin. The hollows between the gravel ridges were now filled with *sabkha,* the flat salt-pan that is one of the hazards of the coastal regions of the Gulf. For some *sabkha* is firm and hard and provides a perfect surface for motor travel, while other stretches, identical in appearance, are only a thin crust covering a treacherous morass. We followed previous wheel-tracks across the wider salt-pans, and climbed a last gravel ridge to the village of Khor.

Khor is the Arabic word for fiord, and indeed there is something Scandinavian about Khor which has attracted the members of our Danish expedition in all the years since this first visit. The white houses of the village crowd the edge of dark rock slabs that slope steeply down to the waters of the narrow inlet. At the water's edge the boats are drawn up, and a dhow rides at anchor farther out. In the air is the sharp tang of salt and of drying seaweed.

The police fort stands at the inland edge of the village amid the roofless shells of abandoned houses. Khor was once larger than it is today. When pearl-diving was the main source of wealth in the Gulf, Khor was a prosperous and expanding town, with its own fleet of pearling dhows. Now the younger men seek the oil-fields and the growing capital city, and the desert encroaches on the outskirts of the town.

We drank tea and coffee and ate sweet biscuits at the fort, while the sergeant in command reported back over the radio to Zubara that we had arrived. As soon as we left he doubtless reported to Doha fort that we were on our way. The network of police radio-communication in Qatar was to save us much anxiety and even expense in later years. Originally built up by Ron as an Early Warning system against Bedouin raids, it soon proved its more day-by-day worth as a saver of lives. More and more the Arab uses the automobile in the desert; and with a sublime faith in the mercy of Allah he will start on a journey across a waterless waste in a ramshackle truck or a battered limousine, with no thought of a survival kit and little enough thought of gasoline. But wherever he goes the police radio network follows him. When the following year we began serious reconnaissance in Qatar we thought it a necessary precaution to have two vehicles—but we soon found that we needed only one. Whenever we stopped, as we often did, to reconnoitre a stretch of desert on foot, within two or three hours a police truck would nose over the horizon, sent out to find why we were overdue. A mechanical breakdown, which in other circumstances might have meant death by thirst, or at best a day-long journey on foot across waterless desert, was reduced to a minor inconvenience—all the more so as the police were largely recruited from those very Bedouin they were originally conceived as a protection against, and they know every inch of the desert and, I believe, the individual tire tracks of every vehicle that frequents their "beat."

We ran into Doha in the late afternoon, across the salt-flats of the east coast. Doha had changed since I was last there six years before. Then we had had to leave our vehicles outside the town, as the streets were too narrow for anything but donkey-carts. Now broad paved roads met at the new mosque by the half-completed new palace in the centre of the town; the ring-road was half-finished, and was already marked out for its dual carriage-way.

We were driven straight through the capital and on to the new police fort in the outskirts, with its crenellated walls surrounding an immense parade-ground. It was typical of the Qatar view of the fitness of things, we found, that first priority in the use of the new oil wealth was given to the building up of mosques and of the land's defenses. Third on the list came the largest and most modern hospital in the Gulf—and only fourth the ruler's new palace.

Ron came out to meet us at the door of the headquarters building. Though his beard was gone he looked more hawklike than ever in Arab headcloth above the maroon-braided khaki uniform. He discussed eagerly the possibilities of a serious archæological expedition the next year, while at the same time he dragged us across the parade-ground to see his new toys, the squadron of tracked infantry-carriers. Ron was clearly in his element as commandant of the Qatar police. I recalled him as superintendent in Bahrain, sitting with his flat visored cap on the desk before him and worrying out problems of traffic control. Here he commanded an army in all but name, and the armoured vehicles only served to emphasize the fact that Qatar was part of mainland Arabia and had very different police aims from Bahrain. Here was no problem of checking petty theft or keeping an eye on political hotheads. Here was the age-old question of the relative strength of the townsfolk and of the desert nomads. The desert of Qatar, to within sight of the coastal villages, formed part, and merely part, of the grazing grounds of powerful Bedouin tribes, the Na'im, the Manasir, and above all the Murra, whose range went deep into Saudi Arabia, as far as the oasis of Jabrin, 200 miles from the coast. These nomad tribes had never given more than nominal allegiance to the sheikhs of the coastal

125

towns, and then only in so far as the sheikhs of Qatar could effectively control the grazing grounds and prevent encroach-ment by other nomads. *That* was a police job after Ron's heart.

The next day we took the direct oil-company road back across the peninsula to Dukhan. We had spent the night at Umm Said, the oil town by the loading terminal on the east coast south of Doha, and the road followed the oil pipeline that zigzagged across Qatar from the oil-field on the west coast. The black road ran straight and almost deserted across the featureless gravel plains. But on our left, on the southern horizon, marched a range of hills. They were sand dunes. Here in the southeast of Qatar the sands of Arabia, in their imperceptibly slow wandering, have made an attempt—or a beginning—of an invasion. Here the towering, crescent-shaped dunes are separate entities, with long stretches of gravel plain between the foremost and the next. Farther to the south, in the direction of the Empty Quarter of Arabia, the Rub' al-Khali, they coalesce, riding up on each other in wave of sand upon sand. But even here, and even in the distance, they have a menacing aspect, as though they might any moment change their millimetre-slow advance and roll forward to overwhelm the stony desert, the road, and all the works of man.

We could have crossed the peninsula in two hours on the paved road, but we had the day before us, and much to see. Halfway across the peninsula we turned south on a sandy track toward Karana, where Sheikh Ali of Qatar was said to be hunting. Karana is one of the most pleasant spots in Qatar. Low sandy hillocks and wide sandy hollows are here clothed with a sparse growth of grass, so sparse that, close at hand, the single blades scarcely show against the brown sand. But seen from a distance the hills and valleys are green, and in every hollow there are bushes and acacia trees.

In the shade of the largest grove of trees stood the white hunting lodge of Sheikh Ali, a couple of rooms with a wide porch. A major-domo told us that the sheikh was expected back soon from the day's hunt and bade us be seated on the rugs spread out on the porch. Some half hour later Sheikh Ali arrived and came

out immediately to greet us. With the courtesy that good breed-
ing demands of an Arab of the desert he conversed with us for
half an hour, while coffee was sipped, though he was probably
completely uninterested in our visit, clearly dead-tired, and was,
though neither he nor we knew it, already seriously ill. Not many
months later he collapsed and was flown to India for the medical
treatment that saved his life. After months in hospital he returned
to Qatar, but soon afterwards relinquished the reins of government to his son, Ahmed. In retirement his health has improved,
and he now finds time, between the hunting trips that custom
demands of an Arab sheikh, to devote to his true interest, the
collection and study of rare Arabic manuscripts.

After due exchange of courtesies we took our leave, and for an
hour strolled around the groves and wells of Karana, looking for
signs of early habitation. There was nothing, no flints, no tell, no
potsherds. Even the wells were to all appearances modern, without the cut-stone facings that we had learned in Bahrain to
expect. We drove back to the main road and turned west again.

Now we could see ahead of us the rugged limestone chain of
hills which lines the west coast of Qatar south of the oil-drilling
headquarters at Dukhan. Where the road topped that crest and
turned sharply northward to follow the ridge to Dukhan we came
in sight of the sea. Below us the land fell away in rocky terraces
to the stretch of sand, scarcely half a mile broad, which sloped
down to the bay which here separates Qatar from mainland
Arabia. The bend in the road has a name—Umm Bab.

Umm Bab will always for me be a ghost town. And indeed one
isolated house lay here, an unmotivated block of one-room dwellings. It is the sole reminder of a project that came to nothing.

In 1948 the oil company in Qatar found itself in possession of
quantities of oil, with no way of getting it out to the markets.
Much of its energies in that year went to prospecting the coasts of
Qatar, in order to find some way of getting the oil to the tankers.
Qatar is surrounded on all sides by shoals and reefs, and approach is impossible for vessels with the draught of modern
tankers. But finally a channel was found which, by dint of heroic
blasting, could enable tankers to reach comparatively deep water

off Umm Bab, and the site was selected as the loading point. Whatever the disadvantages of the site from the navigation point of view it was an ideal site for a town, and the architects enjoyed themselves thoroughly drawing up blueprints of the town that was to arise on the ridges and terraces overlooking the beach. Complete plans were made, with the church and school and country club crowning the ridge, and the villas and bachelor flats occupying the terraces. We all looked forward to moving into Umm Bab. Then just before the first construction gangs moved in, the marine survey group discovered deep water, easily accessible, on the other side of the peninsula, at Umm Said, and the whole project was dropped.

The oil town at Umm Said, built on a monotonous plain of sand where only the distant threat of the sand dunes breaks the dead level of the skyline, is a poor substitute for the dream city of Umm Bab, but doubtless the tanker skippers, saved the long haul round the peninsula and the hazards of the tortuous channel, are duly grateful for the change of plan. And only the bend in the road remains to mark the site of what would have been the fairest city in the Arabian Gulf.

We drove on, past the spill-gas flares of the degassing stations —for all the oil wells in Qatar lie along the western ridge—and reached Dukhan as evening fell.

The next day we were to return to Bahrain, but it would be afternoon before the launch left, and we took a morning drive up the coast from Dukhan. Ten miles north of the oil camp a headland juts out into the sea, called Ras Uwainat Ali. And as soon as P.V. saw the shallow bays running in on either side of the headland he called on the driver to stop.

There is an almost instinctive ability that develops in the seeker after flint, and that enables him to recognize at a glance the sites that the hunters and fishers of the Stone Age would have chosen for habitation. P.V. has this ability to an almost uncanny degree. Here at Ras Uwainat Ali he had extrapolated a rise in sea level of some ten feet and seen that the result would be two deep inlets meeting, or almost meeting, behind the sheltering headland. It was an ideal site for a Stone Age fishing encampment.

And almost before we alighted from the car the first sherds of flint discards proved his point.

Before we returned to Dukhan for lunch and the boat to Bahrain we had explored two Stone Age encampments, a couple of hundred yards apart, and had our pockets full of flint scrapers and knives and discarded flakes and blades. The Qatar Stone Age was a reality.

We could not, of course, date the Qatar Stone Age. As with the very similar flints from Bahrain, all we could say was that in shape and style of manufacture they resembled the Late Palæolithic (Aurignacian or Perigordian) of Europe. And that could put them anything up to forty thousand years old. But we could not assume an identity of date between cultures a quarter of the world apart, particularly where, as here, the climate might have encouraged survival, and even fossilization, of cultures that in Europe were forced by the ending of the last Ice Age either to adapt or to perish.

But as we reclined on the carpets spread on the deck of the launch, and watched the yellow sands of Qatar recede into the distance, we were agreed that we had reason enough to be satisfied with our three-day holiday. We were not bringing home any spectacular discoveries, of city tells or buried temples. But the flint sites and the scattering of grave-mounds were enough to show that Qatar *had* a past, and we determined to try the following year to send in a team to look more closely at the peninsula. For Qatar is twenty times the size of Bahrain, and we had only seen a tiny fraction of the whole.

We got back to Bahrain just in time for the revolution. I had just measured out my new *sondage*, a neat 5 × 5-metre square twenty-five metres south of my last digging, and we were removing the topsoil, when we heard the first shots across the bay from Manama.

It was a mild revolution as revolutions go, I believe, and it was unsuccessful. But even mild revolutions are an inconvenience to an archæological expedition. Starting as a market-square protest against the police moving a street-salesman from his pitch, it quickly developed into riots and marches and mass meetings led by a group of young men, the first products of the first school in the Arabian Gulf, which had been started in Bahrain twenty years before. And within twenty-four hours it had crystallized out into a general strike, aimed particularly at stopping oil production and the oil refinery, and a series of demands from the "Higher Executive Committee," as the young men called themselves. The demands were not in themselves unreasonable—their presentation as an ultimatum made it impossible to accept them. A sheikhdom is by tradition a benevolent and paternal despotism, and is in the long run incompatible with an educated and prosperous population. This had been foreseen by Sheikh Sulman, and a process of gradual extension of responsibility, first through elected municipal councils and advisory committees, had been initiated, planned to grow with the growth of literacy and education in the populace. That the first graduates of the secondary schools should wish the process to move faster than planned is a phenomenon common, apparently, to every developing country. It was obvious that both sides in the Bahrain struggle meant well, and obvious that neither side could afford to give way to the other. The affair settled down into a trial of strength—and the completeness of the general strike was one measure of the strength of the "Higher Committee."

Since the first year our workers had come from the villages; and the villages govern themselves, with a headman responsible to the Minister for Rural Affairs, who is a cousin of the sheikh. They are not accustomed to taking orders from the townspeople of Manama or Muharraq. And when, a full day after the strike had paralyzed Manama, the first young men on motor-cycles came to the fort and told our men that they must lay down tools, they came to us in some indignation. They could see the point of their brothers and sons, who worked for Bapco, stopping work in order to stop the government earning money. But if the excavations stopped, surely they were *saving* the government money! However, the next day our two foremen came early to the camp, to tell us that they had held meetings in the villages, and decided that it would be best to stop work, as otherwise there might be reprisals, against the villages or against us, from hotheads in the towns. We accepted their decision, and pointed out that, with the bazaar in Manama shut, we were beginning to run short of food. They promised that the villages would make sure that we were well supplied with eggs and rice and vegetables.

The villagers of Barbar were made of sterner stuff. The foreman of our work-team there was himself the headman of the village, and the villagers were intensely proud of the wonderful stone temple whose terraces were taking shape beneath their spades. When we drove out as usual on the third day of the strike they were there in full force, and only laughed to hear that the workers at the fort had laid down tools.

Little news came out of Manama that day, as we went around the deserted diggings with unaccustomed leisure to get our drawings and measurements up to date. But what news came was disquieting. There had been riots, and burnings of cars, and it was said (it turned out to be untrue) that one of the sheikhs had been pulled from his car and stoned to death. Police were concentrating on holding the road open between Manama and the refinery and the oil town of Awali. Most other roads had been blocked by the rioters with felled palm-trees. The strike was complete—except for the excavations at Barbar. Neither we nor Mohamed bin Ibrahim, our Barbar foreman, realized how seriously such a breach in an otherwise solid strike would be regarded. But next morning, when we took the track to Barbar in our land-rover, we got no farther than a quarter mile from the camp. Where the track crossed the first of the irrigation ditches the culvert had been broken down. We tried another track and another, and finally the main track, which led to the highway and Manama. Every one of them was blocked, with felled trees and demolished bridges. The camp was cut off.

We went back to hold a council of war. We were virtually in a state of siege, and we were somewhat vulnerable. We knew that there was no animosity towards us personally, but it was the object of the strike committee to embarrass the government as publicly as possible, and one obvious way was to show that the police could no longer protect foreigners in the country. We were

most afraid of fire. The *barasti* walls and roofs of our camp were
by now as dry as tinder. One fanatic with one match could burn
the whole camp to the ground. We had seen *barasti* fires in the
villages—we had driven out to try to help once when a fire broke
out in the nearest village, and we had seen how ineffectual our
single fire-extinguisher was, once such an ideally inflammable
building caught fire.

On the other hand, if we were in a state of siege, a fort was not
a bad place to withstand it in. The ramparts of the Portuguese
fort still stood sheer, and they could only be scaled in three
places. And from the top of the towers there was an uninterrupted view for miles. We instituted forthwith a watch-system
from the highest tower by day, while by night two men at a time
would patrol the ramparts, pick-helves in hand.

There was an air of unreality over the next two days. The camp
lay quiet under the bland March sunshine. Beyond the moat the
diggings were still, no workers trundling their wheelbarrows, no
smoke from the water-pipe fire, none of the visitors of whom
there was usually a constant trickle, and who on Thursday afternoons and Fridays, the Moslem weekend, came in their coach-
loads and wandered over the broad top of the tell. Now not a
figure moved, on the tell or in the palm gardens beyond. And
there was no sound. Away in the distance to the south, across the
nearest date-groves and the scrub-desert beyond, ran the line of
the Budeiya road, the east-west asphalted road from Manama
from which the track led off north to our fort. The broken bridges
that cut us off lay on this track between us and the road, but
rumour had it that the Budeiya road too was blocked with felled
trees. We kept the road under observation all day long, but
nothing moved along it, and in the still air there was no sound of
traffic. The road-blocks must be real enough.

The day passed, and the night. It seemed rather ridiculous to
be pacing the ramparts in the darkness. It had a flavour of the
nineteenth century to be waiting and listening for a "native"
attack. Bahrain, surely, was not inhabited by "natives," but by the
Bahrainis whom we had known for years, who drove out in their
cars or rode out on their bicycles to stand on the edge of our

excavations and ask the same intelligent or stupid questions as visitors to our excavations in Denmark asked. Was it really conceivable that these same people would creep up out of the night and fire our camp? We were tempted to call off the watch and go to bed.

There was no attack. Nothing moved all night.

And all the following day nothing moved.

In the evening the siege was raised. For almost an hour of the late afternoon we could hear the intermittent sound of vehicle engines somewhere among the scrub-palms of the dips and hollows between us and the road. And just before sunset a jeep and two trucks climbed the edge of the tell and stopped beside our two land-rovers beyond the moat. Armed police jumped from the trucks and took up perimeter positions, and two police officers came up to meet us as we descended the ramparts. It was very efficient, and very military—perhaps rather spoiled by the absence of an enemy.

But the precautions of the police were not without their cause; they had had to remove or repair four road-blocks on the track between us and the highway, hauling palm-trunks to one side and bridging broken culverts above the dry irrigation ditches.

The general strike was still in full force. No traffic, they said, moved in Manama, and the Budeiya road was blocked at half a dozen points. The police held the Manama fort and the European quarter towards the naval base, and had throughout kept open the road to Awali and the refinery. It was from the Awali road that they had struck north to the Budeiya road, behind the road-blocks, and so northward again to us.

The inspector, a young Bahraini, wanted us to evacuate the camp immediately and return under their escort to the naval base while it was still light enough to see the road-blocks. We pointed out that we could not leave all the results of our digging to the mercy of passing incendiaries. The gathering dusk made a long argument impossible, and finally he agreed that we should be safe enough for another night. Tomorrow morning we must pack our most valuable finds in our vehicles, and be prepared to move at ten o'clock, when they would come out to cover our retreat. He offered to leave us two men with rifles, and we declined with thanks. We did not want any policemen, with nerves ragged from days of patrol hazards in Manama, opening fire on any of "our" villagers who might decide to visit us with information or supplies. We set no watch that night, and went to bed.

Next morning—it was a Friday—we evacuated. With three police vehicles and our two land-rovers we were a formidable convoy, and the precautions taken by the police soon checked any light-heartedness we might have felt at being once more in contact with the world. We were passing through enemy-held country, and to reach "our" lines we had to force those of the "enemy." At each repaired culvert the vehicles had to run a tightrope of two palm-trunks, inching across under the guidance of a police sergeant watching for wheel slips. And while the convoy negotiated these obstacles the police force fanned out to cover the crossing. It took an hour to reach the road, and there we received instructions for the run in to Manama. We were on no account to stop. Any crowds on the roads were to be charged, with horns blazing and as much noise as we could make, to put stone-throwers off their aim. One of the police trucks would lead the way, and another bring up the rear. We tried to show a confidence that we did not feel, and set off. And we never saw a soul until we reached the first of the manned police posts on the Awali road.

That evening the strike was called off. The next morning the shops opened as usual in the bazaar, and we drove back to our camp, past palm-trunks rolled to the side of the newly opened Budeiya road. And our workers were all waiting for us at the camp, eager to resume their work. That same day I started my new test hole.

The digging season was in fact over. It was the end of March, and the really hot weather could be expected any day. Within a week of the end of the strike our party had dispersed on their several ways home, and Yunis and I alone remained, to pack and close down the camp.

It was Yunis who did all the work. I had my hole. And for once I could dig without interruption. The duties of a second-in-command, the almost daily trips to Manama or Awali to arrange visas and tickets and permits, to beg packing-cases or to fix car repairs or to cash cheques, the two-day ordeal of pay-parade—all these were suddenly reduced to manageable proportions. Our labour force of eighty men was reduced to seven, and they were picked men every one. There was my foreman Radi', an upright old man who could spot the minutest change in the texture or colour of an earth layer—and who died two years later; Abdulkarim, tall, broad-shouldered, who was to succeed Radi' as foreman; Ali bin Mohamed, who had dug with me since our first year, and Hasan Mubarak, both proud of being as tall as I am, a head taller than the average Arab. There was Ali bin Hasan, who could shovel earth clean up and over the lip of an eight-foot cut; and Hasan bin Habib, who had eyes like a hawk, and never let a potsherd escape him; and Hajji Hasan, who had had two sons working with us that year, and whose grandson joined our force eight years later. I did not need to watch or instruct these men; I could concentrate on drawing and interpreting the layers as we reached them, and analyzing the pottery they contained.

It will be recalled that I had jumped twenty-five metres southward from my last *sondage*, in the belief that our earliest levels there had been outside the city limits of the earliest occupation of the tell; and that in the new *sondage* we were hoping to find stratified remains of the "Barbar culture." So my new neat square hole, five metres to a side, lay higher up the gradual slope of the tell, not far away from the dry moat that surrounds our Portuguese fort, and we could work out that we had about twenty-four feet of earth between us and bedrock. It would be a deep hole.

I was determined that, though Toto had left for home, my pottery analysis was going to be just as thorough as it had been under her guidance. And it was therefore with some consternation that I found, as the first three or four levels were spread out and noted upon, that the clear-cut picture of our first *sondages* was completely absent. Sherds of the thin glazed and unglazed bowls of phase 2 were mixed with the double handles and Chinese celadon of phase 1. And among them were earlier and later sherds too, red ridged "Barbar" sherds and the blue-and-white china of the Ming Dynasty, sixteenth-century imports from the time when the Portuguese held the fort. If a level is as old as the latest object in it these were Portuguese levels—but they contained far too much older material.

Then I noticed, in the perpendicular sides of the deepening hole, that these levels sloped, running downward towards the northeast. I looked to the southwest, and saw the moat, some twenty yards away. There lay the answer. The earth we were digging was the "spoil" from the moat, the earth thrown up by the Portuguese when they dug their dry ditch around their fort. And it was of course a mixture of all levels all the way down to bedrock.

Sure enough, at the sixth level the sloping layers ended, abutting on an original horizontal ground surface. Now I should meet pure phase 1 and then phase 2.

I did not. In the southwestern quarter of the *sondage* our picks and shovels began to bring up quantities of the thick caramel-coloured bases and pedestals that we had met with in phase 3, while over the rest of the area came the red ridged ware of the "Barbar culture." I stopped work at once, and Radiʿ and I scraped the whole floor of the digging clean with our trowels. Then we could clearly see, against the dark earth, the roughly circular outline of a large pit in the southwest corner.

Here the advantage of picked workers stood out. I could put two men to digging out this pit, while the remainder took the rest of the floor down layer by layer, knowing that they would keep the pottery from the two areas carefully separated. The pit, which of course had to be later in date than the layers into which it had been dug, proved to be over four feet deep, and it contained an inordinate quantity of potsherds. Whatever the reason for digging the pit there could be no doubt that it had been used later as a rubbish dump, filled in with the refuse of a settlement of which there was, as yet, no trace. The pottery was very uniform, and had all the characteristics of a "culture." The pots were all fairly thick-walled, and the clay, tempered with sand, had been fired to a warm honey or caramel colour. We immediately dubbed the pottery "caramel ware." If the people of the thin bowls, the contemporaries of Alexander the Great, had been corn-flake eaters, the "Caramel People" must have lived on beer. They had a few bowls to be sure, but they were thick and clumsy —and comparatively rare (19). Far and away the greater part of the sherds belonged to tall drinking vases with funnel-shaped necks and narrow solid bases that often developed into regular pedestals. There were two main forms, one with a short body and a tall neck (20), the other with a tall body and a short neck (21). And there were objects that I first took to be small flat dishes on a

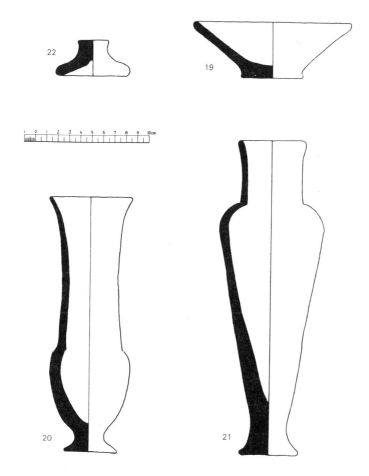

THE POTTERY TYPES OF CITY III, FROM THE CENTURIES UP TO 1200 B.C. THEY ARE WELL KNOWN IN MESOPOTAMIA, FROM THE SAME PERIOD, THE TIME OF THE KASSITES.

tiny pedestal base, until we turned them over and realized that they were lids for the vases (22). It was a very small inventory on which to base a culture. But there was no doubt that it was in itself homogeneous, and completely different from the phase 1 and phase 2 pottery that we had found in our earlier *sondages*. It was a third phase, and moreover it was immediately clear that it was phase 3. For we had met these thick pedestal bases before, among the mixed bag of pottery types which we had previously found underlying phase 2. So that even though phase 2 (and for that matter phase 1) was unaccountably missing in this new hole there was no doubt about the stratigraphical placing of the caramel ware below, and earlier than, both these phases.

That phase 4, the levels into which the caramel-ware rubbish pit had been dug, was earlier still was beyond all doubt. And it was obvious from the start that phase 4 was the "Barbar culture." The contrast with the caramel ware was complete. Instead of thick yellow-brown sherds of small slender vessels the Barbar layers contained thin red sherds of large round-bellied vessels. Where caramel ware was sand or straw-tempered, the Barbar ware was thinned with quite coarse gravel. The change-over was statistically abrupt—even in the topmost Barbar level 92 per cent of all sherds found were of this thin red gravel-tempered ware, and of these over three quarters showed the horizontal ridges that we knew so well from the temple site at Barbar. So far as we could reconstruct them the vessels represented were solely of the two egg-shaped types we have already described from Barbar (17 and 18), the one without a neck, and the other with neck and triangular rim.

I felt an immense satisfaction at having finally located the "Barbar culture" in a stratified context in the city tell. But it soon became clear that I was not only digging a stratified culture—I had landed in the midst of a city. I had forgotten that cities existed. Since, three months before, I had identified and left behind the south wall of the Islamic "palace-fort," we had dug three holes down to bedrock, and this was my fourth. And, apart from a single wall of phase 2 date cutting inexplicably across a corner of my first hole, I had throughout dug down through plain

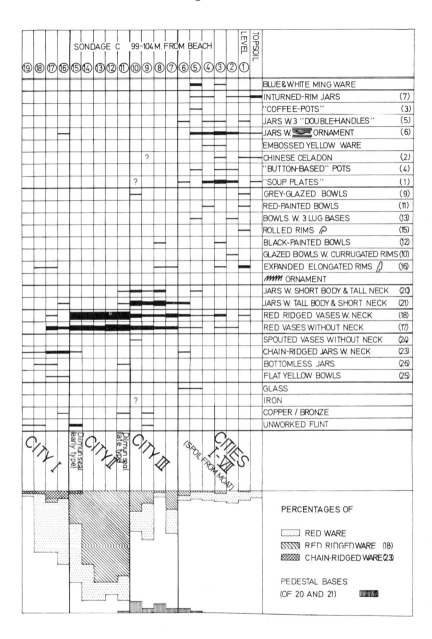

POTTERY ANALYSIS IN THE *sondage* WITHIN THE NORTH WALL AT QALA'AT AL-BAHRAIN. THE THREE SEQUENCE BREAKS ARE SHOWN MOST CLEARLY IN THE PERCENTAGE DIAGRAM.

stratified earth. There had been no buildings, no living floors, no streets, no hearths or ovens or sunk storage jars to suggest that anyone had *lived* in the area I had dug over. And in this new digging I had passed through the spoil from the moat and the rubbish pit. Then suddenly I found myself standing at the corner of a street.

With the removal of the very first "Barbar" layer a fair stone house appeared. Its wall, of cut and shaped stone, ran south from the northern limit of my *sondage* almost to the edge of the caramel-ware rubbish pit, and then turned neatly at right angles and disappeared into the western edge of the digging. And four yards away, along the eastern edge of my hole, another wall ran the full length of the digging, forming the other side of the street. There was a doorway into the house at the corner, and as we dug down a large squared threshold stone appeared. The walls of the house proved to be standing to a height of about two and a half feet.

It is always tempting, when you reach a level with handsome buildings, or even with any recognizable buildings at all, to stop and extend your diggings in area; to follow the streets and see where they go, to enter the houses and trace out the rooms and sift the debris on the floors and find out what each room was used for and what sort of person it was who lived in it. It is a hard-hearted archæologist who can order a wall demolished in order to find out what is underneath. Yet this was a *sondage*, a sounding, a plunge into the depths to see what was there; and it was the end of the season. Yunis had almost finished the packing, and the roof-mats were already removed from all the unoccupied bed-rooms. We lived in the skeleton of a camp and I could not ask for many days more. So we went down deeper—though the need for speed persuaded me not to demolish the house walls, to leave them standing and to dig down in the street outside.

I had expected to find the house walls resting on a stone foundation, a trench dug in the width of the wall and filled with stones as was usual in antiquity (and, I suppose, with the addition of cement, today). Instead we found here a new technique; a trench about three feet wide, twice as wide as the walls, and

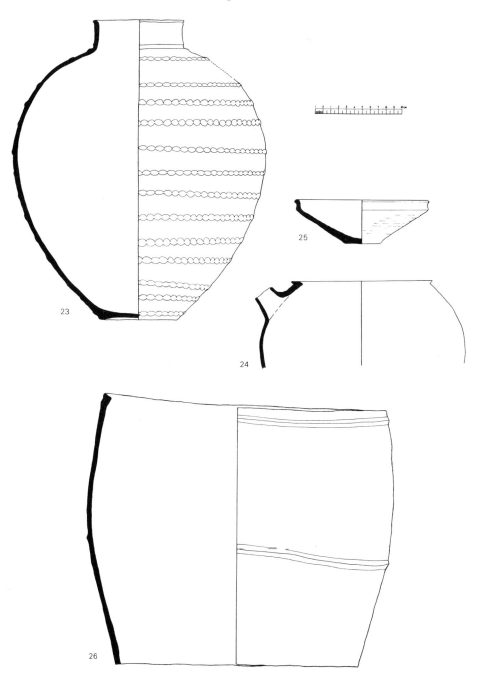

THE POTTERY TYPES OF THE "CHAIN-RIDGE" PERIOD, CITY I, PROBABLY ABOUT
2500 B.C.

some two feet deep had been dug and filled with clean yellow sand, packed hard into place, and the wall had been built directly upon the sand. I have difficulty in believing that the technique was effective, and that it could support a complete stone-built house without danger of subsidence. But perhaps the stone house-walls were never any higher than we found them, and supported a superstructure of wood or *barasti.*

We cut through the foundation and went down, through four feet of well-stratified layers, all full of the characteristic pottery of the "Barbar culture." Another three feet should bring us to bedrock, and I could go home.

Then suddenly there was no more ridged ware. I had not been prepared for that. I had confidently expected that, just as at Barbar, the red ridged ware would go down to virgin sand. Yet here, beyond doubt, was a new phase.

As I examined the potsherds spread out on the tables among the packing-cases in the partly dismantled camp it became clear that the change-over from phase 4 to phase 5 was of a different order from the earlier changes of phase. Previously the changes had been so radical, in colour of clay and shape of vessels, that they suggested a complete change of population and even a considerable lapse of time during which the earlier phase could be forgotten. This time the resemblances between the two phases were quite as significant as the differences. In the new phase the egg-shaped vessels of red gravel-tempered clay continued. The most obvious change was in their decoration. Instead of the horizontal ridges being plain they were now formed in what I came to call a "chain" pattern, alternately flattened and pinched together. At the same time the rim of the necked vessels ceased to be triangular in section, and was much simpler, just slightly rolled (23). The neckless vessels, too, now had a simpler, thinner rim; they had always had a tendency, in the "Barbar culture," to be unridged, apart from a ring or two around the opening, and now they were always plain, and frequently with a short spout, only about half an inch in height, just below the rim (24). In general "chain-ridging" was less common than the plain ridges had been in phase 4, forming scarcely 10 per cent of the total of sherds.

And even the red sherds, which had dominated so completely in the former phase that my workmen used to call me whenever they found a sherd of any other colour than red, formed now only about half of the total. The others were a very mixed bag, thick and straw-tempered, brown or yellow or greenish-white, clearly of fairly large, coarse "kitchen ware," but impossible to put together to any definite shape. Only two further vessel types could be identified in this phase, one a small flat bowl of yellow clay (25) and the other not really a vessel at all. It was of the usual red clay and was cylindrical in shape *without a bottom*. Its only decoration was a single sharp-edged ridge below the rim (26), and it had clearly been intended to be sunk below the house floor, as a storage jar for some dry goods such as grain. The open bottom of the vessel would allow free drainage and would help to keep the contents dry.

THE COPPER COFFEE-POT OF THE ARABIAN GULF. SLIGHT DIFFERENCES OF SHAPE OR BRASS ORNAMENTS DISTINGUISH DIFFERENT PLACES OF MANUFACTURE. THIS COMES FROM THE OMAN.

In this connection it is worth noting that we were now digging in sand, the flour-like drift sand that must originally have covered the bedrock at the time when the first inhabitants had settled upon the site. The cylindrical bottomless vessels could well be used in such a medium, but it was not surprising that they had been given up later, as the stony and rubbish-filled layers of the tell built up.

Everything now was drawing to a close. Only one packing-case remained open, to receive my sherds as soon as they were dug up and analyzed, and the shipping company had been instructed to collect the whole shipment in two days' time. Three quarters of the dining room was full of piled blankets and bedsteads and mattresses and roofing-mats, and for the last day or so Yunis and I had been sleeping under the open sky, since our roofs too had been stripped off. The cook had found another job and left us, and we ate scratch meals prepared by Saleh, our fourteen-year-old kitchen-boy.

We had found a wall in phase 5, following exactly the line of the street in phase 4 above, and showing that the city plan had probably been the same in both phases. And a foot below the wall we reached bedrock. There were hardly any sherds in the final foot of sand, fortunately, for there was only room for a single carton of sherds in Yunis's final packing-case. As the truck from the shipping company rolled up over the edge of the tell, Yunis nailed down the final results of the dig, and I called my seven workers up from where they were brushing clean the rock surface below the sheer twenty-foot walls of earth. They climbed slowly up the steps they had carved in the debris of millennia, and we went away to load the truck.

CHAPTER EIGHT

҂҂҂҂҂

THE FLOWER OF
IMMORTALITY

The months while you are waiting, back at the museum, for the packing-cases to arrive from the Gulf are periods not merely of hard work, but of self-examination. In the intervals of balancing financial accounts, writing letters of thanks, and the endless cataloguing and numbering of potsherds and specimens from the year before and the year before that you speculate over what you have done and what you should have done this year and what you absolutely must do next year. What were the questions you set out to answer? How far have you answered them? And what new questions have arisen?

The 1956 season had brought us a big step forward. In my preoccupation with my stratigraphy and my pottery analysis I had scarcely noticed that one afternoon the biggest question of all had suddenly been answered, the question that had brought us to Bahrain, that of the age of the burial-mounds.

Alun was the Church of England vicar in Bahrain and his parish extended outside Bahrain to Saudi Arabia, Qatar, and the Trucial Coast, an area which, early records tell us, was in pre-Islamic times the diocese of six bishops. He was a wide-shouldered man with a small trimmed beard, and he always went robed in a brown monk's habit belted at the waist with a thick rope.

145

This was no affectation; Alun believed that among Moslems, where religion is a living force and the imams are distinguished by their dress, it would create a wrong impression if Christian priests appeared to be disguising their calling. Alun got around more than most; he was one of the few Europeans of Bahrain who was allowed regularly into Saudi Arabia, and we had come into contact with him a year before when he had brought over for our inspection some flint projectile points that a geologist of the Arabian American Oil Company had found in the great desert of the Rub' al-Khali. Now this year, in early March, he had walked into camp one afternoon with a large cardboard box. They were making a new road up at Buri, he said, and it passed through one of the large mound-fields above 'Ali. He had been driving along it today, and had seen that one of the bulldozers had cut away half a mound, exposing the central chamber. He had stopped and climbed out and pulled a stone or two away to break into the chamber. And there inside lay a pot, which he had brought with him in case we were interested. He opened his cardboard box and lifted out and placed on the table a typical ridged, red, egg-shaped, short-necked, triangular-rimmed, "Barbar culture" vessel. I remember that we gave him a beer . . .

So the grave-mounds, and the Barbar temple, and my phase 4 at Qala'at al-Bahrain were all of the same period. It was not entirely unexpected. Although the vessels that we had found ourselves in the two mounds we had opened two years before did not occur in any of our levels there were generic resemblances, the round bases for example, which made us expect that, if we did find them, they would be in the Barbar levels. And the year before Bob and I had found, in an exposed face in a cut-away tell near the Awali road, a scrap of what we were convinced was grave-mound pottery together with ridged Barbar sherds. (It is worth anticipating here, I think, to say that there is now no slightest doubt of this identification. We have since frequently found scraps—though never more than scraps—of the typical grave-mound vessels in "Barbar" and even in "chain-ridge" levels, and we have seven or eight of the ridged round-bellied Barbar vessels—only those with necks, incidentally—from grave-mounds that we have ourselves excavated. In some cases these vessels are apparently of a rather early type, with the simple, slightly rolled rim which we more commonly find associated with "chain-ridge" ornamentation—but we have never yet found a "chain-ridge" vessel in a grave-mound.)

Now came the heart-searching. If we had solved the "Mystery of the Mounds," which we had set out originally to solve, was there any point in carrying on? To that the first supplementary question must be: Was our solution good enough? The mounds, we could now say, were the burial places of a people who had lived in a city around the present Portuguese fort on the north coast of Bahrain and who had built a temple at Barbar some three miles farther west along the coast. They had used a very distinctive pottery which painstaking research had failed to find anywhere else in the ancient world, so that probably they were a people, a "culture," in their own right, rather than colonists or offshoots from some other known culture. They were in fact a "Lost Civilization." And all this had happened, the city, the temple, and the burial-mounds, somewhere round about 2300 B.C., a date based almost entirely on the evidence of the copper bull's head from Barbar, with its close resemblance to the bulls' heads of the Royal Graves at Ur, which most authorities—except their excavator—ascribed to within a hundred years or so of that date.

Well, that gave two excellent reasons for carrying on digging. One was that the evidence for the date simply wasn't good enough. The other was that if you find a Lost Civilization you don't just walk away and leave it. A new civilization has to be integrated; its position in the history of its time and in the development of world culture has to be determined.

Now, according to theory that was just what my stratigraphic digging had been for, to attach dates, however relative, to the phases of Bahrain's cultures, and to see to what degree the phases were integrated with each other. It was time to look at my notebooks and see how what I had found was to be interpreted.

I had, it will be recalled, five phases, all carefully tied in to changes in the pottery inventory, which I had hitherto counted in numbers downwards from the top. The first thing to do was to change the numbers round and count from the bottom. This is not so meaningless as it might appear. While we had discovered them from the top downwards they had *happened* the other way round, from the bottom upwards. So the renumbering was a change from a subjective to an objective view. This was very necessary. For example, we had talked, and thought, of the plain-ridged pottery of phase 4, the "Barbar culture," changing to chain-pattern ridges in phase 5. In fact the change had been the other way, the chain ridges had given place to plain ridges. If that change had, as it appeared, taken place on Bahrain, then if we were to look for foreign origins for our Lost Civilization we should look for parallels to the chain-ridge ware rather than to the plain ridges.

So we start off with City I: date uncertain, origin uncertain, apparently the founder fathers of the city (though wait; was there not in fact in the earliest levels of the chain-ridge people the same sort of mixture of incompatible pottery—on the one hand, the thin, red, gravel-tempered, chain-decorated ware itself, and on the other, the thick, yellowish, straw-tempered "kitchen ware"—as we had found above bedrock in our first *sondages?* Such a mixture of incompatibles had meant then that we were outside our city, sifting the trampled throw-outs of more than one culture. Might it not mean the same again? Might there be an earlier city deeper in the mound?) We needed to know a lot more about City I.

Then City II: date somewhere about 2300 B.C., perhaps; origin —City I. Perhaps nothing more than a change in fashion of pottery, though probably more. City II had lasted some time, long enough to pile up five levels in the tell, to build and rebuild and rebuild again the Barbar temple, to accumulate something like a hundred thousand burial-mounds. But how long was that? A hundred years, or three, or five?

City III: represented only by the rubbish pit full of "caramel ware." But here the books helped us. "Caramel ware" was very well known indeed. It was the Kassite ware of Mesopotamia. The Kassites were a people who had invaded Mesopotamia from the mountains of Persian Luristan around the year 1750 B.C., and had gradually extended their rule until they held the whole of the valley of the Euphrates and the Tigris from well north of the present-day Baghdad to the Arabian Gulf. The rule of the Kassite kings had finally been put to an end by Assyrian conquest about 1200 B.C. During all this period of over five hundred years the pottery in use in southern Mesopotamia, even in the areas not under Kassite rule, had been surprisingly uniform, showing no change at all from generation to generation. And it was identical with our "caramel ware."

This was very satisfactory, from our point of view. It was of course obvious that our rubbish pit had not taken 550 years to dig and to fill. All that we could say with certainty concerning it was that it had been dug and filled at some date between 1750 and 1200 B.C. But even that, considering that we had started with no dates at all, was an improvement. And it meant that we could now say with certainty that any period antecedent to City III was older than, at latest, 1200 B.C., and that any subsequent period was later than, at earliest, 1750 B.C. That the Barbar period, below City III, was independently dated to, very roughly, 2300 B.C., and "phase 2," above City III, was dated by its Attic pottery to about 330 B.C. gave a very pleasing air of verisimilitude to this deduction. It looked as though the archæology of Bahrain was acquiring perspective.

Had we only had my *sondages* to work with, "phase 2" would have become City IV. But P.V. had now been digging for three years in the centre of the city mound, extending the first excavation that had been made on the site. Where, that first year, there had been the junction of two high stone walls in an excavation six feet wide and twenty feet deep, there was now a building of impressive proportions standing in an excavation of at least adequate size. We appeared to be in a large hall, forty feet across, with walls of cut stone, fifteen feet high, on three sides and running into the face of unexcavated earth on the fourth side. To the north of the hall a broad stairway led upwards, broken off after six steps, and it was below and behind these stairs that we had first encountered the building. It was an impressive edifice, clearly an important building—and it had defied all our attempts to date it.

This was against the rules. It should always be possible to

recover the pottery types associated with any building, and thereby to "place" the building in the sequence of pottery development, and thereby give it at least a relative dating. As I have so often tried to explain to freshman diggers on our teams, there should be four, or perhaps five, types of layers associated with any building. There are the construction layers, foundation trenches for the walls, filling layers to level off floors, and the actual mason's layer of trampled lime and clay and stone chippings; these levels will be sealed by the actual walls and floors, and should contain nothing later than the date of erection of the building. Above the floors come the second type of layer, the occupation levels; they will be fairly horizontal, and may consist of a whole series of new floors laid above the old, with occupation debris between. Thirdly come the destruction layers, the heaps of rubble where the roof has caved in and the walls fallen in or out, with perhaps the thick layer of ash that shows that the building was burnt; these layers will be sloping, running downward from the surviving wall-stumps, and they will effectively seal off the uppermost occupation level, whose contents should record the date of destruction. Finally you will have the layers of abandonment, when the heaps of fallen rubble have gradually been evened out by weathering, with rain-washed mud and wind-blown sand filling the hollows. And here you may also find the robber layers, the holes dug by the searchers for valuables or for salvageable building stone.

Where P.V.'s building (which we were already beginning to call the Palace) broke the rules was in having no occupation levels at all. The thick layers of debris from the collapse of wall and roof sloped clean down to the cement floor of the hall. Apparently the building had stood abandoned for some time before its collapse, and during that time had been cleaned out, not only of anything of value but apparently of all occupation debris. It was odd. It still is.

To date the building it would be necessary to go below the floor. There might be earlier floors below, and the debris between the floors would give us the information we wanted. And if not, the construction level should date the erection of the building.

That was clearly one of the objectives for our next season. In the meantime we had the bath-tub-shaped sarcophagi. It will be recalled that we had found two of these clay coffins during the first year, buried through holes in the floor of the building. They were apparently later in date than the building, but earlier than the collapse of the superstructure. And this year we had found a third sarcophagus. It was the most impressive discovery of the year, for it was unrobbed. When we had found it, behind the staircase not far from the first two burials, its cover, of stone slabs cemented together, was still in place unbroken. It had been difficult to remove, for it had originally rested upon a wooden lid, and the wood had perished, leaving the stones poised precariously above the open coffin, and any careless move would have caused them to collapse upon the burial beneath. Anders had spent three days removing the stones, scarcely daring to breathe as he worked to loosen them one by one and lift them away. And finally we had been able to see the complete burial below.

The skeleton lay, like the others we had found, curled up in the bottom of the deep sarcophagus. And beside it lay a complete drinking service in bronze. There was a flat shallow bronze bowl and a deep bronze vase with a hinged bucket-handle. And there was a bronze "tea-strainer" with a handle ending in an animal's head, and a little dipper, a deep ladle with a long handle hinged to the top of the bowl in such a way that wine could be dipped from a narrow-necked jar and then tipped into a beaker. The wine-jar lay also there, a deep vessel of glazed pottery with a pointed base. When we had drawn and photographed all these objects in position we had carefully removed them from the coffin, and gone on to examine the skeleton more closely. We found that the man had been buried with an iron dagger at his waist, and with a seal of agate around his neck. The seal, a smoky blue in colour, was carved with a scene of a man, or god, standing before a tree, with a winged sun above. The shape of seal and the manner of scene upon it had been typical enough for us, even with our limited experience, to say "neo-Babylonian" as soon as we saw it. Now, while we waited for the wine service to arrive in the cargo from Bahrain, I had the seal before me, for P.V. had taken it home in his pocket; and a study of the reference books left little doubt that the seal should be dated to about 650 B.C., give or take fifty years.

The number of fixed points in our chronology of Bahrain was multiplying very satisfactorily, and I proclaimed the bath-tub-coffin period to be City IV, with the private proviso that City IV might also turn out to be the Palace period.

So the Attic-ware period, the period of the "Corn-flakes People," became City V, and its pottery became in common parlance "Greek," although it was nothing of the sort. The Islamic fort, with its "phase 1" pottery, was now City VI, and the very last phase of occupation that we met in our diggings, the quarrying holes where the Portuguese had dug for stone to build their fort, became City VII. And in that case the fort itself was City VII too.

Seven cities were a nice number to have, the number of the superimposed cities at Troy, and the "Seven-City Sequence" had a pleasing euphony. But it was soon pointed out that there was a City VIII, consisting of a jumble of some dozen *barastis* on the edge of the tell, and a foreign intrusive culture, a Danish settlement, within the ramparts of City VII. We forthwith entitled ourselves the Carlsberg culture.

The working out of the Seven- (or if you like eight-) City Sequence disguised for us for quite some weeks the fact that we had really not got very far at all. Archæologically speaking, we had come a long way—we had seven successive cultures, five of them fairly satisfactorily dated. But, historically speaking, we had little that was new. It was hardly a contribution to world history, or even to Bahrain history, that in the second millennium B.C. the people of Bahrain filled holes in the ground with rubbish; and even the fact that the rubbish they filled the holes with was identical with the rubbish discarded in contemporary Mesopotamia would only gain historical significance if we could show *why* it was identical, what connection there had been between Bahrain and Mesopotamia in Kassite times. We could connect—tenuously —the presence of Attic ware in City V with the voyages of Alexander's captains to the island of Tylos. But did we dare to connect the presence of neo-Babylonian seals in City IV with

Assurbanipal's claim at approximately the right date that Dilmun was a province of his empire? And if so could our "palace" possibly be the palace of "Uperi, king of Dilmun"? And—most important of all—where did City II, the "Barbar culture," fit into world history? It was not early enough for Gilgamesh, even if Gilgamesh were historical.

More digging was required. And one archæological problem in particular obtruded. Why had I found remains of City I and City II and City III in my southernmost *sondage* and not in my earlier ones? When I compared my drawn sections of the three *sondages* the question took concrete form. In my last *sondage* I had streets and buildings of City II at the same level as, farther north, I had found thick levels of City V remains. Yet there was a two-thousand-year difference in date. Somewhere between my last two diggings something radical must happen to these layers. What it was was quite obvious—when I had jumped twenty-five metres to dig my last *sondage* I had jumped clean over the wall that surrounded City II.

It was time to plan the next expedition. The stock-taking of our achievements and of our unanswered questions had to be pulled into shape and put into words. We had to tell our sponsors what we had done with their money, and ask them for support for the next stage of the work. Writing these letters, to the Carlsberg Foundation, to the Bahrain government, and to the Bahrain Petroleum Company, had each year formed the final act of one expedition and the official opening of the next. And this year there were two new letters to write, to the government and to the petroleum company of Qatar.

In many ways these letters begging for funds were the least pleasant part of the expeditions. Although we have never met anything other than a ready and sympathetic understanding of the necessity of our relying for support on grants from governments and oil companies it is never completely enjoyable to go begging year after year. And there were other disadvantages. Our museum's complete lack of endowments meant that we were living from hand to mouth. We could not plan ahead for more

than a year at a time. Any large-scale capital investments in
earth-moving material, dump trucks, or narrow-gauge railways,
were out of the question. To buy a new land-rover meant the loss
of twenty days' digging that year, and if we were to reconnoitre
Qatar we should need two new land-rovers this year.

And that brought to the fore a new problem that was to grow
extravagantly in future years. The Bahrain government would
have every right to object if money which it contributed for work
in Bahrain was employed on work in Qatar. And the Qatar
government and the Qatar Petroleum Company, which both responded generously to our appeal for funds, would naturally
expect their contributions to be used in Qatar and not in Bahrain.
The result was endless petty problems of accountancy. While
the postage on our letters to the Bahrain government and to the
Qatar government should be—and was—charged to the Bahrain
and the Qatar expeditions respectively, who should pay for the
notepaper? And while the air fares of the Bahrain team and the
Qatar team were easy to apportion, how should P.V.'s and my air
fare be apportioned? The work of accountancy began to take up
quite a disproportionate amount of my time in the months between the expeditions.

But the money came in, and the next expedition took shape;
and after the usual anxious struggle with visas and inoculations
through the Christmas and New Year holidays, the 1957 expedition assembled in Copenhagen in early January and boarded the
plane for Bahrain. This year had been more anxious than usual.
For in the fall had come the Suez crisis. The Middle East had
been in a turmoil, and for some months it had looked as though
any archæological work would be out of the question. But the
storm had blown over, and by the time we left the only effect of
the crisis was that we were forced to fly via Iraq rather than via
Egypt.

We were ten men on the plane this time, quite a formidable
expedition as I thought of the party of two who had sparked the
adventure off three years before. Six of us were veterans of our
previous campaigns. Yunis was to run our camp for us; Peder and
Helmuth were returning to their temple at Barbar. P.V. and

Mogens would continue digging their palace, and I was going back to my section trench. One of the newcomers was an architect and would draw plans for all of us, another was a student who would assist me. The remaining two were experienced archæologists. Poul was to make a new *sondage* in the centre of the Portuguese fort; for the thought had struck us that perhaps the fort had been built above the citadel of the earlier cities, and very important things might lie there. And Viggo was to dig a shell-heap on the southwest coast of Bahrain.

We had not forgotten Qatar. But we had decided that an extended reconnaissance of Qatar would best be achieved by sending a large party, about half our number, across for one month out of the three which we would be spending in the Gulf. In this way we could cover quite as much ground as if we sent two men over for the whole period; and we should be able to take one of our land-rovers with us, so that we should only need to acquire one new vehicle.

We were all intrigued by Viggo's shell-heap. Danish archæologists are brought up on shell-heaps, which are found in large numbers near the coasts of Denmark. They are the famous "kitchen-middens," the debris of hunting and fishing communities who settled the Danish coasts about 6000 B.C., long before the first Stone Age farmers entered the country. We had no reason to expect that the Bahrain "kitchen-midden" would be anything similar. This shell-heap had been discovered by P.V. when he was looking for flint sites in the southern desert during our second campaign. It lay out on the coast, with a dangerous *sabkha* between it and solid land, and it was obvious that before the *sabkha* was formed it had been an island. And the shells of which it was composed were the shells of pearl-oysters.

Clearly it was the debris of a pearling settlement, or a pearling camp; a place where pearl-fishers had landed their catch, to be spread out in the sun until the oysters died and the shells opened. This is the practice to this day in many parts of the world, but not in the Gulf. The pearl-divers of the Arabian Gulf stay on board their ships throughout the season, searching the oysters for pearls on shipboard and throwing the opened shells overboard. This settlement must therefore be older than the present pearling technique. And we very much wanted to know how old pearling was in the Gulf.

This brings me to the story of Gilgamesh.

I have already mentioned the ancient Babylonian epic of the hero whose exploits and travels fill twelve long cuneiform tablets. And we have heard how, in his quest for immortality, he visited Utu-nipishtim, undoubtedly in Dilmun, and heard from him the story of the Deluge. But the tale does not end there. After Utu-nipishtim has told Gilgamesh at length how *he* achieved immortality he relents, and gives Gilgamesh instructions for finding the Flower of Immortality. The flower grows on the seabed, or perhaps in the sweet waters of the Abyss beneath the seabed. And Gilgamesh is to attach stones to his feet, and by their aid sink down to the bed of the sea, and there pluck the magic flower. When he eats it he will renew his youth.

This is all very interesting, for the pearl-divers of Bahrain still attach stones to their feet in order to descend to the seabed, and there can be little doubt that the "Flower of Immortality" is the pearl. I have often wondered if some tradition of the pearl being the elixir of eternal life and eternal youth may not have been current in Egypt in classical times, when Cleopatra is said to have drunk pearls dissolved in wine.

The story of Gilgamesh has no happy ending. He does indeed follow Utu-nipishtim's instructions to the letter. He finds and plucks the flower from the seabed, and decides to take it home, to share with the elders of his city, Erech. But while he sleeps, the snake comes up from a water-hole and, as in Genesis, cheats mankind of eternal life. It eats the flower, and thereby achieves immortality, as anyone may observe. For whenever the snake feels itself growing old it sloughs its skin, and emerges young and vigorous again.

The moral of the story is made very plain. How can Man, who cannot even conquer Sleep, hope to conquer Death?

But the story of Gilgamesh, which suggested that pearls, and even the techniques of pearl-diving, were known to the Sumerians and the Babylonians from earliest times, made us interested to check up, if we could, on the antiquity of pearl-fishing in Bahrain.

So every morning four of our workers took their spades and climbed aboard the land-rover, and drove with Viggo the hour-long journey to the lonely white hillock by the sea. It was one of those small excavations with limited objectives that often give valuable results. In this case it exceeded our expectations. Viggo's five sections cut through the mound confirmed our belief that it was a pearl-fishers' encampment. The shells in the heap were almost 100 per cent of pearl-oysters; but scattered through the heap were the hearths and food refuse, mainly fish bones, of the pearl-divers. Around the hearths there was a sprinkling of pot-sherds. And two of the very few pots that could be reconstructed were of the red ridged ware which we knew so well from the Barbar temple.

This was a true addition to the history of Bahrain. At Barbar, and at Qala'at al-Bahrain, we had proved that people were living in Bahrain in the third millennium B.C. Now we could demon-strate one of the reasons why they were there, and show that some of them, at least, gained their livelihood in the quest for the flower of the seabeds.

We had full use, while Viggo was digging pearl-shells, for the expedition's three vehicles. For one of the land-rovers was away with him all day, and the other was in Manama most of the day, while Yunis bought supplies. So the third, a rather aged limou-sine, had to do the odd jobs. It took me to town all too often, to talk with government departments, to procure residence permits from the British Political Agency, and to arrange with oil compa-nies and the representatives of the Qatar government for our forthcoming visit. It took P.V. out into the desert to look for flint, when he could be spared from his "palace" excavation. And it took out Peder and Helmuth to Barbar every day and brought them home.

Barbar was becoming unrecognizable. It was increasingly diffi-cult to realize that we had once stood on the top of a not very high hill of sand, and looked *down* into the temple courtyard. The three metres of sand that had covered the courtyard were gone, and for two years now we had been digging outward from the central area, last year to the east, and now to the south. To the east the object had been to find out what happened to the open spillway that had led away in that direction from the libation stone in front of the altar. This passed through the massive eastern wall of the courtyard, and when we came to dig on the farther side of this wall we found that it went down a good six feet below the level of the courtyard. But at one point a ramp led down into a remarkable complex. At the end of the ramp a wall led off to either side, curving round to enclose a roughly circular area about twenty feet in diameter. In the centre was a large block, built up of stones set in gypsum plaster, and beyond it a smaller circular wall, contained within the larger, but with only about a four-foot diameter. Both the smaller and the larger enclosure were filled with a dark-grey mass of striated sandy clay, clearly water-laid. They were not only filled with this deposit; they were completely drowned in it. For the deposit had overflowed beyond the walls, and still farther out a third retaining wall had been built to contain it. This third wall was oval, enclosing an area a full thirty by fifty feet. It looked very much as though the ramp had originally led all the way to the smaller central wall, and that the space to which the ramp had led had been twice extended. But what the deposit was, and how it had got there we could not explain, and still cannot to this day. It had no connection with the spillway. For the spillway ran by way of a drain down the outer side of the high courtyard wall to a stone-roofed aqueduct most resembling the *qanats* we had found in the desert which passed beneath the oval structure and on towards the sea to the north.

To the south of the temple courtyard the structures that appeared this year were equally complex but more capable of explanation. Immediately south of the courtyard wall a flight of steps appeared, leading due south. It was followed down with the excitement that steps descending into the unknown always arouse, but after eight steps it stopped short, broken off sheer. In front of it stood a wall, its top level with the topmost tread of the staircase. It went very much deeper than the bottom surviving step, a good ten feet in all. And it was an unusual wall. On the outer, southern side it was well made, of well-fitting cut stones; but the side towards the staircase was very irregular, the stones completely unsquared and unfinished. It looked as though that side was not meant to be seen.

It was indeed not meant to be seen. The wall was the retaining wall of a terrace, and had been filled in behind with sand. The staircase then must be earlier, and had led up to the temple before the terrace was built. The question remained of what it had led *down* to.

As Peder and Helmuth, with their team of workers from Barbar, cleared the outer side of this terrace wall, they found that it curved around towards the west and north. And where the curvature began, they found a second staircase. This did not lead outward like the one behind the wall, but was built against it, running downward towards the south and east. In fact it was clear that its foot would reach the very point where the foot of the first staircase would have ended, had it not been broken off by the terrace wall.

Work was hurried forward to reach this point. But it could not be reached. For directly above that point, at a level with the top of the terrace wall, appeared the coping of a well.

Wells are among the least popular objects found by archæologists. They always appear at the wrong places, at a crucial point in a section, or breaking through an important wall or floor. And they are always of later date than the structures that they disturb. And they cannot be ignored. Dig the earth away around them, and they soon stand like factory chimneys in an excavation. And that they cannot be allowed to do; for a factory chimney is built to stand unsupported, but a well is built within a supporting depth of earth. As they are excavated they have to be demolished. This well was in fact not entirely demolished this year. For it was supported, partly by the terrace wall against which it had been dug, and partly by the unexcavated earth to the other side of our cut. But it was emptied, and as it was cleared the side towards the staircase along the wall was pulled down, to prevent it collapsing into the excavation.

159

It occasioned no surprise that the potsherds found in the well were not of the usual Barbar type, but of a much later date. But we were surprised by the sheer beauty of the pottery. There was a large quantity and most of it was of fine thin ware. There were straw-coloured vases with slender necks and two tall handles. There was the greater part of a very large spherical pot with dark-blue glaze and four lugs. And there were several large bowls, glazed and painted in very fine designs. Two of these, the very finest, had no formal pattern, but were painted in flaring streaks of greens and oranges and yellows, giving an irresistible flamelike effect. All were in fragments, of course, but all the sherds were present. As they grew under Yunis's hands at the camp it was clear that we had collectors' items here, the sort of Islamic glazed ware that many a museum of fine art would envy us.

That they were of Islamic date was very clear, and an exhaustive study of the literature and of many European and Middle Eastern collections has enabled us to anchor the pottery firmly in the ninth century. But just how pottery of this quality came to be thrown into our well is not clear. There are no ruins of Islamic date anywhere near, and such pottery would scarcely form the equipment of the stone-quarrying gangs whose trenches form the only other evidence of later disturbance of our four-thousand-year-old temple site.

It rapidly became clear that the well itself was no Islamic intrusion on the site. For in digging around it Peder and Helmuth found two things that told us all we needed to know. Where the foot of the staircase along the wall-face met the foot of the well stood a square stone basin, upon which the well was built, and into which water began to seep as soon as the sand was dug away. And beyond the well, a yard or so farther south, lay another terrace wall with the same beautifully cut and finished southern face and unfinished inner surface.

We could now reconstruct the whole story. Originally the temple had stood on a small mound, and from it a flight of stairs ran south to a spring at the foot of the mound, with a square catchment basin. Later, the area of the temple was extended, by constructing a terrace running out as far as the spring, and a stairway was built along the terrace wall running down to the spring. And later again the terrace was extended farther, as far as the new southern wall. But this terrace would cover the spring, and therefore the well was built, with its well-head at terrace level, so that water could still be obtained. This well must have been abandoned and filled when the temple was abandoned. But it had been rediscovered in Islamic times, and cleaned out, and then again filled in, with the sand that contained our fine glazed ware.

The system of terraces gave a new dimension to our temple at Barbar. We could now see that the original ground surface, four thousand years ago, must have been eight or ten feet lower than the present surface of the desert, and that the temple must have been much more imposing than we had imagined, standing on its platform above sheer terrace walls. It almost began to qualify as a ziggurat, the terraced temple mounds of Mesopotamia. And, indeed, every time I drove out to bring Peder and Helmuth home at the end of the day's work, the central temple area seemed to stand higher, as the excavations revealed more and more of the staircases and ramps that led up to it.

Equally imposing, in its way, was the excavation at Qala'at al-Bahrain on which P.V. and Mogens had now been digging for four years. Considerable stretches of the walls, ten to fifteen feet high, of the enigmatic "palace" were now laid bare, and the monumental nature of the building was very obvious. The area of the first two years' excavation, in which the three bath-tub-coffins had been found, was now seen as a mere below-stairs alcove in a corner of a large hall over twenty-five feet across.

We should have believed that the hall had been a courtyard, open to the sky, had it not been that the squared stone footings of one of the two pillars which had supported its ceiling were still in position, while the site of the other could be seen as a slight square platform upon the clay floor.

The palace still defied all our efforts to date it. None of us who were digging elsewhere could quite believe so incredible a situation, and we went down time after time into the excavation to satisfy ourselves that there really was no occupation layer. There was none. The destruction level, a layer about five feet thick of broken building stone and large lumps of plaster, which must have been the fallen tops of the walls and the roof, or even an upper story, lay directly upon the clay floor. The upper part of the destruction level contained quantities of potsherds of thin glazed or red-painted bowls, the pottery of the time of Alexander, of my City V. It was clear that at the time of City V the palace had still stood, as a roofless shell, and had been used as a convenient rubbish dump. So we had what archæologists love to call a *terminus ante quem,* an upper limit of date. The palace must be older than about 300 B.C. It was probable, though not quite certain, that the building was older than the bath-tub-coffins, which we felt secure in dating to about 650 B.C. Certainly the three coffins we had found behind the staircase had been buried in holes dug through the floor of the building, and it was difficult to imagine these burials taking place while the building was in use. But it was not quite impossible; there have been periods in Mesopotamia when it was customary to bury people below the floor of their home.

But an upper limit, however exact, was not sufficient. We needed a *terminus post quem* also, a lower limit. I was myself, as we know, inclined to include the palace with the coffins in City IV, between the Kassites, about 1200 B.C., and the neo-Babylonians at 600 B.C., and would have liked to associate the building with King Uperi, who had sent presents to Sargon of Assyria in 709 B.C. P.V. would have liked the palace to be older, much older, but had to admit that in that case it had been in use for a very long time.

The only way to find out was to dig deeper. And in preparation for this the clay floor of the hall was scraped and brushed meticulously clean.

It was then that a number of small circular patches were found, where the floor was of a different consistency and a slightly lighter colour. And probing carefully with a trowel in one of these patches P.V. uncovered an inverted bowl. A little more work showed that the bowl was the lid to another bowl beneath. When the lid was carefully lifted the bowl was seen to be full of sand, and the whole find was sent up to the camp, where it could be investigated with greater care than at the bottom of an excavation. And P.V. started on the second patch.

In the course of a week fourteen patches had been dug out, and on the worktable in the camp stood twelve bowls. Four were lidded with inverted bowls, and four others had a large potsherd as a cover. Three were uncovered, and the last was sealed with a thick layer of gypsum plaster. The two other holes in the ground had been simple holes, but one had been covered with an inverted bowl, and had contained nothing, while the other had been topped with a large potsherd. Below this lay twenty-six beads, of agate and amethyst and faïence. They had originally formed a necklace, for the little silver ring that had been the clasp lay there too.

Here at last we had pottery that was clearly contemporary with

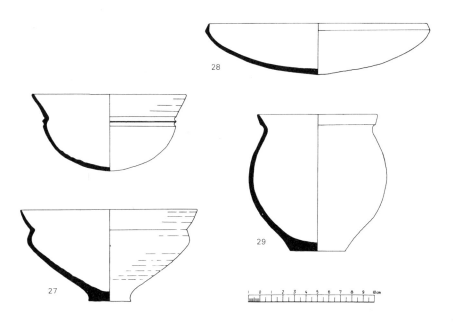

THE TYPICAL BOWLS IN WHICH THE SNAKE-BURIALS ARE FOUND. THE UPPER BOWL OF 27 FORMED THE LID TO THE LOWER BOWL. THEY BELONG TO CITY IV, WHICH WE WOULD LIKE TO DATE TO THE ASSYRIAN PERIOD, ABOUT 700 B.C.

the "palace," shallow bowls of two types (27) and (28) and a deeper type of vessel with a narrow rim (29). But for the moment interest was concentrated on the contents of the vessels. Yunis and P.V. had been working on them every afternoon, removing the sand carefully with camel's-hair brushes and spatulæ. And in seven of the bowls they had found, coiled up in the bottom, the skeletons of snakes.

Three more of the vessels contained a few loose snake-bones, and the remaining two contained only sand. This does not mean that they were empty when they were deposited, but merely that their contents had not been of a nature to survive the millennia.

In over half the bowls there was found in addition, loose among the coiled snake-bones, a single bead, in most cases a tiny turquoise.

On the first two occasions when the bead was found it occasioned little remark, for it is not highly unusual to find beads loose in the sand, and they might have been introduced by accident. But soon it became obvious that the bead was as much a constituent part of the deposit as the snake. And yet oddly enough a considerable time passed before it occurred to us that we had here a clear association with the story of Gilgamesh.

It was not for lack of speculation. It was obvious that the snakes in their covered bowls beneath the floor were of religious or magical significance. It did not need archæologists, who as a class are traditionally prone to see ritual purposes in anything for which they cannot immediately find a practical use, to see that no practical, mundane, everyday explanation was here possible. And we talked of snake-goddesses in Crete and in Bronze Age Denmark, and a mediæval Danish tradition of burying an adder under the threshold to keep evil spirits out of the house. It did not occur to us that it was here, in Dilmun, that the snake had eaten the pearl and achieved immortality; that here in Dilmun, far more than in Cleopatra's Egypt, would the snake and the pearl be regarded as the symbols of that freedom from sickness, old age, and death for which Dilmun itself was famed. In that case to bury a snake beneath the floor of your house would be a potent insurance against sickness and death. And the bead was explained, in a fashion. We should have preferred a pearl, but we are told that the pearl, being calcium carbonate with a trace of organic matter, disintegrates easily in the earth. We have since found a pearl in a later snake-burial, and it is possible that the bowls where no bead was found originally contained a pearl; it is anyway certain that pearls were no less valuable then than now, so that the turquoise may well have been a "poor man's immortality."

Beyond a doubt we have here clear proof that the legend of Gilgamesh was still a living and integral part of the religion of Bahrain at the time when the palace was built and inhabited. We have since found many more of these snake-burials, beneath the floors of other rooms, and their total must be well up into the forties. This is far more than could be accounted for by some single "consecration" ceremony, such as that of our *barasti*-builders when they buried the head and feet of the sacrificial goat beneath the floor of our camp. Perhaps the sacrifice had to be renewed yearly, or on the death or birth of a member of the family who lived in the great house. Or perhaps the building was not a palace but a temple—or partook in some way of both functions—and the snake-bowls are the offerings of suppliants in quest of health or long life. We are at a loss, as we always must be when we pass beyond the relics of the material aspects of life, and meet something which hints of the life of the spirit.

It was difficult to pull half our team from this succession of discoveries in order to fulfil our program in Qatar. And looking at the long array of "finds" on our storeroom shelves, we decided that on our return we would end our season by putting on a public exhibition of our results in Bahrain.

Qatar indeed proved, this year, rather an anticlimax after our work on the city civilization of Bahrain.

I saw little of that Qatar season myself. Once I had seen the party accommodated in a bungalow which the Shell Oil Company was able to lend us in Doha, and had negotiated the purchase of a land-rover from the same company—on very generous terms, for the company had recently suffered the loss in a sudden storm of its seabed drilling platform and would be on reduced strength until a new platform could be built and towed out—P.V. took over the reconnaissance and I returned to my Bahrain diggings.

They covered a lot of ground in Qatar that year, ranging from Doha to the northern point of the peninsula, and again south to the dune country on the border of Saudi Arabia. They had two tents with them, which we had begged from the National Museum in Copenhagen and which had last seen service in central Mongolia, and with these and a stock of food and water they would be out in the desert for three or four days at a stretch before returning to the baths and restaurant of the oil camp. When they returned to Bahrain at the end of March their swathe of exploration had given them a much more detailed picture of what there was to find in Qatar than our two-man two-day reconnaissance of the year before.

It seemed at the time that the negative evidence was more important than the positive. There was no trace in the whole of Qatar of our "Barbar culture," or of any of the cultures that in Bahrain we were inclined to date to the period when Dilmun flourished. There were no city tells, and there were no immense fields of grave-mounds. Several groups of forty or fifty mounds had been found in the northwest, similar to those we had observed the year before. And one of them was excavated. It proved to be a cairn of stones surrounding a shallow stone cist, resembling but little the elaborate alcoved chambers of the Bahrain mounds. And while the Bahrain chambers always lay east-west, this lay north-south. The skeleton, unaccompanied by any objects at all, lay in the same half-contracted position as those of the Bahrain tombs, on its right side, with head to the north and hands before the face. There was no evidence of date, except that the position showed it to be pre-Islamic.

Equally undatable were numerous carvings on exposed slabs of rock in the far northeast. There were rows and rosettes of small, saucer-shaped depressions, the "cup-marks" which are so well known from Bronze Age Europe but which are found over almost all the world. There were carved footprints and linear

designs that resembled closely the arrow-like plan of the wicker
fish-traps that line the shallows along the coasts of Bahrain and
Qatar.

The most significant discovery was that of a further dozen flint
sites, a foretaste of the wealth of Stone Age remains that was to
keep us busy in Qatar for the next six years. It was already clear
that on the windswept deserts of Qatar, where no grass grows to
hide what is dropped, and where even the covering of sand
comes and goes with every wind, the tools and weapons of
millennia of stone-using hunters lay still exposed on the surface.
And here the different shapes and types of artifacts told just as
clearly of different eras and different cultures as did the differences in shapes and types of pottery on Bahrain. On the rocky
coasts and low plateaux of the northwest the flint sites showed a
preponderance of small scrapers, the tool used to prepare skins
for use as clothing. This same preponderance had been noted on
the flint sites of Bahrain, and indeed the two "cultures" were to
all intents and purposes identical. On a rocky ridge overlooking
the eastern sea a completely different style was found, long thin
blades of flint, with among them an occasional arrowhead of
simple type, a blade pointed at one end and chipped to a tang at
the other. And finally, down by the sea in the sandy gullies below
where the dream town of Umm Bab should have been, there
were quantities of the tiny chippings which are the waste from

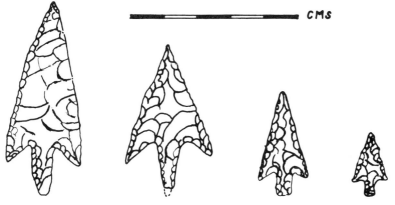

FLINT ARROWHEADS FROM THE MOST RECENT OF THE FOUR STONE-AGE CUL-
TURES OF QATAR. SEE MAP 3.

pressure flaking, the late and very refined technique of thinning and shaping implements by tapping off small parallel flakes from the surface. And here was found one specimen of the finished product, a tiny triangular barbed and tanged arrowhead. It was to be the first of many.

CHAPTER NINE

⟁⟁⟁⟁⟁

"MAY THE WIDE SEA BRING YOU ITS ABUNDANCE"

The Bahrain Exhibition, at the beginning of April, was a considerable success. Sheikh Sulman came, with half his family, to open it in state, and spent an hour looking at our display, listening to P.V.'s explanations, and asking innumerable questions. Then the schoolroom that we had borrowed was opened to the public, and for two days we had no rest as the men of Bahrain poured in to see what we had found. The third day was climactical. That day we closed the exhibition to men and opened it for the women. This was at the suggestion of the directress of the girls' schools, who had told us that there was much interest in our work among the ladies, but that no woman would come to the exhibition while men were there.

We were uncertain what to do ourselves, for we did not wish to cause a scandal, and yet we could not leave our exhibits unguarded. We need not have worried. When the doors were opened and the first party entered, clothed from head to foot in black robes and veils, we stood bashfully in the corners of the room, trying to look as inconspicuous as possible. But the ladies threw back their veils, many letting their robes slip back from their heads to their shoulders; and one of the ladies, taking off her cloak to reveal a smart two-piece costume, came up to us and said in faultless English that "Her Highness would very much like us to explain the exhibition to her." The party of visitors was the other half of Sheikh Sulman's family, his wife and his daughters and daughters-in-law, their children and their governesses, and their ladies in waiting.

All day the women streamed in in their hundreds, and not more than three or four felt it necessary to retain veil or mask when once they came inside. If we had so much as looked at one of these women in the street, though she was veiled and masked she would have pulled her cloak across her face and turned away. But in the temporary museum, convention was dropped with the veil. The ladies discussed the exhibits with us, asked questions, and pulled us aside to tell us of places on the island where they had heard of, or seen, things that might interest us. It was far and away our most successful day.

We had, of course, our snake-bowls on exhibition, as well as a couple of bath-tub-coffins with their skeletons. We had flints from the desert, and pots and pearl-shells from the "kitchen-midden." There were some copper axes and spear-heads from the Barbar temple, and the whole magnificent array of the glazed ware from the well. And there was a long glass case with a score of small objects from my own dig at the Qala'at al-Bahrain tell. Pride of place went to three small stone seals.

The importance of these objects was out of all proportion to their size and number—as I shall try to show.

The excavation along the northern shore had produced other things that could not be brought to exhibition. Chief among them were the defenses of the Barbar-period city. They had not proved difficult to find. Working back from the last *sondage* of the year before I had laid out two of my five-metre-square holes. And in the northernmost of them I met the city wall only two feet below the surface.

It was an imposing construction, a full eleven feet in thickness, constructed of large, roughly squared stones set in gypsum cement. But during the four thousand years and more since it was built it had suffered severely. For the last two thousand years at least it had clearly been used as a convenient stone-quarry. The whole of the outer, northern, face was gone. And here the walls of houses, built up against the raw core of the wall and containing sherds of the thin bowls of the "Greek" period, showed who the culprits had been. Later, the protruding top of the wall had been incorporated in houses of the same Islamic period as my seashore fort, and finally a deep quarry hole, dug through Islamic and "Greek" levels, had taken out a large part of the wall in its full thickness. The blue-and-white sherds of Chinese porcelain in this hole clearly marked the Portuguese as the quarriers, and indeed we could identify stones from the city wall incorporated in the walls of the Portuguese fort within which we lived.

But on the inner face the wall was better preserved, and here we could follow the course of the street of the "Barbar" period in which I had found myself the year before. Then I had stood at a street corner in the middle of a small square hole in the ground. Now, standing at the same corner I could look forty feet north along the street.

We were clearly in no mean city. The street was straight and level, thirteen feet wide and running due north and south. On either side ran the stone walls of the houses, the wall on the right unbroken, only relieved by shallow buttresses. On the left two doorways opened into the street, giving access to the houses. The street was a cul-de-sac, ending against the inner face of the city wall, built of squared stones, here set in a mortar of green clay. And the municipal planning that appeared in the careful orientation of the street was further evidenced. For where the street ended at the wall there was a well, recessed into the corner formed by the left wall of the street and the city wall. And in front of it, in the centre of the street, a large earthenware basin, a full metre in diameter, had been sunk, with its top at street level. It was clearly a municipal water supply. Probably a slave had been employed to keep the basin full of water from the well, so that the people living in the street could fetch water or wash clothes. I had seen something very similar in the streets of Manama, where the enlightened municipality had, not many years before, introduced a public water supply, running pipes from the water-towers to hydrants at convenient points in the streets.

There too they had set up troughs and open tanks, and these public watering points were always surrounded by a throng of black-robed housewives, chattering as they filled their pitchers and scrubbed their laundry. It was not difficult to picture some similar scene here, four thousand years ago, with the women of Dilmun—for this surely was Dilmun—meeting to exchange the gossip of the day at the watering point beneath the towering wall of their city.

We dug very carefully when we approached the level of this street. For it was unpaved, and in the sand that the inhabitants of the city had trod we might expect to find anything that they had lost or thrown away. We found, of course, hundreds of potsherds, all of the red "Barbar" ware, but we were looking for other, more valuable things. And it was, of course, Hasan bin Habib, of the eagle eyes, who made the first find. He came to me and held out his clenched hand. And opened it, to show a circular object of stone, about as big as a silver dollar. It was a stamp-seal, and as I brushed off the sand and began to make out its form I knew that this would be the find of the year. For it was a very special seal, and we knew what was special about it.

A famous French archæologist once stated that the most essential and immediate thing to do when you make an important discovery is to light a cigarette. For at that moment it is vitally necessary not to do anything hasty, not to allow the treasure-hunting instinct to triumph over the scientific, but rather to stop all work and to sit quietly and think over all the implications of the discovery. So I persuaded my team to circulate their communal water-pipe, while I filled and lit my own pipe and sat down on the doorstep of the nearest "Barbar" house, to look at and think about the seal.

It was, as I have said, a round stamp-seal. It was about an inch in diameter, flat on one side, with a design cut in the face, which I could already see depicted two human beings. The other side was a flat dome, pierced by a hole so that it could be hung on a cord. And the dome was decorated with a band of three incised lines and with four incised circles, each with a dot in the middle. The material was steatite, a soft stone of rather greasy appearance and feel, which accounts for its popular name of soap-stone.

Now, we might not have known so much about this type of seal, had it not been that we had seen one before.

It had happened three years before, during our first season on the island. One of the amateur archæologists of Bahrain, an American engineer with the oil company, sent us word that he had found a seal. He had been wandering among the grave-mounds that lie to either side of the road to Budeiya, the road that we could see from the ramparts around our camp. And the seal had simply been there, lying on the surface. We came and looked at it, and borrowed it, and made a plaster cast. And we sent a description of it back to Aarhus, to the professor of classical archæology, to ask him if he could find anything similar in the books. And he replied with a reference to an article by Professor C. J. Gadd, published nearly a quarter of a century earlier, in 1932 (*Proceedings of the British Academy*).

Dr. Gadd at that time had been in charge of the objects from Mesopotamia in the British Museum and part of his work consisted of arranging for exhibition the objects brought home by Sir Leonard Woolley from his excavations at Ur, which were then in their tenth year. The Ur excavations were a joint venture of the British Museum and the University Museum of Philadelphia, and the objects found at Ur were therefore divided three ways, between London, Philadelphia, and Baghdad. But among the objects that came to London were several hundred seals, the great majority of them being the cylindrical seals that were in general use in Mesopotamia from about 3000 until about 500 B.C. Among them was a little handful of circular stamp-seals, and when Gadd looked at the records he found that in fact twelve stamp-seals bearing a certain generic resemblance had been found in Ur. Moreover, in the collections of the British Museum, which for over a hundred years had been a receiving point for a miscellany of objects from all over the world, there were already three seals of the same type, all believed to have come originally from Mesopotamia. It was this collection of fifteen seals which Gadd had published.

Professor Gadd's article is of paramount importance to the

theme of this book, and I could recall its main outlines as I sat in the February sunshine in the doorway of a four-thousand-year-old house. The point of most immediate importance was that seven of Gadd's seals from Ur, and one of the other three, were of identical form to the one that I held in my hand. The designs on the faces were different, of course, though even here there were points of resemblance, for the seven seals also bore representations of men and animals very similar to those on the American engineer's seal and on the one we had just found. But the shape was the same, with the gently domed boss decorated with three incised lines and four centre-pointed circles.

That seals of a type found in Ur should turn up on Bahrain, and now should be found lying in a street of the "Barbar period," was of great significance. Logically it must mean that people from Ur had been in Bahrain, or that people from Bahrain had been in Ur, or that people from some third place had been both in Bahrain and in Ur. But even this paled beside the implications of the other seven seals described in Gadd's article.

These other seals were not quite the same as ours, though they resembled them closely enough for Gadd to be satisfied that they were closely related. They were also round, also of steatite. But the pierced boss on the back was higher and not so broad, leaving a wide flat collar between the dome and the circumference of the seal. And this boss was undecorated, save for a single incised line. It was the design on the face of these seals which was so important and which was the reason why Gadd had entitled his article "Seals of Ancient Indian Style Found at Ur." In every case they bore the figure of a bull, and in five cases—four from Ur and one from elsewhere—the bull was surmounted by an inscription in the unknown language of the Indus Valley civilization.

The Indus Valley civilization is the Cinderella of the ancient world. By a combination of circumstances it has been considerably overshadowed by its elder sisters of the Nile Valley and the Tigris-Euphrates Valley. It is more distant from Europe (and it was from Europe that the discoverers of all the ancient civilizations had come); it was discovered much later; and it has proved more difficult to fit into a coherent history of mankind. Unlike the

I. A small section of one of the six major moundfields of Bahrain. Every mound is the work of man, and every mound covers a stone-built burial chamber. Beyond the multitude of small mounds the giant mounds around the village of Ali—the "Royal Graves"—rise against the darker date plantations beyond.

II. *Above:* The "Royal Mounds" at Ali on Bahrain are a group of some twenty tumuli rising to over forty feet in height, and covering complicated systems of ringwalls and central chambers. Around the one in the middle distance traces can be seen of a perimeter ring, all that is left of an ancient surrounding wall. *Below:* One of the smaller Bahrain mounds, cut through in our first season of excavation, shows details of construction. The central stone chamber (the upper course of its sealing wall displaced by robbers) had stood for some time covered only by a minimal mound, presumably awaiting its occupant. After the burial the mound was raised further, bounded by a ring of rough stones.

III. *Above:* The "holy well" at Diraz on Bahrain, viewed from above. The steps lead down to the well-head, formed of a single block of chiselled stone. Pottery proves the well to date to about 2000 B.C. *Below:* The pair of kneeling animals, of limestone and eighteen inches long, was found on the steps down to the Diraz well. They are probably rams, but were decapitated when the well was destroyed. No traces of the heads were found.

IV. The central courtyard of the Barbar temple. In the foreground is
the double-plinth, two rings of stones framed in a raised oblong. Behind
are the two stone supports of the "throne," standing on a dais, with
before them the square "altar" with a hollow in the top. The "libation-
drain" can be seen passing through the rear wall, while to the extreme
left is the pit in which offerings were found.

V. *Above left:* This bull's head, twenty cms. high and cast in the round, lay in the corner of a room of Temple II at Barbar, together with a heap of copper bands and sheet copper pierced with nails. The eyes were originally inlaid.   *Above right:* Chief among the offerings from the pit before the Barbar-temple altar is this copper figurine of a naked, clean-shaven man in the posture of supplication. He is eleven cms. high, and rivets in the semicircular base suggest that he was originally attached to a stand, or formed the handle of some object, perhaps a mirror.   *Below:* An offering of a later age, these 9th century A.D. bowls, with magnificent flame-like decoration, lay in the main well of the Barbar temple, which had been cleaned out and reused nearly three thousand years after the temple was destroyed.

VI. The south front of the Barbar temple shows the terrace walling of two periods, that of Temple II with the stairway, and to its right that of Temple III which later masked it. To the left the well in which the Islamic pottery lay can just be seen, while the center court of the temple (Plate IV) is at upper left.

VII. *Above:* At the western end of the Barbar-temple terrace a flight of steps leads down to this enclosed tank. Perhaps used for baptism or in purification rites, it was at least not merely the water supply of the temple, for a well lay by the head of the staircase.   *Below:* The tank above may indeed have been a "wishing well," or a communication channel to the god of the nether waters, for it contained seven of the round stamp seals which are the most easily identifiable feature of the Dilmun civilization. The two dark seals were found elsewhere in the Barbar temple.

VIII. One of the ruined towers of the Portuguese fort still looks out to sea over the desolation of the tell of Qalaʿat al-Bahrain. We dug it out one year, revealing two vaulted chambers, which the expedition uses as a banqueting hall on ceremonial occasions. . . .

IX. *Above:* In 1956 our camp was built within the ramparts of the ruined Portuguese fort. Here, under construction, is the main sleeping wing, with the palm-rib framework of walls and roof, later to be thatched with palm-leaves. *Below:* The completed camp, with its library and row of hermit-like cells, has for nine seasons provided a comfortable and surprisingly attractive home for some scores of Danish archaeologists.

X. *Opposite:* The first sondage at the tell of Qala'at al-Bahrain met the massive walls of the "palace" some three feet underground, and followed them down, in a hole much deeper than it was wide, to two bathtub coffins dug through holes in the "palace" floor. The coffins (one has already been removed) were of bitumen-coated clay and can be dated to the time of the Assyrian kings about 700 B.C. The pot beside the coffin is significantly of the same shape as that in Plate XVII, *below.*

XI. *Above:* Six years later the "palace" excavation shows a different picture. From the ramparts of the Portuguese fort we look down into an extensive excavation, in which the walls of the "palace" still rise in places to a height of fourteen feet.

XII. *Opposite:* The magnificent gateway, high but narrow like Arab doorways to this day, of the "palace" at Qala'at al-Bahrain. This is the view from the street outside, which leads direct to the gateway.

XIII. *Above:* By the sea on the northern edge of the tell of Qala'at al-Bahrain lay a fortified Islamic palace of the 11th or 12th century A.D. Its central paved court was surrounded by a symmetrical system of buildings and streets leading to the turrets of the outer wall.

XIV. The outer face of the West Wall of the Early Dilmun city (City II) at Qala'at al-Bahrain still survives to an appreciable height after the vicissitudes of four millennia.

XV. *Above:* Two of the typical pottery vessels of the first city at Qala'-at al-Bahrain (City I—perhaps 2500 B.C.) The pot on the left bears the chain-ridges which are characteristic of this period. Both are of red clay. *Below:* Typical pottery of City II (about 2000 B.C.). Chain-ridges have now been abandoned, and the central pot shows the plain ridges which now dominate. To the left rear is one of the comparatively rare painted vases, in polychrome white and red. The two beakers in right front have been "borrowed" for the picture from the Barbar temple. They belong to this period, though only fragments have been found in the city tell.

XVI. *Above:* A selection of pottery from the gravemounds of Bahrain.
The two large vessels are clearly of the same red ridged type as on
Plate XV, bottom. The two goblets and the three bowls come from one
of the giant "Royal Mounds" at Ali. *Below:* Pottery of City III at Qala'
at al-Bahrain. Of honey-brown clay, they are a complete contrast to the
vessels of the preceding period, and are identical with Mesopotamian
pottery of the period 1800-1200 B.C.

XVII. *Above:* One of the snake-offerings found buried below the floor of the "palace" which represents City IV at Qala'at al-Bahrain. It clearly harks back to the Gilgamesh legend (and even perhaps the Genesis story) of the snake which robbed mankind of eternal life—and incidentally it supplies us with pottery types which enable us to date levels elsewhere to the same Assyrian period.   *Below:* About 650 B.C. a silversmith buried his stock of metal—mainly rings, earrings, and broken bracelets—in a typical pot of the period beneath the floor of the "palace" at Qala'at al-Bahrain. A signet ring of Phoenician origin in the hoard reveals the date. The occasion may well have been an Assyrian conquest of Dilmun by Esarhaddon or Assurbanipal.

XVIII. *Above:* Though this collection is in fact from a grave on Bahrain, it shows the typical pottery of City V, the period of the Seleucid Empire (300-100 B.C.). In front of the two vessels lie a steatite lid and a bone spindle. *Below:* A series of stone weights found in the "customs house" within the north gate of the Early Dilmun city at Qala'at al-Bahrain. They are of the type used in the Indus Valley civilization, and appear to show that Dilmun (originally at least) lay within the economic sphere of India rather than Mesopotamia.

XIX. *Opposite:* The Early-Dilmun period settlement on Failaka island, off Kuwait. While the buildings are far less impressive than the contemporary buildings of Bahrain they contained a wealth of stamp-seals and fragments of carved steatite bowls, which suggest that the island was, then as in later times, an important religious center.

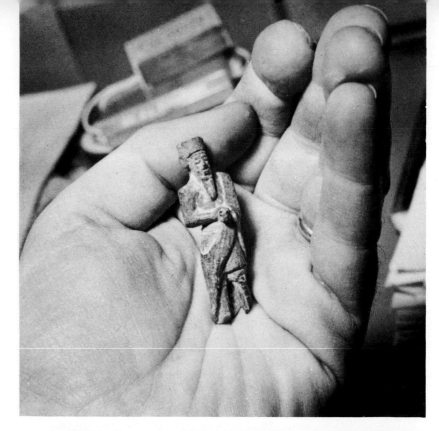

XX. *Above:* This tiny steatite figurine is one of the few sculptures in the round from the Dilmun settlement on Failaka. Like the copper figurine from the Barbar temple (Plate V—*above*) it stands in the posture of supplication. *Below left:* Fragment of a steatite bowl from Failaka, bearing the cuneiform inscription "Temple of the god Inzak." Other fragments of the same bowl show that the two human figures are standing on the back of an animal, probably a ram. *Below right:* Five seals found on Failaka. Their great similarity to the Barbar seals shown in Plate VII is obvious. The reverse sides are identical with those from Barbar.

XXI. The kitchen of a house in the Dilmun settlement on Failaka. Utensils of stone and pottery still stand in position on the "kitchen table."

XXII. In the Seleucid settlement on Failaka, separated by three hundred yards and two thousand years from the Early Dilmun settlement, the main feature is this Greek temple, probably to Artemis. In the center of the inner chamber is the plinth for the statue of the goddess; beyond the pillared porch lies the altar, and beyond the altar the fortification wall of the township. Beyond the wall, at the far end of the excavation the moat is almost lost in shadow.

XXIII. *Above:* Professor Jeppesen, the excavator of the Greek temple on Failaka, is here engaged in deciphering the Greek dedication inscription of the temple. *Below:* This hoard of silver tetradrachms was found in the immediate vicinity of the Greek temple. They date to about 210 B.C.

XXIV. *Opposite:* The shrine of Al-Khidr, the Green Man, on Failaka. This modern shrine, to a saint of Islam said to be immortal, shows a direct continuity of religious belief spanning four thousand years.

XXV. *Above:* The first of the tomb-chambers on Umm an-Nar, in Abu Dhabi. The ring-wall and the complicated system of inner walls can be seen.

XXVI. *Above:* A smaller tomb-chamber on Umm an-Nar, where one of the two triangular entrances still survives. *Below:* Among the stones fallen from the ring wall of one of the Umm an-Nar tombs were two bearing reliefs of animals, to the left a camel and an oryx, to the right a bull. The stones originally flanked the entrance to the tomb, and the stone between the two reliefs was the capstone of this entrance.

XXVII. *Above:* This collection of pottery, together with sherds of at least as many more vessels and the bones of about thirty-six individuals, came from the tomb chamber on Plate XXVI–*above.*   *Below:* Close-up of the vessel shown in rear center above, bearing the painted figure of a humped bull. clear evidence of connection with India.

XXVIII. The small hunting and fishing settlement on Umm an-Nar, dating perhaps to 2700 B.C., contained surprisingly spacious and well-built stone houses. On the escarpment beyond can be seen some of the unexcavated tomb-chambers.

XXIX. At Buraimi, a hundred miles inland in Abu Dhabi, lie tomb-chambers of the same type as those of Umm an-Nar, but built of even more substantial stones.

XXX. *Above:* The top half of one of the seven-foot stones forming the two entrances to the tomb-chamber shown on Plate XXIX. It bears two reliefs, to the right a sexual scene and to the left a figure riding a donkey followed by another figure on foot. *Below:* The bottom half of the same entrance stone, bearing a relief of two lions, or cheetahs, tearing a gazelle. The photograph has been turned to show the stone in its correct relation to the top half—it was in fact standing on edge when photographed.

XXXI. The "impossible" tell at Tarut, in Saudi Arabia, crowned by the ruins of a fairly modern fort, and with the ladies' bath-house in the foreground (with some of the ladies). The surface sherds are of Early Dilmun date, while from the line of shadow near the base came Neolithic flints and Ubaid pottery, probably dating to about 4000 B.C.

XXXII. *Above:* At Jabrin, two hundred miles in the interior of Saudi Arabia, lie extensive fields of grave-mounds, apparently of Second Millennium B.C. date. They lie on the edge of the great desert of the Empty Quarter, and mark our furthest penetration into the mainland of Arabia. *Below:* From the coast of Saudi Arabia come the earliest traces yet found of civilization in the Arabian Gulf—flint implements, obsidian blades, and these sherds of painted pottery of the Ubaid culture, the earliest known culture of southern Mesopotamia, dating to about 4000 B.C.

civilizations of Egypt and Mesopotamia, which had been known by repute to the historians of Greece and Rome, and which were recorded in the Bible, the civilization of the Indus was unsuspected until 1921. In that year the ruins of a large city were located by the Archæological Survey of India at Harappa in the Punjab, besides the former course of a tributary to the Indus. And the following year the site of an equally large city was discovered at Mohenjo-Daro on the banks of the Indus itself, 400 miles southwest of Harappa. Sir John Marshall, the director general of the survey, started excavations at both sites in that year, and the diggings went on for six years. The two cities proved to be almost identical. They were some three miles in circumference, each with a fortified citadel to the west of the main town area. They were built entirely of brick, for the greater part kiln-baked. Noteworthy was the evidence of town-planning. Mohenjo-Daro had been clearly laid out on a grid-iron plan, with avenues forty-five feet wide, running due north-south and east-west, and dividing the town into nine precincts. Although Harappa had been extensively quarried less than a hundred years ago to provide ballast for railway construction, there still survived evidence of a similar town-plan there.

It was clear from the start that these two cities, four hundred miles apart, belonged to the same civilization. The resemblance in layout was mirrored by an identity of material culture. The pottery was identical, and painted in a variety of very distinctive patterns. Tools and weapons were identical, largely of flint but with a fair number of objects of copper, fish-hooks, knives and spear-heads, and flat-cast copper axes. And the clearest evidence of all was that the seals were identical, and very distinctive. They were of steatite, about an inch to an inch and a half across, and square. At the back they had a domed boss pierced for the string and normally decorated with a single incised groove. The picture on the face normally consisted of an animal surmounted by a line of what was obviously script. The animal was most often a bull, either the humped Zebu or the unhumped variety, and the language was otherwise unknown. Several hundreds of these seals were found.

Three of the seals found at Mohenjo-Daro were, however, not square but round, with the same domed boss and with a broad flat collar between the boss and the circumference. They were in fact of the same type as the round stamp-seals with the Indus script found by Woolley at Ur and published by Gadd.

Now, that had been extraordinarily important. For while it was clear that Harappa and Mohenjo-Daro were cities of the same, new, civilization, and must be of the same date, it was by no means clear what that date was. Written records might have told, but apart from the short inscriptions on the seals there were no written records, and the seal inscriptions could not be read. As we saw with the decipherment of cuneiform, long texts are almost essential to the solving of the riddle of an unknown language, and no long texts in the Indus script have been found. It is obvious from the seals that the people of the Indus Valley civilization were literate, but we have not in India had the stupendous good fortune that we have in Mesopotamia, that the ordinary, day-to-day writing was done on an imperishable material. So, as indeed with our excavations in Bahrain, the civilization of the Indus Valley could only be dated by the finding of objects identical with objects found elsewhere in datable contexts. The round seals of Mohenjo-Daro, then, could be dated, if the round seals of Ur could be dated.

This was not quite so easy as might have been expected. The rule that a level is as old as the latest object in it works the other way too. An object may well be earlier than the level in which it is found. Witness the Stone Age axes frequently found in the ruins of Danish Iron Age houses, collected, it is believed, as charms to protect the houses against lightning. Most of Woolley's seals had been found in the course of sifting sand, and could not be ascribed to a level at all. Of the three where the circumstances of discovery were recorded, two were of the high-bossed, Mohenjo-Daro type, and were ascribed respectively to a Sargonid (about 2300 B.C.) and a Second Dynasty of Ur (about 2200 B.C.) level, while the third, of the low-bossed, circle-ornamented type such as Hasan had just found, was discovered in a rubbish level, doubtfully ascribed to the Kassite period (1700–1200 B.C.). So the Indus Valley civilization had been tentatively dated to the last three centuries of the third millennium B.C.

As I smoked my pipe in the Bahrain diggings, and attempted to recall these facts, two further points presented themselves. For the first, that the presence of identical seals at Ur and Mohenjo-Daro proved that there had been contact between India and Mesopotamia at the time of the Indus Valley civilization. And for the second, that the round stamp-seals were "foreign" both in India and in Mesopotamia. In both cases they formed less than one per cent of the total of seals found. The rest were cylindrical in Mesopotamia, square in India.

If they were "foreign" in India and Mesopotamia, was it possible that they were "native" to Bahrain? Had it been travellers from Bahrain, merchants perhaps, who had lost the thirteen round seals in Ur and the three in Mohenjo-Daro? I decided that I was building a rather extravagantly large castle in the air, on a foundation of only two seals, and one of them a surface find. Besides, there were two sorts of round seals, the high-bossed type with the bulls and the Indus script, and the low-bossed circle-ornamented type with designs of humans and animals. Admittedly Gadd had considered them sufficiently alike to publish them together and to suggest that they were related. But the fact remained that the three seals from Mohenjo-Daro were of the high-bossed type, and the two from Bahrain of the low-bossed. The connection with Ur was definite enough, but the connection with India seemed somewhat tenuous.

The pause for a cigarette which the Frenchman recommended was far exceeded, and my workmen were getting impatient. The longer-range problems would have to wait, while I concentrated on ensuring that my find was correctly dealt with archæologically. I thought of Woolley's ten undatable seals; there must be no doubt as to where this one had come from.

Hasan bin Habib had spotted it in a shovelful of earth on its way to the baskets in which the earth is lifted to the wheelbarrows on the lip of the excavation. The shovelful comprised the earth scraped up from an area not more than ten inches square and less than an inch deep. We set off this area on our plans, and

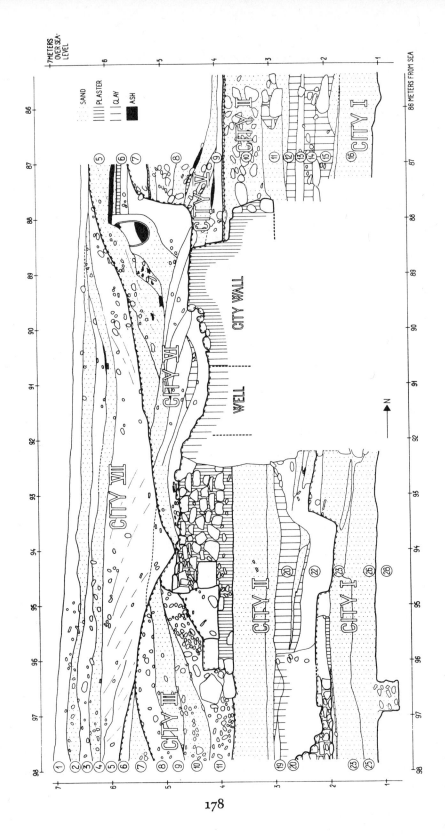

levelled it in. We sifted the earth for half a metre around and two centimetres below the finding-place, and kept every scrap of pottery in a separate box. And I gave Hasan a special reward of two rupees—no less than forty cents—and told him that he should have spotted the seal before it had been scraped up from its original position. I promised five rupees to the man who first found me a seal *in situ*.

There were no more seals lying in the street. But we found a scrap of sawn ivory a day or so later. It was about an inch long, and showed the curvature of the tusk on one side, and the sawn surfaces on either end. It was as though the tusk had been inexpertly sawn off, the saw cut overlapping instead of meeting, and leaving a loose piece to break off as the tusk was being carried along the street. Ivory, too, might point towards India, though there were elephants in Africa, and even, at this time, in Mesopotamia.

We dug down further, below the street level, down towards the "chain-ridge" levels of City I which must lie below. And a week later I found the second seal myself. It was *in situ*, lying up against the inner side of the city wall. Hasan bin Habib insisted, jubilantly, that I pay myself five rupees from the expedition's purse. And I did so, without the heart to tell him that in this case it didn't count. For at this point the original rear face of the city wall had been quarried away at a later date, and the seal lay in the quarry trench, with little stratigraphic significance.

In other ways, though, it possessed significance to make me revise my theories drastically. For it was a round steatite seal with a high pierced boss, decorated with a single incised line. There was the broad flat collar around the boss; and on the face of the seal there was the figure of a bull. But there was no Indus script. Instead there was the incised design of a human footprint

SECTION THROUGH THE NORTH WALL OF THE CITY TELL OF QALA'AT AL-BAHRAIN, AT THE POINT WHERE THE WELL AT THE END OF THE CUL-DE-SAC CUTS INTO THE WALL ON ITS INNER SIDE. TWO THOUSAND YEARS LATER, AT THE TIME OF ALEXANDER, THE PEOPLE OF CITY V CUT INTO THE OUTER FACE, WHILE WITHIN THE LAST MILLENNIUM THE PEOPLES OF CITIES VI AND VII DUG DOWN TO ROB THE WALL OF BUILDING STONE.

and a scorpion. It was undoubtedly of the type of the three Mohenjo-Daro seals; and, after all, two of the three seals from Mohenjo-Daro, and two of the high-bossed seals in the British Museum, had no Indus script either.

It looked as though we perhaps had three types of round stamp-seal and not two. There was the high-bossed *with* Indus script, and the high-bossed *without* Indus script, and the low-bossed, which never had Indus script. All three types were found at Ur, types one and two were found at Mohenjo-Daro, types two and three were found in Bahrain. What then of my theory that type three was native to Bahrain, that those of the low-bossed type were, as I had begun to call them, "Dilmun seals"?

Had my latest type-two seal been brought to Bahrain from outside, or could it too be "native"? After all, Gadd had regarded the two types as related. Perhaps the disturbed stratigraphy of my second seal did not signify, and it was indeed, as its level would imply, earlier than the first. Perhaps the difference between type two and type three was chronological.

Again I was building theories on an absurdly small basis. I simply could not postulate an Early Dilmun seal with a high boss and a Later Dilmun seal with a low boss on a statistical count of one each! It was a theory, a wild theory perhaps, which would fit the few facts that we had. And if archæology is a science, as we like to claim, then theories must be tested by experiment. With more digging, more seals would sooner or later be found. And stratigraphy would determine whether the difference in type corresponded to a difference in date.

A fortnight later Hasan bin Habib won his five rupees. During the fortnight we had been digging steadily downward on either side of the city wall, which now stood up as an eight-foot-high barrier between the two halves of the excavation. We had kept the two excavations approximately level, yet on the northern side, towards the sea, we were digging in City V, among the thin red-painted or grey-glazed pottery of Alexander the Great's time, and on the southern side we were deep into City II, with red ridged pottery which might well be contemporary with Sargon of Akkad, that other great conqueror who had preceded Alexander by exactly two thousand years.

There is a subtle trap in the archæologist's habit of translating history into stratigraphy. It is all too easy to forget to translate back. I had to remind myself that when, in Sargon's and Hammurabi's time, the inhabitants of our city were living and walking our street the city wall at the end of the street was standing to its full height, manned by sentinels who must have stood silhouetted against the sky, with spear in hand and woollen cloak pulled tight against the damp breeze from the sea, as they looked out over the sheer drop of the outer face of the wall, down to the sand of the beach below, a beach which was much lower than the level of the street behind them.

Then two thousand years passed, as long a time as from Julius Cæsar to the present day. And the people of the time of Alexander saw the wall deserted and crumbling, but still standing sheer on the beach side to well above the height of a man. Within the rampart the sand must have lapped the top of the wall, covering the ruins of two thousand years, but outside there was still the sheer drop to the piles of stone and rubble which had once been the wall's superstructure. And the men of the Greek period used this stone and rubble as material to build their houses, and used the long backcloth of the ruined rampart itself as the back wall of their dwellings.

We were working backward in time, back to the time when the wall was built. And we found that point of time—earlier than I had expected. We found a burnt layer. It was a level where the usual sandy soil was darkened by smoke and particles of charcoal. At that level we found a number of round-bellied pots, decorated with the "chain-pattern" ridges. They had been buried in the ground up to their shoulders, and the tops, where they had protruded, had been broken off. They were full of a black burnt mass, and we rejoiced, for here we could get samples which could be dated by measurement of the residue of radioactive carbon. (We rejoiced too soon, for the contents must have been heavily contaminated with bitumen, or some other unthinkably ancient carbon material. For when they were processed by the carbon-14 laboratory in Copenhagen we got quite impossible dates, ranging from nineteen thousand to thirty-six thousand years old.)

When we followed this burnt layer in towards the city wall we discovered that at that level the wall ended, and the layer went on beneath it. And when our digging outside the wall reached that level we met the same layer, with the same "chain-ridged" potsherds.

Now this was, finally, not archæology but history. A city, the city of the "chain-ridge" people, had apparently been unwalled, and had been burnt. And the same people—for there was no real break in the continuity of the pottery—had returned after the destruction and rebuilt the city. And this time they had built a wall, ten feet thick, around the city. It would have been more than a little interesting to have been able to put a carbon-14 date to that event. . . .

Anyway, just within the city wall, and above the burnt level, there was a very local layer of whitish beach sand. It was obvious that, when they wished to build the wall, there had existed a slight hollow here, and in order to provide a level surface for the wall the builders had filled the hollow with a few baskets of sand from the shore. And it was in this sand that Hasan bin Habib spotted the third seal, and showed it to me, still in its original position.

It made confusion even worse confounded, for it was of still another type. The generic resemblance was still there, sure enough, and no one could doubt that all three seals we had found that year were related. But this one was smaller than the others, only about half an inch across, and of black steatite. It had the high boss on the back, though with a double incised line, and there was no room for the wide flat collar, but only for a narrow rim around the boss. And the design on the front was not of a bull but of a goat, or perhaps a gazelle, with above it another goat and a star.

My speculations started again, still with the impossibly slender statistical basis. Perhaps we had here a strictly chronological stylistic development, from small black seals to larger light-grey seals, both with the high boss, and from there to the low-bossed seals with circles on the boss. But obviously we should have to wait for further discoveries before we could confirm or deny any such sequence. It did seem, though, that we could at this stage claim that the dominant form of seal in use in Bahrain was the round stamp-seal. That at least they all had in common.

The sand layer in which this seal had appeared was surprisingly rich in "small finds." Although only covering about two square yards, and only about six inches thick, it contained two fragments of small steatite bowls, both decorated with the same incised ornamentation of the centre-pointed circle as decorated the "later" seals, three tiny turquoise beads, and half of a larger bead of a translucent reddish-brown stone which we recognized as carnelian. In addition, the sand was full of small green nodules. These, on examination, proved to be tiny scraps of copper which had corroded and, in doing so, stained and glued together the sand grains immediately around them. It was all very strange. We wondered if all the sand down on the beach, at the time when the city wall was built, had been equally full of scraps of copper, fragments of carved stone bowls, lost beads, and lost seals. And if so, why?

There is little more to relate of this particular "dig." We went on down, another metre and more, through "chain-ridge" levels and then through grey sand, until we met bedrock. And there we stopped. . . .

I have talked at length, perhaps undue length, about this excavation of the city wall. It was of course my own personal "dig," and I saw more of it than of the others. And the seals were undoubtedly the high spots of the season.

Looked at as a whole the handful of small objects, picked up along ten yards of one of the streets of the First and Second Cities beneath our tell, and now exhibited to the people of Bahrain among a collection of much more immediately fascinating objects, opened up perspectives of incredible width. They had one factor in common. None of them was of a substance native to Bahrain. While the steatite seals, and perhaps the steatite bowls, might have been manufactured in Bahrain, the steatite itself was foreign. It might have come from many areas, for steatite is not uncommon. It is found in the mountains of Persia and the Oman, and in many places further afield. The copper fish-hooks and the innumerable scraps of unworked copper were also of unknown origin; there were strong rumours of copper in the Oman, and copper was also available in India and in Persian Luristan. The ivory pointed more definitely to India, though not with absolute certainty. The carnelian bead, on the other hand, could only have come from India, since the only other areas where carnelian occurs, Central Europe and South America, were out of the question. There was one object, and only one, which could, so far as material goes, have come from Bahrain, and we knew that it did not. It was a perfect cube of polished flint, about three quarters of an inch to a side. And we recognized it immediately for what it was. It was a weight, of the type in common use in the cities of the Indus Valley, and used nowhere else.

Together these objects were evidence that Bahrain had had a very widespread trade network in the Barbar period and before. And it was just the evidence which we would have expected to find, if Bahrain were in truth Dilmun.

I have described at length the cuneiform inscriptions bearing on the historical fact of Dilmun's existence and its historical associations with Mesopotamia. And I have given in detail the textual evidence that Dilmun figured as a holy land in the mythology of ancient Sumer and Babylonia. There is a third class of cuneiform document, however, concerning Dilmun, which needs to be examined closely. There are a large number of extant tablets dealing with the trade between Mesopotamia and Dilmun.

Once again we need to remind ourselves how very lucky we are that the ordinary correspondence of Mesopotamia was written on a material that survives the ages. In four thousand years' time there will be no written evidence, and scarcely any indirect evidence, to show the scope of the business of Lloyds of London or of a New York shipping company. But in the cities of Mesopotamia the contracts and bills of lading, the receipts and general correspondence, were all written on clay. Even so, we should not forget that we have statistically a very small sample indeed of all that was written, and even that sample is not representative.

In any excavation of a Mesopotamian city there is a perfectly natural tendency to concentrate excavation on the most important structures, the fortifications, the temples, and the palaces.

These may be expected to give the richest finds and to reveal most clearly the vicissitudes of history, the successions of kings, the conquests and rebuildings. They will contain the important historical inscriptions, the annals of the deeds of kings, the foundation and restoration documents of the temples, the bricks inscribed with the names of the kings who ordered the building. The temple and palace libraries, too, will contain the liturgies and hymns, and the religious epics, which cast so much light on the beliefs and mythologies of the peoples of Mesopotamia.

Again we are lucky, in the fact that the temples played an important part in the commerce of the cities. In the centuries around 2000 B.C. they even seem to have themselves engaged in large-scale mercantile enterprises, exporting the products of their own workshops and importing cargoes of various staples. In the following centuries trade passed mainly into the hands of private merchants, but even so the temples played the part of commissioners of oaths, preserving copies of agreements between shippers and shareholders, while they also in certain cases seem to have levied import duties or received tithes of cargoes imported. So from the temple archives we frequently get a fair view of the scope and extent of trade.

But the business files of the individual merchants were kept in their houses. And it is very rarely that excavation has touched these ordinary residential and business areas of the cities. It is therefore almost by blind chance that we are in a position to tell the story of a certain Ea-nasir, import and export merchant of Ur, who between the years 1813 and 1790 B.C. was engaged in the Dilmun trade. This is traditionally the date of Abraham, and the two may very well have been living in Ur at this same time. That they would have known each other is more unlikely, as the trading interests of Abraham's family lay towards the west and north.

During the winter excavation season of 1930–1931 at Ur, Sir Leonard Woolley decided to leave for a while his uncovering of the temples and funeral chambers of the kings of the Third Dynasty of Ur, and to excavate a section of the residential quarters of the town. In the area that he chose he found that the

houses were unexpectedly well preserved from the period immediately before the sack of Ur by Hammurabi of Babylon in 1780
B.C., and he excavated an area of some ten thousand square yards,
employing for the purpose about a hundred and fifty workmen.
This is a scale of operation which our finances have never allowed
us to match, and it was made easier by the fact that his streets
and floor levels lay only about two metres underground, compared with the four to six metres which we have had to dig.

In the words of his preliminary report:

> ". . . at this period town-planning was conspicuous by its
> absence. The streets are narrow, unpaved, and wind between
> houses whose irregular frontages depend, clearly, on the acci-
> dents of private ownership. Building blocks are so huge and so
> crowded that to houses situated in the hearts of them blind alleys
> are the only means of approach. The dwelling houses conform to
> one type more or less according to the possibilities of the site;
> the central court entered from a lobby and surrounded by the
> living rooms, with a stairway giving to the upper floor, is the
> basic idea of buildings of very different sizes and of forms ap-
> parently very diverse. Scattered among the residences are
> smaller buildings which can only be shops. The simplest of them
> consist of two rooms only, a booth-like 'show-room' opening
> onto the street sometimes with a front entirely open, and behind
> it a long magazine or store. . . . The walls of all the buildings
> are constructed with burnt bricks below and mud bricks above,
> the wall face originally plastered and whitewashed."

(*Antiquaries Journal*, vol. 11, pp. 360–61)

In this area Woolley excavated about fifty houses and shops on
either side of six streets. In practically every house he found a
score or so of clay tablets, stored in clay jars or in bitumen-lined
pits (for damp, not fire, would be the danger to documents
written on clay), or lying loose on the floors. In some cases they
gave a clue to the identity of the householder and to the business
carried on within the house. There were the account books of the
money-lender, the exercise books of the school—and there was
Ea-nasir's business correspondence.

Ea-nasir's house was one of those which were approached by a blind alley, and on every side its outer walls were also the outer walls of the neighbours' houses. It was of medium size, both by modern and by ancient standards, measuring some fifteen hundred square feet in ground-floor area, with probably an upper floor of some thousand square feet. It was far from being the largest house in the area excavated by Woolley, and it consisted of only five rooms around the central courtyard. Woolley noted

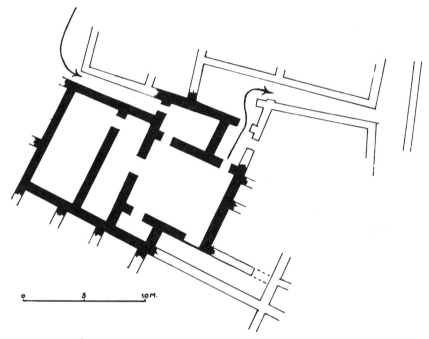

EA-NASIR'S HOUSE IN UR, WHICH PRODUCED TABLETS CONCERNING THE DILMUN COPPER TRADE. EXCAVATED BY SIR LEONARD WOOLLEY IN 1930.

that the house had at one time been larger, but two rooms had been blocked off at one end and incorporated in the next-door house. There was in fact no evidence that Ea-nasir was a conspicuously successful man, and some evidence that he was not entirely succeeding in keeping up with the Joneses.

Ea-nasir is mentioned in eighteen tablets, most of them found in his house. From these it appears that he was a broker in copper, the majority of the documents being letters instructing

Ea-nasir to deliver specific quantities of copper from the holdings of named individuals to other named individuals. Some of these letters are couched in what is clearly plain business language, while others show traces of a certain acrimony, accusing our broker of delay in carrying out assignments, or of delivering poor-quality ingots. One letter, from a certain Nanni, is particularly bitter:

> "When you came, you said, 'I will give good ingots to Gimil-Sin'. That is what you said, but you have not done so; you offered bad ingots to my messenger, saying, 'Take it or leave it'. Who am I that you should treat me so contemptuously? Are we not both gentlemen? . . . Who is there among the Dilmun traders who has acted against me in this way? . . ."

Ea-nasir, then, is a "Dilmun trader," and it is from there that he shipped into Ur the copper in which he dealt. Another document makes this clear. It is a breakdown of a shipment of copper from Dilmun into the various quantities due to various importers in Ur —and, perhaps significantly, it appears that the quantity due to Ea-nasir has not been paid for. The tablet, like so many others, is defective, and there are annoying gaps, but the general purport is clear. My translation is free, as a full transliteration and literal translation has been published (W. F. Leemans: *Foreign Trade in the Old Babylonian Period*, Leiden 1960, pp. 38–39).

> "Of 13,1?? minas of copper according to the standard of Dilmun received by [the name is lost] at Dilmun, 5,5?2⅔ minas by Dilmun standard have been given to us. These weights by Ur standards are 611 talents 6⅔ minas of copper, of which Ala . . . has given us 245 talents 54⅓ minas. Ea-nasir owes for 427½ minas and Nauirum-ili owes for 325 minas, a total of 450 talents 2⅓ minas of copper by the standard of Ur. The balance remaining is 161 talents 4⅓ minas of copper."

This tablet is important for two reasons (and a third will later appear). First because it tells us that the copper acquired in Dilmun arrived there from some other place; and secondly because it gives us some idea of the amount of copper which was moving in the Gulf. For we know the standard weights and measures of Ur, and we can therefore translate the quantities involved into modern terms. The quantities were by no means inconsiderable. The shipment acquired in Dilmun was no less than eighteen and a half metric tons, which at present prices would fetch something like twenty thousand dollars. Of that, Ea-nasir's share was some five and three quarters tons, worth about six thousand dollars.

If we leave Ea-nasir to his creditors, and look at the other tablets from Ur, we find considerably more details about the Dilmun trade. The lists of tithes or offerings to the great temple of Ningal beneath the shadow of the ziggurat of Ur tell us much about the composition of the cargoes reaching Ur from Dilmun. Copper always figures prominently, and there can be little doubt that it was the staple on which the trade depended.

Eight tablets from the Ningal temple concern the Dilmun trade, and they are about a century older than the tablets from Ea-nasir's house. Most of them are dated, and they range from 1907 to 1871 B.C. A typical example reads, with unreadable or missing words in parentheses, and words of unknown meaning in italics:

"(. . .) copper ingots of 4 talents,
4 copper ingots of 3 talents each,
11 shekels of oblong pieces of bronze,
3 kidney-shaped beads of carnelian,
3 "fish-eyes" (pearls?),
8 (. . .) stones,
9 *sila* of white coral,
3 (. . .) stones,
5½ minas of rods of ivory,
30 pieces of tortoise-shell (?),
1 wooden rod with copper (. . .),
1 ivory comb,
1 mina of copper in lieu of ivory,
3 minas of *elligu* stone,
2 measures of antimony (eye-paint),
3 shekels of *merahdu,*

(. . .) counting-boards (?) of Makan reed,
3 shekels of (. . .),
15 shekels of *arazum*,
(. . .) shekels of *hulumum*,
[four lines missing]
from an expedition to Dilmun,
tithe for the goddess Ningal,
from individual participants
[five lines missing, which would include the date]."

The list is indeed variegated, but it is noteworthy that, apart from the copper, it consists of items of small bulk, and undoubtedly high price, belonging to the luxury trade. Apart from ivory, tortoise-shell, and eye-paint, the counting-boards (if that is what they were) of Makan reed (which may be bamboo), and the three unknown items, all the rest are precious and semi-precious stones. Particular interest attaches to the "fish-eyes," which we find mentioned in five of the eight tablets. We can only guess that they are pearls, but it is noteworthy that they are always mentioned by number and not, as are almost all other articles, by weight or measure. This would at least suggest that they were of quite appreciable value.

The other tablets add a few further items to the list. Two mention lapis lazuli and something called "fire-stones," and two mention gold. Silver is frequently mentioned, but in most cases it is specified that the silver was paid as equivalent of the tithe, so that it is unlikely that silver actually formed part of the cargoes from Dilmun.

At first sight these lists do not encourage an identification of Dilmun with Bahrain. For apart from pearls and tortoise-shell none of the articles mentioned can be found in Bahrain. But we draw comfort from the fact that nowhere at all can all the articles be found together. Most significant here is lapis lazuli, for that can only have come from Afghanistan, which could produce but few of the other items, and certainly neither ivory nor pearls. Dilmun is therefore a clearing-house for commodities from further afield, and the majority of the small-bulk luxury items seem to point unequivocally towards the Indian sub-continent.

We have still two very important questions outstanding. One is the source of the copper which was the principal reason for the Dilmun trade. The other is the outward cargo. What did the merchants of Mesopotamia ship to Dilmun, to pay for what they bought? Three further tablets give us the answers to both questions.

In fact only one of these tablets even mentions Dilmun. It is a plain receipt, issued on behalf of a certain Ur-gur, "the captain of a large boat," for "ten talents of different kinds of wool of ordinary quality, put in a boat to Dilmun." It is dated to 2027 B.C., over a hundred years earlier than the tithe lists and nearly 250 years earlier than Ea-nasir. The other two tablets, from 2026 and 2024 B.C., are also receipts, both issued by a certain Lu-Endilla for goods received from the temple of Nannar, the principal temple of Ur. The first is for sixty talents of wool, seventy garments, one hundred and eighty skins, and "6 *kur* of good sesame-oil," described as "merchandise for buying copper." The second is more specific, for fifteen garments and two thirds of a talent of wool, "merchandise for buying copper from Makan."

It would seem, then, that the copper bought in Dilmun came there—in cargoes, as we have seen, of almost twenty tons—from another country called Makan. We shall have more to say about Makan later. And it is clear that the main item of exchange for this copper was wool and woollen piece-goods. That this was still the main export from Mesopotamia to Dilmun a quarter of a millennium later is strongly suggested by another of the tablets found in Ea-nasir's house which records the receipt by him of a total of fifty garments, with their various values in silver carefully specified.

There are moreover two further tablets from Ur contemporary with Ea-nasir—one is dated to 1794 B.C.—but apparently unconnected with his ventures; and they are even more explicit. One reads:

> "Lu-Meshlamtae and Nigsisanabsa have borrowed from Ur-Ninmar 2 minas of silver, 5 *kur* of sesame-oil and 30 garments, as capital for a partnership for an expedition to Dilmun to buy copper there. . . ."

191

The other is less easily decipherable, but concerns a loan of five shekels of silver "for buying 'fish-eyes' and other merchandise on an expedition to Dilmun."

There is a noteworthy practical hard-headedness about all this. These merchants who were raising capital and assembling cargo for the voyages to Dilmun were not investing in some wild argosy to a mythical land of immortality beyond the horizon of the known world. This was routine business; it was the way they made their living.

Nor should we imagine that the trading was carried on exclusively by Mesopotamians. Two of the people recorded as paying tithes to the Ningal temple are specifically listed as natives of Dilmun, so there were probably Dilmunite merchants resident in Mesopotamia and Mesopotamian merchants resident in Dilmun, while ships of both countries would be engaged in the carrying traffic.

Ships of other nationalities, too, would, in these first two centuries of the second millennium B.C., be beating up the Gulf to Dilmun and be beached upon its shores, under the walls of its cities. The ships from Makan would be heavily loaded with their cargoes of copper, while the ships from the cities of the Indus Valley civilization would have cargoes, then as now, of timber (and perhaps, though there is no evidence, of cotton), in addition to their lighter and more valuable stores of ivory, lapis lazuli, and carnelian.

Our little cabinet-full of exhibits made a sorry showing as representatives of this busy international trade, and added but little to the chain of evidence that Bahrain was in truth Dilmun. But after all they were but the objects dropped by chance in ten yards of a blind alley within the city—and they were certainly the *right* objects. The ivory and the carnelian and the copper were there. And the innumerable small grains of copper in the beach sand that had levelled the area within the new-built city wall would be explicable if cargoes of copper were continually being transshipped between the beached vessels outside the wall. We looked at the polished flint weight of the Indus Valley people, and recalled that Dilmun had had a different system of weights and measures from that of Ur—could it have been that of the Indus Valley civilization? And we had the three seals, seals such as those which foreign merchants had left behind them in Ur and in Mohenjo-Daro. It could all be added up to a very convincing total—and there were no loose ends to it. For behind the handful of objects from the street there was a very solid backing of very solid facts. There was a well-fortified and far from inconsiderable city; our tell was over half the size of Ur, and Ur was one of the largest of the cities of Mesopotamia. There was the temple at Barbar, twice during this period built to a larger scale on a broader and more handsome terraced platform. And there were a hundred thousand burial-mounds, the largest of which were monuments which must have taken hundreds of workmen months to construct. This was no isolated agricultural and fishing culture. Prosperity of this order could not be achieved by exploiting the meagre resources of Bahrain alone. Clearly the

THESE BOATS, ABOUT 15 FEET LONG AND MADE OF BUNDLES OF REEDS, ARE USED BY FISHERMEN OF BAHRAIN. THEY ARE BUOYANT BUT NOT, OF COURSE, WATERTIGHT (AND ARE THEREFORE TECHNICALLY RAFTS). SIMILAR BOATS OF PAPYRUS REEDS WERE IN USE IN EGYPT OVER 4000 YEARS AGO.

wealth of Bahrain had come from outside; Bahrain had been a focal point of the far-ranging trade of which the tablets told. As such Bahrain must have been named in those tablets, and there was no other candidate for that name except Dilmun.

The reason for Bahrain's importance on the trade routes was not hard to find. The island was a watering point. In all the length of the Gulf it was only here, and on the Arabian mainland just opposite, that fresh water could be obtained in quantity. That water which the god Enki at the dawn of time had caused to spring forth in Dilmun had indeed, as he promised, brought prosperity to the land. And a variant version of the tale of "Enki and Ninhursag," found like the commercial tablets at Ur and recently published, gives an alternative text of Enki's blessing of Dilmun which has a very strict relevance to the theme of this chapter; for it names practically every one of the import and export commodities recorded in the tablets of the Dilmun trade. It reads, in Professor Kramer's translation:

> "*May the land Tukrish transport to you [i.e. to Dilmun] gold from Harali, lapis lazuli, . . . ;*
> *May the land Meluhha bring you tempting [?] precious carnelian, mes-shagan wood, fine sea-wood, sailors;*
> *May the land Marhashi bring you precious stone, crystal,*
> *May the land Magan bring you mighty copper, the strength of . . . , diorite, u-stone, shuman-stone;*
> *May the Sealand transport to you ebony, the . . . ornament of the king,*
> *May the land Zalamgar transport to you wool, good ore, . . . ;*
> *May the land Elam transport to you . . . wool, tribute;*
> *May the shrine Ur, the dais of kingship, the . . . city, transport to you grain, sesame-oil, noble garments, fine garments, sailors;*
> *May the wide sea bring you its abundance.*
> *The city—its dwellings are good dwellings,*
> *Dilmun—its dwellings are good dwellings, . . ."*

(*Antiquity 146*, June 1963)

CHAPTER TEN

৯৯৯৯৯

THE GREEN MAN

One day, while I was busy digging my street behind the city wall, and while P.V. was away with his party ranging the deserts of Qatar, we had a visitor at the camp. He introduced himself as the British Political Agent in Kuwait. Up in Kuwait, he said, there were among the British community a number of enthusiastic amateur archæologists, and they were proposing to make a trip to the island of Failaka, off the coast of Kuwait, where there were said to be ruins. He asked to see what we had been finding in Bahrain, that they might have some idea what to look for on their exploration.

We showed him our diggings, and we examined with him the displays of type specimens of the pottery of our seven cities which we had mounted on the wall of our work-room. And only a week later we received a parcel containing a box of potsherds from Failaka, with the suggestion that I should stop off in Kuwait on my way home, to see more of the finds and to talk over the future.

Our work was finished for the year in Bahrain. The expedition was over, our team was preparing to leave. And Yunis and I were starting to strike camp once more. It was becoming routine now, and this time I had no last-minute dig on my hands. As soon as the last packing-case was nailed down and corded and stencilled, and loaded aboard the shipping company's truck, I left Yunis to

195

strip the camp alone, and took the little Gulf Aviation machine for Kuwait.

The north shore of Bahrain lay flat below me as we circled to gain height, and the Qala'at al-Bahrain tell, which loomed so large in our work, could be made out as a tiny indentation in the plantations which line the coast. As so often before, and since, I tried and failed to spot the temple mound at Barbar as we swung out over the coast and toward the Saudi Arabian shore. The straits between Bahrain and Arabia seemed incredibly narrow from the air, and I tried hard to get some sort of impression of the Arabian coastline opposite Bahrain. If I could not spot our own diggings, there was little hope of seeing from the air any archæo-logical possibilities on the opposite shore. Yet this was probably as close as we would ever get to investigating the archæology there. It was well known to be exceedingly difficult to get permission to enter Saudi Arabia, and completely impossible if one was sus-pected of being an archæologist. Yet we had it on the authority of Sargon of Assyria that Dilmun was more than an island. There was a land frontier between Dilmun and Bit-Iakin, so that some-where on that forbidden coast there must be settlements similar to those we had found in Bahrain. But all I could see was the dark mass of the date gardens around Dammam and the bay of Qatif, before the plane swung north and began to follow the coastline towards Kuwait.

For an hour we flew low along the coast, where the yellow expanse of the desert met the blue expanse of the sea in a sharp line. Here there was no fresh water and no habitation, nothing but an endless sandy beach. Then we flew in over the land, and saw ahead the waters of the bay of Kuwait. We banked steeply over massed blocks of new concrete houses, ringed by a semi-cir-cle of dual-carriage-way road, with roundabouts strung along it like beads on a string, and we glided into the airport of Kuwait.

I had been only half prepared for Kuwait. I had seen it from the air before, and seen the endless streams of cars on the ring-road. But from the ground, as I sat beside the Agency driver, the mass of the traffic and the signs of explosive constructional expan-

sion were completely bewildering. Kuwait is a phenomenon without parallel in the East.

That its prosperity is founded upon oil is the grossest of plati-
tudes—and tells little. For over ten years I had been closely
associated with Gulf sheikhdoms whose prosperity was founded
on oil. But Kuwait's oil wealth is of a completely different order
from that of Bahrain or Qatar. Statistics of modern oil production
would appear to be out of place in an account of an archæological
expedition. But roughly the position is this.

Bahrain has for over thirty years had a nice steady income from
oil royalties, gradually mounting to a present figure of about
twenty million dollars a year. Since Bahrain is only about 230
square miles in area and has about 140,000 inhabitants, its oil
revenues, amounting to about 150 dollars a year for every man,
woman, and child on the island, make a very adequate contribution to the state finances. They enable a comprehensive program
of public works, public education, and public health to be maintained without any form of direct taxation.

Qatar is very much richer. With over four times the production
of oil and less than half the number of inhabitants it has an oil
income amounting to about 1500 dollars per head of population.
It was immediately obvious, on visiting Doha, that while Bahrain
was prosperous Qatar was booming, but its income was at that
time only ten years old, and Qatar is a much larger country, and
had longer to go to catch up.

But Kuwait has an oil production forty times that of Bahrain.
Every four months it receives in oil revenues more than Bahrain
has received in all the thirty years since oil was discovered there.
With twice the population of Bahrain, Kuwait has a yearly oil
revenue of three thousand dollars per head.

That is impossible to cope with. Try as it might Kuwait could
not spend the money as fast as it came in. The ministries which
had been hurriedly set up when the stream of oil began to flow in
1950 found that, however ambitious their plans for schools and
hospitals, roads and parks and harbours, money came in faster
than their materials could be delivered, faster than their architects could plan and their builders build. While in the rest of the

world time is money, in Kuwait money is time. With any project the decisive factor was not how much it cost, but how fast it could be done.

The town of Kuwait, the whole country, reflected this attitude. There was a feverish atmosphere over the place, everywhere immense unfinished buildings, and immense unsurfaced roads laid out to serve immense suburbs which were not yet even started, everywhere crowded streets of hurrying humanity, and everywhere the streams of new and shining automobiles.

By contrast the British Political Agency was a haven of rest, an island of stability in the frenzy of change. For the Agency was older than the oil boom and, built on a promontory by the shore, had escaped the attentions of the town-planners. And there, in the lofty rooms of a building redolent of the Indian Empire, I could look over what little was known of the history of Kuwait.

It did not take long. Kuwait's known history was scarcely two hundred years old. Carsten Niebuhr, of that earlier Danish expedition just two centuries before, had recorded the existence of the town of Kuwait, also called Grain, here on the southern shore of the deep bay running westward at the mouth of the Shatt al-Arab, where the Euphrates and Tigris enter the Gulf. It was a town of perhaps ten thousand inhabitants, he had said, fishers and pearl-fishers, but at the height of the summer, when the pearl-fishers were on the banks near Bahrain and the camel-trading caravans had left for Damascus and Aleppo, there were scarcely three thousand inhabitants left in the town. The ruling tribe here were the Utubi, who were trying to establish their independence from the powerful Bani Khalid, which dominated the coast from Bahrain to Iraq. When the sheikh of the Bani Khalid sent an army to Grain, added Niebuhr, the inhabitants sought refuge on the island of Failaka, which belongs to their domains.

At this time Kuwait must have been a recently founded town. Grain, more properly Qurain, means "the little horn," and is probably the name given to the promontory between the west-ward-running Bay of Kuwait and the southward-running Arabian Gulf, the promontory on which the town now stands. The name

Kuwait means "the little fort," and its establishment must have been the first step in the movement of the Utubi towards independence. In the years following Niebuhr's visit to the Gulf the movement had been successful. Not merely had the Utubi sheikhs held Kuwait, as they do to this day, but a powerful branch of the family had moved south. We have met it already. It was the Khalifah, who had taken up residence in Zubara on Qatar, and from there conquered Bahrain.

Now, Niebuhr had added, for good measure, that there was a "Portuguese castle" near Grain, and it was largely this statement which had induced the archæological enthusiasts of Kuwait to explore the island of Failaka. For there was without a doubt no Portuguese castle on the mainland; whereas on the north coast of the island of Failaka there were known to be the deserted ruins of a town with a fort. And the town was significantly called Qurainiya.

Failaka lies out in the centre of the entrance to Kuwait Bay, a good three-hour trip by motor launch from the mainland. It occupies in fact a strategic position in relation to Kuwait. From it the headlands on either side of the wide bay are visible, so that no ship can enter the bay unseen. Past Failaka sail all day long the succession of dhows plying between Basra on the Shatt al-Arab and Kuwait. They are one of the main supply lines to the inexhaustible market of Kuwait, but until recently they were Kuwait's lifeline. For they used to carry water. Kuwait had grown up around a few brackish wells, but had soon grown beyond their capacity. From that time Kuwait had been dependent for her very existence on water brought by dhow from the river system of Mesopotamia. With the coming of oil, and the consequent growth of population, the supply line was overstrained and dangerously vulnerable both to the vagaries of the weather and to political pressure. Kuwait had spent her first few millions looking unsuccessfully in its own territory for water—the story that whenever they bored for water they only found oil is apocryphal —and had then built the largest water-distillery in the world. She was now independent of water from Iraq, but still the dhows sail past Failaka, loaded with other goods.

Failaka was itself well supplied with water. By some whim of geology the water from the sparse winter rainfall does not run off to the sea or evaporate, but sinks to a water-table some six feet below the sandy surface of the island. Here it can be tapped by shallow wells, which soon run dry as they exhaust the water immediately around. But a new well dug a hundred yards or so away will tap new water, and so on. Corn had been grown on Failaka, it was said, until a very few years ago.

For many reasons, therefore, it seemed likely that Failaka was an older site of settlement than Kuwait itself. And indeed the island was said to be full of ruins. There was also an important shrine on the island, a place of pilgrimage for the Shi'ite sect of Islam; and that too suggested an antiquity which exceeded two hundred years.

And then, finally, the sole antiquity ever discovered in Kuwait had been found on Failaka—and it stood in the very room in which I sat reading. It was an irregular slab of limestone, on the face of which was engraved an inscription—in Greek. One corner had been broken off, but only one word had thereby been rendered doubtful. The inscription read: "Soteles, the Athenian, and the so[ldiers] (dedicated this) to Zeus the Saviour, to Poseidon, and to Artemis the Saviouress." The stone had been found nearly twenty years before, and entrusted for safe keeping to the Political Agent.

The inscription had caused intense speculation locally. It was clearly of classical Greek date, over two thousand years old. But what was an Athenian, with one or more companions (for the mutilated word which, in the light of later knowledge, is now translated "the soldiers" seemed then part of another name, and a woman's name at that), doing on an island in the middle of the Arabian Gulf? The theory commonly put forward was that they were survivors of a shipwreck, as indeed the designation of two of the deities as "saviours" seemed to confirm.

But it had certainly seemed worth while to look at Failaka, and on Failaka the town of Qurainiya seemed the most promising starting point.

It proved in fact to be the wrong point to start, for Qurainiya was no older than Kuwait itself. Sprawled over a shallow valley on the north coast of the island, its tumbled stone walls had yielded the unmistakable coarse glazed potsherds in turquoise blue which characterize the last two hundred years. And a careful survey of the fort, with a meticulous excavation of one of the corner towers, gave the same result. It was a round tower, typical of Arab fortification, and with no resemblance to the angular towers of the Portuguese forts.

As I studied the photographs and drawings and reports and potsherds of this very well conceived and executed dig I could not help feeling that such energy and enterprise had deserved a more exciting result. Had I known then what the island of Failaka was to yield I should have felt so even more. For it happens all too often in archæology that the professional reaps where the amateur has sown, and certainly in the Gulf we owe practically all the major discoveries to the perspicuity of observant amateurs and to their generosity in passing on their results to us. I hope that Sir Guwain Bell, now I believe Her Britannic Majesty's ambassador in Nigeria, and John Muir, still undoubtedly with the British Council somewhere in the world, are satisfied with our stewardship of the antiquities of the island on which they were the first to dig.

It was John Muir who next day escorted me to the Kuwaiti Ministry of Education, and introduced me to its deputy director, Darwish Miqdadi. Darwish was from Iraq, an elderly gentleman of the old school, courteous, soft-spoken, and scholarly, and it was difficult to credit the rumour that he had played a major part in Rashid Ali's rebellion in Iraq during World War II and served a considerable term of internment in consequence. His bland demeanour covered an astounding clearness of vision, and to him was in large part due the efficiency of the Education Department, which was building and staffing an average of ten new schools a year, had built a secondary school which would be expanded to a university just as soon as students had reached university level, and was converting one of the surviving forts of Kuwait into a temporary museum, at the same time as plans for a permanent museum were being drafted. The prospect of our perhaps finding

something to put into the museum appealed immediately to Darwish Miqdadi, and the obligatory half-hour of small talk over
coffee was followed by half an hour of incisive planning of an
expedition for the following year. When I next day took the plane
for Denmark I had in my briefcase the outline of the application,
already agreed to in principle, which we should make for an
expedition to be financed entirely by the Ministry and to survey
the whole country, with particular attention to the island of
Failaka.

There was nevertheless much to do in Denmark that summer.
With expeditions to organize to Bahrain, Qatar, and Kuwait, I
found myself pinned down to my desk among the shelves full of
potsherds throughout the months when the rest of the museum
staff were out digging in the Danish summer countryside. I was
running in arrears with the numbering of the potsherds; our
conservation department in its temporary hut behind the museum had only time to deal with such of our bronzes as were
actively attacked by corrosion, and the museum had no draughts-
man to bring our plans and section drawings into shape. Already
our expedition was straining the resources of a museum which
had never been planned to cope with large-scale Oriental archæological projects; and there was no lack of sincere well-
wishers to tell us that we should avoid the snare of uncontrolled
expansion of the expeditions beyond the stage with which the
background organization could cope. It is probable that they
were right, but we were already beyond the point at which we
could turn back. We had unwittingly started digging in the
centre of an archæological vacuum, and some law of cultural
ærodynamics was now insisting that we expand to fill that vacuum. When a new problem or a new area was brought to our
attention, and at the same time the means to investigate it were
proffered, we could only have justified a refusal to undertake the
work by convincing both ourselves and our sponsors that it was
completely without connection with the work we were already
doing. But the connections with the work we were doing were
also expanding rapidly, and certainly now included Kuwait. We
had just demonstrated Bahrain's involvement in a vigorous trade

with Mesopotamia in the second millennium B.C., and this trade must have sailed right past Kuwait and Failaka. And somewhere in that direction lay the frontier recorded by Sargon of Assyria in the seventh century B.C. between Dilmun and Bit-Iakin.

I have said little about Bit-Iakin, but in some ways it was a mystery second only to Dilmun. It was a land, as we have seen, south of Babylonia, south of Ur and all the well-known cities of Mesopotamia. The name Bit-Iakin had in Sargon's day been but recently given to the land; it means the House of Iakin, and Iakin had been a chieftain two generations earlier who had assumed the kingship and had been a thorn in the side of the Assyrian kings. But the land was very much older, and had previously been known to the Babylonians simply as the Sealand. As such it was frequently mentioned in the texts from the second millennium B.C. (we saw it at the end of the last chapter as the supplier of, oddly, ebony to Dilmun), and it had even more than once ruled the southern part of Babylonia. In particular in the sixteenth century B.C., when the Kassites conquered Babylon, the Sealand had established a strong dynasty of kings in south Babylonia, and had held the whole of ancient Sumer against the Kassites for more than two hundred years. And yet the Sealand, like its neighbour Dilmun, had disappeared from history, and no one knew where it lay.

So we could not claim an indifference to what there might be to find in Kuwait. The problem of an expedition there was purely one of logistics. And during the summer of 1957 we worked out a program.

We were eleven men who in the beginning of January 1958 left by air for Bahrain. Three were to go on immediately to Qatar, together with P.V., who would spend a fortnight there with them, selecting the sites, a field of grave-mounds and a ruined village in the northwest, and would then return. We had little anxiety for Qatar that year. The party there was in charge of Eigil, who was an experienced leader of expeditions, though in a somewhat different part of the world. He is one of the best-known present-day explorers of Greenland, and the greatest living authority on the prehistoric Eskimo settlements of Peary Land.

In the meantime I was to reopen the Bahrain diggings. This again was no difficult task, as our party was practically unchanged from the previous year. After three weeks, then, P.V. and I were able to leave for Kuwait, and a week after our arrival four further men were to leave Denmark for Kuwait.

That was the gamble. We had a week in which to explore a country about twice the size of Qatar, and to find suitable sites for the new party to dig.

Three days later we landed on Failaka. As we stood on the deck of the launch, lurching in the ground-swell of the backwash from the land, we could see the whole length of the flat white beach of the western coast of the island. It was less than three miles long, but behind the beach we knew from our maps that the island ran seven miles to the easternmost point. On our left the island ended in a rocky point crowned by a little knoll. This was the sanctuary of Al-Khidr, the Green Man, we had been told by the captain of the launch. On our right, to the south, the view was bounded by two low hills, one of them surmounted by a stone building, and these two hills were called Sa'ad wa-Sa'aid. Between the two, and immediately behind the beach in front of us,

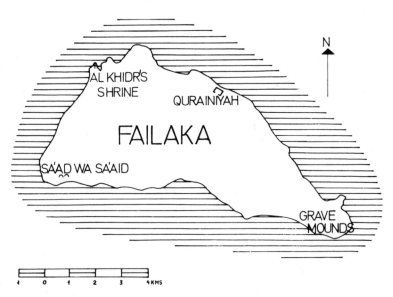

THE ISLAND OF FAILAKA, IN KUWAIT.

was the huddle of brown clay houses which comprised the village of Zor, the only village on Failaka.

There was no harbour, and no jetty. The launch held its position on the edge of the surf, with its engine running at half speed, while our fiercely bearded captain talked over the radio-telephone with the headmaster of the village school, to get a boat sent to fetch us off. For the launch belonged to the Ministry of Education, and was used to carry supplies, mainly of food, to the Failaka school, and to take the schoolmasters on their fortnightly week-ends to Kuwait town.

It was a dugout that came in answer to the radio, a long slim primitive craft hollowed from a single trunk, and it held its position with practised skill alongside the launch while we lowered our bags and tripods, and the ice-ax which I always carried, and finally ourselves. With bare centimetres of freeboard it turned and ran with the waves up and onto the shelving beach. We stepped ashore and were greeted in meticulous English by a foursquare man in a brown business suit, the headmaster of the school. Later, in his large study with the double row of armchairs leading off from his desk in true Arab reception-room style we met the rest of the staff, a half-dozen young men in European garb. They were all Palestinians, refugees from the state of Israel whose existence they refused to recognize, and they were pathetically anxious to emphasize the Western-looking spirit of the Mediterranean Arab. While P.V. and I had worn our *abbas*, the woollen cloak of the Gulf Arab, against the chill wind of the sea-passage, these teachers would make no such concession to the land in which they found themselves. Nor would it have been appreciated if they had. We were here to investigate Kuwait's past, but the Jordanians and Egyptians and Palestinians were employed to shape Kuwait's future, and that future lay in Westernization. The school was modern, built only two years before and still being extended, and the staff were enthusiastic innovators, clearly thrilled by the opportunity to introduce a modern system of education from scratch without regard to tradition or expense. The study was hung with drawings and paintings of local scenes done by the schoolboys, and with charts of attendance and progress. In the corridor outside we had seen glass cases with local collections of plants and birds and insects. We were taken to see the assembly hall with its stage and cinema projector immediately after we had drunk coffee. And even the coffee was the sweet Turkish coffee of the Levant, instead of the cardamom-flavoured coffee of the Gulf.

We were shown our quarters, a classroom on the upper floor which had been converted hurriedly, divided into a bedroom and a sitting-room. And then we were introduced to the doctor, a smiling Indian. He was to take us around the island, for he possessed the only presentable car on Failaka. The only other vehicle was the tank truck used by the school to fetch water from the pump-station on the outskirts of the village. We arranged to start with him after lunch and returned to our quarters to unpack. We were uncertain where and how we were to eat, but we need have had no anxiety. There had been an elderly Indian on the launch with us who had sat huddled miserably in his greatcoat on deck all the way over. It turned out that he was our cook. With the ingenuity which we were to find was the distinguishing quality of all Indian cooks he had established his kitchen at the end of the school corridor, and within minutes of our arrival he served us with a steaming dish of mutton cutlets, fried tomatoes, and French fries, arranged on a spotless cloth set with the monogrammed porcelain of the Education Department.

Replete and not a little somnolent, for we had been called at half past six to catch the launch, we set out to call on the Emir, the representative of the ruler of Kuwait on the island. He was Kuwaiti, and the coffee he served was cardamom-flavoured. And after coffee he and the headmaster climbed into the doctor's jeep with us. We drove along tracks which had been made by sheep and donkeys among sandy hillocks covered with sparse grass and thorn bushes which gave a deceptively green appearance at a distance. We were running along the northern flank of the whale-back of the island, and after a couple of miles turned downhill to the waste of stone walls which was Qurainiya. Here a twenty-minute wandering through the ruins and examination of the trenches dug the year before confirmed the impression of the potsherds. It was not here that we should seek the distant past of Kuwait. We went on, and were soon running along the eastern spit of the island, with the sea on both sides. At the final point there was a group of small knolls which even at a distance looked unnatural in shape. As they grew nearer we looked at each other and said "Grave-mounds." There were only five or six in all, and after our experience in Bahrain and Qatar we were not disposed to hazard a guess at their age without excavation—except that they were older than Qurainiya, older than Islam. We were on the right track, and we marked them down as worth digging, if we could find nothing better. And then we turned back, along the southern shore of the spit and over the backbone of the island to Zor.

The next morning we were up early and slipped away before school began. For it is only on foot that ground can be properly examined, yet an Arab feels that he has failed in hospitality if he does not provide a car for even the shortest trip. We left the southern outskirts of Zor, and crossed the pockmarked area where well after shallow well had been dug. And as we approached the southwest corner of the island the twin mounds of Sa'ad wa-Sa'aid rose smoothly in front of us. They were the most conspicuous landmarks on the whole island, two low broad humps rising from the flat plain about three hundred yards apart. From the sea and from the land they looked like tells.

Close at hand there was no doubt. As we walked up the slope of the taller, westernmost mound, twenty yards apart and with our eyes on the ground, we saw the innumerable potsherds which mark a settlement site. Among them I saw large fragments of flat baked brick, of a so very Mesopotamian appearance that I began immediately to turn them over, to look for the cuneiform stamps with which the kings of Babylonia and Assyria were in the habit of marking the bricks of their public buildings. We had no brick buildings in Bahrain, and my first thought was that we must have here come within the cultural zone of Mesopotamia. But there were no cuneiform inscriptions, and I turned to the potsherds. At this point P.V. strolled over, with the studied nonchalance which I by now knew meant that he had found something of importance. He opened his hand, and displayed three sherds—of thin, red, ridged "Barbar" ware.

As we looked, more and more of the Barbar sherds could be seen, mixed of course with sherds of more modern date, and even rags and cola-bottle sherds and bits of coffee-cups, for the southern corner of the island was a favourite picnic place. But we recalled that on the whole of the tell at Qala'at al-Bahrain we had never found a Barbar sherd on the surface. Here they lay in such numbers that there could be little doubt that the whole tell was of Barbar date, and had never been overlaid by other, later settlement.

Then slowly the shock began to register. This we had not expected. We were over 250 miles from Bahrain, and in fact a hundred miles closer to Ur than to Bahrain. We had expected Mesopotamian influence, perhaps even Mesopotamian colonization, in Kuwait; we had not expected Bahrain influence, or Bahrain colonization. Yet if the "Barbar culture" was the material manifestation of Dilmun, then Failaka too was part of Dilmun. In that case Dilmun was a lot bigger than we had dreamed. The distance from Bahrain to Failaka was the distance from Eridu, the southernmost city of Babylonia, to Eshnunna, its northernmost city. In geographical extent, then, Dilmun could measure up to Babylonia itself.

We had, of course, only two points at the extreme ends of this extent. We had nothing in between Bahrain and Failaka, except sea and apparently barren coastline. But no one had looked at these barren coasts—they belonged to Saudi Arabia, and everyone knew that Saudi Arabia was inaccesssible.

We traversed back across the northern slopes of the west tell, and crossed over the flat ground towards the east tell. Here on the level the fragments of red baked brick were more numerous, and now that our viewpoint was lower we could see a patch of irregular ground between us and the sea, halfway between the tells. We crossed to it, and found that the whole area, roughly square and about thirty yards across, was covered with tumbled bricks. Here and there we could make out the lines of walls. Here there were no Barbar sherds, indeed very few sherds of any sort. We passed on to the eastern tell.

This was lower than the western mound, and roughly rectangular in shape. The mound was higher on the edges than in the centre, clear evidence of defensive walling, and on the southern rim were two grave-mounds. As we walked over towards the northern edge, collecting pottery as we went, it became clear that the settlement here was of a completely different period and type from the first tell. Again there were no Barbar sherds, but the pottery here was just as well known to us as that from Barbar. The fragments I was collecting were those of the thin bowls, glazed or red-painted, which we knew from the so-called Greek layers at our Bahrain tell.

On our way over the tell we had seen a truck come lurching over the rough track from the direction of the village, and at the northern edge of the tell the headmaster and three teachers intercepted us, full of apologies that the truck had not been there when we needed it. With them was a venerable man in Arab dress, who was introduced as the caretaker of the school, a native of Failaka. We explained to them what we had found, that the western tell seemed to cover a settlement probably four thousand years old, of the date of Abraham the Friend of God, whom God preserved. And the eastern tell was more recent, but still ancient enough, of the time of Alexander of the Two Horns. At this the caretaker showed some excitement and, taking us by the hand, he led us along the northern rampart of the east tell to a point where a shallow sand-flooded excavation still showed a jumble of stones. Here, he said, he had himself been present some twenty years before when workers digging for stones to build a house in the village had found the stone with writing that was now at the Agency in Kuwait.

Our reputation was established. That we could, on the basis of a handful of potsherds, attribute a site to the time of the Greeks without knowing that it was there a Greek inscription had been found thoroughly impressed the gathering of schoolteachers. We were without a doubt most learned men.

We were equally impressed. We had not expected such rapid confirmation of our rather hazardous dating of the site. And certainly we had not expected that the site might not only be of Greek date but be actually Greek. Admittedly the theory of the shipwrecked Greek sailors on Failaka had seemed unsatisfactory, and now, as we looked over the evidence on the ground of a very considerable settlement, it was obvious that the "castaways" had been both numerous and energetic. This in fact was a permanent fortification. But could it really be Greek? Alexander's fleet, we knew, had passed this way, and the Seleucid empire of his successors had stretched as far as the head of the Gulf. Was it possible that we were standing here at a frontier post of the Seleucid kings?

One thing at least was clear. We need look no further for a site to dig. Here we had represented two of the most important periods of the history of the Gulf, and they were represented in a most convenient form. For whereas in Bahrain we had to dig away the "Greek" period in order to reach the Barbar period, here the two lay side by side. They could be dug simultaneously.

The digs had to be organized, and there was little time to spare. In three days' time our team from Denmark would be arriving, and one of those days was a Friday, the Moslem sabbath, when no work could be done. We arranged to return to Kuwait on the afternoon of the next day, Thursday, when the launch would be taking the weekend party of schoolmasters to the mainland. There we should have to buy all the miscellaneous equipment for a dig, picks and shovels and measuring tapes and earth-baskets, cord and pegs and notebooks and drawing paper, labels and pottery-bags and brushes and trowels. But first and foremost we needed workmen, and if they had to be brought from the mainland there would be further difficulties of tentage and food and water supply. We raised the question with the headmaster, but immediately the caretaker of the school broke in. There were men enough in the village, he said, who travelled each week to Kuwait to find casual work in the docks and the markets, but who would be glad to work for us here on their own island. When we came back next week he would have thirty men ready for us.

In the early afternoon of the following day we were on our way back to Kuwait in the launch. We had been out to the site once more, to decide where exactly to begin digging. For we had agreed, in a long evening discussion, that we should divide our forces. P.V., with two of the four newcomers, would continue the reconnaissance of the mainland which we had scarcely begun, and I, with the other two, would return to Failaka. I was to dig a *sondage* in the "Dilmun" tell, while Erling and Aage, both experienced excavators, would start on the "Greek" tell and the house site between the tells. After a week P.V. would round off his reconnaissance and come to Failaka with Poul and Torben, who would take over my *sondage,* leaving us free to return to Bahrain.

FROM ONE OF THE FAILAKA SEALS. A MAN HOLDS A MONKEY AT ARM'S LENGTH; MONKEYS WERE IMPORTED AS PETS FROM MELUHHA.

An hour before the launch was due we had borrowed the school's water truck with its driver, and had made the short trip to the northwestern point of the island, to look at the sanctuary of Al-Khidr. On a low rocky promontory, washed by the sea on three sides, lay a tiny steep-sided mound. On its top was a small circular enclosure, a wall about five feet high with a narrow entrance gap. As we clambered up the mound we could see clearly that it was artificial, that it was in fact a miniature tell, with the worked stone of previous buildings protruding here and there.

Within the enclosure on the summit, which was scarcely six feet across, stood a rough stone pillar, and nothing else. That the building was a place of pilgrimage was evidenced by the small flags and pennons and fluttering bits of bright-coloured cloth which had been planted among the stones of the wall, while bones of sheep and chickens lay everywhere around, and the central pillar was smeared with a dark stickiness which can hardly have been anything other than blood.

The driver of the school truck had told us the significance of the shrine, and his story had agreed in essentials with that recorded by the greatest authority on Kuwait, the legendary Colonel Dickson, whom we were later to meet. Al-Khidr, our driver said, was a saint who had been a friend of Moses. He resided normally at Kerbala in Iraq, the holy city of the Shi'a Moslems, but every Tuesday he flew to Mecca, and rested Tuesday night at this island shrine. And if a woman wished to conceive a son then she should spend Tuesday night in prayer at the shrine, and her wish would be surely granted.

I asked how old the shrine was, but he did not know. It had been pulled down several times, he said, by the government in Kuwait. I could well believe that, for the people of the mainland are of the more orthodox and puritanical Sunni sect of Islam, and could hardly tolerate a practice which smacked strongly of idolatry. But the Shi'a inhabitants of Failaka had always built up the shrine again, he added, and many people came to visit it, from as far away as India.

We had been unable to find any evidence, ourselves, of the date of the shrine; the abundance of potsherds was very modern. But scarcely a hundred yards from the sanctuary there lay two large flat mounds, and we had walked over to them. And on both we had found the red ridged sherds of the "Barbar culture."

As we relaxed on the carpet spread on the deck of the launch and looked back at the mounds at the northern and southern ends of Failaka's western coast still clearly visible above our wake, we had speculations enough to keep us wakeful for the whole of the three-hour run across the sunlit sea to Kuwait. Why had the Dilmunites of Bahrain settled here, so far north of their homeland? And what had Greeks—and Athenians yet—been doing there? And who was Al-Khidr? The name, in the Arabic, means merely "the green man," and told us nothing. How did a Green Man fit into the picture?

Three years were to pass before we knew the answers.

CHAPTER ELEVEN

ぺぺぺぺぺ

LOOKING FOR MAKAN

Exactly a month had gone by since the day when P.V. and I had sailed from Failaka on our way to meet our team at Kuwait airport. And now it was Bahrain that was dropping astern, sinking into the blue haze of distance as the little aircraft turned its nose to the southeast. At the window seven-year-old Annette was excitedly looking ahead for the coast of Qatar, while Michael, two years old, stared solemnly from Vibeke's lap at P.V.'s magnificent blue *abba*. All of which requires explanation.

The explanation lay folded in my pocket. It was a telegram which read: TWELVE TUMULI OF BAHRAIN TYPE DISCOVERED ON ISLAND OFF ABU DHABI CAN YOU AND PV COME—TIM.

I had known Tim for many years. In the old days, when I had been working for the Qatar Petroleum Company on Bahrain, Tim used to run down the Gulf from the Anglo-Iranian Oil Company's refinery at Abadan, with a large powered barge loaded with gasoline and lubricating oil. It was one of the anomalies of the oil business that, while our company in Qatar was producing crude oil in almost unlimited quantities, it had to purchase the gasoline to run its drilling rigs and its vehicles from elsewhere. Tim was the Abadan sales manager for the Gulf. Oddly enough, we had neither of us discovered, during these years, that we had in common a passion for archæology.

Since then many things had changed. Anglo-Iranian had been

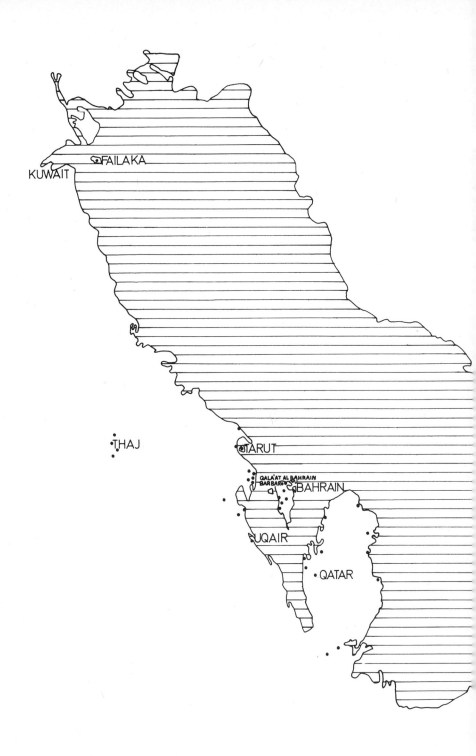

KUWAIT

FAILAKA

•THAJ

TARUT

QALA'AT AL BAHRAIN
BARBAR

BAHRAIN

UQAIR

QATAR

•JABRIN

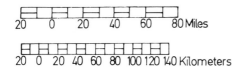

• SITES ON OR NEAR THE ARABIAN GULF
INVESTIGATED BY EXPEDITION

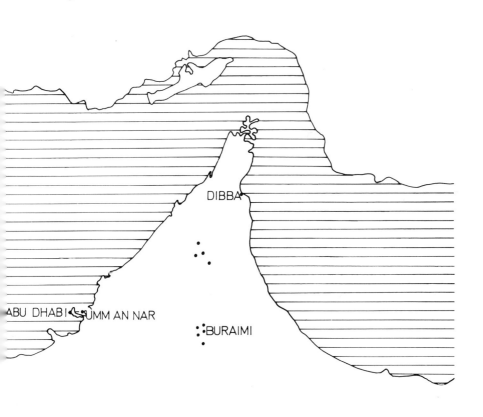

215

forced out of Persia, and had changed its name to British Petroleum. And to compensate for its loss of Persian oil it was expanding hugely elsewhere in the Gulf. It owned half the oil of Kuwait, and, in association with a French company, it held the concession to the seabed off the coast of Abu Dhabi in the "eastern basin" of the Arabian Gulf. And Tim had for some years been in charge of developing this concession.

When we first started digging in Bahrain, five years ago now, Tim had been living in Bahrain, running a house that was periodically invaded by a boisterous crew of French divers investigating the seabed. The following year he was housing an equally boisterous crew of Americans from a seismographic vessel surveying the geological structure of the same seabed. During both these years we had seen much of him, as he frequently visited our diggings and we frequently enjoyed the hospitality of his house. Two years before he had moved to Abu Dhabi, but still kept in touch during his frequent duty visits to Bahrain. Now, it seemed, instead of coming to see our finds he wanted us to come and see his.

The aircraft had now found its height, and droned eastward across the coast of Qatar. We were well north of the oil town at Dukhan, and I looked down on the unlikely chance of being able to spot the brown tents of our party against the brown sand; for it must be about here they were digging the ruins of the village of Murwab, in the hope of finding pre-Islamic remains below the early Islamic walls. But the brown waste continued uninterrupted, and Michael and Annette were falling asleep to the monotonous thrum of the engines.

Vibeke was looking south toward Dukhan, and I knew she was remembering the last time we flew together across the strait from Bahrain to Qatar, when we were leaving the Gulf eight years before. I had promised her then that she would come back.

Just a week ago she had landed in Bahrain with the two small children, a rather incongruous addition to a hard-working archæological expedition; and now they had been especially asked to accompany us to Abu Dhabi. There was reason for that too.

Abu Dhabi was the largest, and the poorest, of the sheikhdoms of the Trucial Coast. It lies beyond Qatar, where the coast of

Arabia begins to trend northward and eastward to the rocky promontory which almost closes the entrance to the Arabian Gulf, leaving only a scant thirty miles to the Persian shore. From there the coast trends southward again, facing out to the Gulf of Oman and to India.

Geographically, this eastern extremity of Arabia gives the impression of not belonging to Arabia at all. It is a mountain massif, joined to the rest of the land-mass by a low-lying plain over which now roll the red dunes of the immense sand desert known as the Empty Quarter of Arabia. The main mountain mass and the eastern seaboard facing the Indian Ocean form the territory of the Sultanate of Muscat and Oman, while the seaboard facing the Arabian Gulf consists of a string of small sheikhdoms whose independence is guaranteed by the terms of a truce imposed on them a hundred and fifty years ago under the guns of a British fleet. Since the signing of the truce the area has been known officially as the Trucial Coast; its earlier designation, the Pirate Coast, was equally well deserved, and it was the repeated raids by the heavily armed privateers of this coast on the ships of the British East India Company which had occasioned the fleet action of 1819.

Of the seven sheikhdoms of the Trucial Coast only Abu Dhabi is of any considerable size. It is the southernmost of the string, and its ill-defined boundaries stretch far into the Empty Quarter to the south, and a hundred miles inland to the east, to where the large oasis of Buraimi lies at the foot of the Oman mountains.

Until very recently the Oman peninsula had been perhaps the most isolated and least explored area of the whole world, and Abu Dhabi was the least known part of the Oman peninsula. When Tim had established himself there two years earlier there had only been one other European in the whole of the thirty or so thousand square miles of the sheikhdom, the British Political Officer. But with Tim's arrival the European population had been quadrupled, for Tim had his wife and infant daughter with him. For two years the little family had been living an isolated existence in the little coastal town which was the capital of the sheikhdom, and as soon as Tim heard that Vibeke and the children were with me he had followed up his telegram with an eager invitation to them to accompany me to Abu Dhabi.

We were now out over the deep water beyond Qatar, an expanse unbroken by the green shallows which line the shore from Bahrain to Kuwait and stretch almost all the way from Bahrain to Qatar. Here the blue of the sea formed a deep bowl to meet the blue of the sky, and we seemed to be flying in the centre of an azure sphere. My thoughts turned to the task ahead.

The area of operation of the expedition was expanding explosively. Abu Dhabi was as far to the east and south of Bahrain as Kuwait was to the north and west, and when we reached our destination we would be five hundred miles from our new diggings on Failaka. Surely Dilmun could not have extended over such an expanse. It was a distance greater than that from Ur to Nineveh, nearly half as far again as from Mohenjo-Daro to Harappa. If Tim's mounds were really "of Bahrain type," then Dilmun was a country the length of Babylonia and Assyria combined, larger than the whole extent of Upper and Lower Egypt, as large as the immense Indus Valley civilization. For a while I toyed with the idea of a Fourth Great Power in the East, and then, reluctantly, turned it down. The evidence was, on balance, against it.

Item, there was the peninsula of Qatar. We had by now reconnoitred sufficiently in Qatar to be able to state with some certainty that there were no remains of our Dilmun cultures there. And it was scarcely conceivable that a "Dilmun Empire" stretching the whole length of the Arabian shore of the Gulf would have had no settlements on the most prominent geographical feature of that shore, and one moreover within sight of its major centre on Bahrain. Item, Tim's twelve tumuli were far from being a sufficient basis for so extravagant an hypothesis. I was by now deeply suspicious of tumuli. Even on Bahrain we were now certain that there were tumuli of two distinct periods. While the vast majority, in the huge mound-fields covering the northern and western slopes of the escarpment, were undoubtedly of "Barbar culture" date, there were several hundreds on either side of the road south of the Portuguese fort which contained burials accompanied by the thin glazed bowls of our "Greek" period. And the tumuli of Qatar, of which we had now dug five, were equally certainly not of Barbar date. They had still produced no datable evidence, for the skeletons were unaccompanied by any grave gifts at all, but the chambers in which they lay were completely different in shape and construction from either of the Bahrain types. In the lands of the Gulf, where there was little depth of soil above bedrock, tumuli were a natural burial form, and could belong to any period.

And item, if there was a fourth great power then there was also a fifth. The Oman was a strong candidate for the site of Makan.

Any investigation into the location of Dilmun leads automatically to speculation about the location of the land of Makan. We have already met Makan, as the land whence came the copper for which the merchants of Ur sailed to Dilmun. But there was more to it than that. Dilmun and Makan were always being named together, often in the same sentence, and often together with a third land, that of Meluhha.

As we flew on over the blue expanse of sea, I tried to remember the more important inscriptions linking Dilmun with Makan. There was the earliest of them all, the boast of Sargon of Akkad, about 2300 B.C., that he "made the ships from Meluhha, the ships from Magan, the ships from Dilmun tie up alongside the quay of Agade." There was even the claim of Naram-Sin, the grandson of Sargon, in a rather suspect chronicle, that he "marched against the country of Makan and personally took captive Mannu-dannu, king of Makan." And Gudea, the famous governor of Lagash around 2130 B.C., at the time when the barbarians of Gutium ruled in Mesopotamia, had imported diorite from Makan to fashion his numerous statues. Some of the statues still existed, with inscriptions carved on them recording the fact.

And then there were the merchants' tablets from Ur, with their cargoes "for the purchase of copper from Makan," "for the purchase of copper, loaded on a ship for Makan." But that was in the earlier tablets, those of about 2000 B.C. By the time of Ea-nasir two hundred years later there were, it seems, no direct sailings to Makan. Now all the trade went through the entrepôt of Dilmun. But Makan was still known as a primary producer. So far as I remembered there were a number of lexicon texts from this very period, lists of produce with their country of origin. And there you met, in the lists of types of stone, "diorite: produce of Makan"; in the lists of metals, "copper: produce of Makan"; in the lists of types of wood, "palm-trees: produce of Dilmun, produce of Makan, produce of Meluhha."

It is all very commercial and matter-of-fact. There are no mythological texts; the gods of the Sumerians, who appear to have been almost more at home in Dilmun than in Mesopotamia itself, never visited Makan.

There had of course been speculation among the learned about the precise location of Makan, and as I recalled there were two major schools of thought. The one would place Makan in the Oman. Their reasons were twofold: there was the general consideration that Makan must be within fairly easy sailing distance of Dilmun, and the specific argument of copper analysis. A large number of copper objects from Mesopotamia of the period 3000–2000 B.C. had been analyzed, and the copper had been found to contain a slight trace, about 0.2–0.3 per cent, of nickel. Nickel is fairly rare as an impurity in copper, and a similar inmixture of nickel had been found in a single specimen of copper ore from what were reported to be "ancient workings" in the territory of the Sultan of Muscat and Oman, more precisely in the valley running from the oasis of Buraimi on the border between Abu Dhabi and Muscat down to the port of Sohar on the Muscat coast. A single specimen was rather slender evidence, but it was the only specimen to have come out of the Oman.

The other school of thought would place Makan in Africa, in the Sudan or perhaps Ethiopia! This rather surprising location was unfortunately based on very definite inscriptional evidence. For Makan, and Meluhha too, were frequently mentioned in the royal inscriptions of the Assyrian kings, in connection with their campaigns of conquest in Egypt around the years 700–650 B.C. And the inscriptions left no doubt at all that Makan and Meluhha were regions in Upper Egypt and further south. That of course seemed to settle the matter once and for all—but it didn't really. The commercial references to Makan and Meluhha ceased by about 1800 B.C., and the Assyrian kings first mention them again over a thousand years later. If Makan and Meluhha had been places of legend for a thousand years it was not at all impossible that the Assyrians, who had never had dealings with either country anyway, had been mistaken in locating them in Africa. After all, the Spaniards had called the islands of the Caribbean the West Indies because they believed they had reached India. And there is a settlement in Greenland called Thule because Roman geographers nearly two thousand years ago told of a land in the far north called Ultima Thule which might have been, but was not, Greenland.

Of course it is rash, and perhaps presumptuous, of us to say that we, over a span of four thousand years, are cleverer at identifying the Makan and Meluhha of the Ur traders than were the Assyrians over a gap of only one thousand years. And the onus of proof rests with us and not with the Assyrians. But it is difficult to fit an African location to the text of the Ur tablets or to the facts of archæology. Distance alone was a factor, and though I had never been conservative in my estimation of the distances which trading vessels could cover I could not ignore the fact that the sailing distance from Bahrain to Africa was twice that from Bahrain to India. Ivory and gold, which were products of Meluhha, could come equally well from Africa and from India, but the carnelian of Meluhha could only come from Rajputana in India. And surely if Meluhha was in Africa there was a very disturbing omission in the trade goods. One of the major imports of the Egyptians from *their* trading expeditions down the Red Sea to the south was frankincense, grown then as now in the Hadramaut in southern Arabia. Surely frankincense would have figured in the texts of imports from Dilmun if the ships from Makan and Meluhha had sailed the whole length of the Hadramaut coast.

Most significant was the evidence of archæology. Most of this evidence, admittedly, was negative; there were no imports from Egypt in the Mesopotamia of 2000 B.C., and no imports from Mesopotamia in the Egypt of that date. There were no settlements of that date discovered in Africa at all, apart from Egypt; no African civilization which could have produced the "Makan chairs" and "Meluhha tables," or the "multi-coloured ivory birds of Meluhha." On the other side there was positive evidence, in the

form of the "Dilmun" seals, that Mesopotamia had traded with
he Indus Valley civilization; we might expect, then, that the
name by which the people of the Indus Valley designated themselves would occur somewhere in the Mesopotamian tablets. The
only likely candidate was Meluhha (and there was even the
suggestive use, by the Sanskrit-speaking Aryans who had entered
India from the north and—probably—overthrown the Indus
civilization, of the non-Sanskrit loan-word *mleccha* to denote
non-Aryans, people who did not worship the Aryan gods, and,
perhaps significantly, users of copper. Could it be that *Mleccha*
was the Indus people's own name for themselves and their
country?).

Ahead of the plane I could see a line of light brown, almost
white, encroaching on the blue. It was the coast of the Oman, and
it was time to abandon speculation. As with so many problems of
prehistory an ounce of exploration was worth a ton of theory. As
with the reading of cuneiform, there comes a time when the
evidence available has been squeezed dry of all that it will give,
and the only recourse is to go out and find more evidence.

Our plane came in low over the town of Abu Dhabi, a brief
glimpse of a white beach, clusters of *barastis*, an imposing tur-
reted fort, and the white sand again. It seemed alarmingly close,
and I looked for the airport. But it was not until we banked in a
sharp turn that I saw two rows of black-painted oil-drums marking the approach to a stretch of salt-flat. Beside them stood a
small hut, and beside the hut a land-rover. Our wheels touched
with scarcely a jar on the packed sand, and the land-rover started
towards us as we rolled to a halt.

"Nice that you could come," said Tim, as we jumped down.
"Come and meet Susan and Deborah."

The heat was a shock after the coolness of the flight, a bright
dry heat, fiercer and more invigorating than the cloying warmth
of Bahrain. A second land-rover drove up as we chatted with Tim
and Susan and the pilot, while four-year-old Deborah and two-
year-old Michael took stock of each other, and the Arab driver
and an Indian clerk unloaded provision boxes and mail bags from
the plane. Other bags were loaded, and the pilot waved his hand
and climbed aboard again. "Back for you in three days," he said

to us, and taxied to the end of the runway, and took off in a plume of dust. We distributed ourselves in the two cars and drove to town.

I shall always be glad that I saw Abu Dhabi before the oil came in three years later. For as Abu Dhabi was then, so must all the towns of the Gulf have been before the great oil adventure started. There had been no passport officers or customs officials at the "airport." There was in fact no air service; the strip had been built by the oil company, and the only planes to use it were those chartered by the oil company. And there was no road from the airstrip to the town. At the edge of the salt-flat the sand began, deep, white, and floury. The land-rovers, on low-pressure tires, ground downward through the low register of gears, ploughing with their four-wheel drive hub-deep through the drift-sand. Ahead, a single line of palm-trees stood incongruously in the sand, with the bulk of the whitewashed fort to the left and with the cluster of *barastis* beyond. We slid between the trees and among the huts, with rangy hens and lean goats scattering before us, and donkeys browsing incuriously on scraps of paper in the shadow of the *barasti* fences.

Winding among the huts, the furrows in the sand which alone marked the road led out to the shore between two white cement buildings, the police headquarters and the office of the oil company. This was the centre of the town, and here stood groups of lean bearded men in brown *abbas,* with crossed bandoliers of cartridges, each bearing in the centre of his belt a dagger in an oddly bent sheath ornamented with silver thread. Women passed among them, less unobtrusively than we were accustomed to from the more northern sheikhdoms, and though they wore the usual long black cloak over their heads they were unveiled.

We turned and ran eastward through the deep sand of the beach, to the outskirts of the town and the large cement house which was Tim's home.

The cool, white, high-ceilinged house, with its tiled bathrooms and deep verandahs, was an unobtrusive monument to the organizing ability of a great oil company. It seemed a little thing that there were electric lamps and flush toilets, and taps that ran water when they were turned. And then you did a double take, and realized that there was no water and no electricity in Abu Dhabi. To obtain running water the company had to put up a distillation plant; to run the distillation plant they had to put up an electricity generating plant; to land the generator and the distillation plant and the cement and the tiles they had had to build a jetty, and to bring it to the site they had had to build a road. The deep armchairs and the spring mattresses, the table linen and the sporting prints on the walls, all had been shipped in from England. As we sipped a before-dinner drink Tim told us of the months while the house was being built, when they had lived in shacks and tents on the site, and the only water was six months old in cask, rainwater collected the previous winter and stored in barely cleaned kerosene drums, and little Deborah had had dysentery and there had been no flush toilets then. . . .

We retired to shower and change for dinner, a dinner for which most of the food had come by air in refrigerated containers from the oil-company operating base on Das Island. But the main dish was local, Tim explained, as he carved what appeared to be a most excellent joint of beef. It was only after we had commented favourably on its taste that he informed us that we could, if we wished, boast that our first meal in Abu Dhabi had been roast mermaid.

It was dugong, he said, sea-cow, the seal-like mammal which is still to be found, though rarely, in the mangrove swamps along the Trucial Coast and which, seen swimming upright by the early mariners in the Indian Ocean, had given rise to the myth of the mermaid.

Dinner had been served early, for at eight o'clock Tim and P.V. and I were to call on the ruler of Abu Dhabi. It was a ritual of the desert sheikhdoms which could not be omitted, and which we had no wish to omit. Every stranger arriving in a town or a tribal encampment, every townsman or member of the tribe returning from a journey to distant parts, calls on the sheikh at the first opportunity after his arrival, to tell his news and to state his business. For the sheikh is the ruler and protector of his people, and he needs to know everything which passes in his kingdom. Morning and evening he holds his *majlis*, his public "sitting" to which anyone may come, to give his news or air his grievance, or merely to greet his ruler, sip a cup of coffee, and slip quietly away again. Even in the rich oil sheikhdoms the custom is still honoured in theory. Though there secretaries and chamberlains winnow the visitors, and the signing of a guest-book is substituted for the ritual arrival visit, the *majlis* is still held night and morning, and the right of the subject to meet his monarch may be discouraged but is never denied. Here in Abu Dhabi, where visitors were still rare, it would have been the gravest discourtesy not to attend the first *majlis* after our arrival.

So in the darkness before moonrise Tim's land-rover ploughed through the deep sand towards the white bulk of the royal fortress, with its crenellated ramparts reflecting the starlight, and halted before the iron-studded gate. The sentries, with their rifles held loosely but unmistakably covering us, shouted for the watch commander, who opened a low portal in the gate and conducted us into the hall of audience. From the upholstered armchair at the end of the room Sheikh Shakhbut of Abu Dhabi rose to greet us.

Sheikh Shakhbut was middle-aged, thin, and black-bearded, with an ascetic, almost melancholy, face and lively brown eyes. My recollection of our first meeting is seriously disturbed by the fact that, some years later when the oil money began to roll in by the millions of pounds, he became deeply suspicious of everyone, including archæologists, but I know that my first impression was entirely favourable. He was intensely curious about our work, with an intelligent appreciation of the problems involved in archæological research in virgin territory and of the light which it could throw on the origins of his people and his country. He knew of the island where Tım had found the mounds. It was called Umm an-Nar, he said, "Mother of Fire," and in his father's day idols had been found on the island, stone figures of animals, which must have been made in the Time of Ignorance before Islam. They had of course been immediately smashed and thrown away. But there might perhaps be more, with inscriptions to tell us who the people were who had made them. We explained that written inscriptions were not essential. Almost every Arab we meet, from our workmen to the sheikhs, is firmly convinced that we are looking either for gold or for *târîkh*, inscriptions, things with writing on them. And we constantly try to explain that things without writing are also evidence. If you look at a copper coffee-pot, I tried to explain, you can see from its shape whether it was made in Dubai or in Niswa, in Bahrain or in Damascus. If we find a pot on Umm an-Nar island we may, if God will, be able to say that it was made in Iraq at the time of Abraham the Friend of God, and so we should know that ships sailed here from Iraq at that time. He looked thoughtful. Maybe you will find things from Ur, he said, and I knew that he was better informed than most.

As the bitter coffee went the rounds in the little handle-less cups Sheikh Shakhbut leaned forward, with the lamplight gleaming on the gold-handled dagger at his belt. Who were the people, he asked, who had lived in Abu Dhabi in the Time of Ignorance? Were they Arabs? It was too early to say, we answered, but we hoped to be able to tell him after we had looked at their monuments.

The next morning Tim and P.V. and I set out for Umm an-Nar. It was a good half-hour's drive, first through the deep sand as far as the airstrip, and then out onto the firm sand-flats. Abu Dhabi town itself lies on an island, separated from the mainland by a narrow strait scarcely covered at low tide. The threat of Bedouin raids has, even within living memory, been very real to the towns and villages of the coast, and most are sited more with an eye to protection from attack from the landward than from the seaward side. (That this has been true throughout history is witnessed to by the fact that all our major sites are on islands, Bahrain itself, Failaka, and now Umm an-Nar. And there are more to come.) The strait which guarded Abu Dhabi had itself been guarded. Out in the water stood a tall round tower, loopholed and with its entrance high up on the seaward side. Here, once the access rope or ladder had been drawn up, two or three men with matchlocks could cover the crossing, and from the flat roof could signal by beacon to the sheikh's fort, which, significantly, covers the southern approaches to Abu Dhabi town.

Now the round tower was deserted, and a narrow cobbled causeway had been built across the strait. But the threat was not forgotten. On the landward side of the causeway lay a modern, whitewashed fort, like something out of *Beau Geste,* and smart khaki-clad police, with repeating rifles and field radios, held the causeway against unauthorized passage. We showed our passports, and our permit from the sheikh, and drove out into the Arabian desert.

We had not far to go. For the last four miles before the causeway we had been able to see the dark whaleback of Umm an-Nar to the left across the salt-flat and the water beyond. Tim had pointed out to us the tiny patch of green on the northern end which was, he said, the only palm-tree on the island, and he had even claimed to be able to see the burial-mounds. Now we turned north along the low limestone ridges of the mainland and then down onto the coastal salt-flats. Umm an-Nar was a low dark hump before us, and between the salt-flats and the island we could see the mast and lateen rig of the sailing boat which had been sent round during the night to ferry us to the island. It was not easy to approach. This was our first taste of the real *sabkha*, the treacherous salt-pan of the coast, and time and again we would drive out on seemingly firm salt, and have to swing sharply back as the surface began to quiver and the wheels of the land-rover to dig themselves in. But a wide circuit eventually brought us out on the drier sand immediately above the beach, where we could remove our sand-boots and stockings, roll up our trousers and wade out to the boat.

The actual crossing was scarcely two hundred yards broad, though scored deep by the tide race, and we waded ashore on the island and crossed the broad tidal flats to eroded limestone cliffs where the island in reality began.

Umm an-Nar is a small island, scarcely a mile in either dimension. In the south low cliffs ring a stony dome, and when we came out upon this plateau we could see why Umm an-Nar had appeared darker than the yellow islets around. Its surface was covered entirely with flint.

It took only a moment to assure ourselves that the flint was a natural deposit. We had met the same phenomenon in Qatar, acres and acres covered with slabs and splinters and broken sheets of flint. For flint is formed by chemical action in limestone, and, since limestone is a sedimentary rock, laid down in horizontal deposits of seashells and skeletons of sea creatures, the flint too tends to form in horizontal layers within the stone. But limestone is a soft rock, easily weathered away by wind and rain, whereas flint is almost everlasting. Here, therefore, as in Qatar, a limestone layer had been weathered completely away from above and below a flint layer, leaving the flint lying on the surface.

We began at once looking for artifacts as we walked over the solid bed of flint, but to look for a needle in a haystack would have been child's play by comparison. We were looking in a haystack for a straw with a knot in it, looking for a piece of flint which had been shaped by man among millions of pieces which had been shaped by nature. You need a special sort of eyes for this type of work, and I have not got that sort of eyes. But P.V. has, and in the ten-minute walk across the flint dome he picked up three discards, pieces struck off during the fashioning of a flint tool. They were enough to show that man had been there before us, during the long past of the Stone Age.

The dome ended abruptly after half a mile, sloping steeply down to a level stretch covered with sparse grasses. Beyond, the ground rose again to a level limestone plateau, not so high as that on which we were standing. And on this plateau the works of man stood thickly. To the west a low wall marked the site of a cistern, dug, Sheikh Shakhbut had told us, in his grandfather's day to collect rainwater. Whenever it rained—which was not every year—they would sail across from Abu Dhabi to Umm an-Nar and fill casks with the water which had drained into the cistern. By the cistern wall stood the scrub palm which was the only tree on the island. The rest of the plateau was covered with grave-mounds. There were at least fifty, heaps of tumbled stone, some quite small, but a few measuring quite twenty yards across and six feet or so in height.

We hurried across the level ground towards the mounds, but halfway across Tim stopped us, to show us the wall-footings of a little square building and, close beside it, a sudden hole in the ground. We might like to look at this, he said; it was admittedly natural, a pot-hole formed by water action in the limestone, but there was water in the bottom, undrinkable now but it was the only water on the island, and it might once have been fresh.

He leaped cheerfully into the hole, and looking apprehensively

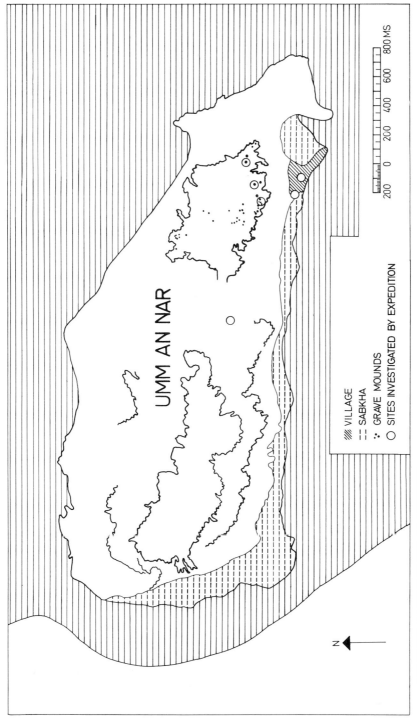

THE ISLAND OF UMM AN-NAR, IN ABU DHABI.

VILLAGE

SABKHA

GRAVE MOUNDS

SITES INVESTIGATED BY EXPEDITION

UMM AN NAR

N

200 0 200 400 600 800 MS

down, we saw him standing in a slope of debris which rose up to within five feet of the surface. We followed more circumspectly and, as our eyes accustomed themselves to the gloom after the blazing sunshine outside, we saw the roof of the cavern arching down towards the foot of the talus slope on which we stood. We scrambled cautiously down, and soon could hear the stones which rolled from beneath our feet splashing into water below us. The narrow pool of dark water between the talus and the wall looked cool and fresh and inviting. But its taste puckered the mouth. Loaded with alkali as it was it could not, even in the worst straits, be used for man or beast. We scrambled up the crumbling slope and clambered out of the fissure at the top, blinking in the light and blanketing heat of the noonday sun.

The plateau, when we reached it, was a naked sheet of rock, with only a thin spread of pebbles and a few sand-drifted hollows. Erosion had been at work along the plateau edges, undermining the rock and forming overhangs and breaking off large bites, so that, though the plateau was scarcely a man's height above the sand plain, it was surprisingly difficult to find a place to climb up.

The burial-mounds were—burial-mounds. More could not be said of them. Cairns of stones, irregularly placed, of irregular sizes, perhaps rather low in relation to their diameter, they looked like stone burial-mounds from anywhere in the world, from any date or culture. On two of the largest we could see traces of a ring-wall, but this meant little. More often than one realizes a burial-mound possesses a ring-wall, a circle of stones set before the mound is built to mark where its perimeter is to be. They prevent the material of the mound from sliding outward, and make the monument more imposing and more regular. So they are the rule rather than the exception. Only in course of time the material of the mound always does in fact slide down and cover the ring-wall, so that in many cases it cannot be seen on a first reconnaissance.

The ring-walls that were still visible on the two large mounds were exceptionally fine. They were cut limestone blocks, a foot high and nearly three feet long, with their outer faces curved to follow the circumference of the mound, and their edges cut to fit neatly against each other. They suggested that the mound-builders had cared more for the appearance of their monuments than the tumbled piles of stones would otherwise indicate.

But of the identity or date of the mound-builders there was no evidence. On or around the mounds there were no potsherds, which alone could have given us a line. This was in itself a promising sign. For it suggested that the mounds had been left undisturbed since they were built, nor were there any telltale hollows in the tops of the mounds such as we find with such depressing regularity on the Bahrain mounds, and which tell of robber pits dug down to the central chamber. If we could find the means to dig these mounds we should almost certainly find the evidence which was so conspicuously lacking outside them.

We gathered by the palm-tree to discuss the matter, and to look at the cistern, a large oblong walled pit with dried and puckered mud in the bottom and with the plaster of its walls piously inscribed with the name of Allah the Compassionate the Merciful. The afternoon was already well advanced, and we had been quartering the ground among the tumuli for nearly three hours in the blazing sun. P.V. pronounced judgment; the mounds were undoubtedly burial tumuli and undoubtedly pre-Islamic. They were rather above the average in size and care of construction, and this was in itself a matter for amazement here on a waterless island off a waterless coast hundreds of miles from any other known pre-Islamic site. They were of some considerable age, for at one point erosion had eaten into the plateau since their building and removed half a mound. They would undoubtedly repay digging, but he did not see how we could dig them.

The more we discussed ways and means the more obvious it became that we could not dig on Umm an-Nar. To establish and supply a camp on the island would require a full-fledged expedition. Provisions and workmen would have to be transported daily from Abu Dhabi town; much of the supplies, and probably even water, would have to be brought from Dubai, the nearest town with a well-equipped market, a hundred miles up the coast. The project would be expensive, and we had no money. In Bahrain and Qatar and Kuwait we had received grants from the sheikhs and from the oil companies, but these three lands were rich with the wealth of oil. The grants they gave us were for work in their own territories, and could not be diverted to Abu Dhabi. It would be useless to ask Sheikh Shakhbut for money which he had not got. The oil companies, undoubtedly, were rich enough; B.P. stood behind Tim, and the on-shore concession was held by a subsidiary of my old company, Iraq Petroleum. But both companies were in the exploration stage here; for perhaps years to come all their entries would be on the debit side of the ledger, and until they paid their own way they could not be expected to pay ours. It was a promising site, we said regretfully, but if it was to be dug it would have to be by a richer museum with independent resources of its own.

In the meantime there was a question which remained to answer. Where had the people lived who were buried in the mounds? Their settlement could hardly have been elsewhere than on the island, and was probably close to the shore. We spread out again, to make our way back to the ferry dhow along the shoreline.

I was crossing a low rocky promontory only a hundred yards from the mound plateau when I noticed that my boots sank more deeply than usual into the sand of the hollows. There was a different feel to the surface, and I began to dig down with the ice-ax which appears so incongruous in the tropics, but which is such a superlative entrenching tool. Only inches below the surface I came upon ash, mixed with scraps of animal bones and a few nondescript potsherds. Here were undoubtedly the ruins of occupation, and I called to Tim and P.V. We had little time for investigation if we were to reach home before sunset and the swift onset of the tropical night, but a cursory examination of the promontory was sufficient to make out the almost buried courses of stone walling. Here there had undoubtedly been a settlement, though whether it was of the same unknown date as the burial-mounds could not be determined. For here too there were no potsherds or artifacts on the surface, and we had no time to dig. Like the mounds, the settlement would have to wait until someone could organize an expedition.

The sun sank lower as we trudged, somewhat wearily, along the beach, until the boat came in sight on the south of the island. Again we waded out and sailed across the channel to the waiting land-rover, and drove home in the gathering dusk.

That evening, over the before-dinner drink, we had much to tell each other. For Vibeke and Susan and the children had also had an eventful day. They had been invited in the afternoon to call on Sheikha Miriam, the young wife of the ruler, in the harem section of the palace to which no man may be admitted. It would be a breach of the privacy with which the Arab surrounds his domestic life were I to repeat Vibeke's description of the sheikh's family and their life. But it is fair to deny a general misconception of a sultry harem life shot through with intrigue, discontent, and sex. Vibeke found the sheikh's wife and sisters gay and charming, full of laughter and curiosity about life in Denmark. She found it odd that they wore their indigo-blackened face-masks even inside their home, but they found it equally odd, and rather shameless, that European women went uncovered, and Vibeke showed proudly the mask which Sheikha Miriam had given her, in order that she might at least observe the proprieties in her own home.

We spent two more days in Abu Dhabi, exploring with Tim the Arabian mainland inland from the coastal *sabkha*. It was a country of rolling white sand dunes and long low limestone ridges, and it was desolate as not even Qatar was desolate. There was no worked flint; there were no cairns or burial-mounds. Only on the track to the oasis of Buraimi in the interior, which we crossed occasionally in our quarterings, was there any sign of man, the half-obliterated tracks of tires, the scattered whitened bones of a camel, and, very rarely, the sight in the distance of a camel train, five or six camels with a man walking ahead and another behind, on their five-day journey from Buraimi with loads of firewood for the coast.

On the second day we returned early, for the plane was due in the early afternoon. It did not come, and the radio in Tim's office reported that it was held up on Das Island with engine trouble. With our bags packed, and the children fidgeting impatiently, we waited as the sun began to decline. It was almost sunset before news came that repairs had been effected and the plane would be leaving to pick us up. We drove out through the sand to the airstrip as the sun sank, and listened for the aircraft engines, while Tim tried to raise the pilot on the radio in the tiny control shack. Dusk was gathering, and there were no landing lights and no provision for night landing on the Abu Dhabi strip. If it got much darker the plane would have to turn back for Bahrain without landing. Finally the pilot came through, cheerful and confident. He would be over us in ten minutes and would see if he could get down. Dusk was falling with alarming rapidity, and we could ourselves no longer see the barrels which marked the ends of the runway. Tim sent his two vehicles to either end of the airstrip and ordered the drivers to turn their headlights onto the surface, and five minutes later we heard the engines of the plane and saw it glide over us like some huge night-bird. It banked and turned and came down, skimming above the roof of the further land-rover, whose headlights shone on the silver underbelly as the plane touched down in a perfect landing.

We said goodbye to Tim as the passengers from Das, four unconcerned Bedouin, alighted with their bedrolls, and we climbed on board for the long night-flight to Bahrain.

In this year of exploration up and down the Gulf we had scarcely had time to look at what was going on in Bahrain—and no time at all for our team in Qatar. So two days later P.V. set forth on a long-overdue visit to Qatar, while I brought myself up to date on the diggings in Bahrain.

In all our excavations buildings had been taking form this year. Beyond the moat of our Portuguese fort, where P.V. had dug his first hole down to the bath-tub-coffins in 1954, there was now, four years later, a very considerable square pit, almost twenty yards square, and almost twenty feet deep. Within it rose the fifteen-foot walls of our putative palace, where the great hall was now cleared. It had proved to be the entrance court, and a monumental doorway stood open in the southeast corner, at the head of a narrow street running along the south wall. A semi-circular channel in the wall, and the hollowed hinge-stone below, showed that the newel-post of the gate had been a considerable pillar of wood, capable of bearing a very massive gate. And indeed the proportions of the doorway, only four feet wide but nine feet high to the lintel, were much the same as those of the gateway to Shalmaneser's palace at Balawat in Assyria. Shalmaneser's gate had been of wood sheathed in bronze, and the bronze sheathing, with its reliefs of Assyrian warriors, is one of the treasures of the British Museum. Here there were no bronze doors, but the resemblance was one more piece of evidence for our tentative dating of the palace to the Assyrian period. Perhaps in very truth Uperi, king of Dilmun, had trod the massive threshold stone on which our surveyor's level was now set up.

Behind the northern city wall, in what had up to now been my own particular dig, Hans had been clearing the houses to the east of the street with the well. They consisted of small stone-walled rooms, built to the same rectangular plan as the street itself. Every wall ran due north-south or due east-west. The room that abutted on the city wall itself was of more than ordinary interest. Here was another well, and behind it, in the thickness of the wall, a flight of steps leading upward towards the vanished parapet. It must have been a guard-room, where the "watch below" could relax from their picket duty. And the well had supplied water to the sentries standing guard in the blazing sun on the ramparts.

I had hoped for more seals from this area, but Hans had none to show me. Instead it was Peder and Helmuth who proudly displayed one of the typical dot-and-circle seals. It was from Barbar—proof, if proof were needed, that the Barbar temple and the "Barbar" levels from the city were of the same culture.

I hardly recognized Barbar when I drove out to see it. The whole southern face of the temple had been cleared, and the walls of the successive terraces upon which the temple had been built stood visible in all their length. I stood at the foot of the stone stairway which mounted to the top of the terrace wall of the phase 2 temple, and far above me I could see the edge of the flagged court with its altar and central plinth. This was the same temple court into which, four years before, I had looked down from the top of the covering mound. Now it seemed immeasurably far above. It began to look as though the Barbar temple was in truth a ziggurat, drowned in sand. For where I was standing

must have been ground level when the temple had been built, yet
I was ten feet below the present desert surface. Ten feet of sand
must have drifted down upon Bahrain in the four thousand years
since the temple was built. What else might ten feet of sand not
cover?

I began to suspect then that the Barbar temple might well be
part of a much vaster complex. It had always seemed implausible
that the temple had stood alone, out in the open country three
miles from our city at Qala'at al-Bahrain. It might well be that it
was the temple-tower of another city, the only structure which
still rose above the encroaching sand. We still do not know how
valid this speculation may be. We have never dared to dig beyond the confines of the temple. For were we to find another city
it would be beyond our resources to excavate it—at least until we
are finished with our present city.

This could take many years yet. When you stood on the edge
or at the bottom of our excavations on the city tell of Qala'at
al-Bahrain, the excavations seemed immense, and the buildings
uncovered within them imposing enough. But stand on the ramparts of the fort, and look out over the wide area of the tell, and
the two holes in the ground sink into insignificance. To the south
and to the west and particularly to the east of our excavations the
tell stretched unbroken. It might hide anything. How could we
be sure that we were digging in the right places? Was the "palace
of Uperi" really the principal building of City IV, the Assyrian
period? Or would we have found equally imposing buildings
wherever we had dug? And where were the palaces of the merchant princes of the Ur tablets, a thousand years and more earlier? And between them City III, the Kassite period, was still
represented by nothing more than rubbish pits. Surely they, too,
had built temples and palaces.

I began to realize how lucky the diggers of Mesopotamian
cities and Indus Valley cities had been. In Mesopotamia the
ziggurat rises unmistakably in every city, the stepped mound of
brick marking the spot where the principal temples and palaces
and royal graves are grouped. In the Indus cities of Harappa and
Mohenjo-Daro the citadels had been unmistakable, built higher

than the residential areas and a little apart from them. Here surface indications could tell us nothing.

We had indeed been struck by the thought that the Portuguese fort itself might have been built above the ancient citadel, or even conceal a ziggurat, and Paul had spent two years digging a deep *sondage* within the walls of the fort a stone's throw from the camp. We had found quite a fine building of our so-called Greek period, City V, digging down with some precision into its bath-room and toilet, and below that we had found nothing—depths of occupation debris of our Barbar city, but no signs of buildings except a few insignificant-looking walls at the very bottom. No important buildings had lain here.

In a way half our work had been accomplished at Qala'at al-Bahrain. We knew now how many cities there were, and the approximate date and salient characteristics of each. We knew the history of the site in depth. Now we needed the history in breadth, the extent, plan, and important features of each of the seven cities. It was a large order. In fact it was work for a permanent archæological institute running a yearly full-size expe-dition of twenty or thirty experts. And yet it was only a single facet of our frighteningly expanding sphere of operations. The Barbar temple, even if we carefully refrained from finding *its* city, would still take several years to finish. Qatar had been producing more and more flint sites every year, and P.V. had

THE CURVED DAGGER OF THE OMAN, WORN IN THE CENTRE OF THE BELT BY EVERY MAN OF THE BEDOUIN.

gone over there with plans for making a systematic Stone Age survey of the whole peninsula, which would keep three or four men busy for three or four years. And Kuwait looked like developing into another Bahrain, with several sites each deserving full-scale attention.

And now there was Abu Dhabi. I still did not see how we could possibly dig the grave-mounds of Umm an-Nar. But it seemed a pity to turn our backs on the only known prehistoric site on the Oman peninsula. Perhaps, another year, four or five of us could hitch-hike down on an oil-company plane for a weekend, and dig out one of the smallest tumuli ourselves, and be flown back in time for the start of the week's work in Bahrain.

Then one day we had visitors. It was no unusual occurrence, for we were, after all, one of the show-places of the island. Not only did residents of Bahrain visit our digs in large numbers, but visitors passing through the island were frequently brought out to see the island's ancient monuments, and our guest-book in the camp contained a surprising number of famous autographs. These visitors were two very eminent persons, who at their own express wish must be nameless. And while I was showing them round our excavations they mentioned that they had spent some days in Abu Dhabi, and that Tim had taken them out to see the tumuli on Umm an-Nar. "He said that you would very much like to dig the tumuli," said one of the visitors. "How much would you need for a season's digging there?"

I had to think fast. Three men, say—a *barasti* built on the island—hire a truck and a driver to carry workmen back and forth, and to bring provisions and water—about a dozen local workers—food—fares, freight, insurance. "I think we could put in a season's work for two thousand pounds," I said. And they said no more.

But when we closed the camp a fortnight later, and when I got back to the museum in Aarhus at the end of April, a letter was lying on my desk from our two distinguished visitors. Providing we could get permission from Sheikh Shakhbut to dig on Umm an-Nar, it read, they would be willing to contribute up to the amount of two thousand pounds.

We were going to look for Makan, after all.

CHAPTER TWELVE

IKAROS

I stood on the edge of the excavation, and looked down into the temple courtyard, with a strong feeling of *déjà vu*. Somewhere, all this had happened before. And then it came back to me. Six years before, the Barbar temple had looked like this. There was the same flooring of rectangular stone slabs of varying sizes skilfully fitted together, the same walling of squared and chiselled limestone blocks, preserved to the same height, one massive course about two feet high and an occasional stone of the next course. And just as clearly as in the case of Barbar, this was a temple.

But it was a very different sort of temple. And as I looked up from the excavation and around, the sense of familiarity faded. Here was no steep-sided mound with palm groves below, but a bare flat mound surrounded by bare flat desert, and beyond it the bare flat blue of the sea. Behind me, a scant three hundred yards away, was the other tell, higher and somewhat steeper, with Oscar's chequerboard of square excavations spreading out over the summit and down the slopes.

It was 1960, and two years had gone by since I had dug the first two squares of that chequerboard on the western tell of Sa'ad wa-Sa'aid on Failaka, and Erling had begun to trace the perimeter walling of the eastern tell on which I was now standing. We had had reason to believe even then that the eastern tell might well cover a settlement of Alexander's Greeks. And looking down

239

again at the temple I could see that there was no longer any doubt. The temple below me was as Greek as the Parthenon.

When I had remarked, rashly, that the resemblance to the Parthenon was more apparent than real, Kristian had been to some pains to prove to me that the resemblance was more real than apparent. There was the same "cella," or inner precinct with its plinth for the statue of the temple deity. There was the same entrance hall, and the two pillar bases at the entrance showed that there had been a pillared facade with a typical triangular gable. He proceeded to point out the capital to one of the pillars, which even I could recognize as Ionic, and a set of "acroters," the free-standing ornaments above the gable, the angles of which gave him the slope of the roof. As he described it the temple rose again before me, a little shrine—it measured only twenty-five by forty feet—of what appeared to me to be of purely Greek charac-ter (though Kristian could spot, he said, Persian influences). And all this over fifteen hundred miles away from Athens.

The reader has met Kristian before. In fact he too had looked down on the emerging Barbar temple, and had worked on its excavation for three years. He is an architect, and a classical archæologist, and I have presaged earlier that we would, in the fullness of time, find a use for his special qualifications. He had not been with us during the last few years, for he had been offered a professorial chair in classical archæology. But when, the year before, the first pillar of the Greek temple had appeared in our section trench, we had known upon whom to call. A Greek temple, in a Greek town, in the Arabian Gulf was, we knew, enough to tempt any classical professor out of his study.

That it was a Greek town was now beyond doubt. It had been strongly indicated the first year, when we had dug the large brick house between the tells. It had turned out to be a workshop for the production of terra-cotta figurines. We had found the kiln in which the figurines were fired, and we had found a large number of fragments of the moulds in which they were formed. Some moulds we could reassemble, and with plaster of Paris ourselves manufacture copies of the products of the foundry. The range was entirely Greek. There were draped and undraped female figures, one not unlike the Venus de Milo, one an almost perfect miniature of the Victory of Samothrace. And there was a man's head in shallow relief that we could all recognize as Alexander the Great himself, represented as the sun-god with rays radiating from his head.

The second year had clinched the matter. For that year brought a wine-jar handle, stamped with the vintner's name in Greek and with the rose which was the trade-mark of Rhodes. That they drank Greek wine was of course not conclusive proof that the inhabitants of Failaka had been Greeks, but it did determine the date as third century B.C., just the period when Alexander's successors, the Seleucids, had ruled the whole sweep of land to the north of Kuwait, from Syria through Mesopotamia and Persia to India. And we knew that some, at least, of the inhabitants wrote Greek, worshipped Greek gods, and bought—or perhaps sold to passing sailors—Greek terra-cottas.

Now the Greek town lay before me, the clean-cut plan of the temple, with the plinth of the altar across the road opposite the temple entrance (I think it was Kristian who informed me that the altars of Greek temples always stood outside the temple proper), and beyond the altar the fortification wall of the town, of stone and seven feet thick. Beyond the wall there was a clear field of fire twenty-five feet wide, and then an immense moat, fifteen feet wide and fifteen feet deep, V-shaped and stone-lined.

On either side of me, and behind, swept the ramparts of the little fortified town, with corner towers and with gateways to north and south. Erling, who had begun the excavation here two years before, was still following the wall, and was even now engaged in clearing the south gate. The fortifications were of complex structure, and showed signs of having been altered and added to during a fairly long period of use. The north wall in particular could be shown to be later in date than the rest, and Paul had just demonstrated by a deep cutting that the original north wall could be traced below the later houses in the northern part of the town, that the town had been extended to the north some time after its first establishment. The original town had in fact been precisely square, with its walls running due north-south and east-west. It began to look like a military encampment, and it may very well have originally been just that.

My speculations were interrupted by the blowing of whistles, and the workers began to climb up from their excavations and stream over towards the tents which dotted the flat area between the tells. It was lunch-time, and the sharp blast of a horn behind me called me over to the expedition truck which was waiting to take us back to town. Imran, who was driving the truck, greeted me boisterously, for I had only arrived from Bahrain that morning, and I had not seen him since the year before.

Throughout the three years Imran had been the official representative of the Kuwait Museum on our dig, though this year he had been joined by a new representative, the director-designate of antiquities, Tareq. Tareq was a young and debonair and enthusiastic Kuwaiti; Imran was a Palestine exile and an ex-taxi-driver.

Imran's was a typical story of Kuwaiti improvisation to achieve modern standards with utmost speed. When the Israeli-Arab struggle for Palestine ended in 1948 Imran found himself in Jerusalem, and he got a job as driver to the American School of Archæology there. For many years he drove archæologists to and from their diggings in Jordan, often helping them in their work, often showing visitors around the excavations. He thereby picked up the archæological jargon and a considerable knowledge of practical archæology, as well as an ability to recognize and date the commoner types of architecture and pottery. But after nearly ten years he left Jerusalem, like so many Palestinian refugees, to seek his fortune in the new Kuwait El Dorado. He became a taxi-driver, but soon found that Kuwait was flooded with taxi-drivers, and that no fortunes were to be made in that trade. It was just at that time that the Kuwait Museum was opened. It was not an archæological museum—there was at that time no archæology. But with praiseworthy vision the Education Department had seen the importance of preserving, in the maelstrom of modernization, a picture of Kuwait as it had been before the oil adventure began. They had taken over an old fort, engaged an expert from the Egyptian museum service, and given him six months and unlimited funds to collect and exhibit what could be rescued of old Kuwait. He had done a magnificent job. House architecture, ship building, pearl-diving, and Bedouin life were all illustrated by original artifacts and accurate scale models; the oil company had contributed a geological wing, and there was an incipient natural-history collection of the plants and animals of Kuwait.

Imran quoted his Jerusalem background, and got a job as one of the custodians of the new museum. And then our diggings started.

Kuwait reacted to the acquisition of a prehistory, complete with ancient monuments, by the application of a three-phase routine which they have employed with success in many fields. They appointed the nearest available man to look after the problem temporarily; they imported the greatest authority available to carry out a survey and make recommendations; and they put out a call for an interested young Kuwaiti who could be sent abroad to train to take over. In that way the problem is covered on an emergency basis, while a permanent organization is planned. And by the time the permanent organization is ready to function a permanent Kuwaiti controller will be trained to operate it.

Thus the director-general of antiquities of one of the major archæological countries of the Middle East had advised on the blueprinting of a model Directorate of Antiquities for Kuwait. And Tareq had spent a year with us in Denmark learning the trade. But Imran had been Kuwait's emergency solution to the problem of what to do about archæologists who, contrary to expectations, turn up two forgotten civilizations in your backyard.

And with us at least he had established his reputation as an archæologist almost at once. For he taught us to recognize mud-brick.

Mud-brick, walling built of clay formed in a mould and then dried in the sun, is one of the archæological traps of the Middle East. The ancient towns of Mesopotamia and Syria were built almost exclusively of these bricks, and the earth of the tells of these countries is largely composed of the disintegrated and collapsed remains of mud-brick houses. In this clay fill, it is almost impossible to distinguish the mud-brick walls which are still standing; and the books of reminiscence of even the most distinguished archæologists almost all contain some cautionary tale of walls dug away before they were recognized. It had been worse with us, for we were not expecting mud-brick. We had come from Bahrain, where the ancient architecture is entirely of stone, and when we came to dig the fortification wall of the Greek town on Failaka we had cut a very neat section to expose the full width of a very satisfactory stone footing of the wall. And then Imran came along, and borrowed a trowel, and began scrapping the exposed sides of our section trench. And as we followed his work we began to see the regular lines of clay mortar between clay bricks, and realized that we had dug clean through a substantial mud-brick superstructure to the wall. From that moment we forgot that Imran was "only" a taxi-driver—except when his skill at repairing the ramshackle jeep which Kuwait had lent us reminded us that he had other valuable abilities.

This digression had occupied my mind as we bumped over the rutted road toward the village, and swung in before our headquarters.

Here too Kuwait had shown what can be done when expense simply does not signify. During our first season we had been quartered in a classroom in the school. Last year, on arrival, we had found a block of rooms built and waiting for us at the far side of the school-yard. Bedrooms and a bathroom, common-room and kitchen, storeroom and office were complete and furnished, with an Indian staff of three to make us comfortable. This year a new wing had been added, to give us a bedroom each, a dark-room, and a laboratory.

The position of the expedition in Kuwait was very different from in Bahrain. In Bahrain we received our grants from the government and the oil company, and we were left alone to use them as we saw fit. While Sheikh Sulman and many members of the government showed a keen interest in our work it was a private and personal interest. If we wanted to borrow a bulldozer or a crane from the government it was always possible, but it was arranged on a personal, man-to-man basis with the state engineer or the head of the Transport Department. The absence of official cognizance of our existence in Bahrain was at times somewhat worrying; we were never sure whether we had in fact permission to dig where we dug, or to camp where we camped. I recall the occasion when we were to dinner with the Bahrain chief of police, a cousin of the ruler, and over coffee he mentioned that he owned the temple tell at Barbar, where we had been digging for five years in the belief that it was public land. He accepted our rather bewildered apologies, and cheerfully gave us his belated permission to carry on. There was in fact no one in the Bahrain government with the duty of supervising our activities, or of looking to the safety of Bahrain's antiquities. As a result, although our agreement with the government there called for a fifty-fifty division of what we found, we had no one to divide with, and for years we had taken everything back to Denmark, on the clear understanding that the division would be made just as soon as a museum was built or an antiquities director appointed.

In Kuwait things went very differently. There the Education Department had assumed full responsibility for our excavations from the start. They not merely paid all the expenses of the expedition and supplied our luxurious board and accommodation. They had recruited our workmen, and themselves dealt with all their pay and food and accommodation. This relieved us of a very great deal of administrative work, for we had now over sixty men working for us, and these were very many more than the single village of Zor could supply. The call for workmen must have gone out throughout the Gulf, for our men were of all Arab nationalities from Iraqi to Muscati, with even a few from Aden and Somalia. Many of the Iraqis were even professional archæological workers, who had dug with the German expeditions at Warka before the war. There was no accommodation in Zor for so many men, and the government had put up a tented camp on the level between our two tells. Food and water were supplied by boat from the mainland, a three-hour sail away. Had we had to arrange all this ourselves we should have needed two extra men on the expedition staff purely for administrative work. As it was, every member of our fourteen-man expedition in Kuwait could concentrate on the archæological problems.

Nor was it only the expedition which was thus cossetted. The sites too were looked after. After the first year fences had been put up around each of the diggings, and now a perimeter fence was going up around the whole area. The disposal of the earth dug up in the course of excavation is always a headache, for unless it is dumped a very expensive distance from the diggings it always proves to have been piled precisely where you want to dig the following year. But in Failaka dump-trucks went to work as soon as the expedition had finished each season's work, and all the loose earth from the diggings was carted away and dumped in the sea.

So Kuwait was a luxury dig, as we from Bahrain never tired of pointing out, with none of the problems which beset the normal expedition. On the other hand the government also extended its guardianship to the objects dug up, and after the second season an Antiquities Law had been promulgated, similar to the laws generally current in the Middle East, laying down that all ancient objects found in the State of Kuwait were the property of the State of Kuwait, and could not be removed without its permission. This is as it should be; it is manifestly unreasonable that irreplaceable treasures of a country's history should be the property of a museum half the world away. But this was the first season that we were to operate under the new law, and it remained to be seen how literally it would be applied. We hoped that the Education Department would realize that there was in reality no conflict of interests involved. We had no desire to fill our museum's galleries with the treasures of Kuwait—our museum had no galleries available. At most we should like, some time in the future when we had room, to fill a small gallery with typical artifacts and pottery from all the cultures we had found throughout the Gulf—and when that time came Kuwait was more likely to complain that we gave too little space to *their* culture, than that we displayed objects which should be in Kuwait. What we needed to take home were the scientific specimens, the boxes of stratified potsherds, the collections of animal bones, the soil samples and carbon samples. And for Kuwait's own sake we hoped to be allowed to take to Denmark the objects which required conservation treatment which Kuwait could not give, the objects of bone and of metal.

Among these was one of the two major finds which P.V. and I had come from Bahrain to see. Kristian took it out of its labelled box while we sat at the common-room table and passed it to us. It was a solid lump of purplish metal, but we knew that the purple colour meant silver. And the shape of the lump revealed its nature. It was a hoard of silver coins, thirteen in all, corroded together into a single mass. To Kristian's experienced eye the size and weight of the coins told their tale. They were silver *tetradrachms*, undoubtedly Greek. Before they were cleaned of their corrosion and separated from each other, more could not be said. They might have been minted by Alexander himself, or by any of the following Seleucid kings. When that could be determined they would give us a very certain line on the date of the Greek town on Failaka.

The hoard had been found the week before, outside the temple and a little way north of the altar. And by great good fortune it lay just where Kristian had cut a north-south section through the altar and out to each side of his broad excavation. So its stratigraphic relationship to the temple was absolutely certain. The section was now dug away—it was while digging it away that the silver hoard had come to light—but his drawings showed clearly that the hoard was later in date than the temple, contemporary with a series of later walls that had been built over the clear space which had originally surrounded the temple complex.

The same section had, on the other side of the altar, encountered the second big find, one which would certainly not be taken out of the country.

Our team had been puzzled, when they excavated the temple, over an odd block of stone just by the southeast corner of the temple, to your left as you entered the building. It was an oblong block, clearly still standing where it had always stood, and in the upper surface was a square hole, as though to take a post. Now we had the explanation. For the new find south of the altar was a large rectangular slab of stone, with a square projection at one end which exactly fitted the hole. The slab had originally, then, stood upright outside the entrance to the temple. And upon the slab was engraved line after line of Greek.

It was a long inscription, forty-three lines in all, and while Lennart, our photographer, was shooting it from every angle and at every angle of the sun in order to get as clear a definition of the lettering as possible, and Gunnar, our conservator, was preparing to take a latex impression of the slab for later study, Kristian was doing his best, without aid of lexicons, to read the message. It was not easy, for the slab was badly weathered, and when it had been wrenched from its position and thrown down by the altar it had been broken into seven pieces, and some of the surface had flaked off. Already, though, the general nature of the inscription, and some of its phrases, were beginning to appear.

The first six lines were in the form of a letter from a certain Anaxarchos. Then, after a space, the rest of the inscription was another letter, addressed to Anaxarchos from a man named Ikadion. Immediately after the opening greeting came the only two lines which were reasonably clear: "The king concerns himself with the island of Ikaros, for his ancestors. . . ." Damage again intervened, and for the rest of the inscription only a word or two on each line could be made out. There seemed to be frequent references to a temple and to ceremonies, and mention of "the inhabitants of the island" and "the letter."

The interpretation seemed to be that Anaxarchos had been the local governor and had received a letter from his superior, Ikadion, instructing him in the king's name to build, or perhaps to maintain, the temple on the island of Ikaros. He had sent on the letter to the commandant of Failaka with a covering note of his own, ordering that the king's command be carried out, and that, when it was done, both letters should be inscribed on stone and set up outside the temple. What we had found was in fact the foundation document of the temple.

Naturally Kristian had been looking with all his might for a date on the inscription, or for the name of the king who had "concerned himself with the island of Ikaros," but it had proved impossible to find either. But what we had was important enough. We knew now that we were standing on the island of Ikaros.

We had long suspected it. And to explain why will require one of the digressions of which this book is so unavoidably full.

The first discovery of traces of actual Greeks on Failaka had diverted us from our search for cuneiform references to Dilmun to a search of the classical authors for any mention of the Arabian Gulf in classical times. They proved to be quite numerous.

In the course of five hundred years, from before 300 B.C. until nearly A.D. 200, about a dozen writers, historians, geographers, botanists, and just plain travellers and sailors, had recorded what they knew of the Middle East, the area which lay to the south of the empire of Alexander, and later to the east of the Roman Empire; and all of them included the Arabian Gulf in their survey, sometimes briefly, sometimes at length. Almost half of the works are no longer extant, but they are quoted, sometimes verbatim, by later authors, so that probably very little which was ever recorded is now lost. Both Strabo, who lived during the last sixty years B.C. and wrote a geography in Greek, and Pliny, who lived a hundred years later and wrote his *Natural History* in Latin, give particularly full accounts of the Arabian Gulf, based largely on three or four lost writers of the previous two centuries. Their accounts of the Arabian shore of the Gulf are not entirely consistent with each other, and both contain a number of names of bays and headlands which we have difficulty in identifying today. But they mention the island of "Ichara," not far from the mouth of the Euphrates, though without giving us any information other than the name. And they tell of an island further south, called Tylos, which cannot be other than Bahrain. This identification has been regarded as certain for many years, and we had known of it long before we began work on Failaka. It is clinched by the fact that a smaller island off Tylos is given the name of Aradus, and we all knew the village of Arad on the island of Muharraq across the causeway from Manama on Bahrain. Attempts have even been made to derive the name Tylos from the name Dilmun—which by the vagaries of the Babylonian script can equally well have been pronounced Tilmun—but the possible connection is too flimsy to bear any weight.

A third place mentioned by both writers has roused much interest, the city of Gerrha. I shall have much to say about Gerrha later, when we began to look for it. It was a large and important walled city, it was said, on the mainland of Arabia not far from Tylos, which traded by sea with Babylon and overland with the frankincense lands of southern Arabia. But Pliny and Strabo differ radically in their accounts of its location, Pliny setting it upon the coast and Strabo sixty miles inland.

At the moment, though, our main interest was in Ikaros, and here we found our fullest information in the latest of our authorities. Around A.D. 170 a historian named Arrian wrote an account, in Greek, of the campaigns of Alexander the Great five hundred years earlier. Fortunately for us he sought out contemporary records, and for the greater part of his description of the coastal regions from Babylonia to India he availed himself of the log of Alexander's Cretan admiral Nearchos. After Alexander's campaign through Persia in 326 B.C. he had crossed the Indus River in present-day Pakistan and pushed deep into the Indian sub-continent before turning south to the coast near the present site of Karachi. There he constructed a fleet and, while he himself marched back with his army through southern Persia, he ordered Nearchos to take the fleet back along the coast of Baluchistan and Persia. The log of Nearchos gives a very detailed description of this coastline, sufficiently accurate to enable almost every natural feature to be identified with certainty. After Nearchos rejoined forces with Alexander at Babylon he was given the task of exploring the coastline of the Arabian peninsula. For Alexander was planning a campaign of conquest against Arabia, incited, says Arrian, by reports of the wealth of the peninsula in myrrh and frankincense, cinnamon and spikenard, and also by the fact that the Arabians had sent no envoys with offers of submission. Nearchos went methodically to work, it seems, sending out three successive ships to cover successively more distant stretches of the coast of Arabia. The first ship reached Tylos, and the third the entrance to the Gulf, at Ras Musandam.

Though Arrian says that the aim was to send a vessel completely around Arabia, the reconnaissance to the mouth of the Gulf was apparently sufficient for the immediate campaign, which was at this point set in train. And then, three days before the Arabian campaign was to begin, Alexander caught fever and died. Nothing more is heard of the plan to conquer Arabia—nor indeed of Nearchos, a circumstance which produced its crop of romantic daydreams among the more fanciful antiquaries of the nineteenth century. Nearchos is supposed to have set sail according to plan and, receiving no orders of recall, to have carried on to found white colonies in the heart of Africa or to initiate the Polynesian colonization of the Pacific.

Be that as it may, his reconnaissance in the Arabian Gulf gives us, via Arrian, a most trustworthy account of our Arabian coast of two thousand years and more ago. Alexander, says Arrian, was "informed of two islands in the sea near the mouth of the Euphrates. The first was not far from its outlet, being about 120 stadia from the shore, and from the river mouth; it is the smaller of the two, and covered all over with thick wood; there was in it also a shrine of Artemis, and the dwellers about the shrine themselves performed the daily services; it pastured wild goats and antelopes, and these were reserved as sacred to Artemis, and no one was allowed to hunt them save any who desired to sacrifice to the goddess: on this excuse only might anyone hunt, and for this purpose hunting was not forbidden. This island, according to Aristobulus, Alexander commanded to be called Ikaros, after the island Ikaros in the Aegean Sea. . . . The other island was reported to be distant from the mouth of the Euphrates about a day and a night's sail for a ship running before the wind; it was called Tylos; and it was large, and neither rough nor wooded for the most part, but the sort which bore garden fruits and all things in due season."

So the Ikaros on which we stood had received its name by command of Alexander himself, and it had held a temple of Artemis before ever the temple which we were excavating had been built. That temple had presumably not been in the name of the actual Greek goddess, but of some deity which the Greeks identified with their own Artemis. What deity that had been we did not know, perhaps a moon-goddess such as Ningal of Ur. Nor did we know where this earlier shrine would have lain. For it was not below the Greek temple. Kristian's section trenches proved that.

There was one place where it could have lain. And it was the one place where we could not look. But more of that later.

In the meantime there was the other of the twin tells of Failaka. While we had been examining the Greek temple inscription in the yard of the archæologists' wing and discussing it over the lunch table, Oscar, who was in charge of the diggings on the other tell, had been biding his time. Finally we turned to him and asked for news from his excavations. For answer he waved a hand to a sheet of paper on the wall above the dining table.

At first sight it was a simple home-made calendar, a list of the dates since the excavation campaign began. But opposite each day there was a number, one or two or three, occasionally four, and opposite one day, ringed around with red, the number seven. Just occasionally there was a blank. We looked our enquiry. "Seals," said Oscar, modestly. We stared incredulously, silently totting up the figures.

We had known there were seals to be found on F3, as we called the western tell of Sa'ad wa-Sa'aid. From the moment when we had found "Barbar" sherds on the surface two years before we had expected a settlement of that seal-using culture to lie there. I had even found the first seals myself, in my first *sondage* on the tell in 1958, three stamp-seals, two of which were of the typical "Barbar" dot-and-circle type, while the third—the first to be found—was a new variant, lens-shaped and double-sided. And the year before the first large-scale excavation of the tell had given the first indication that seals were very much more numerous here than in Bahrain. Thirty-five seals had been found that year, more than twice as many as had at that date been found in all Bahrain. But the total shown by the calendar on the wall was incomparably more than that. My first rough total was eighty-five, and the season was hardly half over. And now Oscar began to produce tray after tray full of matchboxes, each carefully numbered and each containing a seal. In the time at our disposal we could not examine each one in the detail which it deserved, but he picked out the more exciting specimens for us: a double-sided seal with a cuneiform inscription, a seal showing a woman playing upon a harp ornamented with a bull's head like the one of copper which we had found in the Barbar temple, and a seal bearing upon its face an inscription in the unread characters of the Indus Valley cities. Apart from the four or five double-sided seals and—significantly, perhaps—the seal with Indus script, every seal was of what I thought of as "type 3," the latest of my series of forms, that with the four dotted circles and three grooves. The one with Indus script was of no known type, thin and flat with a little high boss.

A SINGLE SEAL FROM FAILAKA BEARS AN INSCRIPTION IN THE UNREAD INDUS SCRIPT.

And then Oscar produced other trays, full of the other objects which had come from his excavation. There were beads and amulets, copper needles mounted in bone handles, and fragments of stone bowls of the same steatite as was used for the seals, many ornamented with figures of men and animals in relief. And among them was a fragment showing portions of two standing human figures, with between them a short inscription in cuneiform characters.

Now Oscar was more at home with runes than with cuneiform,

while it happened that I had, many years before, studied the script of Mesopotamia. My abilities were hardly sufficient to read any inscription at a glance, but as I looked at this fragment I realized that this was not necessary. I had seen this inscription before. It was identical with the first line of the inscription which Captain Durand had found upon Bahrain eighty years before:

e_2-gal ᵈIn-zak—"the temple of the god Inzak."

This was an inscription hardly less important than the dedicatory inscription of the Greek temple. For it meant that this bowl had been part of the inventory of an earlier temple, which probably lay beneath the F3 tell, a temple dedicated to Inzak, the tutelary god of Dilmun. And it went far towards explaining the phenomenal number of seals found in a tell which up to now had produced only the remains of quite humble houses.

So four thousand years ago there had been a temple of Inzak on Failaka; and two thousand years ago a temple of Artemis, as well as a factory for producing votive figurines of Greek gods and goddesses. It began to look as though Failaka had for some millennia been a holy island, a place of pilgrimage. As the idea went home I suddenly recalled that Failaka was still a holy island, still a place of pilgrimage. Was it possible that there was here a bridge across a gulf of four thousand years?

I recalled the shrine of the Green Man, of Al-Khidr, on top of its tiny tell on the northwest point of the island. The Education Department had more than once suggested that we should excavate the shrine and the tell beneath, and I knew that the government would have no objection to its disappearance. For though Al-Khidr is one of the saints of Islam, and as such a perfectly respectable figure, in the eyes of the Kuwaitis of the Sunni sect the rites and traditions associated with the shrine were idolatrous. But though the shrine might well cover that earlier temple of Artemis of which Alexander had heard, we did not dare to undertake its excavation. We had too many friends among the people of Failaka, who like the pilgrims are of the Shi'a persuasion, and to interfere with their sanctuary would alienate the whole island.

But as I considered the mounting evidence that Failaka had for millennia been sacred I decided that I would have to look more closely at the figure of Al-Khidr.

Like so many other lines of enquiry, the investigation into Al-Khidr was shelved through pressure of events; and it was some years later that I first came back to the question—and then in the course of quite a different piece of research.

What happened was this. A member of the film unit of the oil company on Bahrain, John Underwood, conceived the idea of making a film of our work in Bahrain, and for two years cameramen followed our excavations at Qala'at al-Bahrain and Barbar, while John himself collected footage in Denmark and the British Museum. The film, when it was finally submitted to our inspection, proved to be a major work of art. It did far more than present our diggings. John, who was brought up in archæological circles, had summarized the whole argument for the identification of Bahrain with Dilmun, and for the importance of Bahrain in Sumerian mythology and as a waystop on the ancient trade routes. Inevitably he emphasized the importance of Bahrain's plentiful springs of fresh water, and—quite casually—offered an explanation of the name Bahrain. *Bahrain* is good Arabic, and means simply "the two seas"; and no one has ever been able to explain the reason for the name. John suggested in his script that the one sea was the salt water of the Arabian Gulf, and the other was the fresh water which here welled up to the surface.

This explanation, apparently so far-fetched, struck me forcibly, for I knew that the Sumerians and the Babylonians believed in the existence of a sea of fresh water which underlay the earth and the salt sea, that *abzu* or Abyss which we have already met, and which appears in the Bible as "the waters under the earth." And I had already noticed that the Abyss kept cropping up in the wings, as it were, of all the myths about Dilmun: it was Enki, the god of the Abyss, who had given water to Dilmun; it was Enki who intervened to save Ziusudra from the Deluge, and Ziusudra settled in Dilmun; the text of the Gilgamesh legend even suggested, as Professor Lambert had once pointed out to me, that the Flower of Immortality had really grown in the sea-beneath-

the-world, and that Gilgamesh had dived through a hole or channel in the bed of the Bitter Sea to obtain it. Now, these holes in
the seabed, where fresh water wells up from below into the salt
sea, are one of the things for which Bahrain is famous, and they
were mentioned, I knew, by many of the early geographers of
Islam.

It began to seem obvious that, for any people who believed in
the existence of the Abyss, of a fresh-water sea beneath the
world, Bahrain was bound to be renowned as a place, perhaps the
only place, where the fresh sea and the salt sea met. And "the
two seas" would be an obvious name for that place.

There was an unfortunate snag: there was no evidence that the
name Bahrain was older than the beginnings of Islam, and there
was no evidence that the belief in the sea-beneath-the-world had
survived the subjugation of Babylonia to the Persians, and the
replacing of the Babylonian gods by Zoroastrianism, Judaism,
Christianity, and Islam. There seemed to be a gap of a thousand
years or more between the religious myths that could give a
reason for the name Bahrain, and the original use of that name.

Moreover, it was well known that the name Bahrain had only
within the last six hundred years or so even been applied solely to
the island; before that it had been the name for the whole stretch
of coast from Kuwait in the north to the Dhahran peninsula and
the present Bahrain in the south. And too, if our theories were
correct we knew that Bahrain was not called Bahrain in Babylonian times—because it was called Dilmun, and later Tylos. But
the puzzle persisted. No one had ever been able to explain the
name Bahrain, and Underwood's explanation was so obvious, if
only the thousand-year gap could be bridged. I even began to
wonder if perhaps the name Dilmun might, in the unknown language of Dilmun, mean "the two seas." After all, the old extent of
"Bahrain" from Kuwait to Dhahran, including the islands off the
coast, was probably the old extent of Dilmun too, and the fresh-
water springs on land and in the sea were not confined to Bahrain
Island; they also occurred on the mainland opposite and off its
shores.

But the gap in time remained, and one of the things which
determined it was how old the name Bahrain was.

Now, one of the oldest extant Arabic texts is, of course, the Koran. And it does not mention the land of Bahrain. But it occurred to me to check whether there occurred in it the Arabic word *bahrain*, "two seas," at all. And the word does occur, three times, and in very fascinating contexts. In the Sura of the Angels (Sura 35, verse 13) we find:

> "Nor are the two seas [*al-bahrain*] alike: the one fresh, sweet, pleasant for drink, and the other salt, bitter; yet from both ye eat fresh fish, and take forth for you ornaments to wear, and thou seest the ships cleaving their waters that ye may go in quest of his bounties, and that ye may be thankful."

It is interesting to find that the two seas are in fact the one salt and the other fresh, but both are here fished and sailed upon; there is clearly no tradition surviving here of the waters under the earth. Only the mention of "ornaments to wear" may suggest that the pearl fisheries of the Arabian Gulf were in the Prophet's mind.

The next occurrence, in the Sura of Al-Furkan (Sura 25, verse 55), is closer to the mark:

> "And He it is who hath let loose the two seas [*al-bahrain*], the one sweet, fresh; and the other salt, bitter; and hath put an interspace between them, and a barrier that cannot be passed."

Here there does appear to be a survival, garbled perhaps, of the Babylonian belief in the underwater sea, and it makes it very likely that the geographical name Bahrain was in fact a survival into Islamic times of that belief. But it is the third reference which raises some *very* interesting speculations. The word *bahrain* appears at the opening of a long story, in the Sura of the Cave (Sura 18, verses 59–81), which is worth quoting in full:

> "Remember when Moses said to his servant, 'I will not stop till I reach the confluence of the two seas [*al-bahrain*], or for years will I journey on.'
> But when they reached their confluence, they forgot their fish, and it took its way in the sea at will.

And when they had passed on, said Moses to his servant, 'Bring us our morning meal; for now have we incurred weariness from this journey.'

He said, 'What thinkest thou? When we repaired to the rock for rest I forgot the fish; and none but Satan made me forget it, so as not to mention it; and it hath taken its way in the sea in a wondrous sort.'

He said, 'It is this we were in quest of.' And they both went back retracing their footsteps.

Then found they one of our servants to whom we had vouchsafed our mercy, and whom we had instructed with our knowledge.

And Moses said to him, 'Shall I follow thee that thou teach me, for guidance, of that which thou too hast been taught?'

He said, 'Verily, thou canst not have patience with me;

How canst thou be patient in matters whose meaning thou comprehendest not?'

He said, 'Thou shalt find me patient if God please, nor will I disobey thy bidding.'

He said, 'Then, if thou follow me, ask me not of aught until I have given thee an account thereof.'

So they both went on, till they embarked in a ship, and he staved it in. 'What!' said Moses. 'Hast thou staved it in that thou mayest drown its crew? A strange thing now thou hast done!'

He said, 'Did I not tell thee that thou couldst not have patience with me?'

He said, 'Chide me not that I forgat, nor lay on me a hard command.'

Then went they on till they met a youth, and he slew him. Said Moses, 'Hast thou slain him who is free from guilt of blood? Now hast thou wrought a grievous thing!'

He said, 'Did I not tell thee that thou couldst not have patience with me?'

Moses said, 'If after this I ask thee aught, then let me be thy comrade no longer; but now hast thou my excuse.'

They went on till they came to the people of a city. Of this people they asked food, but they refused them for guests.

And they found in it a wall that was about to fall, and he set it upright. Said Moses, 'If thou hadst wished, for this thou mightest have obtained pay.'

He said, 'This is the parting point between me and thee. But I will first tell thee the meaning of that which thou couldst not await with patience.

'As to the vessel, it belonged to poor men who toiled upon the sea, and I was minded to damage it, for in their rear was a king who seized every ship by force.

'As to the youth his parents were believers, and we feared lest he should trouble them by error and infidelity.

'And we desired that their Lord might give them in his place a child, better than he in virtue, and nearer to filial piety.

'And as to the wall, it belonged to two orphan youths in the city, and beneath it was their treasure: and their father was a righteous man: and thy Lord desired that they should reach the age of strength, and take forth their treasure through the mercy of thy Lord. And not of mine own will have I done this. This is the interpretation of that which thou couldst not bear with patience.'"

Now, this meeting of Moses with "one of God's servants" has been extensively commented on and explained in the series of "Recollections" of the doings and sayings of the Prophet which were collected during the generation or so after his death. And the "Recollections" tell that the servant of God whom Moses met at "the meeting-place of the two seas" was none other than Al-Khidr, the saint of the Failaka shrine. Al-Khidr, they say, had formerly been the vizier of Dhu'l-Qurnain (which means "the One with Two Horns"); and he had drunk of the fountain of life, by virtue of which he still lives, and will live till the day of judgment.

Now, "the One with Two Horns" is the usual epithet among the Arabs for Alexander the Great, perhaps because Alexander was often represented, as we have seen, with the rays of the sun surrounding his head. But if the Koran is here claiming that Moses met the vizier of Alexander the Great something is seriously wrong with the Koran's chronology, for Alexander lived nearly a thousand years later than Moses. Can Dhu'l-Qurnain be some other horned entity? If so there are many claimants. The Babylonians and Sumerians consistently represent their gods with horns, or with horned helmets. Gilgamesh is generally represented as horned, while he travelled in the early portion of his epic journeys together with a being, Enkidu, who was not merely horned but was half bull and half man. In that connection it is worthy of note that, immediately following the quotation from the Sura of the Cave above, the Koran goes on to tell of Dhu'l-Qurnain, that he traveled to the setting of the sun and then to the rising of the sun, where he built a wall of brass as a defense against the giants Gog and Magog, and this is very reminiscent of the travels of Gilgamesh and his bull-man companion. But if Dhu'l-Qurnain is Gilgamesh or Enkidu or a Babylonian god, who then is Al-Khidr? That he achieved immortality suggests strongly that he might be identical with Utu-nipishtim/Ziusudra.

In fact, if we are to look for consistency, we could well identify "the One with Two Horns" as Enki, a god famous for his wars with monsters on behalf of mankind, and Al-Khidr, his vizier, as Ziusudra, whom Enki saved from the Deluge. But in that case the man who visits Al-Khidr to learn his secret but is unsuccessful in his quest ought not to be Moses—but Gilgamesh. It looks as though we have here an alternative story of Gilgamesh, rather different from the Babylonian and Sumerian versions, and transferred by the Koran from the hero Gilgamesh, who was forgotten in the Prophet's time, to the hero Moses, who was known to every Arab.

Whatever the truth may be, it is certainly odd that a story of a man who achieved immortality should be associated in the earliest Arabic text with "the meeting-place of the two seas," when the place now called "the two seas" was associated in Babylonian times with the only man ever to have achieved immortality.

We walked once more to the sanctuary of Al-Khidr that afternoon, and looked out over the sea to the dhows dipping down from the mouth of the Shatt al-Arab towards Kuwait town. And we talked of the two inscriptions which we had seen that day. The temple at which we stood, and the two temples in which the two inscriptions had had their place were at intervals of two thousand years from each other, like milestones on the otherwise featureless road which led back to the ancient gods of Dilmun.

Perhaps now this road is not quite so featureless. For the story of Al-Khidr in the Koran was written down by people who were nearer in time to the temple of Artemis than to us. And midway in time between the temple of Artemis and the temple of Inzak are the snake sacrifices of the Bahrain palace, with their clear message that the legend of Gilgamesh and the lost Flower of Immortality was not at that time forgotten.

Surely the women who pass the Tuesday night vigil at the shrine of Al-Khidr in prayer for a child are also seeking immortality of a sort. And the faith that their prayer will be answered is one with that which led Gilgamesh, forty-five centuries ago, across the seas to the servant of the Horned One, to Ziusudra, the immortal dweller in Dilmun.

IT IS TEMPTING TO SEE HERE, IN A GROUP FROM A FAILAKA SEAL, MAN'S FIGHT FOR IMMORTALITY WITH THE SNAKE.

CHAPTER THIRTEEN

𝇊𝇊𝇊𝇊𝇊

THE TOMBS OF UMM AN-NAR

The work in Bahrain had entered upon a new phase. It was 1960, and the seventh successive expedition. For five years we had been living for the first three months of every year in our camp within the Portuguese fort. For seven years we had been digging the Barbar temple and the city around the fort, Qala'at al-Bahrain. The Kuwait dig, in its third year, could still produce sensations, as we have just seen. But the Bahrain dig was becoming routine. And in routine there are dangers.

It was all too easy to follow the same pattern; each year to extend a little the central excavation, where you could now walk for thirty yards along a narrow street with the cut-stone walls of P.V.'s "palace" rising high on your right, with the doorways and doorsteps of lesser houses on your right; each year to unearth more rooms and streets in the Second City quarter behind the north wall. Each year would bring its new crop of potsherds, re-establishing afresh that the Seven-City Sequence was really so. And each year we would have a double-handful of beads and terra-cotta figurines, and even seals, to show for our work. But the first seal had been a sensation. The twentieth was—routine.

To an extent routine was unavoidable. We could not leave sensations unchecked. We had to show, by finding more seals where we expected to find more seals, that the first was not a flash in the pan, a single specimen dropped by chance by a foreigner, a visitor perhaps from Failaka four thousand years ago. And Egon had proved this conclusively last year by digging out a seal-cutter's workshop, with debris of sawn steatite and half a seal, broken in the making and discarded. We had to prove, a second time and perhaps a third, that our pottery sequence was valid over a statistically adequate area. But we must not go on and on and on, hoping that the next metre would bring us something new, a hoard of tablets or a silver treasure or a rich and un-touched burial.

That was the insidious temptation, the horrid thought that we might be stopping inches short of something decisive. I recalled the time, three years before, when I had been scraping a sheer section wall at the end of my excavation, cleaning it up before I drew it—and a whole slab of the sand wall had fallen away beneath my trowel, to reveal a bath-tub-coffin standing a centi-metre further than I had dug. It was not a sensation—we had by now six bath-tub-coffins ranged in rows in our storeroom in the basement of the ruler's palace—but it gave us an idea of what we might be missing only inches from where we stopped.

Yet somewhere we had to stop. Not through lack of material—there would still be city here to dig if we dug a thousand years—but it would be unreasonable to expect Sheikh Sulman and the Bahrain oil company to continue indefinitely contributing to a project subject to the law of diminishing returns. And on the edge of our consciences loomed the question of publication.

It was General Pitt Rivers, the founder of scientific method in archæology, who had said, "A discovery dates only from the time of the record of it, and not from the time of its being found in the soil." Now that we knew where we stood in Bahrain, now that we had something to tell, it was our moral and scientific duty to tell it. Too often there are exaggerated delays in the publication of excavation results, gaps of up to a generation after excavation is finished, before the material is made available for use of excava-tors elsewhere. We thought of Ur, where the last volumes are yet to appear thirty years after the last excavation team packed up and went home. And that was not due to any unnecessary tardi-ness. An immense material takes an immense time to work through and to publish. But we too were amassing an immense material—it would take many years to publish, and the sooner we could begin the better. For our yearly reports in the almost unknown journal of the Jutland Archæological Society gave little more than the fact that our expedition had taken place, and the barest account of the most salient results.

Once we began to think seriously of publication, however, we realized how inadequate our material from Qala'at al-Bahrain in fact was. We had dug two tiny areas on the vast tell, and we had no reason to believe that they were the most important areas. We could give an account of the city in depth, but our knowledge in breadth was woefully inadequate. We could say that City I and City II existed, the cities that had been the contemporaries of the grave-mounds and the Barbar temple and the seal-rich temple village of Failaka—but we could not say how large they were, nor point to their important buildings. City III, the city of the Kassite pottery, was even less than this, its existence merely deduced from pits filled with its rubbish. Only for City IV did we have substantial buildings, the "palace" in the centre of the tell, but there, by contrast, we had no remains on the outskirts of the tell. City V, of the time of Alexander and his successors, was a collection of odd scraps of houses on either side of the city wall, and down by the shore, and a thick layer of rubbish above the "palace"; compared to the clearly delineated and documented Greek fort on Failaka it was amorphous and nebulous. And over all the tell, apparently, obscuring all traces of what had gone before, had stretched the straggling Islamic City VI of the twelfth and thirteenth centuries A.D., crowned by the obtrusive bulk of the Portuguese fort, which was City VII.

We had planned a new series of campaigns designed to increase our knowledge of each of these cities, and within a reasonable number of years to round off our work to the point where we could publish more than a glorified *sondage*.

We had two immediate objectives. The one was to go below the central "palace" over as large an area as possible, in the hope of finding substantial buildings of the earlier periods. The other was to trace the course of the city wall on the other edges of the tell, to find the limits of the city area at its various phases of occupation. To that end we had moved over this year to the extreme western edge of the tell.

It was a surprisingly complete change of scene. On the north wall we had been working in the light, with the glare of the sun on the open tell in front and on the open sea behind. Here on the west there was only a narrow strip of tell. Here the sheer towers of the fort frowned down on a scant hundred yeards of open ground beyond its moat. Then the tell dipped sharply down to level ground, and at the foot of the slope stood a thorn hedge, with behind it the garden of Sheikh Ibrahim.

Sheikh Ibrahim is a cousin of the ruler, and he is an agricultural and industrial innovator. Far to the south, on the edge of the mound-fields, his lime and gypsum plant has modernized a local industry which we could prove was all of four thousand years old. And in his garden he was experimenting with acclimatization of strains of fruits and flowers imported from Florida and California, citrus trees and grape vines and roses. His garden was a glorious place to walk in—and when we had first built our camp he had invited us to frequent his garden as freely as we wished. Shady walks led beneath towering *lowz* trees and between thickets of hibiscus, past groves of banana palms with their immense purple flowers, and bushes of pepper with their tiny waxy red blossoms. Spindly papaya trees with their incongruous bunches of green fruit at the crown and the half-grown citrus trees loaded with huge yellow fruit lined the water-channels, and between and beyond the trees were the irrigated plots of roses in full flower, of tomatoes and alfalfa, with the banks between the plots planted with vines and melons. And among them all stood the date-palms which not even the most versatile experimenter would dream of omitting. For they are the certain cash crop, the bearers of the Dilmun dates which were famous in Mesopotamia in the time of Gudea of Lagash.

Our diggings were almost in the shadow of the garden, on the crest and down the steep slope of the edge of the tell.

It had been obvious, of course, that the western fortification wall of the city ran beneath the crest where the tell began to slope sharply down, and that this steep slope was but debris, fallen down when the wall collapsed. But it did not turn out that way. We—Svend and I—laid out two parallel trenches across the top of the crest and down the slope, trenches four metres apart. For here we were going to repeat the level-by-level digging that we had carried out four years before on the northern wall, but on a larger scale and by an improved method. The trenches were only preliminary. When they were dug down to virgin soil, both sides of the four-metre block which lay between would be drawn in section. And then the block itself would be cut away, level by level, with the section drawings as guides to ensure that each level was taken cleanly and accurately.

That was what Svend was engaged upon when I came back from Failaka. And by then we knew that the city wall was not where we had expected. It lay further out, at the very foot of the slope that edged the tell, and its top was below the level of the ground upon which Sheikh Ibrahim was growing his roses. We pushed our trenches further out, right up to the garden fence, and went down on both sides of the wall. And just as at Barbar, we had to go down ten feet below the present ground surface before we came to the bottom of the wall, here based firmly on bedrock.

It was a magnificent sight. Here, in contrast to the north wall, where the outer facing stones had been quarried away to build Seleucid-period houses, the outer facing was intact as high as the wall still stood. And in sheer exuberance we cleared back from our section along thirty feet of the wall face, to show the monumental structure in all its glory. Built of large squared stones, it rose high above us, as it must once have risen above the inhabitants of Dilmun approaching their city from the west, from the direction of the Barbar temple. On the garden side of our trench rose the ten feet of earth which had accumulated during the four thousand years which separated us from them—and it was from that earth, from its pattern of accumulation, that we must try to find out what had happened in the interval, why it had happened, and perhaps when. But first the wall itself. As we looked at the masonry of its outer face we began to make out an irregular break in its construction some halfway up. Below, the stones

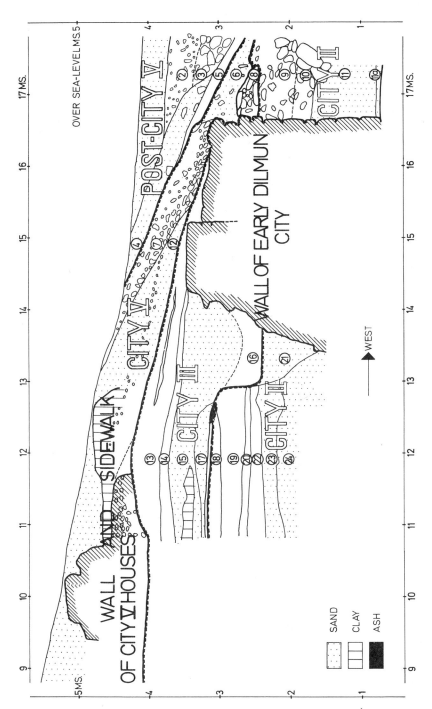

SECTION THROUGH THE WEST WALL OF THE CITY TELL OF QALAʿAT AL-BAH-
RAIN. THE ROBBER PIT WHICH REMOVED THE INNER FACE OF THE WALL IS
VERY PLAIN.

267

were large, regular, well-laid. Above they were smaller, more irregular, more weathered, in less accurate alignment. Clearly the stones of the lower level had been cut to fit the job to be done; in the upper courses the mason had used such material as was to hand. The reason was clear. The original wall had been demolished, or had fallen into ruins, and it had been rebuilt on its original footings, using the same materials, the fallen and broken stones of the earlier wall. And then of course it had fallen again, when the wall went out of use the second time. But this time the fall had not been so disastrous. In fact when we climbed to the top of the wall we found that the second destruction had only been superficial. For the first four feet from the outer face of the wall the top consisted of irregular stonework, clearly the broken top of a broken wall. But behind this the top of the wall was paved with a strip of level cement. Clearly this was the parapet on which the garrison guarding the wall had stood and walked. It was the original top of the wall, and all that had fallen was the four-foot-thick breastwork which had protected them. Or perhaps —after all, four feet was somewhat thick for a breastwork—perhaps there had been *two* parapets, the outer one at a higher level than the one on which we stood, with a thin curtain wall carrying the outer face of the wall still higher. That question was to be answered two years later.

The inner edge of the parapet broke sharply off. For while the outer face of the northern wall had been quarried, here it was the inner face which had suffered from stone-robbers. The inner side of the wall was a jumbled mass of broken stone, and our section showed clearly the outlines of the trench dug down from a later level by the robbers. And following the level back from the top of the stone-quarriers' trench we could see clearly who the robbers were, and why they needed stone. For at this level there lay, on the crest of the tell above the slope, a whole street of small houses. They were tiny, and followed a uniform plan. From the street a narrow doorway with a stone threshold gave entrance to a square room, and from this room a further doorway led to a smaller room. In the larger room the footings of a stone staircase showed that there had been access to an upper floor, or perhaps to a flat roof. And that was all, but the same pattern repeated itself as far as our excavation extended along the street—we had four of these two-room houses, and a portion of a fifth. The houses stood with their backs to where the wall had been, with the street beyond, and clearly the stone dug from the wall had been used to build them, at a time when the wall lay buried beneath the debris of the tell, no longer in use as a fortification.

The history of the site at this particular point was unusually clear. Now we only needed the evidence of pottery from the various levels in order to be able to put some sort of date to what had happened. And as the levels were dug and the baskets of potsherds were washed and spread out for inspection, the dates indeed emerged.

Within the wall the lowest level was a thick layer of fine white sand, which had clearly lain there before the wall was built, and which had been cleared away only along the actual building line to give the wall a firm foundation on the rock below. The sand was almost sterile, but did contain a few sherds of "chain-ridge" ware. Above came the first levels of brown "occupation-earth," and the potsherds here were of Barbar type, as were those in the bottom levels outside the walls. So the wall had been built by the Barbar people. The first destruction of the wall was marked by fallen stones in the next level outside the wall. And above these stones, as well as within the wall at the level of the break, lay the typical honey-coloured Kassite ware. Thus it was in the "Kassite" period that the wall had been rebuilt (and perhaps it was an invasion of the people using the Kassite pottery which had resulted in the destruction of the wall which they had made good). After the "Kassites" the wall had fallen into disrepair, as a further jumble of fallen stones outside the wall showed, and the wall had in fact disappeared from view below the "overflow" from the tell. And then had come the quarrying, and the building of the block of tiny houses. And both were dated unmistakably by the pottery to the Seleucid period, City V, the last two or three centuries b.c. And that brought us to the present surface. There were no Islamic remains here, apart from a well, less than eight hundred years old, to judge by the pottery recovered from it, which had been dug down through the middle of one of the Seleucid houses.

What we did not find was perhaps as important as what we did. In the Barbar and Kassite levels within the city wall there were no traces of houses or streets such as adjoined the northern wall. The area within the wall had either been unoccupied during these periods, or else the dwellings of its inhabitants had been of materials too flimsy to leave any trace.

This, then, was the tale of the western wall.

I was glad that this dig had gone so easily, and given such clear-cut results. For in three days I was due in Abu Dhabi, to look at the results of two years' digging. But before I went I had time to pay a visit to Barbar.

I saw all too little of Barbar. Every morning Yunis drove Peder and Helmuth out to the temple site, and every evening he fetched them home. And only two or three times in a season would I beg the privilege, and a chance to see the site. Each time so much had been done that it was like visiting a new excavation, and, looking back, I have static pictures of stages in the excavation, rather than a progressional view of an excavation campaign. Yet that was what it was. We had established, in the first two years, the fact that the structure was a temple and had been built and rebuilt three times on a successively larger scale, all within the time limits of City II at Qala'at al-Bahrain. And once these basic facts were established Peder and Helmuth had followed a methodical plan; they had dug the central area, then the eastern edge, then the southern edge, and then the western edge. Now they were working on the northern side of the site, and it looked as though Barbar, at least, could be "rounded off" within at the most one or two years more.

The southern side was the most impressive. Here the whole stretch of the terrace walls of Temple II and Temple III stood exposed, the two walls running parallel to each other in an elegant curved sweep of very fine masonry. By what seemed almost a happy chance the wall of the Third Terrace was lower in the middle—it had been quarried away, probably in the tenth century A.D.—and thereby gave an unobscured view of the flight of steps which led boldly up the face of the Second Terrace. They helped give the temple its appearance of a mini-ziggurat.

Where the terrace walls curved round to form the southwest corner, just past the well which had figured in the architecture of all three phases, there was something new to look at. We had long ago found a ramp at this corner, leading down from the central paved court of the temple toward the western part of the mound. We had followed it downward, to find that it broke off short just after passing between the broken stumps of two stone pillars. We were fairly confident that this ramp was the main approach to the temple on the top of the terrace. And our guess had seemed confirmed when, last year, Peder and Helmuth had met the same structure at a lower level beyond the break, but now in the form of a handsome flight of stone steps. They had followed them downward with the usual anticipatory excitement.

They did not stop at the level of the foot of the terrace wall, which must have been ground level then. They went on down. They met the water-table. And they went on down, our workers baling up a mixture of sand and water and wading up to their knees in quicksand. A wall had been found to edge the steps on their northern side, a fine wall of polished limestone slabs, as high as the top of the terraces. And while the waterlogged sand was being shovelled off the lower steps this wall was followed. After twelve feet it turned squarely south, and after another twelve feet squarely east, and ran until it abutted on the terrace wall, thus completely enclosing the foot of the steps. Far from digging out the temple gate we had expected, the excavators found themselves clearing a small stone-lined room almost three feet deep in water. And the water welled out from a pierced stone pipe, or bottomless stone jar, standing in the centre of the room. Clearly the water was meant to be there; the structure was a tank or bathing pool. It was nothing so simple as the temple water-supply. Had it been that, the well close by would not have been so elaborately preserved through the rebuilding of the temple.

Such an ablution pool was a very un-Sumerian feature in a temple which otherwise was not un-Mesopotamian in character. And we thought of the Great Bath on the citadel of Mohenjo-

Daro, and of the washing places which are an indispensable feature of every mosque to this day. But perhaps there was more to it than that. To the Sumerians, and probably even more to the people of Dilmun, such a spring was not a natural phenomenon. Here were the waters of the Abyss, here the sweet waters of the sea-beneath-the-world broke through to the surface. This might be the very spring which Enki, the Lord of the Abyss, had caused to gush forth in Dilmun, at the behest of the goddess Ninhursag.

The spring might indeed be the reason why the temple lay here at all. It might even have been a wishing well. We had recalled the coins thrown into the Trevi fountain, when we found seven of our Dilmun stamp-seals at the bottom of the pool. . . .

The airfield at Abu Dhabi was unchanged. The tiny Heron of Gulf Aviation still touched down on the hard-packed sand between the guiding lines of painted oil-drums. But now Sadiq was waiting with our own land-rover to take us to the camp on Umm an-Nar. Arne was with him, while Knud had stayed on the island to look after the digging. Both Arne and Sadiq were old acquaintances. Arne comes from the Faroes, the rocky Danish-administered group of islands in the north Atlantic on which I had spent two years of garrison duty during the war, and he had dug with us on Failaka the year before. Sadiq was of Persian family, though born in Dubai a hundred miles up the coast, and he had been driver to P.V. and me on an adventurous trip through the Oman the year before. Now he was driving for us again, bringing our workers and supplies each day from Abu Dhabi town to our island. He was a cheerful young man who spent every spare moment caring for his vehicle, and who had the gift of making himself understood, by the use of clear simple Arabic and an abundance of gesture, even to the least experienced Arabist among us. He was to be an invaluable asset to our expeditions in the years to come.

As we drove over the sand-flats toward the causeway to the mainland Arne told us of the work. Much had happened in two years of digging since P.V. and I had first driven out with Tim to see the grave-mounds of Umm an-Nar. We had sent three men to the island last year, and had built for them a smaller replica of our Bahrain camp, a single long *barasti* hut with a living room and kitchen at one end and three small sleeping cabins at the other. There they had spent two months, under exceptionally arduous conditions. The local market had been able to supply little in the way of food, and we had been allowed to draw on supplies of canned goods from Tim's oil company, which was at that time establishing itself on an island in the middle of the Gulf, halfway to Qatar. But these supplies arrived irregularly, a case or two at a time of bulk items. I recalled that on my visit last year the available supplies had consisted of a case of canned bacon, a case of tomato ketchup, and three cartons of tonic water. This last item was serious, as the available water had been standing six months in kerosene drums, had a scum of kerosene on top, and was completely undrinkable. We were heartily sick of the taste of tonic water by the time the next plane came in with cartons of beer and lemon squash. Their cook too, though willing enough, had been incompetent, and they had only managed to exist by buying up the few eggs locally available, and frying them themselves when they got back each day from work. This year, Arne told me, things were better. They had a superlative cook, and a grocery store had opened in town—and he assured me that there was no tonic water in the camp.

Last year our team had started with high hopes. They had expected that the grave-mounds, like those of Bahrain, would contain a central chamber, and they had started to dig quadrants in two of the mounds, as well as a section trench across the settlement tell. But it had not turned out that way. Just within the perimeter of the two grave-mounds they came upon a perfect circle of cut limestone blocks, each two or three feet in length and over a foot high. Their outer surfaces were ground to a smooth finish, curved to the curvature of the circle, and fitted so closely together that the proverbial knife-blade could not be inserted between them. Here and there a block of a second course of similar stones still stood in position. And outside the circle lay many other blocks of the same type, lying where they had fallen

273

outwards, sufficient in number to have formed an original circular wall four courses high. But within this ring of incredibly fine masonry lay an amorphous welter of stones, thin slabs, and roughly squared blocks piled and tumbled in absolute confusion. There was no sign of a central chamber.

Now Anders, who was in charge of the team, is one of the most meticulous excavators of our time. We were fortunate in having him engaged on this incredibly difficult assignment. No stone was moved until its precise relation to the stones below and on either side had been determined. And thereby it gradually appeared that in the first trench to the centre of the mound there were a number of dry-stone walls, scarcely distinguishable from the stones which lay between and above them, criss-crossing the trench in many different directions. The work of tracing the walls could not be left to the workmen from Abu Dhabi. First Mogens was called in from the second mound to help with the first, and then Risgaard from the settlement trench. When the season finished, instead of two mounds and a settlement excavated, only half of the first mound was completed. But it lay there, cleared, with every wall intact, and with the fallen stones from the outer wall cleaned and lying in position. The plan of the mound was fully comprehensible.

And it was clear that it was not a grave-mound at all. It was a sepulchral building. There had been no original mound of stones or of earth covering a chamber. Every stone in the heap had originally been part of the construction. And the construction had been possibly the most elaborate provision for the disposal of the dead ever made. Not the largest or richest or finest, of course; it was no pyramid. But even the pyramids of Egypt are in fact burial-mounds, piles of blocks around a central chamber.

Here the outer wall was backed and buttressed by a thick dry-stone wall all the way round, except at two points opposite one another. Here there had been two entrances, and the fallen wall-stones at these points had cutaway portions showing that the entrances had been small rhomboid-shaped doorways or portholes. And together with the doorway stones lay the actual doors, thin rhomboid-shaped slabs of stone with stone handles carved in

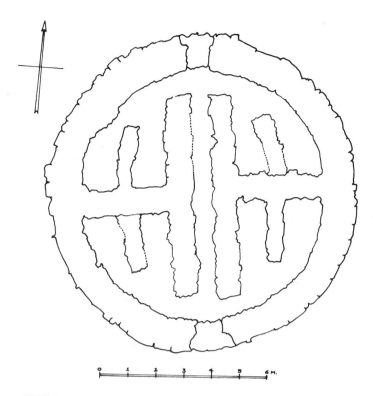

PLAN OF THE FIRST TOMB TO BE EXCAVATED ON UMM AN-NAR.

one piece with the door. Across the diameter of the circular building, from door to door, ran a narrow corridor, with dry-stone walls on either hand. But these walls did not join the circumference wall. They stopped a little short at either end, giving access to a narrow corridor running within the perimeter. But not running clean around. Midway between the doorways it met a cross-wall, joining the circumference wall to the diameter wall, and this cross-wall had, in turn, a short projecting wall on either side. This is difficult to explain in words, but the diagram will make it clear. In effect, the interior of the circular building was divided by a system of walls into eight small alcoves and a transverse corridor. Both the corridor and the alcoves were paved with slabs, while the walls gradually widened from their bases upwards, showing that the alcoves and the corridor had originally been vaulted, or, more precisely, corbelled. It must have been an eery experience, when the building was new, to crawl through the tiny entrance from the bright sunshine into the darkness of the interior, and to stoop along the passages beneath the curve of the roof, from one alcove to another. And the contents of the alcoves would not make the experience less awesome. For thick on the flags of the alcoves lay the bones of the dead.

There was little discernible order in the human bones which Anders excavated on these flagged floors. But this was not due, as in Bahrain, to the depredations of robbers. It was in the nature of things. While the Bahrain grave-mounds are single tombs for single burials, the Umm an-Nar mortuary chambers were designed for repeated use. Body after body had been buried in these tombs, borne in through the port-hole stone and deposited in the alcoves. And in the process the previous occupants had been treated with scant reverence. Their bones had been pushed aside, piled along the wall footings, trampled underfoot. And not merely the bones. Among the human remains lay the gifts which had accompanied them to the tomb, gifts of pottery and of copper weapons. And these too had been trampled and broken and cast to one side.

The pottery led me seriously astray that year. In my defense I may claim that there was little of it, and not enough to put together a single complete pot. It was unusually fine ware, thin, well fired, and thrown on a fast wheel. Some sherds had barely discernible geometric patterns in black paint above a reddish burnished wash. Thin ware, with a red wash and with burnish, we had hitherto only met in our "thin-bowl" period on Bahrain, our City V of the period of Alexander. And so I had told Sheikh Shakhbut that the graves of Umm an-Nar appeared to be about two thousand years old.

The excavations of Knud and Arne this year showed that I had underestimated by over a hundred per cent. The graves were more than twice as old as that.

They had done a lot of work during the two months they had been living on their desert island. It was of course easier this year. Once Anders had established the basic pattern of the tomb structures it was no longer so difficult to clear them. Once inside the circular perimeter wall the technique is to dig down at once to the flagged floor and then to work inwards. The inner dry-stone walls can only with difficulty be made out among the confusion of tumbled stone if you are digging downward from the top, but they are unmistakable when you meet them from the side. Knud and Arne had not only finished clearing Anders's first tomb—they had completely excavated five others. They were much smaller tombs, admittedly, but that too was deliberate. We now had a series of excavated tombs, ranging from the smallest to the largest. And we could see that the pattern of interior walling varied with the size of the tomb. The largest of the five new structures had the same two entrances and central passage, but the space behind the passage was divided by a simple cross-wall, providing but four alcoves. The next had two entrances, but no way of getting from one to the other. A cross-wall divided the whole interior into two, and a short cross-piece in the centre divided each half into two alcoves. The third had but a single entrance, and an interior divided by a projecting wall into two alcoves. And the last two were simple ring-walls with no interior divisions. There was even some doubt as to whether the smallest of them all was a tomb at all.

Of these five smaller tombs, only one—the second largest of the five—had an outer wall of ground and finished masonry; the others were of roughly squared, unfinished stone. But the finely built one had its walls preserved in places to six courses of masonry, and one whole doorway still stood intact, the courses projecting inward to form a blunt-apexed triangle.

All the tombs, except the very smallest one, contained human remains and pottery. But by far the richest in both were the newly excavated half of Anders's original mound and the fine tomb with the preserved doorway. This latter tomb, though only fifteen feet across inside, with a floor area of about 135 square feet, contained the remains of at least thirty-six individuals, far more than could have been accommodated if they had all been buried at one time. And in addition there were over forty pottery vessels, of which twenty-two were unbroken. The new half of Anders's cairn had yielded twenty-three vessels, many of them unbroken, and the bones of fifteen burials, while the other tombs produced only about sixteen further vessels between them.

This was the tale of the excavation, as I learnt it, at first sketchily from Arne as we drove with Sadiq at the wheel, and later in the afternoon as I saw it for myself after the scorching walk across the sun-blasted plateau of the island. But before that I had sat for an hour or more in the dappled shade of the *barasti*, as Knud produced one complete pot after another from the boxes in which they were packed. And I knew as I looked at them that the tombs on Umm an-Nar were much older than I had thought.

I could not of course immediately "place" the pottery. I have never had the photographic memory that can unerringly match a pot fresh from the earth with an illustration or a drawing in a book seen years before. But the general attribution of these delicate thin vases, with their black-painted patterns of criss-crossed triangles and chains of semi-circles and zigzag bands on the polished reddish-brown ground was unmistakable. They belonged to the range of wares found in Iran and Baluchistan, and designated generically as "chalcolithic." These wares had a spread in time—with very uncertain limits, for little excavation has been done in these areas—from the fourth to the second millennium B.C.

Some of the pottery could give a closer dating. There were a couple of small cracker-barrel-shaped jars in grey, covered with bands of the black designs from shoulder to flat base, which even I could recognize as typical of the Kulli culture, while a shoulder-sherd of a larger red-brown vessel bore the painted figure of a humped bull, the Brahmin bull of India, which was equally typically Kulli. This needs explaining.

To the west of the Indus Valley civilization, in Baluchistan and up to the borders of Afghanistan, around Poona, a large number of separate cultures, distinguished by different shapes and decoration of pottery, have been identified during the last forty years by British, French, and American archæologists, the earliest and most famous of whom was the British explorer Sir Aurel Stein. These cultures, which, for all their finely decorated pottery, represent only village communities of probably semi-nomadic herdsmen, appear to have been the matrix out of which the Indus Valley civilization developed, and much discussion has been devoted to the question of which, if any, of these cultures was in truth the racial antecedent of the Indus people. Of these cultures, the one designated as the Kulli culture has emerged most clearly as a widespread unity, with villages and even quite considerable towns in south Baluchistan. It was not the Kulli people who

THE TOMB POTTERY FROM UMM AN-NAR IN ABU DHABI. THE BARREL-SHAPED VASES ARE GREY, THE OTHERS RED.

279

THE ZEBU BULL, FREQUENTLY DEPICTED ON INDUS SEALS AND KULLI POTS, HERE
ADORNS THE NECK OF A VASE FROM ONE OF THE UMM AN-NAR TOMBS.

originated the Indus civilization—on the contrary, the Indus civilization in its period of greatest expansion reached out and colonized much of the territory held by the Kulli villagers. But at least there was general agreement that the Kulli people had been the western neighbors of the Indus Valley people, contemporary with them or perhaps a little earlier in date. Now it began to appear that the people of Umm an-Nar had been the western neighbors of the Kulli people, and had imported some at least of their pottery.

The argument could be taken further. Umm an-Nar was contemporary with Kulli, and Kulli was contemporary with or somewhat earlier than the Indus Valley culture. But the Indus Valley culture was contemporary with our Barbar culture, with Early Dilmun, City II on Bahrain. Therefore Umm an-Nar in turn was contemporary with, or somewhat earlier than, the Barbar culture.

Yet it was quite certain that it was *not* the Barbar culture. No pottery similar to that which I was turning in my hands had been found on Bahrain. And the difference in the type of grave and in the burial practices was fundamental. Two hundred and fifty miles northwest of Bahrain, on Failaka, the culture contemporary with City II *was* the culture of City II, with exactly similar seals and pottery. Failaka had been just as much a part of Dilmun as Bahrain.

But here, 250 miles southeast of Bahrain, the culture contemporary with Early Dilmun was completely different. Whatever Umm an-Nar was, it had not been part of Dilmun. As I laid the pots back in their boxes the possibility became more and more obtrusive that we had here on Umm an-Nar the first outpost of the second "lost civilization" of the Lower Sea, the copper kingdom of Makan.

Five days later, in the early dawn, we waded ashore from Muhamed's ferry boat and boarded Sadiq's land-rover for the journey to Buraimi.

CHAPTER FOURTEEN

卍卍卍卍卍

THE EMPTY QUARTER

The expedition to Buraimi was the second of many. My own seventh trip, and up to now my last, was made in 1968. My first, and the expedition's first, had taken place in 1959, the year of the first digging in the grave-mounds of Umm an-Nar.

That year P.V. and I had flown down from Bahrain to look at the progress of the dig, and the first evening we had called on the ruler of Abu Dhabi. It was the beginning of the month of Ramadhan, when the strict Moslems of the Gulf may neither eat nor drink nor smoke between sunrise and sunset, and Sheikh Shakhbut was holding his court after nightfall.

The next day we were at the diggings, watching our dozen lean brown Omanis removing loose stones and baskets of earth from the mound, when we saw in the distance a man coming over the dark crest of the island from the direction of the camp and the ferry. As he came closer we recognized Ian, the tall athletic Scot who had relieved Tim as oil-company representative. He came up and pulled us aside. "You're going to have distinguished visitors in about half an hour," he said. "The ruler is coming out to look at what you're finding."

We were not perturbed. We were accustomed, from Bahrain, to the active interest of the sheikhs, and we knew from our talks with Shakhbut of Abu Dhabi that he followed our work with keen attention. There was not even the problem of hospitality—

in Ramadhan in the middle of the day it would have been a breach of manners to offer coffee or any refreshment at all. We waited. A short while later we saw a group of white-robed figures descending the slope towards us and we went forward to meet them.

The visit lasted half an hour, and Sheikh Shakhbut showed great curiosity about our work, speculating over what manner of people these could have been, who had built their village and their tombs on the island in his territory during the Age of Ignorance. He was accompanied by his two sons, Sayyid and Sultan, and by his brother Zayid, a tall, lean but broad-shouldered man with the hawk-like visage of the true Bedawi and a short black beard, carefully trimmed. Zayid had come down to the coast to observe Ramadhan, but was usually away in the interior, ruling as vice-regent over the villages of the Buraimi oasis. His was a name to conjure with—he was a mighty hunter and a renowned desert fighter. But his chief fame rested on the story that, when Saudi Arabia laid claim to Buraimi ten years before, they had offered Sheikh Zayid a bribe of ten million dollars in return for recognizing their claim and handing the oasis over to them. And he had refused, and in 1955 had taken an active part in expelling a Saudi force which had established itself in one village in the oasis.

Zayid was just as interested in our work as his brother and followed our explanation, fluently translated into Arabic by Ian, with attention. But it was obvious that, in his mind, nothing in the coastal regions of Abu Dhabi could compare with his realm in the interior. After we had shown him the extent of our mound-field, he turned to Ian with a remark. "If you want to see mounds like these in their hundreds," translated Ian, "Sheikh Zayid says you should come to Buraimi." We replied, enthusiastically, that there was nothing we should like better to do. And there the matter rested, and a few days later P.V. and I returned to Bahrain.

But after a week there we had received a visit from the manager of the British Petroleum Company, Ian's opposite number in Bahrain. In accordance with Sheikh Zayid's wish, he informed us, his company in Abu Dhabi had arranged a trip for us to Buraimi, which he hoped we would undertake in the very near future. He had provisionally booked seats for us on the charter plane leaving for Abu Dhabi in two days' time.

So on seventeenth March, after a brief visit to our team on Umm an-Nar, P.V. and I set forth on a luxury safari such as only an oil company could have arranged. The convoy consisted of two large land-rover station-cars. We were alone, apart from an interpreter, a cook, and the two drivers, Sadiq—whom we now met for the first time—and his brother Rashid. So we could spread ourselves on the broad front seats, each to his own car, while the cook and the interpreter sat on the rear seats, together with our luggage, and blankets and mattresses and spare cans of water and gasoline, and food enough for a regiment—which was only a reserve supply in case we failed to arrive on time at the appointed stopping places where real food would be awaiting us. And the cook carried carefully a large parcel, which we only several days later discovered to contain two complete place settings of porcelain, soup plates and entrée plates and dinner and dessert plates, all meticulously packed in cloth in case we should need them. They were never used.

We were heading southeast, away from the coast into the immense wilderness of the Empty Quarter. But first we had to negotiate the coastal *sabkha*, a salt-pan which at high tide becomes an impassable quagmire, where the abandoned wrecks of cars and trucks, drowned above their wheels in salt-caked mud, served as warnings and as markers for the scarcely discernible track. I thought of the Aamand, and the warning stone by the Viking causeway in Jutland. We could have used a wooden causeway here.

We climbed the escarpment, over sharp-edged slabs and shoulders of sand-drowned limestone, and came into the loose powdery sand beyond. Sadiq grinned, and rang the changes on his gears with a virtuoso's skill, charging the slopes at speed, changing down without checking his impetus, and going into high to career down to other side. After an hour of ploughing up and down the loose slopes of sand he reached into his pocket, pulled out a pack of cigarettes, and, after fingering it thoughtfully for a while, came to a decision and lit one. Thankfully I relaxed and lit one of the long Indian cheroots which I at that time favoured. It was Ramadhan, and a good Moslem will not smoke during daylight hours. But the rule prohibiting smoking, eating, and drinking is relaxed in certain circumstances, for children, for the sick, and for bonafide travellers. And Sadiq had apparently decided that we were travellers.

For hours the sand continued, broken occasionally by a patch of the inland *sabkha,* hard salt flat which must, ages ago, have been a lake. Occasionally, too, there were stretches of gravel, or areas where ragged broad-leaved bushes had obtained a foothold in the sand and banked it into hummocks.

In one of these areas of scanty vegetation we rounded a dune and came upon a red pick-up truck drawn up beside the thickest bushes. In its shadow sat five men, with their *abbas* over their heads to give greater shade. We pulled up, and one of the Arabs rose and walked over to talk with Sadiq. Sadiq alighted, and went over to the truck, lifted its bonnet, and tried a few connections. He shrugged his shoulders and came back to us. "Dynamo no good," he said. "No al-ectric." We questioned him further. The truck had set off from Buraimi the day before, and had been stranded here for over twenty-four hours. We were the first people they had seen since the breakdown. "But—shouldn't we do something?" we exclaimed, as Sadiq started the engine, preparing to drive on. He explained that he had promised to give word to the owner of the truck at Buraimi, and he would send a dynamo out, if he had one, the next time a car was leaving Buraimi. "But have they food, and water?" I asked. Sadiq shrugged again. "No food, water in radiator," he replied casually, and added, "*That* way—maybe three miles, Bedouin well." I thought of our waggon-load of reserve provisions. "But we have food, and water," I said. "As you will," said Sadiq, and spoke to our cook, who rummaged in the boxes in the rear, and presented the leader of the stranded party with a can of pineapple slices. The Arab accepted it gravely, shook hands, and went back to his truck, where he tucked the tin of fruit under the luggage in the back and squatted down again with his companions.

We drove on. Clearly P.V. and I were the only ones who were

in any way concerned. To sit alone in the desert, where one car might pass in the course of a week, was no reason for anxiety among these Abu Dhabi Arabs, to whom the desert was home. Sooner or later they would be picked up, for God is merciful; and until then they would exist on what the desert could provide, whether it was edible roots, or lizards, or tins of pineapple. But of course they would eat none of these before sundown, for they had been stationary for over twenty-four hours, and were not therefore, technically, travellers.

As we proceeded, the sand gradually changed color. Near the coast it had been white, looking against the sun like an endless snow-field. Now gradually it changed to a reddish buff, the famous red sands of the central desert. The slopes gradually took on the crescent shape of true wind-formed dunes. And the dunes got higher and steeper, so that we charged up seemingly sheer slopes, to twist sharply at the top and roar along below the crests, before slithering down another sheer slope a hundreds yards further on. Occasionally Sadiq would sound his horn, and then we would take a slope at speed, shoot over the crest and straight down the other side. The horn blast was a warning, in case another car might be doing the same from the other side. It could not, of course, have been heard; but God was indeed merciful.

From the top of one of the dunes Sadiq gestured with his cigarette. "Hafit," he said, and looking in the direction he pointed I could see on the horizon a long dark whaleback, seemingly immensely remote and immensely high. Jebel Hafit is the mountain, a western outlier of the main Oman massif, which frowns down upon Buraimi from the south, and it was as we gradually came nearer, and the shoulders and ridges of Hafit began to etch themselves in sun and shadow, that I discovered that I was already in love with Buraimi.

I grew up among mountains, but in the green woods and dales of Denmark I have learned to do without them. I do not miss them—until I see a mountain. And then I realize suddenly that the landscape is *right* again, that there is once more a world to be looked up to rather than down upon, that crags and buttresses are a necessary part of the scene, to challenge heart and lungs and sinews, and the spirit of man.

I was in a poetical haze as we fell off the highest dune yet, into Buraimi.

We had far to go still. Before us was more sand, but low and rolling, with bushes and tussocks of grass, and occasional clumps of half-buried acacias. And now we crossed donkey-tracks ever more frequently, and even the wheel-tracks of other cars. And as the clumps of acacias and tamarisks became more frequent we met our first camels, grazing on the lower branches of the trees.

I had always associated camels with the open desert, and with domesticity. And indeed the long strings which we occasionally passed on our way to Umm an-Nar, swinging along loaded with bundles of brushwood for Abu Dhabi town, had accorded exactly with my preconceptions. But here, where I saw them free and untethered, grazing in droves among the trees, I realized that the camel is in truth an animal of the savannah, a tree-grazer by nature, with in fact the same disability as the giraffe, that its neck is better designed for reaching up than for reaching down. Here in a landscape which, as we proceeded, resembled more and more the open bushland of East Africa, the camel seemed ecologically to fill the place of the giraffe, seemed to be in its natural homeland. Two years later we were to find evidence that that might indeed be the case.

By now we were driving along rutted tracks amid shoulders of wind-blown sand clothed with a thin grass. On the horizon before us, and to the right toward the bulk of Jebel Hafit, the tops of palm-trees appeared, solid masses of dark olive green. And in front of them, scarcely distinguishable against the yellow-brown sand, were yellow-brown clusters of clay houses. They were the scattered villages of the oasis, seven in number. Four of them were under the government of Sheikh Zayid of Abu Dhabi; the other three belonged to the Sultanate of Muscat and Oman. Beside and between the villages rose yellow forts of sun-dried brick, some in ruins, some visibly sliding down into amorphous clay tells, some in good repair and flying the flag of their allegiance, the red flag of Muscat, or the red and white flag of Abu Dhabi. We drove up to one of the latter. We had arrived.

The single sleepy sentry blinked at our enquiry for Sheikh Zayid. It was mid-afternoon, in Ramadhan. They were all asleep,

he said. We said we would wait, but he called in to the officer of
the watch, and shortly afterward a slim young man with a short
trimmed beard came out, yawning. "Sheikh Tahnun, bin Muhamed bin Khalifah," whispered Sadiq to us, and we knew that
honour was being done us. Sheikh Muhamed bin Khalifah and his
family are held in high respect in Abu Dhabi. Sheikh Muhamed
was now old, but in his youth he had personally killed a usurper
who had driven his uncle, Zayid's and Shakhbut's grandfather,
from the throne and into exile. And instead of taking the throne
himself, as it was in his power to do, he had called the rightful
ruler back from Sharjah. There was an unmistakable mediæval
air about these tales of black treachery and uncompromising
loyalty, just as there was about these four-square castles with the
hawks drowsing in the sun on their perches outside. But the
sentry was armed with a repeating rifle, and four khaki-painted
jeeps stood in the shade of the straggling palm-trees. . . .

Tahnun led us into the audience hall, seated us on the cushions
along the walls, and clapped his hands. And servants came in
with trays of fruit. We protested; it was Ramadhan, and the sun
was up. It was unlawful to eat. "No," he replied gravely, "you are
Christians. Your religion does not forbid."

So we ate a token meal, and drank a token cup of coffee, while
Tahnun sat by. And then the young sheikh summoned a guide,
who would take us to the guest palace of Sheikh Zayid. And we
went out to our cars and drove away.

The guest palace was at the other side of the southernmost
village of Al-Ain, and was a conspicuous building. It was the
latest of the forts ever to have been built for purely defensive
purposes in the oasis, and it towered on the top of a bare knoll
like a ziggurat. It was three tall stories high, and only the upper
story had windows. Below there were rifle-slits, and at ground
level there was but one narrow doorway, giving onto a steep
narrow stair which one man could have held against a multitude.
There was a sentry on the door, and two of Zayid's servants, who
carried our bedrolls up to the upper floor.

While the servants, under the eye of our cook, made one of the
thick-walled rooms ready for us, P.V. and I went on, up a stout

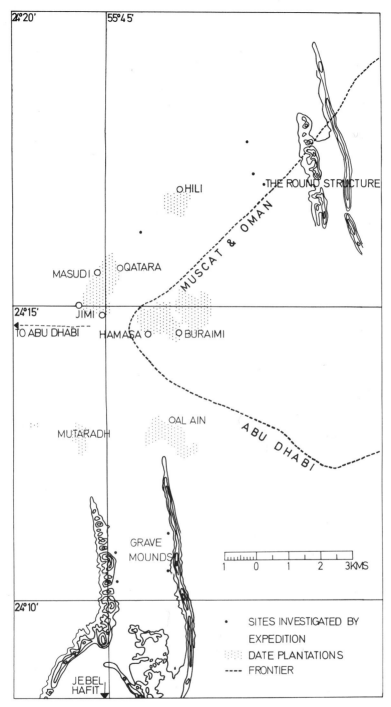

THE OASIS OF BURAIMI (OR, AS IT IS NOW CALLED, THE OASIS OF AL-AIN), WHERE
WE NOW DIG ON THE BORDERS OF MUSCAT.

wooden ladder to the flat roof. From this vantage point we could look out over the southern stretch of the oasis.

Almost at our feet were the gardens of Al-Ain. They were sunken gardens, reminding us of the sunken springs of the Bahrain desert, ringed by high walls which held back the surrounding sand. But these covered an immense area, perhaps a square mile in all, and they were a vivid green, with vegetables and alfalfa growing between carefully spaced date-palms, the tops of which we had seen on our approach standing up above the retaining walls. But here there were no springs, for these gardens were not at the source but at the outlets of the *qanats*, the underground watercourses which we had first seen in Bahrain. Looking down we could follow the course of several of these *qanats*, tracing the line of short chimney-like structures which were the shafts leading down to the artificial channels which led the water from its underground springs in the surrounding hills. One of these channels ran immediately below us, and as we looked we saw one of Zayid's servants emerge from the building to draw water on a bucket and rope for our washing.

Beyond the gardens, to the south, Jebel Hafit towered into the sky, its foot still four or five miles distant, and from its northern end two chains of steep crags ran out towards us, diverging as they approached, so that the gardens and village of Al-Ain lay at the mouth of the deep valley which ran between them. To the north the land was more level, with rounded sandy hills and beyond them a flat tree-scattered plain running to the more distant mountains of Muscat. And on the horizon to the northwest were the dark masses of palm-trees which marked the sites of other villages, Mas'udi and Buraimi itself, villages on Muscat territory.

As we looked over the landscape and tried to identify which of the sandy hills might be prehistoric tells, the sun sank lower toward the western dunes, and we were called down by our interpreter with the news that a messenger had come from Sheikh Zayid. We were asked to attend him, after the sunset prayer, for the dinner that would break the daylong fast.

Accordingly, two hours after nightfall we drove away, in the darkness, for Zayid's palace, and as we passed the unlighted village we met another vehicle driving towards our guest house. It stopped, and we were hailed, in Danish. It was Anders and Mogens and Risgaard, just arrived from Umm an-Nar.

We had been half expecting them, for they had said they would come if they could persuade their driver to make the journey. That had by no means been certain, for Khalifah would have to drive his pick-up alone, without the support of a second car. His vehicle, though powerful, had no four-wheel drive. And half the journey must be made in the darkness, for they could not start until digging was over for the day. We were very conscious of the fact that Buraimi was back of beyond, that until a scant score of years before "no white man had set his foot" there, or at least only two "white men" in a hundred years. We had a proper respect for the desert, for the Great Unknown.

We might have known that our respect would not be shared by Khalifah, or Sadiq, or any of the desert-runners whose fathers led their pack-camels along all the routes through the dunes, and who themselves are opening up the same routes with their power-wagons and land-rovers. Khalifah would without doubt have been panic-stricken at the idea of driving from Long Beach to Manhattan, but he had seen nothing perilous in facing the Empty Quarter of Arabia by night and alone.

The trip had almost been harder on the passengers, in the open body of the truck. They were thick with dust, and half-choked and half-blinded by the swirling sand. But they turned their vehicle and followed us to Zayid's palace. After all, he could not be unaccustomed to visitors arriving travel-stained and dust-covered.

Zayid rose to greet us as we entered his audience chamber, and his entourage rose with him. He seemed taller and more broad-shouldered than when we had met him on Umm an-Nar, and his brown robe and simple black *agal* differed in no way from the dress of the common Bedu. Only the gold-hilted daggar in the centre of his belt marked him as a man of consequence—that, and an indefinable presence which could be seen as much in the deference of the others in the room as in the sheikh's own frank smile and cool appraising glance. For the others in the room were no band of obsequious courtiers. They were as tough a company of self-reliant warriors as one could wish to meet.

Most of them were young, lithe, and direct of gaze, clean-shaven or with carefully trimmed, almost foppish black beards. Most wore bandoliers in addition to their daggers, and some carried deadly looking automatic rifles with telescopic sights, the muzzles and breeches protected with leather against the sand. There was a sprinkling of elder men, and one white-bearded and hawk-visaged old man by Zayid's right hand, who was introduced to us as Muhamed bin Khalifah, Tahnun's famous father. He courteously made room for us, and we took our places on the cushions beside Sheikh Zayid.

For half an hour we were questioned by Zayid on our results from Umm an-Nar and on the whole problem of the early history of Arabia. And then we ate. I was by now fairly accustomed to the dinners of the desert sheikhs—it was ten years since, at the celebration of that first shipment of oil from Qatar, I had first seen the mountain of rice on its metal dish on the floor mats, surmounted by the whole sheep, roasted and steaming. But I had not feasted in this way so often that I had ceased to be surprised, each time, by the fragrance of the rice, and its dry heat as one dug into the mound with the fingers of the right hand, nor the tenderness of the meat as it tore away from the bone. And here for the first time I sampled what the Arab considers the best part of the feast, the sheep's brain. For there is a trick of opening the skull of the sheep, using the lower jawbone as the key, which every Arab knows of but few have mastered. I had seen it attempted, unsuccessfully, before, but now Zayid took the head and the jawbone, and inserted the end of the jaw at some point in the skull. He twisted sharply and the skull broke open, and he leaned over to offer the contents first to P.V. and then to me.

Though we ate hugely there was still a mighty mound of rice and the greater part of the sheep left when we rose from our haunches and gave place to the body-guard who would take the second sitting at the meal. And after we had washed our grease-covered hands beneath the stream of water from the ewer held by one of the servants we went out into the courtyard. There we took our places on a terrace, and after a moment or two a cinema projector sprang to life, projecting a film on the whitewashed wall of the courtyard. We had already remarked the electric light—Zayid's palace possessed the only generator in Buraimi—and we learnt later that the real reason why Zayid had transported the generator with immense difficulty over the desert road to Buraimi was in order to have power available for his film projector. The film was in Arabic and lasted for hours, telling the swashbuckling story of the mythical Arab hero Antar, a warrior who had led a resistance movement against the Byzantine emperors. The time was two o'clock in the morning before the film reached its dramatic climax with a running sword-fight through the imperial palace in Constantinople, and we could scarcely hold ourselves awake. When they began to show a second film we threw in our hands, and begged Sheikh Zayid that we be excused. We were to be up early next day, we explained, in order to see what Buraimi had to offer of archæological remains. Zayid smiled and nodded. "I shall come and fetch you at seven o'clock," he said.

That was in less than five hours' time, and we agreed among ourselves, as we drove home, that the rendezvous would probably be kept with a few hours' delay, for appointments mean little to most Arabs. But we felt it politic to be ready at the appointed time all the same, and we stumbled sleepily out of our blankets at a quarter to seven. It was as well we did. For promptly at seven two open jeeps roared up before our ziggurat, with Zayid himself, looking spruce and wide awake, driving the leading vehicle. We climbed into our two land-rovers and followed behind, along the steep-sided *wadi* which skirts Al-Ain, and out on the rough track along the valley leading toward Jebel Hafit.

On our left rose steep crags, and on our right a gentler rocky slope led up to a bluff overlooking the green valley. And as we approached the bluff we could see that the whole slope was covered with burial-mounds, steep-sided cairns of stones clustering most thickly along the very edge of the bluff. Zayid's jeep turned up the slope and stopped in the middle of the largest group of mounds. We dismounted and looked around.

Zayid's boast of hundreds of mounds was not idle. Around us on the ridge stood quite that number and as our eyes accustomed themselves to the landscape we could see mounds on every crag and crest and spur, all the way to Mount Hafit itself. Zayid turned to us with a lift of his eyebrows. "Yes," we said, "grave-mounds, from the Age of Ignorance."

That was in truth all we could say at that stage: that they were burial-mounds, and from before Islam.

There is no hard and fast rule for identifying and dating burial-mounds, which often disappoints people who take us to see those they have discovered. Burial-mounds are one of the most common cultural phenomena existing. There is scarcely a people which has not, at some stage in its history or prehistory—often at several widely separated stages—buried its dead under mounds; there is scarcely a part of the world which does not contain mounds raised at some period by its inhabitants. And mounds are nor-mally built of the materials to hand. In a grass-grown valley there will be turf mounds, on a gravel plain the mounds will be of gravel, on a rocky ridge they will be of rocks. Whatever their age, whoever their builders, they will tend to look like any other mounds. And any original distinctive features—even so distinc-tive a type as the circular mortuary buildings of Umm an-Nar—will be smoothed out and obliterated by the passage of time, as the material of the mound gradually seeks its own natural angle of repose.

These mounds were amorphous, like most mounds. All we could say was that they did not *appear* to be like the Umm an-Nar mounds. They might be earlier, or later.

But they certainly should be dug. If we could raise enough money to come back another year and dig them.

Now a year had passed, and we were going out again to look at the Buraimi mounds. Not to dig them.

We were faced with a problem of logistics. Up to now, if we had had two places, or more, that we wanted to dig, we had asked for, and received, the money to dig them simultaneously. That very year we were digging simultaneously at two sites in Bahrain and two in Kuwait and one in Qatar. Here in Abu Dhabi we had two sites, but the situation was very different from that in our other countries. Here the two sites were over a hundred miles apart, and the Buraimi mounds were in practically unexplored territory. The problems of supply in Buraimi were far greater than we had met elsewhere. The greater part of our supplies would have to be transported over the difficult road from the coast. There was no gasoline or oil available in Buraimi, and the tiny market in the village of Al-Ain could supply no foodstuffs except Japanese canned peaches. Moreover, our grants had been given to us for work on the island of Umm an-Nar, and new and substantial grants would be needed for work in the interior. And Abu Dhabi was no rich oil sheikhdom. Admittedly in this very year it became known that the off-shore drillings had struck oil in commercial quantities, and my old company was making its first test borings in a new area of the mainland west of Abu Dhabi town. But they had tried two areas before without results, and disappointment had made both the oil companies and the government cautious. There was little chance of an increase in our grants.

We had decided to work out a plan for successive digging at our two Abu Dhabi sites, to investigate the feasibility of digging for a month on Umm an-Nar and then moving our expedition to Buraimi for a further month. And the trip this year, 1960, was largely undertaken to investigate the possibilities of this plan. We needed to know whether it was possible to rent accommodation in Al-Ain village, and to find out what local supplies—of such things as bread and eggs and meat and vegetables—could be obtained in the area.

We need not have worried. Looking back now, after five seasons of work in Buraimi, we have difficulty in believing that we ever can have thought that the oasis could not support us. For Buraimi is the garden of Abu Dhabi, and for our expedition it has become a legend of sybaritic existence. Nowhere else in our working areas are the chickens so tender, the eggs so large and fresh, the fruit and vegetables so plentiful. Nowhere else can you, at close of work, lie and soak in a bathing pool at the outlet of the *qanat*, with running fresh water that is cool in summer and warm in winter.

After a single season in a hired house in Al-Ain we realized that even that degree of civilization was unnecessary; and, as we had done in Bahrain, we moved our dwelling to our digging sites. Now our two large villa-tents (a gift from a Danish manufacturer) are pitched each year among the acacia trees, looking out over low green foothills to the mountains of Muscat in the blue distance. Even Bahrain, with all its lushness, does not have the freshness and charm of Buraimi. Bahrain is a land of pleasure-gardens beside a turquoise sea—but Buraimi is an untouched savannah. As, in the sunny early morning, you watch the camels browsing sedately through the light clumps of trees in the middle distance, you forget the sea of sand that laps the oasis, still encroaching here and there. This, surely, is how the whole of Arabia once was.

(In the last few years we have found our researches tying in more and more closely with those of the climatologists and hydrologists, who are interested in the history of Arabia's weather and vegetation. But of that more later.)

From these sylvan encampments we have seen, year by year, civilization invading Buraimi, irresistible as the march of the sand dunes. We have seen it with sorrow, for civilization in the oil-lands is inseparable from constructional works, the building of roads, houses, palaces, schools, hospitals, water-works. The contractors and their machines move in, and it is all very well. For much of what they build is necessary. But the contractors never move out again. Constructional work becomes self-perpetuating. Increased royalties bring new and grander plans to supersede the old and half-completed. The immigrant workers themselves need houses and schools and hospitals. Building never stops.

There is a generation growing up in the Gulf, in Kuwait and in Qatar—to a lesser degree in Bahrain, where the tempo has always, wisely, been slower—in Saudi Arabia, and now in Abu Dhabi, which must regard bulldozer-scarred landscapes, houses half-built or half pulled down, streets unsurfaced and half-blocked by unfinished sewage and draining systems, as the natural order of things, who will never have known and never know either the clean simplicity of the oasis village or the broad vistas of the finished Garden City. They are the construction-camp generation, and it is a heavy price to pay.

Buraimi is to be held captive in a network of roads. A gridiron master-plan has been laid out, and for a month during our latest season our camp witnessed the march of progress, as the road-head went by. The roar of machinery ceased only for four hours during the night. Immense bright-yellow graders ploughed their way through the scrub, followed by a choking cloud of sand. For generations the vegetation of Buraimi had fought a gallant battle to subdue the sand blown in from the surrounding desert; but now the wind had found an ally. As the graders worked, a thick film of dust laid itself over the savannah, and over our camp. Given a little while, and it would have choked the life out of animal and plant life, and let in the desert. But progress moves fast. As we watched, the road grew. Between sunset and sunrise, a hundred yards of new road would appear. The new status-symbols of the oil-lands, the roundabouts, sprang up at regular intervals like mushrooms. And the storm passed: the roadhead went on into the distance, the roar of the caterpillars subsided to a muttering, and the dust-clouds were nothing but thunderheads upon the horizon. Peace descended once more on our little corner of Buraimi, a peace that had lasted four millennia and more, since last there had been building activity here. We went back to digging, without use of graders and steam-shovels, our four-thousand-year-old status-symbol, which oddly resembled the roundabouts along the new road. We called it in fact the Round Structure, for we had been uncertain at first of its true nature.

We had found it in 1962, the year in which we first began to dig in Buraimi. Our main objective had been to dig Sheikh Zayid's tumuli on the northern foothills of Jebel Hafit, and in two years we excavated twenty-seven of them. They proved to be totally unlike the burial chambers of Umm an-Nar on the coast, and equally unlike the mounds of Bahrain. Here a beehive-shaped chamber of dry-stone walling had been surrounded by a more or less carefully piled cairn of stones. A short entrance passage giving access from without to the chamber suggested that the tumuli were perhaps intended for more than one burial, but the tombs had been so thoroughly plundered that only in one case was it possible to conclude with some certainty that there had been at least two burials in the chamber. It was this mound, too, which gave us both our richest finds and the probable date of the mounds.

In Abu Dhabi we were meeting the same problem as we had met in Bahrain in the early years. Archæologically we were in *terra incognita,* and no settled chronology existed. In Kuwait we had found that our Bahrain chronology applied, for the settlements on Failaka had been of the same civilizations as those of Bahrain. But Abu Dhabi was clearly no colony of Bahrain. Just as the Umm an-Nar pottery in no way resembled that of Barbar, so

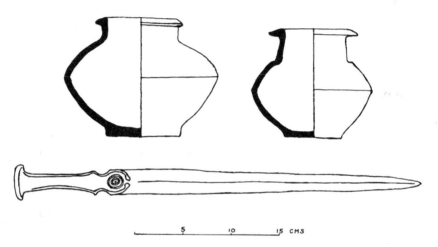

TYPICAL POTS OF THE CAIRNS ON THE SLOPES OF MOUNT HAFIT AT BURAIMI, TOGETHER WITH THE "LURISTAN" SWORD WHICH SUGGESTS A DATE OF ABOUT 1300 B.C.

the pottery of the Hafit tumuli of Buraimi resembled nothing from Bahrain (nor indeed from Umm an-Nar). They were pots with sharply angled (so-called carinated) bodies and a flat collar-like rim. They were not, of themselves, datable. But the bronze sword which we found, together with two of these pots, three bronze bowls, and an ornamented soap-stone dish, in tumulus number twenty, was not entirely unknown. It was a short sword, only seventeen inches long, with a flat pommel recessed on both sides to receive a wooden hilt-grip. And at the junction of pommel and blade there were two semi-circular cut-outs and below them, at the top of the blade, a raised decoration of two concentric circles. Somewhat similar swords are known in the Middle East. They are found in northern Syria, in southern Turkestan, and particularly in Luristan in northwest Persia. Here they occur together with the famous Luristan bronzes, the animal-ornamented "standards" and horse-trappings which appear to mark the arrival of Indo-European-speaking charioteers in the middle of the second millennium B.C. This sword, then, would appear to date the tumuli of Buraimi to about 1300 B.C., but at the same time poses a question which we are still nowhere near solving: how did a sword of this type reach Buraimi? Was it merely in the course of trade, or did the second-millennium invaders of Persia go further, and cross the Strait of Hormuz into east Arabia?

Oman was at this stage beginning to acquire a prehistory. We had two fixed points to which it could be attached, the "Umm an-Nar culture" on the coast at about 2500 B.C., and the Hafit mounds at Buraimi perhaps a thousand years later. But it was a precarious anchorage from which to fly the kite of theory. The two points were a hundred miles apart, and did not necessarily have any historical connection. The Umm an-Nar village might, for all we knew, have been a short-lived settlement of colonists from the Persian coast opposite, who had come and a generation or so later gone without having had any contact at all with the indigenous people of the interior; if indeed there had been any people in the interior until a thousand years later.

The Round Structure settled the matter. Knud and Arne were taken out to see it in 1962 by an emissary from Sheikh Zayid. It lay at the opposite end of the oasis from the Hafit mounds, well to the north between the village of Hili and the first range of Muscat mountains, in the midst of the green scrub-land that we now know so well. It lay there like a miniature Stonehenge, a rough circle of large stone slabs, most of them fallen but one still standing on edge. The circle was some twenty-five yards in diameter (Stonehenge is forty yards) and the stones of which it was composed were impressively large. The one still in place was six feet long and four feet high, and some of the fallen ones had clearly been even larger. Two immense stones at opposite sides of

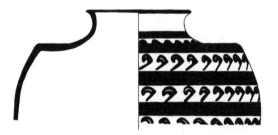

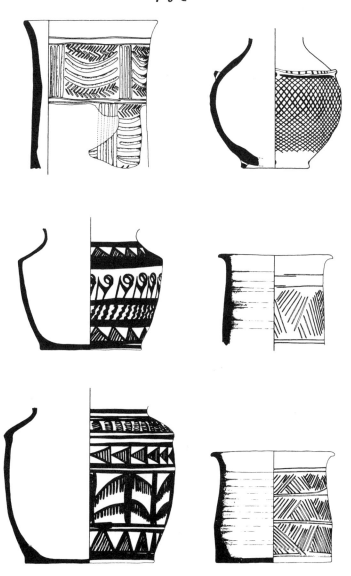

THE GREY PAINTED AND INCISED POTTERY FROM THE ROUND STRUCTURE—A
TOMB OF UMM AN-NAR TYPE—AT BURAIMI (THE PENDANT VASE AT TOP RIGHT,
HOWEVER, IS OF RED WARE). THIS POTTERY HAS CLEAR PARALLELS AT UMM
AN-NAR AND IN SOUTHEAST IRAN.

the ring, each broken into three pieces, had clearly been originally a good nine feet high and had had a "port-hole" entrance, of
a rounded triangular shape, through their centre. It was this
which already suggested to us that, despite the differences in
construction, we might here have a burial chamber of the same
type as that of Umm an-Nar.

This was confirmed the following year when Jens and Vagn
carried out a preliminary investigation while at the same time
digging Hafit tumuli at the rate of one a day. The surface of the
slight mound on which the great stones lay was thick with potsherds of the same grey and red wares with decoration in black
that we knew from the Umm an-Nar graves. And in 1964 and
1965 Jörgen excavated the whole structure.

All the work in Buraimi was done in "half-seasons," which in
practice rarely turned out to be longer than a month. Opening of
the camp on Umm an-Nar, its packing for removal to Buraimi,
and the final packing and despatch of the cases containing our
results, all took place at the coast, and the digging program on
Umm an-Nar always took longer than planned. There was always
too little time to spare for Buraimi.

Our work on Umm an-Nar changed during these subsequent
years. We were no longer digging the burial chambers, but had
turned to the settlement on the low ridge a hundred yards away
to the east. We had expected little of the settlement. We were not
even sure that it was of the same early date as the tombs, and in
any case the bare rock was showing through in several places.
There could be no great depth of soil. We began to dig, at the
south end of the ridge, where the outlines of the stone walls of a
one-roomed hut could be made out on the surface.

The hut turned out to be surprisingly well-built. The walls,
where the soil had protected them, were of limestone courses laid
in plaster, and they stood over three feet high. And then two
doorways were found in the walls, and two more rooms were
found beyond, with doorways leading to other rooms. Before the
season was completed, a large stone house over three hundred
square yards in area had been excavated, containing seven rectangular rooms each ten feet wide and up to thirty-five feet long.

We had to revise our opinion of the rude fishermen of prehistoric Abu Dhabi. This was a finer house than any in contemporary Abu Dhabi except the Sheikh's palace itself.

In the next two years, the two years during which the Round Structure at Buraimi was also being excavated, we dug further sections of the Umm an-Nar settlement, in the centre and the north of the village area. And in both areas we found well-built, spacious stone houses. They were filled, of course, with the debris of occupation, and from this we could try to learn more about this surprisingly substantial village and its inhabitants.

The first we learned was that they were in truth the builders of the burial chambers; for we found the same painted pottery in the houses as in the graves. But when the funeral cortege had left one of these houses for the cemetery it had taken with it the best of the family pottery. The fine ware which was found in such abundance in the tombs was rare in the houses, and the greater part of the pottery was thicker, coarser ware, sherds of large round-shouldered vessels with sharply out-turned rims, sometimes decorated with simple patterns in black paint, sometimes with an undulating pattern of raised ridges.

A spindle-whorl of bone suggested that spinning and weaving were not unknown, and two or three rubbing querns witnessed to the milling of some form of grain. But the presence of a large number of net-sinkers, stones of local limestone pierced with a hole, and a half-dozen copper fish-hooks, told us that fishing was one of the major occupations of the villagers. This was borne out by the large number of fish-bones which we collected, together with several boxes of animal bones. When these came to be analyzed by the zoologists in Copenhagen (the work is not yet completed) we got two considerable surprises. The bones of domestic animals, goats, sheep, and cattle, were rare, though not completely missing. But the bones of camel were common, as were those of gazelle. And the vast majority of the bones, apparently about eighty per cent of the total, were of the dugong, the sea-cow.

The dugong, the seal-like creature about the size of a man which is supposed to have given rise to the legend of the mermaid, is now exceedingly rare in the Arabian Gulf. I have told how Tim had served it to us on our first visit to Abu Dhabi in 1958. In the ten years since then I have seen a single skeleton, and heard of two dugong being caught in fishermen's nets. Four thousand years ago they must have been as common as seals in the Arctic, common enough to be the staple of life for a coastal community.

The other surprise was the camel. And yet it did not come entirely unheralded. In 1961, in the third year of digging on Umm an-Nar, our team had gone back to the large tomb-chamber which Mogens had had to leave the first year, when work was concentrated on elucidating the construction of a single mound. It had proved to resemble the first mound almost exactly, but it produced one new thing. Two of the outer slabs, which to judge by where they lay had originally stood one on either side of the southern port-hole entrance, had been ornamented with figures of animals in low relief. On the one was depicted a bull, notably of the straight-backed western type, and not the Indian humped bull such as was depicted on the pottery; on the other were the figures of an oryx and a camel. And now we had camel bones.

This is interesting, because the camel appears late in the register of man's domestic animals. It was unknown in Mesopotamia and Syria, in Palestine and Egypt, until about 1500 B.C., when the Aramæan invaders rode north into the Fertile Crescent from the interior of Arabia—on camels.

Like most general statements in archæology this needs qualification. There is a copper pin from the earliest levels at Ur, the levels called the Al-Ubaid culture, which bears as its head a perfect, though tiny, figure of a kneeling camel. We shall meet the Al-Ubaid culture again, in a context which may make the camel-pin more than a little significant.

Anyway, it is now clear that the inhabitants of the village on Umm an-Nar knew—and ate—the camel a thousand years before it was introduced into the civilized regions further north. It is not proven, of course, that the camel was domesticated in Umm an-Nar. The carving shows no traces of harness; the bones do not tell us—yet—whether the camels were wild or tame. But the fact that the camel was well known in the Oman at this early date makes it likely enough that it was in this region that the camel was first tamed.

Our picture of the "Umm an-Nar culture" was by now surprisingly detailed, more detailed than our picture of the "Barbar culture" of Bahrain on which we had been digging so much longer. This circumstance illustrates the difference between *sondage* and "area" digging. In Qala'at al-Bahrain we had our seven cities piled one above the other. We were in the course of obtaining a practically complete historical sequence—something we entirely lacked in the Oman—but the areas we dug were too small to give us a picture of the life of the city at any one time. On Umm an-Nar we had a small village with only one period of occupation, complete with cemetery. Even the intensive archæology of northern Europe seldom meets such a fortunate combination. But when it does it is astounding what can be discovered by complete and detailed investigation. Size of population, average life expectancy, prevalent illnesses, size of flocks and herds, diet, occupations—these are but some of the results that can be obtained from a "total" area excavation. Our excavation of the Umm an-Nar community was not total. But we were getting to know

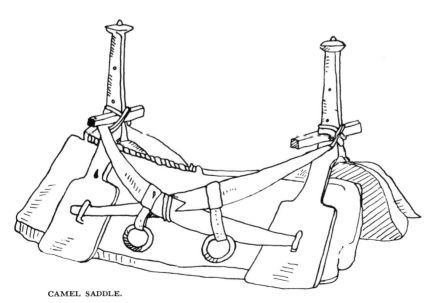

CAMEL SADDLE.

them quite well. And the better we knew them the more an anomaly obtruded itself. Here we had a village of perhaps a score of solidly built stone houses, closely packed in the centre, with more spacious houses on the outskirts. It was an industrious population, the men out all day, fishing, hunting the sea-cow in the creeks or the gazelle on the plains; the women spinning, weaving, making pottery or bead-embroidery; the children tending sheep and perhaps camels. Occasionally a pack-train of donkeys, or again perhaps of camels, would leave the village for the interior, on the five-day journey to Buraimi, with its load of dried fish, or return with dates or firewood. On the way they would pass the cemetery, its pill-box structures of even finer masonry and covering a larger area than the village. The living must have been dominated by the dead.

It was a well-rounded, consistent picture. But it did not fit into Abu Dhabi as we knew it, and certainly not into Umm an-Nar. On Umm an-Nar there was no water for a village. For miles there was no grazing for the flocks and herds we were postulating. The coastal sand-flats could never support the quantities of game evidenced by the bones we were digging up. And the fisherman or herdsman of Abu Dhabi today does not build houses of stone. On the coast he builds palm-leaf *barastis;* in Buraimi he builds of sun-dried brick. Stone houses are an unnecessary luxury in a country with a rainfall of about two inches a year.

And there lay the answer to the anomaly. The community we were excavating was one which was geared to a different climate, in particular to a greater rainfall, than that of the present day.

CHAPTER FIFTEEN

𝇁𝇁𝇁𝇁𝇁

LOOKING FOR GERRHA

For fifteen years two lands had been tantalizing us. Sitting before our tents of an evening in Buraimi we could see the setting sun gilding the mountains of Muscat; and in the mornings the same mountains stood black against the dawn sky, the burial tumuli along their crests thrown into sharp relief. Muscat was forbidden territory, and those tumuli must not be investigated, not even approached. Jörgen had climbed up to them once, believing that the frontier ran along the actual ridge. But he had been turned back by a posse of Muscat soldiery. Muscat was barred to us.

There was a disturbing possibility. Since we had discovered the Round Structure, and identified it as a tomb of the Umm an-Nar culture, we had been looking, in vain, for the tell which ought to cover the town or city in which the people buried there had lived. But half of the Buraimi oasis lies in Muscat territory. The frontier, ill-defined though it is, ran within a mile of the tomb. And it began to look more and more as though the settlement we sought might lie in the wrong country, in the area in which we must not look.

Behind it all was the wider picture. We had demonstrated, with our discovery that our "Umm an-Nar culture" was also to be found in the interior at Buraimi, that there had existed an indigenous civilization in the Oman in the third millennium B.C. And there was a strong possibility that this was the missing land of

Makan, the land that had supplied copper to Mesopotamia during the height of the Bronze Age. If this were really so, then the copper mines and the cities of what must have been one of the richest civilizations of the ancient East, certainly the richest still undiscovered, must lie beyond the closed frontier to the east.

The Sultanate of Muscat and Oman comprises the greater part of the Oman peninsula, the eastward projection of Arabia which divides the Arabian Gulf from the Indian Ocean. It includes almost the whole of the mountain massif east of the Empty Quarter, and almost the whole of the coastline which looks towards Baluchistan and India. We have twice written to the Sultan, asking for a permit to look for prehistoric remains in his country. Twice we have been politely but firmly refused. On the whole I do not blame him. For some years there had been sporadic trouble in the interior of the Oman, where a religious leader with some historic claim to some degree of autonomy had been pretending to an absolute autonomy to which he had no historic claim. For some time there was what amounted to civil war in the interior, and after the Imam was finally expelled in 1958 there had been occasional guerrilla activity, including a disturbingly large number of land mines positioned on the few tracks passable for motor vehicles. I could understand that the Sultan might well feel that there was no great urgency about the rediscovery of a civilization which had been lost for four thousand years, while irresponsible archæologists roaming at will in the interior might well be an embarrassment, and at best would require a large and well-armed escort.

But Muscat still beckons us across the green ridges of Buraimi, with its promise of the proof that we here in Oman have the land of Makan.

Saudi Arabia had been beckoning us longer and more enticingly. Any night we could see from the ramparts of the Portuguese fort the lights of Dhahran, the oil-company town, across the twenty miles of water that separate Bahrain from the mainland. Every day four planes flew each way the twenty-minute run from Muharraq airport to Dhahran airport. In Qatar we were even closer; driving south from Umm Bab, where the bay of

Bahrain really begins to narrow, you can see the Saudi Arabian coastline apparently only a stone's throw away. Holger, who had been quartering the peninsula for four years surveying the Stone-Age sites of Qatar, even claimed that he had been across the frontier, driving for miles through the desert due south from the last of the Qatar police posts until even his police guide admitted that they were beyond Qatar territory.

Saudi Arabia is *big*, on a scale that overshadows even Muscat. It comprises almost the whole of the Arabian peninsula, a territory over two-thirds the size of India, larger than Mexico, and it lay behind and between all the states in which we had hitherto been working. Often I felt that our investigations in Kuwait and Qatar, in Bahrain and Abu Dhabi, were mere nibblings along the edge of the vast territory of Great Arabia, that whatever we found was dwarfed into insignificance by the huge area beyond about which we knew nothing.

For our researches in the Gulf an exploration of the eastern coastal area of Saudi Arabia was not merely desirable; it was practically essential. We had found our "Barbar culture" in Bahrain, and on Failaka. Between the two lay 250 miles of unexplored coast—of Saudi Arabia. It was impossible for us to test our theories on the relationship between the two sites of our culture without some idea of whether other sites lay in the intervening territory. Something with a bearing on our work there must in any case be. For Sargon of Assyria had conquered "Bit-Iakin on the shore of the Bitter Sea as far as the border of Dilmun." So, in Assyrian times at least, at the time of our Bahrain City IV, there had been settlements on the mainland, perhaps frontier posts and fortifications. We could not regard our work as adequately performed until we had looked at Saudi Arabia.

But it was axiomatic that we could not get into Saudi Arabia. No one could get in. We had made enquiries, in the early years. Bahrain government officials and British Political Agents had shrugged their shoulders. You can apply, they said. There is admittedly no one here you can apply *to*, but you can write to the Ministry of the Interior or the Foreign Ministry and apply. You will not get a reply, they said, or if you do it will be after six months and it will be a request for further information. No one ever gets as far as getting a visa.

We had asked our friends among the sheikhs of Bahrain and Qatar. For we knew that they regularly travelled to Saudi Arabia on hunting trips. And they professed astonishment that there could be any difficulty. We will send a letter, they said, or give you a guide, and you will be able to go in without difficulty. But somehow the letter or the guide was never forthcoming at a time when we could use them. We had relegated any thought of entering Saudi Arabia to some hypothetical future when the Saudi Arabian government would become "progressive." And just as others had told us that it was impossible to get into Saudi Arabia, we told others the same. We did not, of course, waste our time applying.

It is in fact quite easy to get permission to enter Saudi Arabia. And I ought to have known how.

There is a system of travel among the tribes of the Arabian peninsula which is certainly older than Islam. To enter the territory of a tribe with which your own tribe is not explicitly in alliance is highly dangerous—unless you have a sponsor. A sponsor is a member of the tribe in question, rarely a person of consequence and often merely a paid guide. But his presence is sufficient to ensure your safety. For he has assumed responsibility for you: if you are killed he is in honour bound to avenge you, to track down your killer and slay him; if you are robbed honour demands that he recover or reimburse your loss. At the same time he assumes responsibility for *your* good conduct, and if *you* kill someone the resultant vendetta will be directed against him and his family.

This system I knew well. I had to explain it every year to our new expedition members who could not understand that our watchmen slept all night and most of the day. It was not necessary to watch, once they had assumed responsibility for us and our goods, I used to say. We, as strangers, were fair game, but no one would infringe our watchmen's honour and risk their vengeance by stealing from us, once we had appointed them. But I had not realized that in Saudi Arabia the system has been developed on a national level. To obtain a visa all you need is a sponsor within the country.

Had we realized this we could perhaps have done something about it, though we in fact knew no one within Saudi Arabia whom we could have asked to act. But fortunately knowledge of our presence in the Gulf and of what we were finding was being noised abroad. As in the case of Qatar and Kuwait and Abu Dhabi, the initiative came from within the country itself. In the summer of 1960 Al and Doris visited us in Aarhus. They were from the Arabian American Oil Company in Dhahran, and they told us of a buried city at a place called Thaj, sixty miles inland and halfway between Bahrain and Kuwait. The same summer Jack and Betsy, also of Dhahran, called in with a concrete proposal. P.V. and I should visit Dhahran during our next season in the Gulf, deliver a lecture to the oil company personnel, and then spend some days exploring.

I confess that we did not take the proposal seriously. We knew that it was impossible to get into Saudi Arabia. So we wasted another season without taking action, and it was only in 1962 that energetic action on the part of Jack and Bert and Marny gave results. We got a telegram in Bahrain, about a fortnight before Christmas, that we were expected, and that visas would be issued on arrival in Dhahran.

The composition of the party had been changed. P.V. was in Kuwait, but Vibeke was with me in Bahrain once more, as well as Michael, now seven years old. It was to be a family party.

I had not at that time realized the strength of the archæological faction in the oil town of Dhahran. When I looked over the packed gathering that was assembled in the cinema to hear me tell of our findings in the Gulf I began to understand the numbers of the enthusiasts, and next day when I learned that a spotting plane was at my disposal it was clear that archæology in Dhahran commanded a respect to which we were by no means accustomed.

There is a phenomenon in Aramco known as "pot-picking." Early every Thursday morning, at the beginning of the Moslem weekend, desert-going vehicles leave the gates of the oil town in large numbers, bound for distant, and often secret, destinations in the desert. There whole families will spend hours quartering the sand, looking for interesting or attractive potsherds or other objects. Some *cognoscenti* specialize in one or other of these "other objects," in beads, or flint arrowheads, or even coins. At the time of our visit this collecting was widespread but largely uninformed. Obviously some of the things found were more important or more interesting than others. But few of the pot-pickers had any idea which. The large attendance at my lecture was not so much caused by a desire to know what we had found in the Gulf states, as to know whether what we had found bore any relation to what they had found. That, of course, was what we wanted to know too. And now some score of the more serious pot-pickers had banded together to show us their best collecting areas. And as this number included some very senior members of the oil company, among them the president and at least four vice presidents, some very excellent facilities for viewing these areas could be laid on. The spotting plane was an ideal beginning.

But as we flew low over the sand dunes, with Michael gazing spellbound out of the window, we began to appreciate the sheer size of our new field of operation. A dimension had been added. Saudi Arabia possesses not merely 350 miles of coastline between Kuwait and Qatar; behind the coastline lies a hinterland stretching 750 miles to the Red Sea, and south of that hinterland lies as much again.

We were not going to look at all that today. In a sort of briefing before the flight it had been explained that we would merely look at sites within a convenient day's journey from Dhahran. We would fly about seventy-five miles north and south along the coast and about sixty miles inland. That meant that we should only look at some nine thousand of the nine hundred thousand square miles of Arabia. But that was thirty-six times the area of Bahrain, which it had once taken us a month to explore indifferently well; it was over twice the area of Qatar, whose investigation had already taken us six years and was to take us one year more.

That year we had twenty-six archæologists working in the Gulf, three in Abu Dhabi, three in Qatar, ten in Bahrain, and ten in Kuwait. We were not only stretched to the limits of centralized organization—we were stretched to the limits of what Denmark could supply of archæologists. The archæological crisis of the High Dam at Aswan, with its prospect of flooding important historical areas of Egypt and the Sudan, was upon us, and the Scandinavian team working in the Sudan on an emergency survey of the area soon to be lost had already robbed us of Yunis and taken several other prospective members of our teams. We had had to recruit beyond the Danish frontier, and two Norwegians were working with us in Kuwait. If we were to extend into Saudi Arabia we would be faced with an organizational and manpower problem of a magnitude equal to the size of the new areas.

As we swung up the coast, after cruising over an extensive mound-field south of Dhahran—which looked for all the world like the mound-fields of Bahrain—I shelved the problems of organization and looked down upon the palm groves and culti- vated fields of Qatif. Most of the coast of Arabia north and south of the rocky peninsula on which Dhahran stands is barren, with yellowish white hillocks of sand forming a barrier between the copper-green shallows of the sea and the brownish-white salt flats which run parallel to the coast. Where there are wells, or where modern borings have supplied artesian water, there are villages and small, labouriously irrigated date plantations. But the Qatif area is different. It is Bahrain all over again. Water in abundance here comes to the surface without help from man, and an area the size of the northern, cultivated part of Bahrain is covered with the same unrestricted vegetation. But the area is under siege. To the north and west great crescent-shaped dunes press hard against the plantations, and in places the first wave has already broken against the palms. Among the dunes the chimneys of abandoned wells suggest that cultivation once covered a greater area.

The Qatif gardens lie along the coast of a deep bay, and our plane now crossed the short stretch of shallow water to the island of Tarut in the centre of the bay. From the air Tarut seemed almost artificial. It is circular and about five miles across. Salt marsh and reed swamps around the coast ring an almost circular

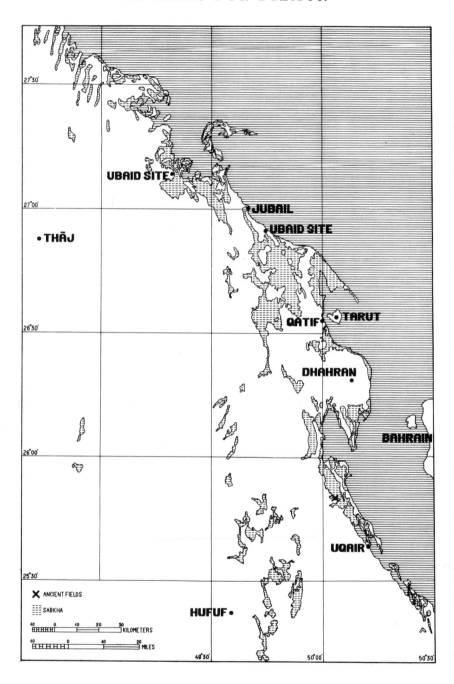

THE EASTERN PROVINCE OF SAUDI ARABIA.

area of palm groves, and in the very centre of the island and of the palm area lies the village of Tarut. In the centre of the village a ruined fort crowned a small steep-sided hill, the only elevation on the island. We were interested in Tarut, for it is named by the earliest Arab geographers, while the town of Darin, on its southern shore, is recorded as the seat of a Nestorian bishopric before Islam.

Now we turned inland across the salt flats, dipping to circle once over Jawan, an island of rock in the *sabkha* where the only archæological excavation yet conducted in Arabia had taken place. The outcrop had been leased by Aramco as a quarry, and the bulldozers had found a settlement tell and a large grave-mound. With the permission of the government Aramco had been allowed to excavate the grave-mound, and Ric Vidal of their staff, who is an archæologist by training, had excavated with great skill what the bulldozers had left. The mound had been completely removed in the process, and as we circled we could see the large cruciform chamber, in the floor of which Ric had found four plundered graves and a quantity of human bones from later mass burials. In the angles of the cross, outside the chamber proper, we could see the stone-built graves which no one had expected, and which had therefore escaped the attention of grave-robbers. From them Ric had recovered some very fine jewelry of gold and precious stones, which dated the graves to the first century A.D.

We flew for twenty minutes due west, soon crossing the pipeline road which ran straight as an arrow to the northwestern horizon on its thousand-mile journey to the Mediterranean and the old Phoenician port of Sidon. Built to service the pipeline carrying Dhahran's oil to the markets of Europe, the road had become the main traffic artery for the transport of fruit, vegetables, and all manner of goods from the Mediterranean to the Arabian Gulf. In Kuwait and Doha, the capital of Qatar, we had often seen the big heavily laden trucks with Lebanese or Jordanian license-plates which regularly made the trip. The wastes of sand and stone below us now, lifeless save for a sprinkling of sparse bushes, would have been slow and difficult to cross without the road. Yet camel tracks, and even vehicle tracks, could be frequently seen. The country was not impassable—it was not even considered by the Arab to be desert at all, for camels and sheep could graze here all the year round, and wells were less than a day's journey apart. I began to wonder if, in our preoccupation with sea-trade, we had thought too little of the land routes across Arabia. Certainly the city of Thaj, for which we were heading, must have lain on some such precursor of the Trans-Arabian Pipeline route.

Ahead lay three mesas and a jumble of low hills, and suddenly we were over Thaj. I had seen air-photographs, and knew what to expect. But I was not prepared for the scale. Below lay a considerable city, the parallelogram of its defensive walls plainly visible. And around it stretched fields of tumuli, many of the mounds oddly ring-shaped, a circular rampart with a hollow in the middle. We flew back and forth over the site half a dozen times while I took in the scene. There were no standing walls or buildings, apart from a cluster of obviously recent stone houses. Everything was covered in sand and rubble, but the general outline was clear. And one thing was completely obvious.

Thaj was a city on the edge of a lake. It stretched for almost a mile along the lake-shore, and half a mile or more inland. Only there was no lake . . . to the northern side of the city stretched a large salt-pan, a *sabkha*.

Now, *sabkhas* are areas of salt mud which clearly once have been water. They are dried-up lakes. They are useless to man. There would be no reason to build a city beside a *sabkha*. Therefore this one-time lake had still been a lake when Thaj was built. This was going to tie up with our speculations on the prehistoric climate of Arabia, for only a higher rainfall, or at least a higher water-table, could have held water in the lake-bed. We needed to date Thaj.

I finished making notes and taking photographs, and we turned south for the fifty-minute flight to Hofuf. The territory was monotonous, the same stretches of stone and scattered bushes, followed by miles of sand dunes where it was useless to look for signs of prehistoric settlement. Then came a metalled road, and cliffs dropping down to a sandy depression, and ahead of us were date plantations again.

Hofuf is the largest oasis in eastern Arabia. I had expected something like Buraimi, for Hofuf covers much the same area, lies forty miles inland against Buraimi's one hundred miles, and like Buraimi is rather a collection of small oases than one single area. But the similarity did not survive inspection. Hofuf has no mountains, nor any of the stretches of sparse grass and thorn trees which give their charm to Buraimi. Hofuf is more like Bahrain or Qatif, with intensive cultivation of dates and even of rice for miles around each spring, and naked sand desert in between. Nor were there any obvious signs from the air of pre-Islamic remains, of earthworks or fortifications or grave-mounds. Hofuf itself was a large walled city, but its walls, we knew, were of fairly recent date, and its motor roads and streets of shops showed no signs of surrounding or overlying an earlier city.

This was to some extent disappointing. For there was reason to believe that there ought to be something at Hofuf. Hofuf ought to be the oasis of Attene—particularly if Gerrha was at Uqair. As we flew the forty-odd miles toward the coast and Uqair, I reviewed once more the "Gerrha problem."

We had come across references to the great Arabian city of Gerrha when we were looking into the question of the identification of Failaka with the classical island of Ikaros. And now I tried to recall what we had discovered then from our reading of what Greek and Roman writers had said about the Gulf. There was more about Gerrha than about any other place in Arabia, but even so it was not more than could be committed to a small sheet of paper. Oddly enough, in Arrian's description of Alexander's preparation for his campaign against Arabia, including the coastal explorations of 323 B.C., there was not the slightest mention of Gerrha. But Eratosthenes, writing about a hundred years after Alexander, tells of the merchants of Gerrha carrying their spices and incense overland to Mesopotamia. This is contradicted by Aristobulus, says Strabo, who tells that the merchants travelled by raft to Babylonia. Strabo, who wrote in the last two decades B.C., quotes Artemidorus, of the previous century, as saying: "By the incense trade . . . the Gerrhaei have become the richest of all tribes, and possess a great quantity of wrought articles in gold and silver, such as couches, tripods, basins, drinking vessels; to which we must add the costly magnificence of their houses; for the doors, walls, and roofs are variegated with inlaid ivory, gold, silver, and precious stones."

The historian Polybius about the same time tells of a campaign of the Seleucid king, Antiochus III, who took a fleet along the Arabian coast in 205 B.C. with the intention of conquering Gerrha; but he was persuaded, by large presents of silver and precious stones, to leave the city unharmed.

There was thus little doubt that in the first, second, and third centuries B.C. Gerrha was an exceedingly wealthy city, trading overland and by sea in aromatics, presumably the frankincense of the Hadramaut. Strabo even tells us where Gerrha lay, but his account is difficult to interpret. Gerrha, he says, is "a city situated on a deep gulf; it is inhabited by Chaldæans, exiles from Babylon; the soil contains salt and the people live in houses made of salt. . . . The city is 200 stadia"—about sixty miles—"distant from the sea." And you sail "onward," he says, from Gerrha to Tylos and Arados, which are the Bahrain islands.

The elder Pliny, writing in the middle of the first century A.D., is more explicit, and I knew his description by heart. Describing the Arabian shore of the Gulf he comes to the island of Ichara, which must be our Ikaros, and then the Gulf of Capeus, and then the Gulf of Gerrha. "Here we find the city of Gerrha, five miles in circumference, with towers built of square blocks of salt. Fifty miles from the coast, lying in the interior, is the region of Attene, and opposite to Gerrha is the island of Tylos, an equal number of miles distant from the coast; it is famous for the vast numbers of its pearls. . . ."

Tylos, we knew, was Bahrain, and the region of Attene fifty miles inland was normally believed to be the Hofuf oasis which was now disappearing in the heat haze behind us. On the coast, on the direct line between Hofuf and Bahrain, lay the village of Uqair, and beside it the ruins of a large walled town. It had seemed obvious to many modern theorists that Uqair must be Gerrha, and the identification seemed clinched by the fact that, in the local dialect of Arabic, the letter *q* is pronounced as *g*. Uqair is pronounced Ogair, which was close enough to the Greek name to be convincing. Admittedly it was known that a walled city had been built at Uqair in Islamic times, but this was believed to lie on the offshore island where the present Uqair village stands. In any case, we knew of other sites not so far away where Islamic cities lay beside or above cities of Seleucid or earlier date.

There were dunes below us, continuous waves of sand upon sand, but ahead we could see the waters of the Gulf, with a broad belt of *sabkha* and lagoon between sand and sea. A single clump of palms and a ruined tower marked the site of the abandoned city of Uqair. As we traced its walls, quartering back and forth, we could see that it was a larger city than Thaj, as indeed would be expected if Pliny's dimensions were to be trusted. Its walls traced a polygon, running out at either end across the salt flats to large square towers by the water's edge. Looking back, with the benefit of hindsight, I think I felt then that there was something wrong with that.

We had one more call to make on our way back up the coast to Dhahran, sixty miles or so to our north. Twenty miles north of Uqair there was a large area, where the dunes scattered and broke against the *sabkha*. Aramco had been carrying out a seismic survey here some years ago, and had photographed the area from the air in that connection. And the air photographs had shown an odd network of markings, too regular to be natural, covering the whole area. They were scarcely visible from the ground, being ridges in the salt flats scarcely more than six inches high, but because of what appeared on the air photographs the geologists had investigated them, and were inclined to believe that they were ancient irrigation ditches. If that were so, there had been an area under cultivation here at least as large as the garden area around Qatif.

It proved difficult to find from the air. It was seven or eight miles inland, on the landward side of a very extensive *sabkha* which ran north from the lagoon at Uqair right to the root of the Dhahran peninsula. And when we did find it the sight added little to the photographs—except to emphasize that it was only by chance of wind and sand that the area was visible at all. Inland and to north and south the sand dunes spread unbroken, and for all we knew the former irrigated fields might extend under the sand all the way to Uqair, or for the matter of that to Hofuf.

Our pilot set his course for the Dhahran airport, and I fell to thinking of sand and *sabkha*. Thaj lay on a *sabkha* which, when Thaj was a living city, must have been a living lake. The culti-vated area at Qatif had been greater once, before the sand moved in. The area of former cultivation we had just seen was drowned in *sabkha* and half-covered in sand. Clearly *sabkha* had been winning ground at the expense of water, and sand at the expense of soil. But how fast? and how continuously? and how long ago?

In Buraimi we had sand encroachment; on Umm an-Nar we had a former settlement dependent on water where today there is no water. On Qatar we were finding Stone-Age sites lining the "shores" of extensive *sabkhas*. In Bahrain the Stone-Age sites ran along the ten-metre contour, suggesting that the sea lay that much higher (or the land that much lower) at the date of the flint sites, which could be anything from twenty to forty thousand years ago.

Climatic changes and changes of sea-level could act and react on each other, cancelling or reinforcing their various effects. And man could cancel or reinforce the effects of nature, keeping cultivation in being when it would otherwise have died, by dig-ging deeper for his water, or creating a desert before it was climatically unavoidable, by over-cultivation and over-grazing.

My speculations were becoming unrealistic. If they were to test out, the first necessity was to put a date to the phenomena. The putative lake at Thaj could be dated only by dating Thaj; the disappearance of cultivation north of Uqair by dating the irriga-tion channels. And that could not be done from the air.

The next morning around ten o'clock we were dating Thaj. We were squatting within the hollow of one of Thaj's ring-mounds, and I was looking at the neck of a large jar which Al had just dug up, and which bore an inscription in black paint in a script which I did not know. Then Al suddenly looked up at something behind me. I turned, to find myself gazing into the muzzle of a rifle carried by a black-bearded Arab.

Like so many events in Arabia, it turned out less dramatically than it can be made to sound. Tom, whose Arabic is fluent and idiomatic, unconcernedly wished our visitor good-day. "Digging is forbidden by the government," said the man, and asked us where we came from. Tom explained that they were of the oil company, and they had a learned man with them who could tell them the history of Thaj merely by looking at bits of pottery. The Arab slung his rifle and squatted beside us. To dig up pots from the ground, he explained, one must have a *firman,* a piece of paper from the Emir in Dammam. We must leave these pots where we had found them. But there were many bits of pot on the surface by the village, and in the village there were stones in the house-walls with writing on them. If we wished, he could show them to us.

As we walked to the village amid the ruins of Thaj we learned that he was the headman and represented the government here. He in turn looked curiously at the five vehicles of our party and said, shrewdly, "Yesterday there came an aeroplane that flew many times over our houses; and today you come in many cars. I think you are planning to bore for oil or water here." We protested that we were interested only in history, and he nodded, half prepared to accept our story, for academic knowledge is traditionally held in high esteem by the Arab. We entered a dark stone house, and our guide pointed to the upper corner of one of the walls. As our eyes grew accustomed to the gloom we could see that one of the stones bore a carved inscription, and gradually we could make out the lettering of the so-called South-Arabian script.

The script is called South-Arabian, or Sabæan, because it was first found in the area of the ancient Sabæan kingdom in south-west Arabia. It has of later years been found in a considerable number of places throughout Arabia, either on gravestones, as this one undoubtedly was, or carved on cliff faces. It is a script, not a language, and, being alphabetic, it presented none of the difficulties of decipherment that we have seen in the case of Babylonian. The language of the inscriptions is Semitic, and closely related to Arabic. Philologists can find minor variations between the languages written in the script in north and south Arabia. Whether these languages deserve separate names is not a matter for an archæologist to express an opinion on. There would seem to be grounds for calling the *script* merely pre-Islamic Arabian. For that is what it is. It seems to have been in use from about 800 B.C. to about A.D. 400.

So that was the first approximation to an age-bracket for Thaj. Though in fact we knew as much already, for three other inscriptions in this script had been found at Thaj some fifty years before and published, and the Aramco pot-pickers knew of four more on the site. A closer dating would still have to depend on potsherds. And we spread out over the site, still accompanied by the headman.

Now, for the pot-pickers of Aramco, each site had its speciality. And the speciality of Thaj was figurines. As on all settlement sites the ground surface was covered with hundreds of thousands of potsherds, but here there lay among them a very large number of fragments of small terra-cotta statuettes. Almost immediately our searchers began finding such fragments. They were mainly of animals, often legs or heads of unidentifiable beasts, but the fragments of bodies almost always bore the hump that identified them as camels. Frequently harness could be made out, represented by lines or chains of circles grooved into the clay. There were also fragments of human figurines, almost always of kneeling naked women, their hair arranged in three braids, one on each shoulder and a central one down the back. The figurines varied a little in size, but were mainly about six inches high. The fragments were small, and often badly weathered, but such was their number—fifty must have been found within the hour—that it was not difficult to make out what the complete figure had looked like.

The figurines I could not date; we had found figurines in Bahrain in many different levels, and none exactly like these. But it was not necessary. The pottery we knew very well indeed. With the first fragment of a thin bowl, red painted and radially burnished inside, I was on familiar ground. This was the pottery which we had found in the Greek town on Failaka, and in our Fifth City on Bahrain. It belonged beyond a doubt to the third century B.C. There were also numerous fragments of the square four-legged "incense-burners" characteristic of this period. The matter was clinched with the finding of eight fragments of glossy black varnished pottery, pieces of small ring-based bowls. They were Attic ware, imports from Greece itself. Some of them were, even rouletted, decorated with a close pattern of semi-circles made with a toothed wheel, a characteristic which proved their Greek origin beyond a doubt.

We had not much time to spend in Thaj. We had started in the dark an hour before dawn, and we arrived back at Dhahran in the dark an hour after sunset. But we covered three hundred miles out and back, eight hours driving and five hours on the site. At three in the afternoon we had to start the homeward trip. By this time the headman was infected with our enthusiasm for the relics of his city; he had taken us to see the two mighty wells, twenty feet across and at least twenty feet down to the dry sandbed in their bottom. They lay south of the town, each with a complicated system of cisterns and aqueducts still discernible around the well-head. And he had shown us the cap-stones of a grave recently discovered west of the town, and seemed almost disappointed that we had neither time nor permission to excavate it. We promised to return one day, and started on the sixty miles of deeply sanded track which we must traverse before we could reach the pipeline road a hundred miles northwest of Dhahran.

This was the pattern of the following days. Next day we started toward the south. Today we were to look for Gerrha, driving to Uqair sixty miles down the coast. It is no easy route. North of Uqair stretches the immense salt flat which we had seen from the air, between the sand dunes along the coast and the sand dunes of the interior. We had to force a neck of the dunes to reach the flat, roaring and sliding through powdery sand in lowest gear and four-wheel drive. And the *sabkha* beyond was treacherous, clearly one of the coastal flats which vary in bearing power according to the state of the tide. It was deeply rutted by the wheels of heavy traffic, for this is the main route to Qatar for the fruit and vegetable trucks from the Lebanon which have fol-lowed the pipeline road. Time and again we met with water-filled pits in the track, where vehicles had gone through the surface crust and had been dug out; and cautious detours had to be made around these places, over *sabkha* which had not even the doubt-ful advantage of having been compacted by previous traffic. It was hazardous to leave the beaten track through the salt-marsh. But we left it, at the point, some twenty miles north of Uqair, where the area of former irrigation should have been easy to find. It was not. We plunged into a maze of sand-hillocks, complicated by bushes and small patches of *sabkha,* and completely lost our way in a matter of moments. One after another our desert-going vehicles ploughed into sand to their hubs, and had to be pushed and pulled clear by the united efforts of all twenty or so of our party. Only seven-year-old Michael, I think, really enjoyed himself. His kindergarten had never had a sand-pit like this.

We made our way with difficulty eastward again to the *sabkha,* and gingerly across it until we hit once more the Uqair highway.

The ruined city of Uqair stretches more vastly on the ground than it had appeared from the air. As I followed the northern wall across the *sabkha* toward the shore, the ruined tower—certainly a modern addition—which marked the southwestern corner seemed immeasurably far away, and the other pot-pickers, moving toward it each by his own route, were already dwarfed by distance. Ahead of me the wall ended at a coastal tower, like the wall only a course or so high, by the narrow strait, and beyond the strait lay the mud-brick houses and yellow fort of the present village. The wall beneath my feet was broad, and built of the coral-like conglomerate which the inhabitants of the Gulf quarry at low tide from the seabed, and which they call *farush.* And that felt wrong, just as the fact that the city wall traversed the *sabkha* at all felt wrong. I recalled how, the day before, we had followed the city wall of Thaj until it reached the *sabkha,* and stopped. I was already beginning to believe that anywhere where there was *sabkha* today there had been water even as recently as two thousand years ago. If that were true, then this wall could not be as old as the wall of Thaj. And, again, in the city of the "Greek" period on Bahrain, and the temple town of the Seleucids on Failaka, *farush* was never used. The walls there were always of quarried limestone. I turned off the wall, and began to cross the city toward the southwest tower.

By the time I got there, with a bag-full of potsherds, I was convinced; and an examination of the sherds picked up by the rest of the party confirmed the diagnosis which not only I but all the rest of the party had come to. After all, most of us had been at Thaj the day before. There we had collected sherds and figurines and scraps of "incense-burners" of the very centuries when Gerrha had flourished. We could all have recognized the same pottery and the same artifacts if we had seen them here. But there were none. There were sherds of glazed pottery, and of incised yellow ware, fragments of ring-bases and of handled vessels. It was a typical Islamic assemblage. Of course there might, as in Bahrain, be an Islamic city built upon a Seleucid-period city, and in that case the Islamic pottery would predominate. But here there was nothing at all of earlier date. Negative evidence, admittedly, proves little. And over much of the city the sand dunes had rolled in to a depth that could well cover an earlier city. But at least the city which appeared on the surface was not Gerrha. And if Gerrha lay beneath the sand dunes it might lie anywhere. Gerrha was still a lost city.

It is still a lost city. Much has happened, archæologically, in Saudi Arabia since that first reconnaissance in December 1962, but Gerrha, with its riches of gold and silver and its houses inlaid with ivory and precious stones, still awaits its discoverer.

Back in Denmark in 1963 we made formal application to extend our researches to Saudi Arabia. There was no department of the Saudi Arabian government at that time entrusted with the care of the antiquities of the country, and our application went apparently unheeded. But that year a commission was appointed to investigate the setting up of a department of Saudi Arabian antiquities.

In 1964 I again spent five days in Dhahran, and this time P.V. came too. We looked once more at Thaj, and this time crossed to the island of Tarut.

The year before we had seen, from the air, the tiny steep-sided tell, crowned by its ruined castle, in the centre of the town which lies in the centre of the island of Tarut. Now we saw the tell from the ground: it looked highly promising—and completely impossible. It was exceedingly steep, and on three sides it was completely hemmed in by houses, built into and dug into the tell, so that the hill-side in fact ran down to the *tops* of their back walls.

When we tried to go round to the fourth side, where there seemed to be a more open area, we were turned firmly away by the men of the town. That side was *haram*, they said, forbidden. It was for the women, where they washed and laundered. We must not look at the women.

We found a narrow alleyway between houses which led up to the permitted side of the tell, and climbed onto the narrow strip of steep bare hill-side between the tops of the houses below and the foot of the massive walls of the summit ruins. And immediately I picked up a rim-sherd of our typical "Barbar" pottery. Everywhere upon the tell lay our well-known red ridged sherds. Once more we were in Dilmun.

There was nothing we could do. We had no permission to dig; we had no time to dig—and had we had permission, time, and money to dig, we should not have known how to begin on such a totally enclosed site. We collected a bag of sherds to prove that this was indeed a site of the "Barbar culture," and therefore the oldest town by far in Saudi Arabia. And we returned to Dhahran.

The next day we drove three hundred miles to Riyadh, the capital of Saudi Arabia. The commission on antiquities was still considering its recommendations, and it was a measure of the growing interest in archæology that we had been asked to lecture to the historical faculty of Riyadh University on our work in the Gulf states.

The road to Riyadh was well-kept and fast; with no towns and little traffic our American limousine covered the distance in four hours flat, gliding between endless sand dunes, descending a rocky escarpment, and then crossing a hundred miles of gravel plain. Fifty years before an earlier Danish explorer, Barclay Raunkiær, had travelled the other way, from Riyadh to the coast at Uqair, by camel caravan, and had taken fourteen days for the journey. We had seen his sketches of Riyadh, a tiny walled town with a large fort rising above the low clay houses, surrounded by palm groves. Now the fort alone survives, a national memorial whose dramatic capture by Abdul-Aziz ibn Saud in 1908 marked the beginning of the Saudi conquest of almost the whole of Arabia. Around the fort a modern capital has grown up, with an imposing avenue along which the ministries stand, each in its

own grounds, each vying with the others in architectural magnificence. And it was in a large and very modern lecture theatre that
I gave my account of ten years of archæology along the eastern
borders of their country. The large audience of students and
professors listened intently, and then spent a full hour in questions and discussion, all revolving around one point, how to make
a start on the archæology of Saudi Arabia itself. We were left in
no doubt that the younger generation of Arabia, at least, was
eager to see us extend our researches to their country.

Again that summer we addressed an application to the government. And again we received not even an acknowledgment. But
when in 1965 I again crossed over from Bahrain to Dhahran, to
lecture once more to Aramco, I learned that a department of
antiquities had been set up under the Ministry of Education.

It was during this trip that the search for Gerrha was taken a
step further. On the second day Bert and Marny drove me out to
the area twenty miles north of Uqair which we had failed so
signally to find two years before.

Now there was no difficulty. The area had been opened up by
the pot-pickers, and we followed a well-worn trail across the
sabkha to the edge of the dunes. Here the dunes encroached
upon the *sabkha,* so that hundreds of small "lakes" of flat salt-pan
lay surrounded by low hills of fine white sand. And across all the
low-lying pans we could see the regular rectangular patterns of
irrigation ditches, sometimes showing as sand-filled depressions,

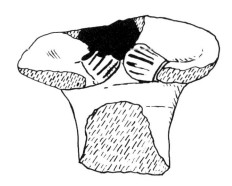

FRAGMENT, 2¼ INCHES HIGH, OF ONE OF THE "MOTHER-GODDESS" FIGURINES
FROM THAJ. THAT ALL THE DAMAGE IS NOT RECENT IS SHOWN BY THE PATCH
OF BITUMEN AT THE NECK, AN ANCIENT REPAIR OF A BROKEN-OFF HEAD.

sometimes standing up a foot or so above the level of the surrounding salt. We followed the usual program of reconnaissance,
the program which we had followed on every new site for a
dozen years. We spread out, twenty yards apart, and began to
look for potsherds and other surface objects. When we gathered
again, for chicken sandwiches and coffee from paper cups, we
had a mixed bag to consider and compare. There was a copper
coin, undecipherable. There were two leaf-shaped bronze arrowheads, and one barbed and tanged flint arrowhead. There were a
few beads. And there were a score or so of potsherds. And these
did not belong anywhere in our sequence.

There was no glazed ware, and nothing of Islamic character;
but there was no Thaj ware either, nor Kassite, nor Barbar. Such
rim-sherds as there were were of necked vessels with a rim turned
outward and down. They could not, in the present state of our
knowledge, be dated. Clearly it was a pre-Islamic site, but
clearly, too, everything was not of the same date. The coin could
not be older than about 500 B.C., the bronze arrowheads were
probably about the same date or a little earlier, the flint arrowhead could hardly be later than 3000 B.C. The area itself seemed
almost entirely agricultural. We had found a fort, a small rectangle of ramparts protruding scarcely two feet above the surrounding *sabkha,* but otherwise no trace of buildings. There was no
city.

But we had only looked at a tiny portion of a truly vast area of
cultivation. And inland the irrigation ditches disappeared beneath dunes running to a hundred feet in height. The place had
no name on the maps, and we agreed to call it "Gerrha," in firmly
inverted commas.

The next day I flew to Riyadh, to meet the department of
antiquities. It consisted, I discovered, of a group of four enthusiastic young men, recently graduated in history or Islamic architecture from Cairo University. And they were very eager to
receive advice on how to organize their department. We spent
two days in conference on essential equipment, on organization
of an archive system, and on the possibility of gaining practical
excavation experience. And then I returned to Bahrain.

Three years were to pass before I saw "Gerrha" again.

៛៛៛៛៛

CHAPTER SIXTEEN

៛៛៛៛៛

"THE DOCK-YARD HOUSE
OF THE LAND"

There were a few years in the beginning of the 1960's when it seemed as though expansion was the natural law of our expeditions in the Arabian Gulf.

In Kuwait the expeditions grew in size from year to year. Kristian was still working on the environs of his Greek temple, which was now very firmly dated by the inscription slab and by the hoard of silver coins.

When Kristian came to study the casts of the inscription in Denmark he found that it was indeed, as was to be expected, dated. The second figure of the year was not very clear, but it appeared to be 73. This would be reckoning from the beginning of the Seleucid era in 312 B.C., and the temple was therefore erected in 239 B.C., in the reign of Seleukos II Kallinikos.

The coins were treated by the conservators of the Coin and Medal Department of the National Museum in Copenhagen. The report of the director of the Department, Otto Mørkholm, is worth quoting *in extenso*:

"It occasioned some immediate disappointment that no less than twelve of the thirteen silver tetradrachmas into which the lump of metal had resolved were of the same type. But just this circumstance will be seen to be of especial importance.

"The dating of the hoard is dependent upon the one outsider in the collection. This can be said with certainty to have been minted by the Syrian king Antiochus III, who ruled the Seleucid Empire from 223 to 187 B.C. We can come even closer. The portrait of the monarch on the obverse shows Antiochus III as a very young man, and our knowledge of the development of his portraiture allows us to place this coin in the beginning of his reign, to about 223–12 B.C. . . . The coin is still in such excellent preservation that it can hardly have been in circulation for very many years. If we therefore date its burial, and with it that of the whole hoard, to about 210–200 B.C., we shall certainly not be far from the truth.

"The remaining twelve coins must be approximately contemporary with the Seleucid coin, as they are just as well preserved as it. . . . The coins were . . . minted in the name of Alexander the Great, even though there must have been an interval of about a hundred years between his death in 323 B.C. and the date of their striking.

"A comparison with a coin from the time of Alexander also shows that much water must have flowed through the Persian Gulf since his time. The coins from Failaka are in every respect barbaric in style. This can perhaps be seen most clearly in the strangely distorted seated figure on the reverse of the coins, but the representation of the head of Herakles must also cause any philhellene to shudder. Moreover the die-cutters were clearly not entirely sure of their Greek script, as there is in the inscription a happy lack of precision in the use of the letters A, Λ and Δ. The letter P is more often written as ϙ." (The latter sign, I may say, is a letter of the 'South Arabian' alphabet.)

"It will perhaps appear remarkable that at this period the coin-types and name of Alexander the Great were still used on the coins, but the explanation is not far to seek. A consequence of Alexander's enormous minting of gold and silver coins of very high quality was that his coins were for several hundred years the favourite medium of payment in international trade. . . . In the third and second centuries B.C. they were therefore imitated in many places. . . .

"Where, then, can it be supposed that the barbarianized Failaka coins originate? . . . A closer examination of the hoard shows that no less than eight of the twelve Alexander-coins have been struck with the same obverse die, and that the same reverse die also occurs in several cases. Such a concentration of dies in a single hoard normally means that the coins have gone by a fairly direct route from the mint to the place of burial without having been in circulation in the interim. It indicates, too, that the place and time of burial is not far removed from the place and time of minting, even though there can naturally be no certainty on this point. The problem is thus to find a locality in the East which lies outside the frontiers of the Hellenistic kingdom (where, of course, coins were struck in the name of the reigning king) but which at the same time was so closely associated with the Greek world as to make it reasonable to expect an 'à la grecque' minting there. It should moreover lie on one of the main trade-routes in that area, for without trade there would be no coins. It would be tempting to indicate Failaka itself as the location of the mint, but an argument against this identification is the fact that Failaka appears precisely at this period to have been under Seleucid rule, as appears from the inscription also discovered in 1960. Another hypothesis is attractive. The leading trading people in eastern Arabia at this time were the Gerrhaeans, an Arab tribe whose capital, Gerrha, lay on the Arabian mainland just opposite Bahrain. From the geographer Strabo, who lived in the time of Augustus but who used earlier, Hellenistic source-material, we know that this people made enormous incomes by trading the precious wares of Arabia and India, in particular spices, and we learn in addition that their trade-route ran from Gerrha to the mouth of the Euphrates and the Tigris (in other words immediately by Failaka), and on up these rivers to the large cities of Seleucia and Susa. From there the enterprising traders proceeded along the upper course of the rivers and on by the ancient caravan routes to the coast of Syria and Phoenicia. They even reached as far as Delos in the Aegean Sea, as is shown by inscriptions on this island from the middle of the second century B.C. In this connection it is worthy of note that Antiochus III felt it necessary in 205 B.C. to make a large-scale military demonstration against the Gerrhaeans, with the object of securing for himself a reasonable proportion of their trade. There is no suggestion, however, of a subjection of their territory, and peace appears to have been speedily re-established. It is tempting to see a connection of some sort between the burial of the treasure on Failaka and this campaign. But however this may be, it can be said that there is a reasonable probability that the barbarianized Alexander-coins in the Failaka hoard originated in Gerrha."

In their little "Barbar culture" township a stone's throw away on Failaka, Poul and Oscar had, by 1962, found a total of 290 Dilmun stamp-seals. This township had also produced a dozen or so cuneiform inscriptions, on seals, on tablets, on fragments of steatite bowls, and on the rims of pottery vessels. On two of these stood the same inscription as that previously found: "Temple of the god Inzak" and at least four others named this tutelary god of Dilmun. One steatite inscription, broken and barely decipherable, even named Dilmun itself. Our conclusion that the "Barbar culture" was the culture of Dilmun seemed thereby proven beyond a doubt.

In Qatar, Holger was systematically quartering the peninsula, with two or three companions, mapping in each year twenty or thirty new flint sites. Holger belongs to the sagas. Then nearly seventy years old, with piercing blue eyes and a jutting white beard, he had for years worked as an amateur flint-archæologist with the Danish National Museum, and was a recognized authority on the Danish Stone Age. Now he was becoming a respected and loved figure in Qatar, known to all the sheikhs and the Bedouin as the leader of the remarkable group of Danes who *walked* the peninsula, where even the meanest Arab rides at least a donkey, and who always could pull from their pockets handsful of flint scrapers and arrowheads.

In the Oman we were working at Buraimi, on the easternmost edge of Abu Dhabi, and in those years we still had hopes of penetrating Muscat. And one year we did indeed cross the mountains to the eastward, though not in Muscat.

The Trucial States, of which Abu Dhabi is one, lie for the most part along the western seaboard of the Oman peninsula. But one, Sharjah, extends across the northern end of the Oman mountain chain, to touch the eastern coast at Dibba; while another, Fujaira, lies entirely on the eastern seaboard, cutting the main territory of

Muscat off from its foothold on the headland of Ras Musandam at the entrance to the Arabian Gulf. In 1964 P.V. and I drove north to Sharjah and over the mountains to Dibba.

It was a hair-raising journey. As far as the crest of the mountains the route followed a broad *wadi,* where our land-rover as often as not was driving in the bed of the shallow stream which wound down it. On either hand were steep cliffs of gravel, cut through by the stream, and as we mounted these were replaced by rock escarpments, with a vista of precipitous hills beyond. The country was wild and beautiful, with bushes and trees and a wealth of flowering plants. Finally we swung into the village of Musafi, dominated by a ruined fort upon a sheer-sided mount, and into the encampment of the Trucial Oman Scouts on the edge of the village.

The Scouts are a local regiment with British officers whose task is to keep the peace among the unruly tribes of the Trucial States. We had met them at their fort in Buraimi oasis, and it was there that we had heard of Dibba. It seems that the Scouts, in the course of exercises there, had dug trenches and stumbled on an ancient site with potsherds and a large number of fragments of ornamented soap-stone vessels. We had visited regimental headquarters in Sharjah, and obtained permission from the colonel— grudgingly and after some hesitation—to go to Dibba and be shown what they had found. It was clear that the colonel was not at all sure that Dibba was a good place for civilians.

As we sat over a warm beer on the *barasti* verandah of the officers' mess at Musafi we were told why. Up in the mountains of Ras Musandam, said the squadron adjutant, lives a tribe of shepherds and small cultivators known as the Shihu. They are fiercely independent fighters, fanatical Moslems, and, while recognizing the authority of the Sultan of Muscat, they allow no stranger to enter their territory. I listened with interest, for I had heard of the Shihu before. Many years ago, in the old oil-company days, Ron and I had often discussed them. Ron had been our representative in Dubai, and a student of the obscurer dialects of Arabic. And he had been intrigued by the rumour that the Shihu spoke a language which no Arab could understand. I too, as an incipient

333

archæologist and a former cuneiform student, was intrigued. In this furthest corner of the Arabian peninsula anything could have survived, as Celtic has survived in the Welsh and Scottish mountains and Basque in the Pyrenees. Here we could even have a survival of Sumerian, or of the still unknown language of Dilmun.

With great caution and at some risk Ron had made the acquaintance of people in Ras al-Khaima on the border of Shihu territory who had contacts with the "lost tribe," and even of two or three "renegade" Shihu who had crossed the frontier and settled in Ras al-Khaima. And he collected some sixty words of the Shihu language, as well as two of the tiny iron axes on a long tough shaft which every Shihu male carries. The language had proved somewhat disappointing. It was a dialect of Persian—as I suppose as an archæologist I should have suspected; for the bearers of the Indo-European languages, of which Persian is one, who spread over Europe and Asia in the second millennium B.C. were also bearers of battle-axes. And if the Shihu were indeed a fossil survival, then their little iron battle-axes indicated that they might be a survival of this wave of invasion.

Now the Shihu were massing, the Musafi adjutant told us, in the hills above Dibba. The boundaries between Muscat and Sharjah and Fujaira all met at Dibba, and had never been defined to the satisfaction of all parties. The Shihu claimed that Sharjah had occupied part of their territory, and were threatening to redress their grievance by force of arms. For two months a squadron of the Scouts had been sitting encamped on the plain south of Dibba, hoping that tempers would cool and negotiations take the place of threats. But tribal war could break out at any time.

We went on. And the character of the landscape changed. The Oman mountains have their gentler slopes on the western side, the way we had come. On the east they fall precipitously to the coast. Almost at once we entered a steep *wadi* whose sides quickly became cliffs towering above us and almost cutting out the sunlight. The gorge widened a little and we passed through a village, with mud-brick houses clinging to the steep slopes. And then the track narrowed again, and steepened, and degenerated into a jumble of boulders, through which wandered the little

334

stream which was all that remained of the water masses which must have carved the chasm. Our progress slowed to a crawl, and less than a crawl, with stops to negotiate the way ahead or investigate the depth of the hidden drop beyond the next boulder, and reversals to escape from impassable rock traps. Like a mule the land-rover picked its way down from boulder to boulder, scraping the sheer walls of the cleft, and leaning and twisting at impossible angles. Wherever there was a talus slope or a break in the cliffs lay tiny millet fields, hardly larger than window-boxes, with the soil held in place by massive dry-stone walls. And along the cliff-face and across the track ran irrigation channels, ingeniously built and engineered to carry water to the miniature fields.

Our descent seemed to continue for hours. Then abruptly the canyon turned a corner, and the cliffs fell away on either hand. Before us stretched level ground, a grass-clad gravel plain which, we knew, extended six miles to the sea, formed by outwash from such gorges as that we had just traversed.

The Scouts had their camp by the beach; and there we symbolically dipped our trowels in the Indian Ocean, as Sargon of Akkad and Hammurabi and Tiglathpileser had dipped their swords in the Mediterranean, to mark the limits imposed by nature on their empire. Eastward of us lay India, five hundred miles distant. It may have been imagination that the Indian Ocean was a deeper blue than the Arabian Gulf; but concretely beneath our feet were the magnificent shells, leopard-spotted and many-fingered pink, which the shallow waters of our Gulf have never produced, but which we find time and again in our diggings, to show that sailors to the Indies have changed little in five thousand years. To the north and south the mountains ran out in steep headlands into the sea; for Dibba's gravel plain is ringed on three sides by the mountains. It is only approachable from the sea, and by the hazardous route by which we had come.

The site, when we drove out in the early evening to see it, was as featureless as the plain which surrounded it. There were no surface indications that anything lay below. But at the bottom of the zigzag line of trenches, perhaps a metre below the surface, bones and potsherds could be seen protruding. The site was not easy to interpret. Nothing looks so unscientific as last year's excavation, with the sharp delineations weathered away and obscured by falls of sand, and with the layered sections baked by a summer's sun to a uniform brick-white. These trenches had been dug two years before, and not with any scientific rectangularity in the first place. Although we scraped and scraped with our trowels we could find no stratigraphy in the cement-hard sides of the trenches, nothing to suggest that these were graves, dug down from a surface somewhere near the present. With all due reservation I give now as my opinion that the Dibba site (it is about a mile and a half southwest of Dibba itself) will prove to be a settlement, a town or village site, and that the three feet of gravel above it has accumulated as a result of flash floods.

Our scraping in the trenches produced a large quantity of potsherds, soap-stone fragments, and animal bones. The pottery was mainly fragments of deep bowls with a slight shoulder below an out-turned rim, rather the same shape as the bowls in which the snakes had been offered in Assyrian-period Bahrain. But here many were painted in geometrical patterns, black designs on a plum-red ground, or red on buff. In many cases the decoration was on the inside of the bowls. The soap-stone vessels were mainly the beehive-shaped pots which we meet so often, in steatite and in alabaster, in the Seleucid period. There was a leaf-shaped bronze arrowhead resembling closely those we were to find the following year at the "Gerrha" site in Saudi Arabia. And there were two buttons of shell, one of them two inches across and decorated with hollows surrounded each by two incised circles.

Such an assemblage, differing radically from anything we had found up to now, and in an area distant from any in which we—or indeed any archæologist—had previously worked, is difficult to date with confidence. It was clearly pre-Islamic, and equally clearly unconnected with our third millennium B.C. cultures of Barbar and Umm an-Nar. The bronze arrowhead suggested an early first millennium B.C. date, and when we got back to our books in Denmark that year we found a shell button, very like the one from Dibba, which had been found at Nineveh, in layers dating to the Assyrian period, about 900 B.C. It is a dangerous parallel, for Nineveh is a thousand miles away, and shell buttons are not the kind of article with definite schools of decoration. But we must do the best we can with what we have, pending further investigation. And further investigation in Dibba presents logistical and financial problems of a very extreme nature.

In the meantime, our work in Bahrain went on; year by year the same grants from the government, and the oil company, and the Carlsberg Breweries. Year by year a team of the same size, though changing more than I should have liked in composition, followed the program that was meant, one of these years, to round off our work to a point where we could pause and publish.

After all the early vicissitudes we had settled down to a pattern, after all. The team was always seven strong, of whom one ran the camp for us. Since Yunis left us, Vibeke had taken on that job for two years, but now the children were in school, and Svend's wife, Lillian, had taken over. And six archæologists worked in three teams of two.

We had finished excavating the Barbar temple, and had bulldozed the sand back to cover it once more. This may well have been a mistake from the viewpoint of public relations. But though the government and the sheikhs were proud of their temple, there was still no authority in Bahrain which could effectively guard the island's antiquities. Stone-robbing was as rife as it ever had been, and even if vandalism could be avoided only an efficient antiquities service could prevent the temple walls from collapsing through natural weathering of the exposed sand beneath.

So now we could concentrate on the city tell, and even spare manpower for some of the projects on our "waiting list."

One team dug in the "palace" area in the centre of the Qala'at al-Bahrain site; one team followed the fortification wall around the city. And the third team was our tactical reserve, to be thrown in as opportunity offered or circumstances demanded. In 1963, when a land-reclamation project had resulted in the gravel being bulldozed off the top of several hundred grave-mounds, this team had opened over fifty of the exposed chambers, and for the first time collected a really comprehensive assemblage of the typical pottery of the grave-mounds. The robbers had been there before us, in apparently every case. Nothing of intrinsic value remained, save a single link of a gold chain. There were no seals, and this was rather odd, for one would have expected seals to have been a peculiarly personal possession, which might well—as in other lands and other periods—have accompanied their own-ers to the grave. It was made odder by the fact that we found two "mock seals," objects of the size and shape of seals carved from the inner whorls of conch shells, with the spiral inner surface of the shell forming a "mock design" on the obverse of the seal. But in almost every tomb chamber we found the fragments of two or three or four pottery vessels, and sometimes even undamaged pots. The egg-shaped, necked vessels of red ridged Barbar ware were common, common enough to leave us in no doubt that the grave-mounds were of Barbar date. Most common of all were the high, bag-shaped vessels of red clay, with cylindrical rilled necks, such as the one we had found in the first tomb we had opened in 1954. It seemed to be a type of pot used almost exclusively as funeral furnishings, for in all our diggings at Qala'at al-Bahrain and at Barbar we had only found a scattered handful of sherds from this type of vessel. And among the hundred or so vessels there were three or four—round-based splayed-necked beakers—which the books told us were of Mesopotamian type, and these belonged to the time of Sargon of Akkad and his successors, or to the succeeding period of the dynasties of Isin and Larsa, the period 2300–2000 B.C., to which we had already dated our "Barbar period."

The following year P.V. took a team out to dig into two of the huge "Royal Tumuli" near Ali village. We had always hesitated to tackle these immense mounds, up to forty feet high. For they were of limited number, perhaps thirty or so in all, and most of them had been opened, with gaping tunnels or shafts leading into the huge stone chambers in the centre. Some of this digging was the work of our predecessors, Durand and Prideaux and

Theodore Bent, but of most there was no record. We could only justify excavating one of the "Royal Mounds" if we could do better than they had done, digging it scientifically with section drawings and plans, which would involve removing the greater part of the mound. This was the sort of project which would take a whole season or two for our full team. And we had never had a season to spare.

But now events forced our hands. The contractors had been at work. Bulldozers had attacked two of the apparently unopened giant tumuli, cutting back into the skirts of the mounds and removing the earth for the land-reclamation projects. Well into the mounds they had hit a solid masonry wall, ten feet high and encircling the mounds, without a break except on the western side, where the ring-wall met the entrance to a passage-way leading into the heart of the mound. This wall had also been largely removed by the contractors, for quarried stone is worth money and the monuments of the forgotten kings of Dilmun are not. But there even the contractors had stopped. For behind the ring-wall towers the bulk of the mound, and it could defend itself. Any attempt to dig further would result in falls of sand and gravel that could overwhelm the attackers.

P.V. cut in at the exposed passage-way, in half its width in order to leave a section to show how the mound was built up. And in the first mound he found himself immediately cutting along a robber tunnel. Though choked with sand it showed clearly in the section face, driven straight down the entrance passage a little above its floor. The robbers had entered the chamber, but we did not. For when P.V. reached the end of the passage, forty-five feet into the mound with the stone retaining wall now towering fifteen feet above him, he found the cap-stones of the chamber broken under their own weight and sagging downward, held up by the sand which filled the chamber. To support these stones, each several tons in weight and with the whole weight of the mound above them, while emptying the chamber of sand, would have required hydraulic jacks and girders which we did not possess. We called in the state engineer, and the oil-company engineers, to look at the problem, but they too had no equipment capable of coping with the work of the engineers of four thousand years ago. We turned back at the massive threshold stone. But the robbers had got in, and from their tunnel we recovered proof of the treasures which had lain within the grave, and which perhaps still lie there. One of the robbers had dropped his load. It had broken, and been left where it lay. It was a little heap of potsherds. We assembled them in the camp, and found that they comprised a nest of three small bowls of egg-shell thinness and two pedestal cups, wine-glass shaped, ornamented with chevrons and triangles in black paint on a wine-red ground. They were a table-service worthy of the kings of Dilmun.

The second tumulus went exactly as the first. Without removing the whole of the upper thirty feet of earth and gravel it was impossible to prop the broken cap-stones of the chamber in such a way that the chamber could be excavated without serious danger to our workmen. But one season, if Allah will, we shall go back, with foreknowledge and full equipment, and find out what the robbers have left us of the "Royal Graves" of Dilmun.

In the meantime, back in the capital city of Dilmun we were beginning to get involved with the Kassites.

Any patient reader who cannot at this point immediately say, "Ah, yes, City Three," may be forgiven. We had difficulty ourselves in remembering our sequence of cultures at Qala'at al-Bahrain, even though it was basic to our whole prehistory of the Gulf. We, too, had to start from the beginning, with "City One—chain-ridge ware; City Two—Barbar, seals and grave-mounds; City Three—Kassite ware; City Four—the 'Assyrian palace'; City Five—Greek ware; City Six—the Islamic period; City Seven—the Portuguese." And of all the cities the one we knew least about was that of the Kassite ware.

To call it a city at all was a misnomer. The patient reader cannot be expected to remember, but we had not forgotten that in the *sondage* that gave the Seven-City Sequence the Kassite ware was only found in rubbish pits dug down into "Barbar period" deposits. Rubbish pits argue some sort of habitation not far away, but we had found no traces of buildings of that period.

We believed that that was as it should be. The period was approximately dated, for the pottery was identical with that used in Mesopotamia during the period of about 1700–1200 B.C., when northern Babylonia at least was dominated by the Kassite invaders. And an article had been written by A. L. Oppenheim in 1954 called "The Sea-faring Merchants of Ur" (*Journal of the American Oriental Society 74*), which had shown, on a basis of the Sumerian trading tablets, how Mesopotamian trade with Dilmun, Makan, and Meluhha had continuously regressed. In the time of Sargon, about 2300 B.C., ships from all three countries dock at his capital; by the Third Dynasty of Ur two hundred years later, only voyages to Makan are recorded; two hundred years later again our friend Ea-nasir only sails as far as Dilmun. And after that there is silence—save for two letters of the Kassite period concerned only with local production of dates—until the expansion of the Assyrian kings brings them to the Dilmun border. Oppenheim's theory was that Dilmun's prosperity had depended on the transit trade of luxury goods from the Indus Valley civilization and of copper from Makan; that the Indus trade had been disrupted by the sack of the Indus cities (the Aryans were increasingly being blamed for this, and the date 1600 B.C. increasingly mentioned as likely), and that something, perhaps a similar invasion of Indo-European speakers, had at the same time disrupted the Makan copper trade (to myself I thought, "The Shihu?"); and that Dilmun had stagnated. It looked that way to us too. The Barbar temple had been abandoned, grave-mounds had ceased to be built, the houses by the northern wall of Qala'at al-Bahrain were given up. We imagined the people of Kassite times—they might even *be* Kassite invaders, at that—living in the patched-up ruins of their Barbar-period predecessors, scavenging the ruins for building stone, and filling the resultant holes with rubbish.

But now our Kassites were beginning to obtrude. In 1962 we had cut completely through the west wall of the city, and found Kassite sherds embedded in the upper, rebuilt portion of the wall, to show that the Kassites had at least repaired their defenses. In 1963 we dug at three points to find the south wall of the city. All three *sondages* were interesting, though too small to tell us all that we would have wished. The westernmost hit the corner of a square tower jutting from the Barbar-period wall, below a whole series of later fortifications, some as late as Islamic times. In the centre *sondage* the Islamic fortification, a massive concrete structure which it would have required dynamite to demolish, lay immediately over the Barbar-period wall. It would have been impossible to investigate the lower wall had we not found a narrow gateway in the later wall, making a gap in which we could go deeper. And there we found, to our incredulous surprise, that the "Barbar" wall was here preserved in its full original height.

There could be no doubt. We reached first a narrow, round-topped wall, some eight or nine inches thick, and four feet further down we found that this stood on the outer edge of the city wall itself, with the walk for the sentries immediately behind, its cement worn smooth by their tread and renewed three times. Below, the wall went down a further eight feet. Parapet and breastwork were here fully preserved, and from the outside we could look up the sheer plastered side of the city wall and see it as it must have appeared to attackers approaching from the landward side. The inner side of the wall was quarried away. The parapet broke sharply off, and the edges of the quarry pit stood out clearly in the sides of our *sondage*. In the narrow space behind the stone-robbers' trench, at the level of the foot of the wall, lay the burnt and dismembered bones of at least six individuals, scattered in complete disorder. Precisely what these bones were doing here we never discovered. Our *sondage*, five metres square to begin with, had been reduced to half of that by the wall and further reduced by substantial buildings of City IV date which we had decided to leave undisturbed. And then—by what I believe is known as Finagle's Law, which says that what can go wrong will go wrong—an Islamic well had been driven down precisely on the line which we had chosen for our main section. The area left to us when we reached the "charnel house" level, sixteen feet down, measured eight by four feet. The bones may well represent the sack of the Barbar-period city, but to be sure would mean extending the *sondage* over a wider area. We have added the skeletons by the south wall to the long list of things which ought, someday when we have more time and money, to be investigated more fully.

The third *sondage* was far to the east, near the southeast corner of the tell. Hitherto we had dug only on the western half of the tell, and this new hole was three hundred yards or more from our nearest previous excavation. We laid out a long trench down the side of the tell, crossing an extension of the line on which we had located the wall in the two previous *sondages*. And we found a wall, but it was not the wall we now knew so well. It was not so wide as the Barber-period wall, though substantial enough—a full six feet across—to be undoubtedly a fortification. And at the foot, on the outer side, there was a glacis, a sloping footing designed to hinder the placing of scaling ladders. Within the wall, to its full depth, were four metres of occupation earth, full of quantities of Kassite pottery. So this was a Kassite wall, and it looked as though the Kassite city had extended over a larger area than the city which had preceded it. That changed our view of the Kassites.

The diggings going on at the same time in the centre of the tell were changing our view of the Kassites too. Year by year the "palace" had been growing, each year's excavation adding three or four new rooms. We were inclined to consider the term "palace" by now somewhat exaggerated. For it began to look now as though we had two adjoining palaces, which was rather a contradiction in terms. There were at least two entrances, each with a threshold stone which must have weighed two tons, and there was a party-wall without any doorway separating the two complexes of rooms. Both were exceptionally large, if looked upon as private houses, and faced, toward the street, with incredibly fine masonry. The first one had, to one side of the entrance hall, a chapel with an altar, at just the place, to the right of the main entrance, where chapels always stood in the houses in Ur from 1800 B.C. The adjoining "palace" had one very large and finely proportioned room with double doors at either end and in the centre of each side, which we immediately dubbed the "throne-

343

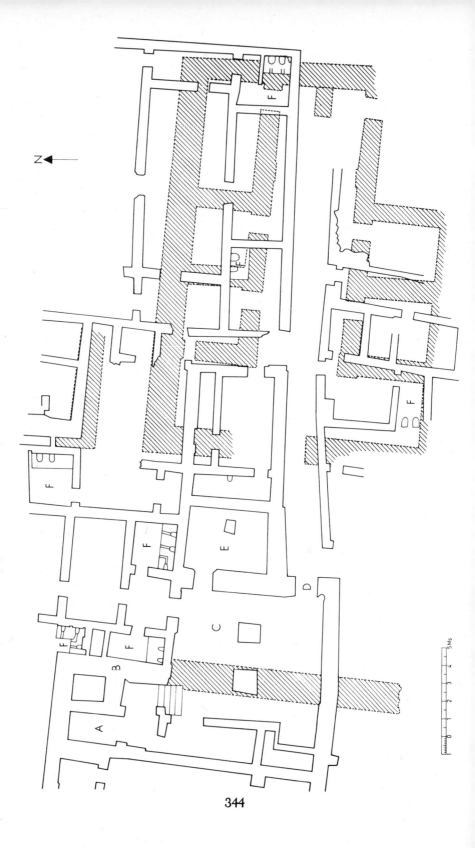

344

room." Both had at least three toilets, each with two or three "Oriental-type" earth closets, which we felt was rather excessive provision for a purely private house. Palaces or no, these were undoubtedly the residences of very wealthy and prominent citizens.

We were still worried about the dating of these buildings. They could not be later than the bath-tub-coffins buried through their floors, of which we had now found four. And these were dated to about 650 B.C. But we were not sure how much earlier than this the buildings could be. In 1962 we started a series of trenches through the floors, in order to date the levels below, and thereby obtain a bracket. And there we met the Kassites.

Immediately below the floor of the eastern "palace" we encountered massive walls of cut stone, walls almost a yard thick, which was nearly twice the width of the "palace" walls above. We followed them down to a cement floor three feet further down. And as our trenches continued they gradually revealed a large rectangular building of regular plan. It consisted of a long narrow central courtyard with a row of five small square rooms on either side.

Just so clearly as the building above was a dwelling, this clearly was not. Here were no chapels, or throne-rooms, or toilets, just the series of uniform rooms opening off the long central hall or court. And whereas the building above had been completely emptied of its contents when it was abandoned, this building had

THE CENTRAL EXCAVATION AT QALA'AT AL-BAHRAIN. THE WALLS OF THE ASSYRIAN-PERIOD "PALACE" (CITY IV) ARE SHOWN PLAIN, THOSE OF THE KASSITE WAREHOUSE BELOW (CITY III) ARE SHADED.

A. HERE, WHERE THE EXCAVATION STARTED, WERE FOUND THREE "BATH-TUB" COFFINS.

B. THIS WALL SURVIVES, TO A HEIGHT OF TWELVE FEET, FROM THE KASSITE PERIOD, AND WAS INCORPORATED AS IT STOOD IN THE "PALACE." A STREET, FORTY FEET WIDE, SEPARATES IT FROM THE KASSITE BUILDING TO THE EAST.

C. THE GREAT COURT, WHERE THE FIRST SNAKE-BURIALS WERE FOUND, WITH ITS TWO PILLAR-BASES.

D. THE MAIN GATE.

E. THE CHAPEL, WITH ITS ALTAR.

F. THERE ARE NO LESS THAN SEVEN "POWDER-ROOMS" IN THE "PALACE" COMPLEX.

its contents still in place. The reason was obvious. The Kassite building had been burnt. The walls were blackened to a height of two feet above the floor—the rest of the walls had probably projected above the ruins and been washed clean by rain—and a deposit, in places quite two feet thick, of black carbonized material lay on the floors. Clearly the rooms had contained large quantities of organic material, and in two rooms at least this had obviously been dates. The greater part of the burnt material consisted of date pits.

Archæologists have always liked conflagrations. There is rarely time in a fire to rescue the contents of burning buildings, and it is rarely worth while to rake through the ashes afterwards to recover burnt possessions. So we expect to find most of the non-inflammable contents of the building waiting for us. Of recent years the archæologist's liking for fires has been enhanced. Fires mean carbon, and carbon can be dated, by measuring its residual content of the radioactive isotope carbon-14. We had been unlucky up to now in our search for carbon-14 datings. Since my three samples from the fall of City I which had proved to be contaminated with bitumen and had given wildly impossible dates, we had fought shy of anything other than recognizable carbonized wood—and that proved to be rare. But now the date pits from the Kassite building could supply carbon which could not have been contaminated, and we filled a plastic bag. After due process, in the course of the following year, the dating came through from the radio-carbon laboratory in Copenhagen (K-827). Our building had been burnt in 1180 B.C., with a possible error of 110 years.

This date suited us very well indeed. However certain you are of an identification (and we were *very* sure that our "Kassite" ware did resemble to the point of identity the Kassite ware of Mesopotamia) it always gives a thrill of satisfaction to have your identification independently confirmed. The Mesopotamian Kassite period lasted from 1700 to 1200 B.C. Thus, our new building was as late as it could be in the Kassite period—and the bracket of dates for the "palace" was correspondingly shortened. The "palace" was later than 1180, earlier than, say, 600 B.C. This bracket comprises the Assyrian and Neo-Babylonian periods of Mesopotamia, and confirmed our hope that the Fifth City was the city of Uperi, who was reigning around 710 B.C.

The quantities of dates stored in the Kassite building gave us an indication of its purpose. It must have been a warehouse or store, perhaps a merchant's business premises. We should perhaps not place too much significance on the nature of the contents. Admittedly the two documents from Nippur of the Kassite period imply that Dilmun was at that time exporting dates, and "Dilmun dates" were highly prized in Babylonia. But we need not see here an export warehouse. Dates were certainly, as they are today, also a staple commodity of internal consumption.

We have some slight indication of the work carried on in the building, of a type which we had hitherto, rather surprisingly, lacked. We found six or seven fragmentary cuneiform tablets.

In Mesopotamian excavations inscribed clay tablets are so common that the Iraq Antiquities Law insists on an epigrapher being included in every expedition to decipher them. In the average house dug there will be six or seven tablets; temples and palaces will normally give hundreds and, exceptionally, tens of thousands. We had found none in the temple at Barbar, none in the "palace" or in the north-wall houses at Qala'at al-Bahrain. It seemed hardly possible that the inhabitants of Dilmun were illiterate, and we were forced to the conclusion that they had written on something other than clay, something which perished with the passage of millennia. But in the Kassite period, at least, it seemed that some of them wrote on clay, and wrote in Babylonian. Perhaps, of course, the warehouse belonged to a Babylonian, a foreigner with foreign habits and language. Indeed, the first tablet we found seemed to be a school text, a student's copy of Babylonian proverbs, and I recalled the school texts in English which every ambitious Arab clerk working for a British firm in Bahrain keeps in his desk. Was this the possession of an ambitious Dilmun clerk working in a Babylonian firm? The rest of the tablets are still being worked on. They are too fragmentary to be easily decipherable, but one appears to list commodities issued, and strengthens the warehouse theory.

347

But whoever they were, they were substantial traders, who could erect these four-square fortress-like establishments. The one we had excavated did not stand alone. Across a narrow alley running along the northern side lay the outer wall of another building of apparently the same character. And if you stood in the main entrance at the western end of the warehouse you looked out onto a thirty-foot-wide street—and streets that wide had elsewhere only been found in the cities of Harappa and Mohenjo-Daro on the Indus. Across the street the faced stone walls of other buildings of equally imposing construction would have frowned down on you. In fact they still do frown down on us. For one of the inner walls of the "palace," which had always puzzled us by its unusual thickness and the fineness of its stone facing, was now shown to be a survival, across the street from the Kassite warehouse, from the buildings of that earlier period, incorporated as it stood in the later structure.

The 1963 season was over before we had finished putting the Kassite warehouse, and the Kassites, on our map. And the time seemed appropriate for stock-taking once more. We had been in the field for ten years. It looked as though we should not be able to continue digging in Kuwait. The Kuwait government now had a fully-fledged Antiquities Department, and had had an expert in from Syria who had pointed out the unusualness of a government in the East financing a foreign expedition. The Antiquities Department did not entirely accept this view, but they were insisting—very reasonably—on a detailed report of our five years' work, preferably in published form, before further work was done. Such a report would, with our limited resources at home, take several years to produce.

In Qatar another year's work would see the Stone Age survey completed, and there was little point in continuing thereafter.

On Umm an-Nar the end was in sight, though Buraimi still offered unguessable possibilities. And Sheikh Shakhbut, who in the beginning had been such an enthusiastic spectator of our digging, was changing. Oil revenues were now flooding into his country, and with them a host of salesmen of every type and quality. The dilemma which faces all newly rich oil sheikhs was upon him, of distinguishing the developer from the exploiter.

Shakhbut realized clearly that even the most honourable firm was seeking its own profit, and saw the hand of the exploiter in every proposal. He retreated into himself, seeing traps in every contract, signs of bad faith in every delay. Even the oil companies, the source of his wealth, found him increasingly suspicious and difficult to deal with. And we too came under his suspicion. For we, like the oil companies, were not asking him for money. Instead we, like the oil companies, were taking things out of his country. Granted the axiom that all foreigners were in his country for what they could make out of it, it was obvious that what we were taking was very valuable. We had had one or two surprise raids on our diggings on Umm an-Nar, when police officers had insisted on our emptying newly found pots of their contents in their presence, and had shown open astonishment when they proved to contain nothing but sand. But the fact that what we were finding had no obvious value only increased the ruler's suspicions. Either we were very very clever at concealing the gold we were finding, or else the objects we were known to be finding had some great and unsuspected market value. In vain we protested, in vain we returned a third of the pottery from the graves and promised the rest as soon as it was catalogued. We explained that we were seekers after knowledge, investigators of the history of his own country. Five years earlier this explanation of our aims had resulted in long and interested discussion; now it was met with bland disbelief. No European was to pull the wool over his eyes. It seemed that our days in Abu Dhabi, too, were numbered.

In Bahrain we had been ourselves trying for years to reach a point where we could call a halt. We had no wish to stop permanently. Dilmun was a new civilization, and new civilizations cannot be investigated for ten years and then dropped. After all, Assyria and Babylonia, which were new civilizations in 1843, had been continuously investigated ever since, and Dilmun was not necessarily less than they. But we needed a year or two to catalogue, digest, and—first and foremost—publish our results. Researchers in neighbouring areas could not forever rest content with the brief interim reports which we published each year.

There was one big gap which remained to be filled in our work

349

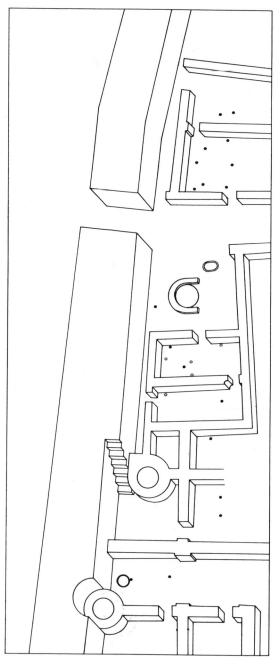

ISOMETRIC VIEW OF THE CITY II AREA WITHIN THE NORTH WALL AT QALA'AT AL-BAHRAIN. AT BOTTOM THE CUL-DE-SAC, AND AT TOP THE CITY GATE, WITH, BETWEEN THEM, THE GUARD-ROOM WITH ITS WELL AND STAIRCASE TO THE RAMPARTS. FINDING-PLACES OF SEALS (•) AND WEIGHTS (○) ARE MARKED, SHOWING THEIR PREPONDERANCE IN THE ROOMS ON EITHER SIDE OF THE GATE.

in Bahrain. We knew too little about the earliest periods on the Qala'at al-Bahrain site. Buildings of the first two cities, of the chain-ridge and the Barbar periods (which we were beginning to lump together and call Early Dilmun) had only been found in our diggings behind the north wall. Elsewhere our *sondages* had been oddly unproductive on these periods. Within the west wall and the south wall there had, it is true, been levels with the well-known red ridged ware, but there had been no buildings. It seemed that, when the Barbar people built their fortification wall, they had enclosed an area far bigger than the city itself. Only in the north did the streets and houses lie close against the wall. Even where we had been able to dig below the "palace" and the Kassite warehouse in the centre of the tell we had found no buildings of Barbar date comparable with those of the northern excavation. So we decided to return to the north wall, and to devote two years to exposing a large area here, adjacent to our previous excavation, which would give us a "wide view" of the city in its earliest phases.

The results were exciting. For we stumbled straight onto the city gate.

The area we had chosen was a stretch of the city wall running some twenty metres eastward from the area where we had first found the northern wall. The wall itself would form the northern edge of the excavation, and the area we should investigate would extend ten metres to the south, within the wall. We divided the area into two, with a baulk two metres wide running north-south between them, to give us a choice of two sections for drawing. This was in fact the only stretch of the north wall available to us, for further to the west it had been quarried away by the Portuguese, and further to the east the wall, and indeed the tell, broke off short, where an area along the shore had been levelled, probably to make gardens in more recent times.

It will be recalled that our original diggings here, four to six years before, had revealed a cul-de-sac street running north to the wall, with substantial stone houses on either side and a well and sunk basin at the end of the street. It had shown signs of municipal planning, contrasting sharply with the winding alleys and haphazard houses of contemporary Ur, and resembling the gridiron plans of contemporary Mohenjo-Daro and Harappa. We were eager to see whether the new area would reveal the same planning on a larger scale.

The digging in 1964 certainly did not. Else and Svend dug down through levels disturbed by one quarrying hole cutting into another, while six metres south of the wall over the whole area appeared a single immense excavation, filled with practically sterile sand, which halved our excavation area from the start. In the six metres available a medley of fragments of house walls and floors ran in every direction. Even the periods seemed here to be confused, for fragments of rooms and houses of Islamic date appeared at the same physical level as other rooms and houses of the Seleucid period. This we had expected, for we believed that the city wall had been standing in ruins above ground for two thousand years after it had been abandoned as a fortification, until in fact the Portuguese had razed it to ground level—and below—less than five hundred years ago. And the people who had occupied the site had used these ancient fortifications as the people of Istanbul use their ancient city wall today, building their houses up against it, tearing out the facing stones and the rubble core, even digging out cave-like rooms within the very fabric of the wall.

In these disturbed levels there was one undisturbed construction. Precisely on the line of our section baulk a cement-surfaced road of the Seleucid period ran north to the wall. In the wall there was a gateway with a threshold stone and hinge-holes for a gate. The gateway had been narrowed at a later stage, and finally completely built up.

This did not excite us unduly. The wall had not, at the time—perhaps 300 B.C.—of this road, been in use as a fortification. Houses of the same period, we knew, had been built beyond the wall, and against its outer face. This was not a city gate, but merely a way through an obstacle.

But the following year we went deeper, below the Seleucid levels, into Early Dilmun with its neatly stratified layers of Barbar pottery. And once again, as in the earlier dig adjoining us to the west, we found ourselves in an orderly, planned municipality. Again all the walls ran due north-south or due east-west. And again we found a street running due north toward the city wall. But this street, one block east from that we had found before, was no cul-de-sac. It lay beneath the street of Seleucid date, and, like it, ran to a gate in the wall.

This was the real thing, a gate in the city's perimeter, a gate out to the uninhabited foreshore. It did not lie exactly beneath the Seleucid gate. For some reason the later gate had been moved a metre further east, so that, while the two overlapped, they did not coincide. Both gaps in the wall were about ten feet wide, though constricted by the hinges of the gates to a little under eight feet. For by the lower gateway, too, there were a pair of hinge-stones, this time of polished black diorite, stones about twenty inches across with cups to accommodate the hinge-posts hollowed into their tops. The lower gate, also, had been blocked, before it was abandoned, with a wall of rough stones built across it.

When we dug deeper we found that even this was not the earliest gate. The wall had been extensively repaired in the middle of the Barbar period, and below the line of repair a third gateway appeared. And this again overlapped but did not coincide with the one above, its gateposts standing a further metre to the west. This lowest gateway had never been blocked, and across the gap the strata of sand curved slightly downward where traffic had hollowed out the roadbed.

We were tempted to "open" the gates, to dig through and see what the outer face of the wall looked like here. But the overlap of the gates made this impossible. It would be necessary to demolish the later superstructure of each wall in order to reach the gate beneath. The project was added to the list of "things to do later," and we turned to the clearing of the area within the gate.

I had always claimed that a gate in the city wall would be an important discovery, pointing out that much of the commercial and municipal activity of a city took place immediately within the gates. Yet somehow I had never really expected that the facts would conform to my theory, which was based on accounts of other excavations. It was a shock to find undoubted signs of just such activity as I had predicted.

Enter the city by the gate from the foreshore, and you will see immediately on your right a little open square. In its centre is a well, and beside it an oval cement-built trough. Clearly this is a halting-place for pack-animals, where donkeys can be watered while they are being loaded and unloaded. But why should pack-animals halt here, just within the city gate, which leads only to the beach? The answer was furnished by the contents of the adjoining buildings.

On either side of the square were two houses, each of two rooms. And in one building we found no less than nine stamp-seals; and in the other three seals and five stone weights. Two of the weights were easily recognizable as such. They were small cubes of polished chert, one measuring less than a centimetre a side and the other incredibly tiny, no more than four millimetres a side. We knew what they were, for we had found one weight of this type before, in the dead-end street a block away. They were the normal weights in use in the cities of the Indus civilization. The other three we did not immediately recognize as weights. They were larger, spheres of polished marble with two flattened sides, and we talked for some time of mace-heads or unfinished marble bowls. It was only when we saw the three together that it became clear that they were weights, and only when we returned home to our reference books that we found that the larger weights of the Harappan civilization were precisely of this type. At home, too, we could weigh them. The largest weighed 1370 grams, and the others were respectively 685 grams, 170 grams, 13.5 grams, and 1.7 grams. The one we had found earlier fitted into the series, being of 27 grams. The smaller ones were thus a half, an eighth, a fiftieth, a hundredth, and an eight hundredth of the largest. And these weights agreed, to within less than one per cent deviation, with the weights found in the Indus cities.

We can now say why the donkeys carrying loads between the beach and the city halted just within the city wall. The two buildings on either side of the square must have been municipal offices, where loads were weighed, and either the loads themselves or the clay documents accompanying them stamped with the seals of the clerks who checked ingoing and outgoing cargoes. We have probably here the customs house and port authority of Dilmun. It was all very modern and efficient. And it was hard to realize that the civil servants who had checked way-bills and consignments in the harbour offices of Dilmun had been dead these four thousand years.

ONE OF THE SEALS FROM THE TEMPLE-TANK AT BARBAR, A REVOLVING WHEEL OF GAZELLE HEADS.

A puzzle remained. Why had Dilmun used the standard weights of the Indus Valley? The Babylonians and Sumerians used a completely different system. Not only were the weights different, but they worked on a different ratio, in thirds and tenths and sixtieths. There could only be one of two explanations. Either the first commercial impulses to have reached Dilmun must have come not from Mesopotamia but from India, or else India was a far more important commercial connection with Dilmun than was Mesopotamia.

We went on digging. For even here, at the earliest period of the wall, we were still five feet above bedrock. And we found, as we had found before, that in this area the city had existed before ever the wall was built. The pottery changed to our chain-ridge ware, and we found house-walls that ran on under the wall. And between these walls and the city wall lay once more the burnt level which showed that the unfortified city had been destroyed by fire. We even found one socketed copper spear-head. . . .

Finally we reached sand, and two feet further down rock, and we thought that that was the end. But now we had a larger area exposed than we ever had had before in these earliest levels. And when we swept the rock clean we could see that it was composed of *farush*. This conglomerate of shells, coral, and other detritus, which we have met before, is a sort of incipient limestone which forms, apparently very quickly, in the shallow tidal waters of the Gulf. It can be prised up in large thin slabs, and is used in quantity today as building material. When we brushed it clean we could see that potsherds were embedded in it. We broke up this *farush* over an area of several square feet, and found sand below. And in this sand there were still potsherds.

So we went on. And for over two feet more we found alternate layers of *farush* and sand, all containing quantities of sherds, until we reached a layer of sterile green clay, the very clay which the chain-ridge and Barbar peoples had used as mortar in their buildings; and below this came more sand, this time containing no potsherds.

We had reached the end. But we had six boxes of layered sherds, which must be earlier than any sherds we had yet found in Bahrain. And very few of these sherds were of the red chain-ridged ware. Most were of a thicker, straw-coloured ware, with rims and bases of a completely new type. We had here a new and quite unexpected culture, earlier than the cultures which we had, perhaps prematurely, called Early Dilmun.

೫೫೫೫೫

CHAPTER SEVENTEEN

೫೫೫೫೫

GREAT ARABIA

The campaign of 1965 was ended. And for a time it looked as though the expeditions were ended. Kuwait and Qatar were definitely terminated. Sheikh Shakhbut of Abu Dhabi had finally gone so far as to declare our presence unwelcome. In Saudi Arabia our second application was gathering dust together with our first. And, concerning Bahrain, one of our major backers, the Carlsberg Foundation, had put its foot down. No more money would be forthcoming for further digging until the definitive publication of our results was at least in train. For that, and for that only, would they continue our grants.

In some ways it was a relief. For a dozen years three months and more had been spent each year in the field; three months or more in clearing up after the field-work, straightening out accounts, writing letters of thanks, and clearing and unpacking our cases of material; three months or more in preparing for the next expedition, raising funds and despatching equipment, gathering our team and arranging visas and passages and inoculations. There had been little time left for cataloguing our material, and no time at all for digesting it, assembling it into a coherent whole, and publishing something more than the bald summaries which was all that we had been able to put out. It was pleasant to be able to relax and start on the scientific study of our shelves of material.

And immediately results began to show, unexpected connections began to appear.

A minor discovery concerned the weights which we had found during our latest season. Having shown by archæological evidence that Dilmun used the Harappan-culture system of weights, I discovered that I should have known it all along. In Chapter Nine I told of the mercantile tablets concerning the Dilmun copper trade found in the house of Ea-nasir in Ur. And I gave the details of the most significant tablet among them, that which records the purchase, and subsequent distribution, of a cargo of some 18½ tons of copper. The document gives some of the quantities involved in "minas of copper according to the standard of Dilmun," and others in talents and minas "according to the standard of Ur." And neither I nor, apparently, anyone else, had realized that a very simple calculation would thereby give the ratio between Dilmun minas and Ur minas, and—since we knew the value in grams of the Ur mina—the actual weight in grams of the Dilmun mina.

Let us look at the problem. The tablet says (translating for clearness rather than for literalness):

> "Of 13,1?? Dilmun minas of copper received at Dilmun, 5,5?2⅔ Dilmun minas have been given to us. Expressed in Ur weights, 611 talents 6⅔ minas were received, and 245 talents 54⅓ minas given to us. 4271½ minas [in Dilmun weights] are owed for by Ea-nasir; and 325 minas [in Dilmun weights] are owed for by Nauirum-ili. The total of these issues is [in Ur weights] 450 talents 2⅓ minas, leaving unissued [in Ur weights] 161 talents 4⅓ minas."

Since the Ur talent contains 60 Ur minas, and the Ur mina weighs 504 grams, we can set up the following equations:

A. 13,1?? Dilmun minas = 611 Ur talents 6⅔ Ur minas = 36,666⅔ Ur minas = 18,480,000 grams

B. 5,5?2⅔ Dilmun minas = 245 Ur talents 54⅓ Ur minas = 14,754⅓ Ur minas = 7,436,184 grams

C. 4596½ (4271½ plus 325) Dilmun minas = 450 Ur talents 2⅓

Ur minas minus 245 Ur talents 54⅓
Ur minas = 12,248 Ur minas =
6,172,992 grams

The solution is complicated by the fact that the tablet is dam-
aged and two of the figures for Dilmun minas are uncertain
(fortunately within narrow limits). It is made further complicated by the fact that the solutions do not agree. The least
possible weight of a Dilmun mina according to equation *A* is
greater than the greatest possible weight for it according to
equation *B!* But working it out as best we can, we find that the
least possible weight for a Dilmun mina is 1329 grams and the
greatest possible weight is 1411 grams. The mean of these two
figures is 1370 grams, which is precisely the weight of the largest
of our "custom-house" weights. (The deviation of the two ex-
tremes on either side of this mean is only three per cent, which is
well within the limits allowable by the somewhat inaccurate
standards of the time.) The average of all the weights of this size
found in the Indus Valley is 1375 grams.

It is always pleasant to receive confirmation of what one knows
already. But the next result of our work in the back-rooms of the
museum in Aarhus was a completely unexpected discovery of
very considerable importance.

Our packing-cases from the Gulf had arrived, and for a fortnight we stood amid planks and wood shavings, sorting the boxes
of potsherds and bones, the cartons of matchboxes containing
seals and coins and lumps of bronze and fragments of worked
stone, the plastic bags of earth samples and charcoal and shells.
As the lists grew the piles on the floor lessened, until everything
was on the shelves, numbered and accessible. As soon as the floor
was swept I pulled out again the six boxes of sherds from the
farush levels within the north gate of the Bahrain city, to examine
more closely these earliest of all potsherds. At the same time, in
the next room, Jörgen and Vagn were working through their
pottery from the last three seasons' work on the village site on
Umm an-Nar.

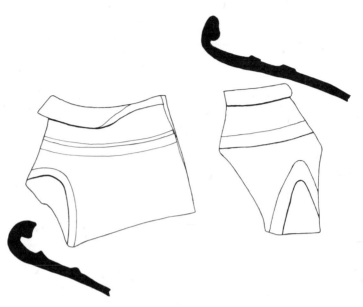

THESE TWO RIM-SHERDS ARE (LEFT) FROM THE NEW LEVELS BELOW CITY I AT QALA'AT AL-BAHRAIN, AND (RIGHT) FROM THE SETTLEMENT AT UMM AN-NAR. THERE IS NO DOUBT OF THEIR VIRTUAL IDENTITY.

It took about a week before we realized that we were working on the same culture.

Once we began to look at the sherds together and side by side there was no doubt about it. The greater part of the pottery consisted of large spherical or egg-shaped vessels, of thick buff or straw-coloured ware. The rims were heavy and elaborate, bent sharply outward, with no neck at all. The bases were unusual, a deep ring-base applied to the round bottom of the vessel. And many of the vessels were decorated with applied ridges, a single or a double rounded ridge which meandered over the upper part of the pot.

Now, this was the first connection of any sort which we had found between our excavations in Bahrain and those in Abu Dhabi. Up to now they might have been at opposite ends of the world, instead of only 250 miles apart, or separated by millennia instead of being, as we were inclined to believe, virtually contemporary. Now the connection was there, and we had to try to explain what it implied.

It did not imply complete identity of civilization. Between the "Barbar cultures" of Bahrain and of Kuwait there had been complete identity, of pottery, of seals, of stoneware, and of weapons. Here there were significant differences. In all the earliest levels on Bahrain the chain-ridge ware persisted side by side with the new pottery. Even in the lowest level of all it still comprised ten per cent of all the sherds. But not a single sherd of chain-ridge ware occurred in the settlement on Umm an-Nar. And in all three levels of the Umm an-Nar setttlement occurred sherds of the painted ware which we had found in such abundance in the burial chambers there. But, though the Bahrain material did contain a scattering of painted sherds, they were not at all like those of Umm an-Nar. It looked as though the people whose potsherds had been scattered on the tide-washed northern shore of Bahrain before the first city was built were already a mixture of cultures. The Indus weights had suggested that the first mercantile impulses had come from the east. Could it be that immigrants from the Oman, using and making Umm an-Nar pottery, had found here an already existing population using and making chain-ridge ware, and that the two in fellowship had established the first trading station here on the coast?

Certainly it now seemed that the "Umm an-Nar culture" of Abu Dhabi must be older than the mature culture of Early Dilmun. And about the same time two small indications turned up to confirm this. One was a further "back-room" discovery of our own. Cleaning and examining the potsherds from the Umm an-Nar village, Vagn found one bearing ornamentation. A cylinder seal had been rolled along the wet clay below the rim.

It is odd that cylinder seals were not more often used in this simple way to decorate pottery. But it is a fact that this use of seals is unknown in Mesopotamia, but has been found on the edge of the Mesopotamian world, in Syria to the west and in Elam to the east. In Elam, which is the most likely source for our specimen, the practice was known only in Early Dynastic times; and our impression, with its attacking animals and stylized rosette, is very Early Dynastic in conception. The date to which it might best belong is perhaps 2800 B.C. So we have a sort of

tentative date for the Umm an-Nar village, and thereby of the
first settlement at Qala'at al-Bahrain. And 2800 B.C. is, incidentally, about the date of Gilgamesh, if, as seems increasingly likely,
there is some foundation in history for the mythological hero.

The second discovery was not made by us. In the Yale Babylonian Collection a tablet was discovered bearing the imprint of a
Dilmun seal, in fact so closely resembling an imprint which we
had found the year before in the upper "Barbar" levels of our
north-gate dig that you had to look two and three times to be
sure that they were not impresses of the same seal. The tablet
probably came from Ur, and is very like in text those mercantile
tablets which tell of the Dilmun trade. This one does not mention
Dilmun, but it records the investment of wool, wheat, and sesame
in a trading venture. And it is dated to the tenth year of the reign
of Gungunum of Larsa, to the year 1923 B.C.

So the merchants of Dilmun had their agencies established in
Ur in the twentieth century B.C., just as in the twentieth
century A.D. they have their agencies and branches in London
and New York. And our Early Dilmun period is seen to span just
about a thousand years. The customs officers sealing cargo in

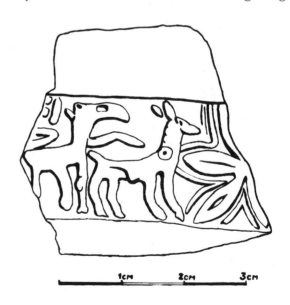

THE POTSHERD FROM UMM AN-NAR WITH ITS SEAL-IMPRESSION.

362

their office by the north gate four thousand years ago were citizens of a city even then as old as Windsor Castle, three times as old as New York.

For two years there was no expedition. And towards the end of that time our relief at not having to organize and run an expedition began to wear noticeably thin. And at the same time we marked a new attitude around us. For a while it had looked as though not merely we, but everyone, had been a little tired of our expeditions. They had appeared to be going on forever. And then with two years to think about it everyone was discovering that they *had* to go on, if not forever, at least without any hard and fast termination point. The work done could not be left hanging in mid-air. Bahrain had antiquities exposed which could not be ignored, museum exhibits which could only leave a Danish museum if there was a museum to house them in Bahrain. And if anything were to be done about the antiquities and the museum, then continued research was a natural consequence.

In Abu Dhabi Sheikh Shakhbut had been deposed, and the new ruler was his brother Zayid, the very man who had first shown us the grave-mounds of Buraimi. And the first intoxication of oil royalties was passing; the continued flood of unlimited oil money was becoming a matter of course. As the more immediate projects of roads and schools and hospitals, of food supplies and water supplies and electricity supplies, were set in train, archæology ceased to be an impertinent irrelevance.

In Saudi Arabia our importuning had caused a Directorate of Antiquities to be set up, and a Directorate of Antiquities has to have antiquities to direct.

We had started something in these lands which now moved forward with its own momentum. And in this movement there was a place for us. We found ourselves in the unaccustomed position of being regarded as letting the Gulf down if we did *not* send out an expedition.

The first move came from Saudi Arabia. In the beginning of 1967, just two years after we had left the Gulf, a letter arrived from the Directorate of Antiquities. They noted that we had previously applied for permission to explore in the Eastern Province, and they would be pleased if we would renew our application, as there was now a strong possibility that it could be granted. Our bluff was called. Now we had to decide, and decide fast, whether we dared tackle an area of a hundred thousand square miles, twenty times the total area we had worked over during the last thirteen years, and how, if we dared, we should set about it.

The problem was essentially one of what Sir Mortimer Wheeler has called "strategic archæology." It would be no use dissipating our strength trying to cover the whole area. But at the other extreme there was the danger of getting bogged down on a single site, however important. What we needed, it seemed to me, was a mobile force of specialists, capable of making swift probes at selected points, and extracting the maximum of information in the minimum of time. There would have to be a ruthless timetable, moving the party from site to site whatever the temptation to remain. And yet, in such a reconnaissance in unknown territory, there would have to be sufficient flexibility to allow unexpected discoveries to be exploited. It would not be easy.

We started with one inestimable advantage. The "pot-pickers" of the oil town of Dhahran had already been over the whole area with a fine-tooth comb. The preliminary reconnaissance of surface indications had been done for us. No useful purpose would be served by our trying to duplicate their work. What we could do, and must do, was dig, and dig at points where the surface indications suggested that digging would supply new information. I picked out four areas where digging might be expected to give specific answers to specific questions.

While the government of Saudi Arabia was considering our application to dig, our application for assistance, financial and logistic, was sent to the oil company in Dhahran. And at the same time as the government approved our plans, Aramco replied that their Exploration Department had been authorized to organize the practical side of our expedition, while the Arab Affairs Department would "take care of the more impractical things, such as money."

Now, when it comes to making a ground survey of the Moon, or of Mars, the Space Administration might do worse than to put the matter in the hands of the Exploration Department of Aramco. It is accustomed to making everyday routine out of desert journeys which thirty years ago would have earned their performers an F.R.G.S., a knighthood, and undying fame. It establishes, and keeps supplied with all comforts, camps in the middle of that most inaccessible of all deserts, the Rub' al-Khali, the Empty Quarter of Arabia.

Our intrepid venture deep into archæologically unknown territory was to them, we found, a jaunt within the normal picnicking area around Dhahran, for the most part well within commuting range. It could be organized in odd moments of relaxation from arranging really serious expeditions.

Yet our preparations were put afoot with the same light-hearted attention to detail as the bigger projects received. For Exploration works on a very simple principle. The man in the field is always right. He knows what he wants; the man in the depot only has to see that he gets it. Order ten thousand gallons of diesel oil, or ask them to change a library book or send a birthday telegram. It will be done. Radio in an indent for six cans of asparagus tips by special truck, and a truck will arrive with six cans of asparagus tips. There will be no query as to whether it could not wait for the regular supply truck; if you ask for special delivery you have a reason, and that is enough for Exploration.

So when in January of 1968 we set off for Thaj, the first point on our list, we were equipped to a standard to which archæologists are not accustomed. Ahead went what Exploration called a Bobtail, an immense ten-wheel-drive stake-bodied truck, with a cab like the bridge of a steamboat (including a lanyard above the driver's head to sound the siren) and with a smoke-stack puffing out the white plume of steam which, I suspect, has given the vehicle its name. It towed a two-thousand-gallon tank of water and carried a dozen or so drums of gasoline, oil, and kerosene, as well as our six tents and the greater part of our camp equipment. Bobtails are the new ships of the desert, and their drivers are a special breed of men, akin to—probably the sons of—the great

Bedouin guides of thirty years ago. They travel immense distances across Arabia, often alone and guided only by God, the stars, and their instinct for direction and distance. They are the sinews of Exploration's communication system.

Behind followed our two land-rovers, each with its radio-transmission aerial nodding to the movement, and our three-ton truck. We had never had a truck at our disposal anywhere before, but the Fargo was scarcely large enough to hold our stock of provisions, beds, mattresses, chairs, and cook-stoves. Our personnel rode the land-rovers. Our party was thirteen strong, a mechanic and two drivers, three cooks, and seven "scientists." Christian and I were the only dirt-archæologists.

I had, for better or worse, my party of specialists. Holger, who had tramped the length and breadth of Qatar and had just published, on his seventy-first birthday, the first of our definitive reports, on the Stone-Age cultures of Qatar, was to range the desert within a day's drive of our camps and work out the Stone-Age cultures of Arabia. Erling, our geologist, was to answer, we hoped, a lot of our questions about climate: why was Thaj built on the shore of a *sabkha?* Where had the coastline been at the time of Gerrha—and of Early Dilmun? What had happened to the irrigated area north of Uqair? Where had the sand come from, and when? Ole, our surveyor, who had mapped our city tell on Bahrain as a student and who was now a professor, was cradling his theodolite on his knees. His biggest job would be to make the town-plan of Thaj, his most difficult job making sense of the wide scattering of irrigation channels at "Gerrha." Bente was our draughtswoman, who up to now had been drawing pottery in the museum in Denmark. This time everything we found must be drawn on the spot, for nothing would come back to the museum in Denmark. The infant Department of Antiquities in Riyadh was playing it safe. They did not wish to jeopardize a hard-won position by risking charges that they were giving national treasures to foreign museums. Everything we found was to be handed over to them. In this we were in full agreement. We had been too long the Cinderella of our own museum not to appreciate the difficulties faced by a department trying to do what had not previously been done; and we felt rather like godfathers to the Antiquities Department. We had watched its advent and teething troubles with solicitude, and we were prepared to go to a lot of trouble to strengthen its position.

Abdul-rahman was the representative of the Department in our party, a specialist in Islamic architecture and archæology, but as anxious as we to get his teeth into the pre-Islamic past of his country. Christian and I would have to do any digging that was to be done, though we still hoped that P.V. would be able to escape from running Danish archæology to join us for part of the season.

The immediate archæological problem with Thaj was straight-forward, and could be answered by a single carefully placed *sondage*. Did the city of the time of Alexander, which surface indications showed to exist, overlie a city or several cities of earlier date? The longer-term historical problem was immensely more complex. What was this city? What part did it play in the history of Arabia, or the history of the world? Who had lived in it? Why was it where it was? These questions we could not hope to answer in a single season. But because they were important questions, we would look at Thaj, and survey Thaj, with a view to full-scale excavation. For that was what would be needed if the historical questions were to be answered. And in our preoccupation with Dilmun we should not lose sight of the fact that in Thaj we had a site of historical importance, architectural promise, and even potential tourist attraction which many an archæologist would consider more than sufficient for a lifetime's work.

The weather was wet and bitterly cold. The tents were snug, but the beds were hard to leave on a chill blustering morning. I reminded myself that in April in Jabrin we should look back in sheer disbelief to a time when we wished that the weather was warmer. But that did not help. What did help was to go and shovel soil and sand up the three-metre-high wall of our *sondage*. Sited just inside the south wall of the city, it measured only two by two metres, and was already deeper than it was wide. I had promised the Department to dig no holes larger than two metres square, and to fill them in when we left. For the Department was afraid that the ignorant and prejudiced local inhabitants might object to any excavation, which could disturb djinns and malignant spirits. I had told them that I did not believe their people to be more custom-bound or superstitious than those we knew so well in the Gulf states. And when, digging down along the inner side of the squared-stone wall, we had found the first bowl, lidded by another bowl, just as we had found them in the "palace" in Bahrain, I lifted it up and showed it to the group of young Bedouin squatting on the edge of the excavation. "What, think you," I asked, "is under the lid here? A djinni?" One of them grinned. "If God will," he said, "there will be gold." "There will be nothing," said another. "If God will," said I, "there will be a snake." They laughed. Foreigners are so full of superstition. And they were right. There was nothing but sand. We found four more pairs of bowls like the first, but none of them contained anything but sand. There may be a connection of some sort between the snake-bowls of Bahrain and the empty bowls of Thaj —though the Thaj bowls are three or four hundred years later in date—but the snake, at least, had by then ceased to figure in the offerings.

There was no earlier city at Thaj. Three metres down, we were below the foundations of the city wall, in a pit that had been dug before the wall was built into the sterile sand which at that time covered the site. Five metres down we came to the bottom of the pit. And the pottery was identical from first to last. Thaj had had but one period of occupation, and that had not lasted more than perhaps four hundred years. We have carbon samples from the lowest and the uppermost levels which may give us the span in time of the city. The ash layers in the upper levels are indeed so thick that it is likely that Thaj died by fire and the sword.

The city proved even more imposing on examination than at first acquaintance. The city wall is fifteen feet thick, faced with stone both out and in, and with towers at regular intervals jutting out from the line of wall. On excavation the walls would still stand seven feet high, and would be an imposing ancient monument. It must have been even more imposing to the caravans from the Hadramaut two thousand years ago which, after forty

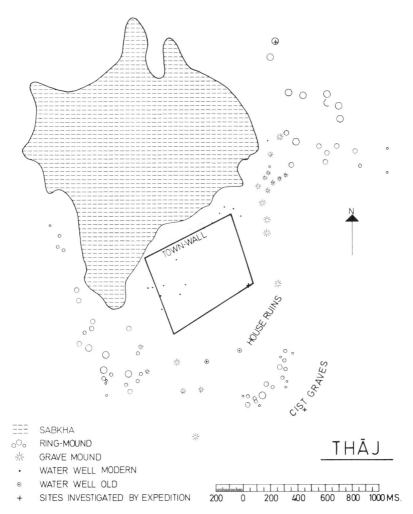

SABKHA
RING-MOUND
GRAVE MOUND
WATER WELL MODERN
WATER WELL OLD
SITES INVESTIGATED BY EXPEDITION

TOWN-WALL

HOUSE RUINS

CIST GRAVES

N

THĀJ

200 0 200 400 600 800 1000 MS.

THE CITY AND ENVIRONS OF THAJ, IN SAUDI ARABIA.

days in the desert, saw the crenellated walls rising to their full height above the palms and gardens south of the city, with the blue waters of the lake beyond.

We were sorely tempted to clear a section of the outer wall, to show what could be done. But we radioed for the Bobtail instead, and moved down the coast.

We encamped on the fringe of the Qatif oasis, opposite the island of Tarut. And our real aim was the island. The tell in the centre of the town of Tarut was still the only settlement of Dilmun date, and of the Dilmun clutures, in Saudi Arabia, still Saudi Arabia's oldest town. And we had hopes that—now that we were "official" and accompanied by a government representative —we could somehow circumvent the tabu on approaching the *haram* side of the tell.

We had an interview with the Emir, where Abdul-rahman pleaded our case; and the retired mayor of Qatif, a local anti-quary of unimpeachable respectability, was summoned to accom-pany us to Tarut. After protracted negotiations with the elders there it was agreed that our examination of the tell in the pres-ence of the ex-mayor could cast no slur on the honour of the ladies of Tarut, and, after suitable warnings had been issued, we were permitted to wander at will over the tell—for the space of two hours.

Rarely have we worked so fast. Ole set up his theodolite, and in the two hours produced an accurate sketch-map of the tell. Bente was instructed to take photographs—on the assumption that the ladies of the town, who showed no inclination to flee our pres-ence, would be reassured by a lady photographer. And Christian and Erling and I worked on the exposed southern face of the tell. The sun-baked soil was iron-hard, and only Erling's geological pick-hammer was capable of making much impression on it. But we could work out at least four layers of occupation, each with exposed stumps of squared-stone walling, and we started digging into the lowest exposed layer.

In the middle of our work we were called by the ex-mayor to see the innermost holy of holies, the women's bathing-pool. Leav-ing Erling to dig, we passed through a maze of walls to find, hard up against the steepest side of the tell, a large natural rock basin full of clear bubbling water. It was one of the natural springs such as we knew from Bahrain. The water was over twelve feet deep, and eight feet below the surface could be seen the footings of a mighty wall of immense square stones. This pool was clearly the reason for the existence of the settlement on this spot, and must have supplied the town with water for over four thousand years.

When we returned to our digging, Erling could prove to us that the occupation of the town stretched even further into the past. From the bottom stratum on which he was working he had recovered a nondescript sherd of yellowish pottery and three pieces of worked flint, including an undoubted flint knife-blade. We were back to the Neolithic.

It was slender evidence on which to push the history of Dilmun this further step backward in time. But it was ineluctable. On all our previous "Barbar" sites, at Barbar itself, on Failaka, at Qala'at al-Bahrain, we had found no worked flint. A large number of flint nodules, yes, and a few flakes of flint, and even one flint core from which blades had been struck, but not a single piece of flint with the secondary chipping, the *retouche*, which shows that it was formed for use. That three retouched fragments had appeared in the course of a hurried, almost casual, burrowing into an exposed stratum could only mean that worked flint was in very common use at the time of that stratum.

We had no date for the level. The Neolithic is a long period, and, off the main stream of progress, tends to persist. We knew too little about Tarut to say whether it had been a backwater, but it was unlikely. In fact one of our main tenets of faith was that Early Dilmun had *not* been a backwater, that on the contrary it had ridden the main stream of progress precisely during the time when Mesopotamia was equipping itself with bronze. If any country might have been expected to have left the Stone Age for the Copper Age *earlier* than Mesopotamia it would be the country which supplied Mesopotamia with copper.

During the following weeks, while we looked at Seleucid-period cemeteries on Tarut and on the coast, and later when we moved camp to the puzzling area of abandoned irrigation channels north of Uqair, I speculated vainly on the problem of digging the Tarut tell. At a stroke it had become not merely the oldest town in Saudi Arabia but the oldest town-site in the Gulf. And it could not be dug. It was brought home to me how lucky we had hitherto been. Elsewhere in the Middle East the important ancient site which is still inhabited is a common problem. *Sondages* dictated by property rights, trenches governed by chance free areas, compensation to land owners, and the actual purchase of excavation areas belong to the ordinary headaches of the expedition leader. In all our work in the Gulf we had never before met these problems. We had met them now, and in an extreme form. We had never commanded the sort of money which would be needed to buy up the centre of Tarut town. In any case, the women's bathing-pool, the communal washing-place and the main water supply of Tarut, was not for sale.

I thought of putting in an all-woman team. We had women archæologists enough. In a week or so I was going east to visit Karen, who this year was running our dig in Buraimi. She could well dig Tarut. But it would not work. We could not use a feminine labour force. Only government decree could open Tarut to us, and a government decree would be highly unpopular locally; not among the women, who had watched our reconnaissance with interest and with no trace of shyness, but among the men. We could only wait for education and the change in the Moslem attitude to women which is slowly taking place. It might take generations.

The problem was to become of even greater importance within a few weeks.

In the meantime we were encamped in a hollow among white sand dunes and flowering desert bushes, twenty miles north of Uqair. Our third problem was to determine whether the area of abandoned irrigation channels could have any connection with the lost city of Gerrha—or whether alternatively Gerrha lay beneath the ruined Islamic city at Uqair.

We did not find Gerrha (unless indeed, as P.V. and Christian think, the walled city at Thaj may be Gerrha). At Uqair three *sondages* showed the Islamic occupation extending down to the footings of the ruined city wall, which must therefore itself be Islamic. And there was nothing below. Further north, we quartered the area for five miles around our camp, mainly on foot. All this area had been harshly eroded by the sand and the wind (which blew down our tents one savage night). We found village sites where the walls and even the floors of the houses had been scoured completely away. Nothing would have remained to show that houses had once stood there, had it not been that, where the hearths had stood, the clay floors had been baked to a hardness which had resisted the sandstorms of two millennia. Among the hearths, now standing a good two feet above the general ground level, were the beads and coins and half-eroded potsherds of the settlements. The pattern of the fields, too, could be worked out, even the palm-gardens where rings of darker earth marked the irrigation pools around each vanished tree. We found and dug two small forts. And everywhere the date was right, the potsherds were of the classical period, but nowhere was there a city.

As we worked it became obvious that we were exploring a coast-land. We were almost ten miles from the sea here, with the wide and treacherous *sabkha* stretching to the east, as far as the narrow strip of sand hills that divided the *sabkha* from the sea. But the characteristics of a coast-land were unmistakable. Our village sites lay at the head of arms of *sabkha* running into rocky coves. The forts stood on low headlands. The largest stretch of irrigation channels could even be identified as reclaimed land, and Erling could show from his section trenches how the dykes had finally broken, and the sea taken back the polder.

Erling's researches were beginning to pay off, and to tie up with earlier geological investigations of the coastal *sabkhas* of Qatar and the Trucial Coast, which had shown that the *sabkhas* there were only about two thousand years old. It began to look as though the coastal area of east Arabia had been slowly rising throughout the last many thousands of years. It was not unlikely. Some millions of years ago, in the Late Miocene, during the last great mountain-building period of the world, the Persian massif had lunged southward, tipping the whole slab of Arabia. In the east Arabia had been pressed down below sea level, forming the Arabian Gulf. And in the west the slab had been cracked off from Africa, forming the deep chasm of the Red Sea, the Rift Valley of East Africa, and the crack which was now the Gulf of Aqaba and the Jordan valley. It was not unlikely that a recovery had been going on ever since, that Arabia was gradually returning to the horizontal.

It would explain many things in the historical record. Such a rise of east Arabia would reduce the flow of underground water from the high land to the west, would in extreme cases, as perhaps here at "Gerrha," cut off the flow altogether. The exposed sea bottom would dry out and blow away as sand and dust, which would choke the vegetation on the land, already threatened by the diminishing water supply. Dust-bowl conditions would result, adding more sand to the dunes. The supply of pasture for grazing animals would diminish, and what there was would be over-grazed, giving more denuded areas, and more sand. Perhaps the whole of the sand of Arabia could not be accounted for by this one single cause, but everything would contribute to the same end. And the process had been culminating during the time when man was trying to establish his civilizations along the coast. Dilmun and Gerrha had been fighting a losing battle.

Now the fight is being taken up again, with oil to hold the dunes in check, with deep borings to tap new water supplies, with organized establishment of vegetation coverage to hold down the surface and retain the air humidity for which the Gulf is notorious. It is a slow process to reverse the judgments of nature, but it had only been a very slight change in the environment which had originally tipped the balance fractionally against man; if the efforts of man could reverse the tip, then all the processes would build up the other way. Archæological research began to have an unexpected relevance.

By chance we did a lot of travelling from "Gerrha." Holger and Abdul-rahman and I drove the long desert road to Qàtar, a trip we had dreamed for years of making the other way, and pre-sented Holger's Stone Age book to the ruler. And Holger and Ole joined a Dhahran party making a five-day trip to Qaryat al-Fau, a region of rock-inscriptions 600 miles to the southwest and less than a hundred miles from the borders of Yemen. It was twice as far as our investigations had been planned to range, but then we were only archæologists—our companions were members of the Exploration Department on a weekend trip.

And I was in Buraimi for a week, where the bulldozers were raging by day and by night, and where Karen and Eivind and

Henning were digging a very curious building, with yard-thick walls of mud-brick, a hundred yards from the "Round Structure" which had turned out to be a burial chamber of the Umm an-Nar culture. The Trucial Oman Scouts were helping them to turn over the immense stones of the collapsed outer facing of the Round Structure, and they had found that the two colossal door-stones were decorated on their outer faces with reliefs.

Now, outside Egypt pictorial reliefs of this period are practically non-existent. They are unknown in the Indus Valley, though India is full of reliefs and rock-carvings of a later day; and in Mesopotamia the great stone reliefs of the Assyrian kings are two thousand years later in date. We had found reliefs before, the animal carvings on the facing slabs of the Umm an-Nar tombs, but the carvings of Buraimi were larger and finer and much more varied. There were two cheetahs, or perhaps lions, tearing a gazelle; there were two oryx standing face to face, with two human figures hand in hand beneath their heads; there was a very Indian scene of sexual intercourse (hardly the thing for grave-chamber decoration, we thought); and there was a man leading a donkey upon which another human figure was riding— which Karen immediately titled "The Flight into Egypt." Eivind was busy making papier-mâché casts of the carvings when I left for Bahrain.

We were not digging in Bahrain that year. But at last the antiquities of Bahrain had been placed officially in the care of the Department of Education, and an Antiquities Office was being organized, and I had been asked to come and discuss when and how we could resume work. Interest was alive again in Bahrain, as it had not been since Sheikh Sulman had died six years before.

I got back to Dhahran to find the party returned from "Gerrha," and prepared to move out next day to the deep south, to Jabrin. And it was then, twelve hours before we were to move off, that the completely unexpected discovery broke, the discovery which —without knowing what it was to be—we nevertheless had to be flexible enough to meet. A note was awaiting me from Grace, a schoolteacher and one of the most enthusiastic of the pot-pickers.

Was I interested in a site with flint arrowheads and painted pottery?

The finds were spread out on the table when I arrived ten minutes later. A score of barbed and tangled arrowheads and as many other flint implements, knives and scrapers and awls. And about two hundred potsherds, of a thin, greenish-yellow ware decorated with geometric patterns in dark-brown paint. I was speechless, for this was beyond our dreams, and I suddenly knew what the lowest level at Tarut was, with its nondescript yellowish sherd and its three pieces of worked flint. Grace was looking anxiously at me, afraid that I would shrug my shoulders and say "Islamic." I stammered out, "But . . . but this is Ubaid."

Somewhere round about 5000 B.C. the first agricultural settlers moved into the waste of swamps along the lower valley of the Tigris and the Euphrates, the region which was to be Sumer, and later still Babylonia. And these first Stone-Age settlers made pottery of a greenish-yellow clay decorated with geometric designs in dark-brown paint. Where they came from no one knows, perhaps from the south, perhaps from the east. During a thousand years or so they gradually tamed lower Mesopotamia, and their pottery spread to the already settled regions of north Mesopotamia and even into Syria. Their culture is called Al-Ubaid, and the nearest settlement of the Ubaid culture to Dhahran, and the earliest of them all at that, was at Eridu, 400 miles away to the north. And now it lay here, in Arabia.

I sat down to think it out. And Grace told me about the site. It was a surface site, she said, a low hill among the sand dunes a quarter of a mile from the coast, about sixty miles north of Dhahran. I knew that stretch of coast. Here, as to the south whence we had just come, there was a large area of *sabkha* between the land and the sea, and a strip of low sandy hills fencing the *sabkha* off from the sea. It must have been a string of islands, I thought, six and seven thousand years ago, when the *sabkha* was sea. There were no traces of buildings, Grace went on, but there were pieces of plaster showing a smooth face on one side and the impress of bound bundles of reeds on the other. She showed me half a dozen pieces, clear proof of the type of houses of these Stone-Age Arabians, and akin to the clay plastering with impress of reeds which had been found on other Ubaid sites. But the largest piece had more to tell. Its smooth side was encrusted with barnacles. "Yes," said Grace, "I found that on the lowest edge of the site."

A fortnight later, when we visited the site, Ole surveyed the height of the spot where the plaster was found. It lay four metres above high-water mark. It was positive proof that the land had risen in relation to the sea.

All this was of paramount importance. It was the biggest new thing that had come out of Arabia since we had found the Umm an-Nar culture. It cried aloud for immediate investigation. But we were after all not flexible enough. We could not break our schedule. We were packed and provisioned for Jabrin. The Bob-tails, two of them this time, had set off the day before, and they had no radios. They could not be recalled.

We set off the following morning—a hundred miles by road to the oasis of Hofuf, and then 250 miles on a compass course through the dunes and across the endless gravel flats; a night rolled in blankets beside the trucks, and then on for another fifty miles through steep eroded hills. This was a journey which even Exploration took somewhat seriously, though Jabrin was to them but a way-halt on the route to the Rub' al-Khali.

Jabrin was our shot-in-the-dark. It is a large oasis, uninhabited except for occasional summer visits by the Murra tribe, and air photographs showed a large number of tumuli on the hills around. This far inland—for Jabrin is over 300 miles from the coast—the tumuli could hardly be of our Early Dilmun culture, unless Dilmun was something very different from the coastal civilization which we believed it to be. So they might be any-thing.

We had planned to spend a fortnight at Jabrin, but we cut it down to ten days, days of fierce heat, with a dust-storm which blew up regularly at noon each day, scourging our faces, clogging our nostrils, and threatening to tear the tents out of the ground. We learned to start work at six, as soon as it was light, and began the long drive back to camp as soon as the yellow clouds ap-peared on the southern horizon soon after eleven.

The tumuli were there all right, in their thousands on every hill

MESOPOTAMIA	RECORDED DILMUN	BC	BAHRAIN	ARABIA	KU
UBAID CULTURE		4250			
		4000		UBAID SITES	
(THE DELUGE)		3750			
		3500			
		3250			
		3000	QALA'AT AL-BAHRAIN / UMM AN-NAR POTTERY	TARUT	
		2750	CITY I	GRAVE MOUNDS	
(GILGAMESH KING OF URUK)	DILMUN FIRST NAMED (UR-NANSHE)	2500	BARBAR TEMPLE I	DILMUN	
SARGON OF AKKAD	SHIPS OF DILMUN MAKAN, MELUHHA	2250		EARLY	FA
GUDEA OF LAGASH	STONE FROM MAKAN		CITY II III		
	TRADE WITH UR EA-NASIR	2000			
HAMMURABI OF BABYLON		1750			
KASSITES		1500	MIDDLE DILMUN		
	2 NIPPUR LETTERS	1250	CITY III		
		1000			
		750	CITY IV	LATE DILMUN	
SARGON OF ASSYRIA / SENNACHERIB OF ASSYRIA / ASSURBANIPAL OF ASSYRIA	CAMPAIGNS ON DILMUN'S BORDER (UPERI KING OF DILMUN) / CONQUERS DILMUN? / DILMUN LAST NAMED (NABONIDUS)	500			
PERSIAN EMPIRE ALEXANDER		250	CITY V / TYLOS / GRAVE MOUNDS	THAJ / GERRHA	IKA
SELEUCID EMPIRE					

378

OMAN	BC	INDIA
	4250	
	4000	
	3750	
	3500	
	3250	
?	3000	
UMM AN-NAR BURAIMI		KULLI
?	2750	
MAKAN ?	2500	MELUHHA
	2250	INDUS
	2000	CIVIL-
	1750	IZATION
		ARYAN INVASION?
	1500	
? GRAVE MOUNDS ?	1250	
	1000	
	750	
DIBBA ?	500	
	250	ALEXANDER

CHRONOLOGICAL CHART, TABULATING THE ARCHAEOLOGICAL RESULTS OF THE EXPEDITIONS AND EQUATING THEM WITH THE HISTORICAL RECORDS OF DILMUN.

top. And down in the scrub of the oasis we found a string of larger mounds, with long chambers of immense stones, the largest chamber forty-six feet in length. These mounds were too large for our little party to tackle, with the nearest available workmen two hundred miles away. But we opened a half-dozen of the smaller hill-top cairns. They were elaborately built of unshaped stones, conical with a rectangular chamber in the centre lined with stone slabs. They reminded us of the mounds on the slopes of Jebel Hafit in Buraimi, but unlike those the Jabrin mounds had no entrance passage.

They had been thoroughly plundered. Five were completely empty, and the sixth contained only a scattering of bones and an overlooked bronze spear-head. There was not a single potsherd, a circumstance so odd that one is tempted to believe that the mound-builders, like the Bedouin of today, used little or no pottery. The spear-head was our only indication of date, and its form, with socket and square shoulders, suggested the middle of the second millennium B.C.

In the mornings, then, we dug our mounds, or collected flint arrowheads on the rich Late Palæolithic site a stone's throw from the large mounds in the valley. In the afternoons, as the canvas of our tents buffeted in the sand-driving wind, our thoughts were, as often as not, six thousand years in the past. The fifth millennium B.C. must, with all reservation, be the date of the Ubaid site on the coast. And it changed all our conceptions of the history of the Gulf. Had civilization reached the Gulf from the north after all, and not from the east? Or had the Ubaid culture originated in east Arabia and spread from there to Mesopotamia? Was there some basis for the old Sumerian legend of the fish-man who had brought agriculture to Mesopotamia from the Arabian Gulf? Whatever the answer, one thing was clear. Civilization was over a thousand years older in the Gulf lands than we had believed, and somehow that thousand years of history had to be filled. It was tantalizing to know that there was one place, and one place only, where the missing centuries could be investigated. The tell of Tarut had Ubaid ware in its lowest, and Barbar ware in its uppermost strata. In between would lie the tale of how the one developed into the other. And Tarut was still as impossible to dig as ever.

The tale of our search for Dilmun ends in mid-air. We have found Dilmun. Where fifteen years ago there was only the mystery of the hundred thousand undated burial mounds of Bahrain there are now cities and temples, dated and documented, along 250 miles of coast and islands from Kuwait to Bahrain and (a discovery of the 1969 campaign, added during printing) extending sixty miles into the interior of Saudi Arabia, to the oasis of Hofuf.

We have a second civilization three hundred miles further to the eastward, in the Oman, contemporary with the beginnings of Dilmun, and indeed perhaps its founders. And behind it all, a thousand years or more earlier in time, we have—to keep us humble—the tantalizing and inspiring riddle of the Ubaid sites.

Archæologically these cultures have been worked out in some detail. But the task of transmuting archæology into history is scarcely begun. We do not know how Dilmun began, nor why it ended. But the investigation which began with the object of explaining why there were grave-mounds on Bahrain has led us into strange by-ways and strange lands. It has given us a richness of experiences that, I think, falls rarely to the lot even of archæologists, who do not normally lead humdrum lives.

The work, of course, will go on. The sea-gate of Bahrain, through which the wealth of the Orient passed and which has been closed for two thousand years, will be opened. The cities of that Umm an-Nar culture which may be the copper land of Makan will be found in Buraimi and, if Allah will, in Muscat. The city of Thaj, and the Seleucid fortress of Ikaros, which faced each other when Alexander the Great was newly dead, will be dug free. The mound-builders of Jabrin will be identified, and even the city of Gerrha will be found. The riddle of the Ubaid settlements will be solved, and sooner or later some way will be found to dig the tell on Tarut.

Whether we shall be the ones to do all this will depend on many things: on the continued good will of the rulers of the Arab states of the Gulf, and of their people among whom we have so many friends; on the sustained generosity of oil companies and other supporters, or the new generosity of new supporters; on the universities which must train, and the museums which must employ, the new generation of Arabian archæologists (dare one call them Dilmunologists?).

HALF A DOZEN OF THE DILMUN SEALS DEPICT TWO GENTLEMEN DRINKING BEER THROUGH STRAWS FROM A COMMON POT, BUT IN NO OTHER DO THE GENTLEMEN APPEAR SO THOROUGHLY TO BE ENJOYING THE PROCESS. IN VIEW OF OUR SPONSORS WE ARE CONTEMPLATING ADOPTING THIS SEAL AS THE CREST OF THE EXPEDITION.

And when, one day, it will all have been said and done, when the last basketful of earth has been carried up from the diggings, and the last word of the last report written—what will it all have mattered? That Dilmun has emerged once more from the mists of oblivion, that we can cross the threshold which Uperi, king of Dilmun, trod, look up at the fortress walls that guarded the emporium of all the Indies—what does it matter? Does it matter who the people were who, in the dawn of our time, opened up the trade routes from Meluhha to Makan, from Makan to Dilmun, from Dilmun to Sumer? For two and a half millennia even the fact that they had been was forgotten, and the world went on happily enough, unaware that it was unaware. Among all the lost volumes of human history, what is one lost chapter more or less?

They are dead and gone, these merchant adventurers of another age; and neither the archæologist's trowel nor the pen of the chronicler can bring back the argosies that once sailed the blue waters of the Arabian Gulf. It can matter as little to them as it does to us, that now once more we know a little of their doings, a few of their names.

And yet I think that Gilgamesh, who sought immortality on Dilmun, and Utu-nipishtim, who found it there, would have approved of what we have been trying to do, of what I have been trying to write.

INDEX

i

Index

iii

Index

Index

Index

A NOTE ABOUT THE AUTHOR

Mr. Bibby was born in 1917 in Heversham, Westmoreland, and educated at Cambridge University. During World War II he served in the Intelligence Corps of the British Army, and was awarded King Christian X's Liberation Medal for his work with the Danish underground movement. From 1947 to 1950 he was Executive Officer of the Iraq Petroleum Company, stationed on Bahrain Island. He later made his home in Denmark and is now Director of Oriental Antiquities at the Prehistoric Museum of Aarhus, Denmark. He has traveled widely in Europe and the Middle East and has taken part in many archæological excavations in Scandinavia, Great Britain, and the Middle East. His book The Testimony of the Spade *(1956), about life in northern Europe from 15,000 B.C. to the time of the Vikings, was a pioneer work in turning prehistory in the heartland of Europe into history. In* Four Thousand Years Ago *(1961), he told the fascinating story of the second millennium B.C. —hitherto known as the "lost" thousand years. His archæological expeditions to the Persian Gulf are scheduled to continue indefinitely.*

A NOTE ON THE TYPE

The text of this book is set in Caledonia, a type face designed by W(illiam) A(ddison) Dwiggins for the Mergenthaler Linotype Company in 1939. Dwiggins chose to call his new type face Caledonia, the Roman name for Scotland, because it was inspired by the Scotch types cast about 1833 by Alexander Wilson & Son, Glasgow type founders. However, there is a calligraphic quality about Caledonia that is totally lacking in the Wilson types. Dwiggins referred to an even earlier type face for this "liveliness of action"—one cut around 1790 by William Martin for the printer William Bulmer. Caledonia has more weight than the Martin letters, and the bottom finishing strokes (serifs) of the letters are cut straight across, without brackets, to make sharp angles with the upright stems, thus giving a "modern face" appearance.

W. A. Dwiggins (1880–1956) was born in Martinsville, Ohio, and studied art in Chicago. In 1904 he moved to Hingham, Massachusetts, where he built a solid reputation as a designer of advertisements and as a calligrapher. He began an association with the Mergenthaler Linotype Company in 1929 and over the next twenty-seven years designed a number of book types for the firm. Of especial interest are the Metro series, Electra, Caledonia, Eldorado, and Falcon. In 1930, Dwiggins first became interested in marionettes, and through the years he made many important contributions to the art of puppetry and the design of marionettes.